FROM THE RUINS OF EMPIRE

ALSO BY PANKAJ MISHRA

NONFICTION

*Temptations of the West: How to Be Modern
in India, Pakistan, Tibet, and Beyond*

An End to Suffering: The Buddha in the World

Butter Chicken in Ludhiana: Travels in Small Town India

FICTION

The Romantics

FROM THE RUINS OF EMPIRE

THE INTELLECTUALS WHO REMADE ASIA

PANKAJ MISHRA

FARRAR, STRAUS AND GIROUX   NEW YORK

Farrar, Straus and Giroux
18 West 18th Street, New York 10011

Printed in the United States of America
Originally published in 2012 by Allen Lane, an imprint of Penguin Books,
Great Britain, as *From the Ruins of Empire: The Revolt Against the West and the Remaking of Asia*
Published in the United States by Farrar, Straus and Giroux
First American edition, 2012

ILLUSTRATION CREDITS

Pages 11–12: Imperial bronze lion sculptures in the ruins of the Old Summer Palace, Beijing, China, 1869 (Hulton Archive/Getty Images); pages 46–47: Street in Old Cairo, c. 1900 (Photo Collection Alexander Alland, Sr./Corbis); pages 124–25: Chinese officers' school in Tianjin, c. 1900 (Hulton-Deutsch Collection/Corbis); pages 184–86: Turkish president Kemal Ataturk visits Eskişehir after signing a treaty with France in Ankara in 1921 (Hulton-Deutsch Collection/Corbis); pages 216–17: Philosopher and teacher Rabindranath Tagore reads to a group of his students in 1929 (E. O. Hoppé/Corbis); pages 242–43: Indian president Rajendra Prasad (*left*) and Prime Minister Jawaharlal Nehru (*right*) greet North Vietnamese president Ho Chi Minh on his arrival at New Delhi's Palam Airport in 1958 (Bettmann/Corbis)

Library of Congress Control Number: 2012940483
ISBN: 978-0-374-24959-5

www.fsgbooks.com

1   3   5   7   9   10   8   6   4   2

For the two Ms

The History of China has shown no development, so that we cannot concern ourselves with it any further ... China and India as it were lie outside the course of world history.

G. W. F. Hegel, 1820

Europeans would like to escape from their history, a 'great' history written in letters of blood. But others, by the hundreds of millions, are taking it up for the first time, or coming back to it.

Raymond Aron, 1969

Contents

A Note on Names and Places

A book that ranges as widely as this over time and space throws up innumerable dilemmas about names of people and places – questions that are actually deeply political in nature, as anyone who uses the old colonial name Bombay instead of Mumbai in the British-built port city will very quickly find out. Romanizing Islamic names necessitates a hard choice between at least three major demotic traditions: Arabic, Turkish and Persian. In the end I decided to use names I thought would be most familiar to readers who read predominantly in English. Hence, I opted for Sun Yat-sen, using the older Wade-Giles system of Romanizing Chinese names, rather than the Pinyin version Sun Yixian. This still leaves some room for debate about whether Zhou Enlai, which I use, is better known than Chou En-lai. And I use Beijing as well as Peking. Consistency in these matters, I discovered, was hard to achieve. I hope that readers will forgive my more eccentric choices.

Prologue

The contemporary world first began to assume its decisive shape over two days in May 1905 in the narrow waters of the Tsushima Strait. In what is now one of the busiest shipping lanes in the world, a small Japanese fleet commanded by Admiral Tōgō Heihachirō annihilated much of the Russian navy, which had sailed half way round the world to reach the Far East. Described by the German kaiser as the most important naval battle since Trafalgar a century earlier, and by President Theodore Roosevelt as 'the greatest phenomenon the world has ever seen', the Battle of Tsushima effectively terminated a war that had been rumbling on since February 1904, fought mainly to decide whether Russia or Japan would control Korea and Manchuria. For the first time since the Middle Ages, a non-European country had vanquished a European power in a major war; and the news careened around a world that Western imperialists – and the invention of the telegraph – had closely knit together.

In Calcutta, safeguarding the British Empire's most cherished possession, the viceroy of India, Lord Curzon, feared that 'the reverberations of that victory have gone like a thunderclap through the whispering galleries of the East'.[1] For once the aloof and frequently blundering Curzon had his finger on the pulse of native opinion, which was best articulated by a then unknown lawyer in South Africa called Mohandas Gandhi (1869–1948), who predicted 'so far and wide have the roots of Japanese victory spread that we cannot now visualize all the fruit it will put forth'.[2]

In Damascus, Mustafa Kemal, a young Ottoman soldier later known as Atatürk (1881–1938), was ecstatic. Desperate to reform and strengthen the Ottoman Empire against Western threats, Kemal

I

had, like many Turks, taken Japan as a model, and now felt vindicated. Reading the newspapers in his provincial town, the sixteen-year-old Jawaharlal Nehru (1889–1964), later India's first prime minister, had excitedly followed the early stages of Japan's war with Russia, fantasizing about his own role in 'Indian freedom and Asiatic freedom from the thralldom of Europe'.[3] The news from Tsushima reached him as he was travelling on a train from Dover to his English public school, Harrow; it immediately put him in 'high good humour'.[4] The Chinese nationalist Sun Yat-sen (1866–1925) was also in London when he heard the news and was similarly exultant. Returning by ship to China in late 1905, Sun was congratulated by Arab port workers at the Suez Canal who thought that he was Japanese.[5]

Excited speculation about the implications of Japan's success filled Turkish, Egyptian, Vietnamese, Persian and Chinese newspapers. Newborn babies in Indian villages were named after Japanese admirals. In the United States, the African-American leader W. E. B. Du Bois spoke of a worldwide eruption of 'colored pride'. Something akin to this sentiment clearly seized the pacifist poet (and future Nobel laureate) Rabindranath Tagore (1861–1941), who on receiving the news from Tsushima led his students in an impromptu victory march around a little school compound in rural Bengal.

It mattered little to which class or race they belonged; the subordinate peoples of the world keenly absorbed the deeper implications – moral and psychological – of Japan's triumph. This diversity was startling. Nehru belonged to a family of affluent, Anglophile Brahmans; his father, a beneficiary of British rule over India, was even rumoured to send his shirts to Europe for dry-cleaning. Sun Yat-sen was the son of a poor farmer; one of his brothers died during the Californian Gold Rush that Chinese coolie labour serviced. Abdurreshid Ibrahim (1857–1944), the foremost pan-Islamic intellectual of his time who travelled to Japan in 1909 to establish contacts with Japanese politicians and activists, was born in western Siberia. Mustafa Kemal was from Salonica (now in Greece), born to parents of Albanian and Macedonian origin. His later associate, the Turkish novelist Halide Edip (1884–1964), who named her newborn son after the Japanese admiral

Tōgō, was a secular-minded feminist. Burma's nationalist icon U
Ottama (1879–1939), who was inspired by Japan's victory over
Russia to move to Tokyo in 1907, was a Buddhist monk.

Some of the numerous Arab, Turkish, Persian, Vietnamese and
Indonesian nationalists who rejoiced over Russia's defeat had even
more diverse backgrounds. But they all shared one experience: of
being subjugated by the people of the West that they had long considered upstarts, if not barbarians. And they all drew the same lesson
from Japan's victory: white men, conquerors of the world, were no
longer invincible. A hundred fantasies – of national freedom, racial
dignity, or simple vengefulness – now bloomed in hearts and minds
that had sullenly endured European authority over their lands.

Bullied by the Western powers in the nineteenth century, and chastened by those powers' rough treatment of China, Japan had set itself
an ambitious task of internal modernization from 1868: of replacing
a semi-feudal shogunate with a constitutional monarchy and unified
nation-state, and of creating a Western-style economy of high production and consumption. In a bestselling book of 1886 titled *The Future
Japan*, Tokutomi Sohō (1863–1957), Japan's leading journalist, had
laid out the likely costs of Japanese indifference to the 'universal'
trends set by the West: 'Those blue-eyed, red-bearded races will invade
our country like a giant wave, drive our people to the islands in the
sea.'[6]

Already by the 1890s, Japan's growing industrial and military
strength was provoking European and American visions of the 'yellow
peril', a fearful image of Asiatic hordes overrunning the white West.
The defeat of Russia proved that Japan's programme of catching up
with the West had been stunningly successful. 'We are dispelling the
myth of the inferiority of the non-white races,' Tokutomi Sohō now
declared. 'With our power we are forcing our acceptance as a member
in the ranks of the world's greatest powers.'[7]

For many other non-white peoples, Russia's humiliation seemed to
negate the West's racial hierarchies, mocking the European presump-
tion to 'civilize' the supposedly 'backward' countries of Asia. 'The
logic of the "white man's burden",' declared Benoy Kumar Sarkar

(1887–1949), India's pioneering sociologist, 'has become an anachronism except only to the blindest fanatics.'[8] Japan had shown that Asian countries could find their own path to modern civilization, and its special vigour. The Young Turk activist, and later minister, Ahmed Riza (1859–1930) summed up this resonant admiration:

> Events of the Far East have put forth evidence of the uselessness of interventions, frequent if pernicious, of Europe reforming a people. On the contrary, the more isolated and preserved from contact with European invaders and plunderers a people is, the better is the measure of [its] evolution toward a rational renovation.[9]

Struggling with institutionalized racism in white-ruled South Africa, Gandhi drew a similar moral lesson from Japan's triumph: 'When everyone in Japan, rich or poor, came to believe in self-respect, the country became free. She could give Russia a slap in the face ... In the same way, we must, too, need to feel the spirit of self-respect.'[10] The Chinese philosopher Yan Fu (1854–1921) recalled a century of humiliations inflicted on China by Western 'barbarians', from the Opium wars to the burning of the imperial Summer Palace in Beijing, and concluded that 'the only reason we did not devour their flesh and sleep upon their hides was that our power was insufficient'.

Japan had now shown how that power could be acquired. For many Asians, tormented by incompetent despots and predatory European businessmen, Japan's constitution was the secret of its strength. Armed by its example, political activists across Asia helped fuel a series of popular constitutional revolutions against ossified autocracies (defeated Russia itself lurched into one in 1905). The Ottoman ruler, Sultan Abdulhamid II (1842–1918), had closely followed Japan's modernization, especially as the ever-rising demands of European powers reduced Istanbul's sovereignty to a pitiable fiction. But many admirers of Japan in the Muslim world were such secular, even antireligious, nationalists as the Young Turk exile and writer Abdullah Cevdet, who wrote of Japan as the carrier 'of the sword, for the oppressors, for the insolent invaders; the torch for the oppressed, for those that shine unto themselves'. Emboldened by Japan's victory, in 1908 the nationalist Young Turks forced Sultan Abdulhamid to reinstate a constitution suspended since 1876. The Persians, encouraged by the sight of constitutional Japan defeating autocratic Russia, created a national assembly in 1906.

In the same year Egypt experienced the first major mass demonstrations against British occupation. For nationalist Muslims in Egypt, Japan was 'The Rising Sun': the title of a book written just before the Russo-Japanese War by the foremost Egyptian nationalist leader, Mustafa Kamil (1874–1908). Students from Muslim countries everywhere now headed to Tokyo to learn the secrets of its progress. The domino effect of Japan's victory was felt even in the Indonesian archipelago which had only recently been unified by Dutch colonialists, where upper-class Javanese set up the first nationalist party in 1908.

The most far-reaching changes occurred in China, culminating in the overthrow of one of the world's oldest imperial dynasties in 1911. Thousands of Chinese flocked to Japan after 1905 in what was then the biggest-ever mass movement of students overseas. Many of post-imperial China's first-generation leaders were to emerge from this group. In 1910, a schoolboy called Mao Zedong (1893–1976) in a small town in China's Hunan province memorized a Japanese song taught by his music teacher, a former student in Japan:

> The sparrow sings, the nightingale dances,
> And the green fields are lovely in the spring.
> The pomegranate flowers crimson, the willows green-leafed,
> And there is a new picture.[11]

Recalling the words perfectly decades later, when Japan menaced China, Mao said, 'At that time, I knew and felt the beauty of Japan, and felt something of her pride and might in this song of her victory over Russia.'[12]

Elsewhere, too, Japan's victory galvanized patriotic sentiment and even pushed it towards extremism. One of the casualties of this new mood was the liberal nationalism that Westernized native elites had ineffectually espoused. The mood in Bengal, which Lord Curzon planned to partition, was already militantly anti-British. Riots and terrorist attacks attested to a hardening of anti-colonial feeling from 1905 that the Indian National Congress had so far only mildly expressed. Radicals in Calcutta and Dhaka began to sponsor Bengali students for trips to Tokyo, and anti-colonial agitators based in

Europe and America established links with Irish and Russian revolutionaries and Japanese and Chinese leaders in order to smuggle arms into Bengal.

The scholar-gentry of French Indochina, too, began to court notions of revolutionary violence. The pioneering Vietnamese nationalist Phan Boi Chau (1867–1940) based himself in Japan from 1905 to 1909, educating many students from French Indochina under the banner of his Dong Du ('Look to the East') society. Social Darwinist ideas of racial war and the struggle for survival came to infect political discourse in Buddhist Ceylon as well as Confucian China and Islamic Egypt. In Cairo, Rashid Rida (1865–1935), whose work later served as an inspiration to Egypt's Muslim Brotherhood, wrote excitedly about the possibility of converting Japan to Islam, and turning the 'yellow peril' of European imagination into a pan-Asian movement for liberation from infidels.[13]

The slaughter of the First World War, a decade after the Battle of Tsushima, would deprive Europe, in Asian eyes, of much of its remaining moral prestige. Japan's conquest of Asia during the Second World War, though eventually reversed, would help detach much of the continent from the weakening grasp of exhausted European empires. In the long view, however, it is the Battle of Tsushima that seems to have struck the opening chords of the recessional of the West.

What Tsushima could not immediately reverse was the superiority of Western arms and commerce which had been impressed upon Asia and Africa for much of the nineteenth century. The twentieth century opened with German soldiers mounting punitive raids against anti-Western Chinese Boxers, the United States suppressing a rebellion in the Philippines, and the British fighting, with the help of Indian soldiers, Dutch settlers in southern Africa. By 1905 these wars had ended with China and the Philippines subdued, and South Africa united under British rule. The West was not to relinquish physical possession of its Eastern territories for many more years. But Japan's victory over Russia accelerated an irreversible process of intellectual, if not yet political, decolonization.

Speaking in 1924, Sun Yat-sen recalled the somnolent last decade of the nineteenth century when the 'colored races in Asia, suffering from the oppression of the Western people, thought that emancipation was impossible':

> Men thought and believed that European civilization was a progressive one – in science, industry, manufacture, and armament – and that Asia had nothing to compare with it. Consequently, they assumed that Asia could never resist Europe, that European oppression could never be shaken off. Such was the idea prevailing thirty years ago.[14]

Japan's defeat of Russia in 1905, Sun Yat-sen said, had infused Asian peoples with a 'new hope': 'of shaking off the yoke of European restriction and domination and regaining their own rightful position in Asia'. And in less than two decades, Sun added, independence movements in Egypt, Turkey, Persia, India, Afghanistan and China had grown vigorous. As Gandhi predicted in 1905, 'the people of the East' were finally 'waking up from their lethargy'.[15] The whispers of the East that Lord Curzon feared would soon swell into full-throated assertions and claims. Scattered and isolated individuals would come together to form mass movements and stoke insurrections. Together they would incite a revolutionary reversal of astonishing swiftness.

From its zenith at the beginning of the twentieth century, Europe's hold over Asia would dramatically weaken; by 1950, with India and China already sovereign states, Europe would be reduced to a peripheral presence in Asia, shored up only by the newest Western power, the United States, and increasingly dependent on an informal empire constituted by military bases, economic pressures and political coups. Europeans, and then Americans, would find that they had underestimated the Asian ability to assimilate modern ideas, techniques and institutions – the 'secrets' of Western power – and then to turn them against the West itself. They had failed to notice the intense desire for equality and dignity among peoples whom Europe's most influential thinkers, from Hegel and Marx to John Stuart Mill, had deemed unfit for self-rule – thinkers whose ideas, ironically, would in fact prove highly potent among these 'subject peoples'.

Today Asian societies from Turkey to China seem very vital and self-assured. This wasn't how they appeared to those who condemned the Ottoman and Qing empires as 'sick' and 'moribund' in the nineteenth century. The much-heralded shift of economic power from the

West to the East may or may not happen, but new perspectives have certainly opened up on world history. For most people in Europe and America, the history of the twentieth century is still largely defined by the two world wars and the long nuclear stand-off with Soviet Communism. But it is now clearer that the central event of the last century for the majority of the world's population was the intellectual and political awakening of Asia and its emergence from the ruins of both Asian and European empires. To acknowledge this is to understand the world not only as it exists today, but also how it is continuing to be remade not so much in the image of the West as in accordance with the aspirations and longings of former subject peoples.

Who were the main thinkers and doers in this long remaking of modern Asia? How did they prefigure the world we live in and the one that future generations will inhabit? This book seeks to answer these questions by looking at the history of the modern world from several different vantage points in Asia (the continent being defined here in its original Greek sense, with the Aegean Sea dividing Asia from Europe, and the Nile as the border between Asia and Africa – a geographical conception not dissimilar to today's geopolitical divisions).

The West has seen Asia through the narrow perspective of its own strategic and economic interests, leaving unexamined – and unimagined – the collective experiences and subjectivities of Asian peoples. It may be disorientating to inhabit this other perspective, and this book will doubtless invoke many names and events that are unfamiliar to its Western readers. But it does not seek to replace a Euro-centric or West-centric perspective with an equally problematic Asia-centric one. Rather, it seeks to open up multiple perspectives on the past and the present, convinced that the assumptions of Western power – increasingly untenable – are no longer a reliable vantage point and may even be dangerously misleading.

From a Western standpoint, the influence of the West can seem both inevitable and necessary, requiring no thorough historical auditing. Europeans and Americans customarily see their countries and cultures as the source of modernity and are confirmed in their assumptions by the extraordinary spectacle of their culture's universal diffusion:

today every society, save some isolated tribal communities in Borneo or the Amazonian rainforests, seems at least partially Westernized, or aspiring towards a form of Western modernity. But there was a time when the West merely denoted a geographical region, and other peoples unselfconsciously assumed a universal order centred in *their* values. Until late into the nineteenth century, people of societies with belief-systems like Islam or Confucianism at their core – much of the known world – could assume that the human order was still fused inseparably with the larger divine or cosmic order defined by their ancestors and gods.

This book seeks to offer a broad view of how some of the most intelligent and sensitive people in the East responded to the encroachments of the West (both physical and intellectual) on their societies. It describes how these Asians understood their history and social existence, and how they responded to the extraordinary sequence of events and movements – the Indian Mutiny, Anglo-Afghan Wars, Ottoman modernization, Turkish and Arab nationalism, the Russo-Japanese War, the Chinese Revolution, the First World War, the Paris Peace Conference, Japanese militarism, decolonization, postcolonial nationalism and the rise of Islamic fundamentalism – that together decided the present shape of Asia.

The book's main protagonists are two itinerant thinkers and activists: Jamal al-Din al-Afghani (1838–97), a Muslim who pursued a long career in trenchant journalism and political exhortation in the Middle East and South Asia in the latter half of the nineteenth century; and Liang Qichao (1873–1929), perhaps China's foremost modern intellectual, who participated in many events that led to the destruction of his country's old imperial certainties and its subsequent re-emergence, after many horrors, as a major world power. Many of al-Afghani's and Liang's ideas ultimately became major forces for change. These early modern Asians stand at the beginning of the process whereby ordinary resentment against the West and Western dominance, along with anxiety about internal weakness and decay, was transformed into mass nationalist and liberation movements and ambitious state-building programmes across Asia.

Many other Asian thinkers and leaders also appear here. Some do relatively fleetingly, like the Vietnamese worker, later called Ho Chi Minh, in his rented morning suit trying to petition President Wilson in Paris in 1919 for an end to French colonialism in Indochina. Others like Sun Yat-sen, the Indian poet Rabindranath Tagore, the Iranian thinker Ali Shariati and the Egyptian ideologue Sayyid Qutb move swiftly across the changing backdrop. Major figures like Gandhi play supporting roles in this drama; his description of modern Western civilization as 'satanic' was preceded by other, more influential such critiques in the Muslim world and China.

The focus on lesser-known individuals is deliberate. It makes it possible, I believe, to see the main political and intellectual tendencies that preceded and outlasted the better-known figures that have come to monopolize, and limit, our sense of India, China and the Muslim world. Liang Qichao bequeathed his obsession with building state power to Mao Zedong and his heirs in Communist China; al-Afghani's fear of the West and obsession with Muslim self-strengthening prepared the way for Atatürk and Nasser as well as Ayatollah Khomeini, and still animates the politics of Islamic societies.

During their long and eventful lives the Asians discussed in the book manifested all of the three main responses to Western power: the reactionary conviction that if Asian people were truly faithful to their religious traditions, which were presumed to be superior to those of all other civilizations, they would be strong again; the moderate notion that only a few Western techniques were required by Asians whose traditions already provided a sound basis for culture and society; and the vigorous determination, embraced by radical secularists like Mao and Atatürk, that the entire old way of life had to be revolutionized in order to compete in the jungle-like conditions of the modern world.

The form of this book – part historical essay and part intellectual biography – is primarily motivated by the conviction that the lines of history converge in individual lives, even though the latter have their own shape and momentum. The early men of modern Asia it describes travelled and wrote prolifically, restlessly assessing their own and other societies, pondering the corruption of power, the decay of community, the loss of political legitimacy and the temptations of the West. Their passionate enquiries appear in retrospect as a single thread, weaving seemingly disparate events and regions into a single web of meaning. So while describing the general intellectual and political atmosphere in Asia in the late nineteenth and early twentieth centuries, I hope above all to retrace their wanderings in the byways of modern history and thought. For these men, though relatively unknown, helped make the world we live in, for better and for worse.

They hold the throne in their hand. The whole realm is in their hand. The country, the apportioning of men's livelihoods is in their hand ... The springs of hope and of fear are in their hand ... In their hand is the power to decide who shall be humbled and who exalted ... Our people is in their hand, education is in their hand ... If the West continues to be what it is, and the East what it is, we shall see the day when the whole world is in their hand.

Akbar Illahabadi, in the 1870s

EGYPT: 'THE BEGINNING OF A SERIES OF GREAT MISFORTUNES'

Early on the morning of 5 May 1798, Napoleon slipped out of Paris to join a 40,000-strong French army sailing towards Egypt. A popular general after his victories in northern Italy, he had been lobbying his civilian superiors for an invasion of Britain. But the Royal Navy was still too strong, and the French were not ready to confront it. In the meantime, France needed colonies in order to prosper, as its foreign minister Charles Maurice de Talleyrand believed, and a presence in Egypt would not only compensate the French for their loss of territory in North America, it could also pose a serious challenge to the British East India Company, which produced highly profitable cash crops in its Indian possessions.

Expanding across India, the British had expelled the French from most of their early bases on the coast. In 1798, the British were locked into a fierce battle with one of their most wily Indian opponents, Tipu Sultan, an ally of France. French control of Egypt could tip the balance of power against the British in India while also deterring the Russians, who eyed the Ottoman Empire. 'As soon as I have made England tremble for the safety of India,' Napoleon declared, 'I shall return to Paris and give the enemy its death blow.' Apart from his country's geopolitical aims, Napoleon cherished his own private fantasy of conquering the Orient. 'Great reputations', he was convinced, 'are only made in the Orient; Europe is too small.'[1] From Egypt he planned to push eastwards in an Alexander-the-Great-style invasion of Asia, with him riding an elephant and holding a new, personally revised Koran that would be the harbinger of a new religion.

Napoleon travelled to Egypt with a large contingent of scientists, philosophers, artists, musicians, astronomers, architects, surveyors, zoologists, printers and engineers, all meant to record the dawn of the French Enlightenment in the backward East. The momentousness of the occasion – the first major contact between modernizing Europe and Asia – was not lost on Napoleon. On board his ship in the Mediterranean, he exhorted his soldiers: 'You are about to undertake a conquest, the effects of which on civilization and commerce of the world are

15

immeasurable.'² He also drafted grand proclamations addressed to the Egyptian people, describing the new French Republic based upon liberty and equality, even as he professed the highest admiration for the Prophet Muhammad and Islam in general. Indeed the French, he claimed, were also Muslims, by virtue of their rejection of the Christian Trinity. He also made some noises – familiar to us after two centuries of imperial wars disguised as humanitarian interventions – about delivering the Egyptians from their despotic masters.

Appearing without warning in Alexandria in July 1798, the French overcame all military opposition as they proceeded towards Cairo. Egypt was then nominally part of the Ottoman Empire though it was ruled directly by a caste of former slave-soldiers called Mamluks. Its meagre armies were not equipped to fight war-hardened French soldiers who outnumbered the Egyptians and were also backed by the latest military technology.

Reaching Cairo after some easy victories, Napoleon commandeered a mansion for himself on the banks of the then Azbakiya Lake, installed the scholars from his baggage train at a new Institut d'Égypte, and set about politically engineering Egypt along republican lines. He thought up a Divan consisting of wise men, an Egyptian version of the Directory that exercised executive power in Paris. But where were wise men to be found in Cairo, which had been abandoned by its ruling class, the Ottoman Mamluks? Much to their bewilderment, Cairo's leading theologians and religious jurists found themselves promoted to political positions and frequently summoned for consultation by Napoleon – marking the first of many such expedient attempts at politically empowering Islam by supposedly secular Westerners in Asia.

Suppressing his allegiance to the Enlightenment, Napoleon vigorously appeased conservative Muslim clerics in the hope they might form the bulwark of pro-French forces in the country. He dressed up in Egyptian robes on the Prophet's birthday and, much to the disquiet of his own secular-minded soldiers, hinted at a mass French conversion to Islam. Some sycophantic (and probably, derisive) Egyptians hailed him as Ali Bonaparte, naming him after the revered son-in-law of the Prophet. This encouraged Napoleon to suggest to the clerics that the Friday sermon at al-Azhar Mosque, one of Islam's holiest buildings, be said in his name.

The devout Muslims were flabbergasted. The head of the Divan, Sheikh al-Sharqawi, recovered sufficiently to say, 'You want to have the protection of the Prophet . . . You want the Arab Muslims to march beneath your banners. You want to restore the glory of Arabia . . . Become a Muslim!'[3] An evasive Napoleon replied: 'There are two difficulties preventing my army and me from becoming Muslims. The first is circumcision and the second is wine. My soldiers have the habit from their infancy, and I will never be able to persuade them to renounce it.'[4]

Napoleon's attempt to introduce Egyptian Muslims to the glories of French secularism and republicanism were equally doomed. Cairenes deplored his dramatic alterations to the cityscape, and the corrupting influence of the French in general. As one observer wrote, 'Cairo has become a second Paris, women go about shamelessly with the French; intoxicating drinks are publicly sold and things are committed of which the Lord of Heaven would not approve.'[5] In the summer of 1798, Napoleon made it mandatory for all Egyptians to wear the tricolour cockade, the knotted ribbon preferred by French republicans. Inviting members of the Divan to his mansion, he tried to drape a tricolour shawl over the shoulders of Sheikh al-Sharqawi. The Sheikh's face turned red from fear of blasphemy and he flung it to the ground. An angry Napoleon insisted that the clerics would have to wear the cockade at least, if not the shawl. An unspoken compromise was finally arrived at: Napoleon would pin the cockade to the chests of the clerics, and they would take it off as soon as they left his company.

The Islamic eminences may have been trying to humour their strange European conqueror while trying to live for another day. Many other Muslims saw plainly the subjugation of Egypt by a Christian from the West as a catastrophe; and they were vindicated when French soldiers, while suppressing the first of the Egyptian revolts against their occupation, stormed the al-Azhar mosque, tethered their horses to the prayer niches, trampled the Korans under their boots, drank wine until they were helpless and then urinated on the floor.

Napoleon, though ready to burn hostile villages, execute prisoners and tear down mosques for the sake of wide roads, actually indulged in fewer atrocities in Egypt than he was to elsewhere; he was always keen to express his admiration for Islam. Still, the Egyptian cleric and scholar 'Abd al-Rahman al-Jabarti, who chronicled Napoleon's conquest of Egypt, described it as 'great battles, terrible events, disastrous facts, calamities, unhappiness, sufferings, persecutions, upsets in the order of things, terror, revolutions, disorders, devastations – in a word, the beginning of a series of great misfortunes'.[6] And this was the reaction of a somewhat sympathetic witness. When the news of Napoleon's exploits arrived in the Hejaz, the people of Mecca tore down the drapery – traditionally made in Egypt – around the sacred Kaaba.

The dramatic gesture clearly expressed how many Muslims would see Napoleon's invasion of Egypt. It had disrupted nothing less than the long-established cosmic order of Islam – something that human history had shown to be more than a widely shared delusion.

The word 'Islam', describing the range of Muslim beliefs and practices across the world, was not used before the nineteenth century. But few Muslims anywhere over the centuries would have doubted that they belonged to both a collective and an individual way of life, an intense solidarity based on certain shared values, beliefs and traditions. To be a good Muslim was to belong to a community of like-minded upholders of the moral and social order. It was also to participate in the making and expansion of the righteous society of believers and, by extension, in the history of Islam as it had unfolded since God first commanded the Prophet Muhammad to live according to His plan. This history began with astonishing successes, and for centuries it seemed that God's design for the world was being empirically fulfilled.

In AD 622, the first year of the Islamic calendar, Muhammad and his band of followers established the first community of believers in a small town in Arabia. Less than a century later, Arab Muslims were in Spain. Great empires – Persian and Byzantine – fell before the energetically expanding community of Muslims. Islam quickly became the new symbol of authority from the Pyrenees to the Himalayas, and the order it created wasn't just political or military. The conquerors of Jerusalem, North Africa and India brought into being a fresh civilization with its own linguistic, legal and administrative standards, its own arts and architecture and orders of beauty.

The invading Mongols broke into this self-contained world in the thirteenth century, briskly terminating the classical age of Islam. But within fifty years the Mongols had themselves converted to Islam and become its most vigorous champions. Sufi orders spread across the Islamic world, sparking a renaissance of Islam in non-Arab lands. From Kufa to Kalimantan, the travelling scholar, the trader and the Friday assembly gave Islam an easy new portability.

Indeed, Islam was as much a universalizing ideology as Western modernity is now, and it successfully shaped distinctive political systems, economies and cultural attitudes across a wide geographical region: the fourteenth-century Moroccan traveller Ibn Battuta had as little trouble getting jobs at imperial courts in India or in West Africa as a Harvard MBA would in Hong Kong and Cape Town today. The notion of a universal community of Muslims, the *umma*, living under the symbolic authority of a *khalifa* (caliph), in a *Dar al-Islam* (land of Muslims), which was distinct from the remote and peripheral *Dar al-Harb* (land of war), helped Muslims from Morocco to Java to imagine a central place in the world for themselves and their shared values.

Itinerant Muslim traders from India were still displacing Hinduism and Buddhism in Indonesia and even Indochina as late as the seventeenth century. Extensive mercantile networks and pilgrimage routes to Mecca from all corners of the world affirmed the unity of *Dar al-Islam*. World trade in fact depended on Muslim merchants, seafarers and bankers. For a Muslim in North Africa, India or South-east Asia, history retained its moral and spiritual as well as temporal coherence; it could be seen as a gradual working out of God's plan.

Though beset by internal problems in the eighteenth century, Muslim empires still regarded Europeans as only slightly less barbarous than their defeated Crusader ancestors. So the success of Napoleon suggested something inconceivable: that the Westerners, though still quite crude, were beginning to forge ahead.

*

Europe was to express, as the nineteenth century progressed, an idea of itself through its manifold achievements of technology, constitutional government, secular state and modern administration; and this idea, which emerged from the American and French revolutions and which seemed to place the West in the avant-garde of progress, would be increasingly hard to refute. Already in 1798, a remarkably high degree of organization defined the post-revolutionary French state as well as the French people, who were coming together on the basis of an apparently common language, territory and history to constitute a separate and distinct 'nation-state'.

Faced with the evidence of Europe's advantages, many Muslims were initially bemused and unable to assess it correctly. 'The newly established republic in France', the Ottoman historian Asim recognized in 1801, 'is different from the other Frankish polities.' But then he went on to say: 'Its ultimate basis is an evil doctrine consisting of the abandonment of religion and the equality of rich and poor.' As for parliamentary deliberations, they were 'like the rumblings and crepitations of a queasy stomach'.[7] Some of this cultural arrogance lingered in the eyewitness accounts of Napoleon's conquest by 'Abd al-Rahman al-Jabarti. The cleric generally found French practices distasteful, even barbaric: 'It is their custom', he wrote, 'not to bury their dead but to toss them on garbage heaps like the corpses of dogs and beasts, or to throw them into the sea.'[8] 'Their women do not veil themselves and have no modesty ... They [the French] have intercourse with any woman who pleases them and vice versa.'[9] Al-Jabarti also mocked French hats, the European habit of peeing in public, and the use of toilet paper. He contemptuously dismissed Napoleon's claim to be a protector of Islam, laughing at the bad Arabic grammar of the Frenchman's proclamations, and he sniggered when the French failed to launch a hot-air balloon at one of their demonstrations of European scientific prowess.

Al-Jabarti's limited experience of political institutions made him misunderstand French revolutionary ideals: 'their term "liberty" means,' he concluded too hastily, 'that they are not slaves like the Mamluks'.[10] He sensed the hostility to his own Islamic values in Napoleon's claim that 'all the people are equal in the eyes of God'.

'This is a lie, and ignorance, and stupidity,' he thundered. 'How can this be when God has made some superior to others?'[11]

Still, al-Jabarti, who had been educated at al-Azhar, couldn't fail to be impressed when he visited the Institut d'Égypte, where the intellectuals in Napoleon's entourage had a well-stocked library.

> Whoever wishes to look up something in a book asks for whatever volumes he wants and the librarian brings them to him . . . All the while they are quiet and no one disturbs his neighbor . . . among the things I saw there was a large book containing the Biography of the Prophet . . . The glorious Qur'an is translated into their language! . . . I saw some of them who know chapters of the Qur'an by heart They have a great interest in the sciences, mainly in mathematics and the knowledge of languages, and make great efforts to learn the Arabic language and the colloquial.[12]

Al-Jabarti was also struck by the efficiency and discipline of the French army, and he followed with great curiosity the electoral processes in the Divan that Napoleon had created, explaining to his Arab readers how members wrote their votes on strips of paper, and how majority opinion prevailed.

Al-Jabarti was not entirely deaf to the lessons from Napoleon's conquest: that the government in the world's first modern nation-state did not merely collect taxes and tributes and maintain law and order; it could also raise a conscript army, equip well-trained personnel with modern weapons, and have democratic procedures in place to elect civilian leaders. Two centuries later, al-Jabarti seems to stand at the beginning of a long line of bewildered Asians: men accustomed to a divinely ordained dispensation, the mysterious workings of fate and the cyclical rise and fall of political fortunes, to whom the remarkable strength of small European nation-states would reveal that organized human energy and action, coupled with technology, amount to a power that could radically manipulate social and political environments. Resentfully dismissive at first of Europe, these men would eventually chafe at their own slothful and uncreative dynastic rulers and weak governments; and they would arrive at a similar conviction: that their societies needed to attain sufficient strength to meet the challenge of the West.

THE SLOW BATTERING OF INDIA
AND CHINA

Napoleon's occupation of a large country like Egypt was always tenuous. Despite his praise of Islam, the population remained hostile. Revolts erupted in the major towns, provoking the French into ugly reprisals, including the vandalism and drunken orgies at the al-Azhar mosque. The British navy finally made Napoleon's position untenable by blockading Egypt, isolating him from France and his supply lines. By August 1799 when Napoleon left Egypt as surreptitiously as he had departed Paris, to begin his ascent to political supremacy in France, his Indian ally Tipu Sultan had also been overcome by the British. There were no more conquests for him to accomplish in Asia. He would now concentrate on Europe, striving, in the fearful words of the Turkish ambassador to Paris, 'day and night like a fiercely biting dog to bring diverse mischiefs on the surrounding lands and to reduce all states to the same disorder as his own accursed nation'.[13]

In retrospect, Napoleon had shot out of the starting blocks too early. By 1798, the Dutch, the Spanish, the Portuguese and the British had all secured crucial footholds in Asian territories. But the European conquest of Asia wouldn't get fully under way until after Napoleon himself was comprehensively defeated in 1815. Exhausted by war, the five great European powers – Britain, France, Prussia, Russia and Austria – would agree to maintain a balance of power in Europe. Their pugnacity at home restrained by treaties, Western nations would grow more aggressive in the East, no longer content with beachheads on the vast continent of Asia. In 1824 the British, ensconced in eastern India, began their long subjugation of Burma. In the same year an Anglo-Dutch treaty confirmed British control of Singapore and the Malay states of the Peninsula while demarcating the influence of the Netherlands over Java. Neither Britain nor the Dutch, in turn, stood in the way of French domination of Vietnam.

By the time of Napoleon's defeat in 1815, the British had conquered a third of India; they would soon be paramount over the rest, inaugurating a potent presence in mainland Asia that was to help them force open China to European traders, and turn the rest of Asia into

a European dependency. The speed and audacity of the British conquests in India seem more astonishing given the low profile they had
kept during their centuries-long presence in the subcontinent. Arriving at the brilliantly adorned Mughal court in Agra in 1616, Sir
Thomas Roe, the first accredited English ambassador to India, had
struggled to keep his national flag aloft. Roe's ruler in England, James
I, who wanted a formal trade treaty with the Mughal emperor
Jahangir, had told him to be 'careful of the preservation of our honour
and dignity'[14] and Roe managed to avoid the bowing and scraping
expected of ambassadors at the Mughal court. But he felt acutely the
shabbiness of the gifts he had brought from England for the aesthete
Jahangir, and he could not entirely overcome the Mughal emperor's
scepticism about a supposedly great English king who concerned himself with such petty things as trade.

As late as 1708, the British East India Company's president felt it
imperative to cringe while addressing the Mughal emperor, declaring
himself as 'the smallest particle of sand . . . with his forehead at command rubbed on the ground'.[15] In 1750 when the Mughal Empire,
weakened by endless wars and invasions, was imploding into a number of independent states, the only place where the British enjoyed
territorial sovereignty was the then obscure fishing village of Bombay
(Mumbai). Their luck finally turned in the next few years. In 1757,
after a battle with Bengal's Muslim viceroy, the East India Company
found itself in possession of a territory three times larger than England. Less than a decade later, the Company had successfully deployed
the same combination of political skulduggery and military force to
undermine the ruler of Awadh, the largest of the Mughal Empire's
provinces.

The British subsequently controlled and ruthlessly exploited economically a large part of eastern India. 'The world has never seen',
Bengal's pioneering novelist Bankim Chandra Chatterji (1838–94)
would write, 'men as tyrannical and powerful as the people who first
founded the Britannic empire in India . . . The English who came to
India in those days were affected by an epidemic – stealing other
people's wealth. The word morality had disappeared from their
vocabulary.'[16] Chatterji worked for the British administration in
Bengal and had to necessarily tone down his criticism. There was no

such inhibition on the righteous rage of Edmund Burke, then a member of the British Parliament. 'Young men (boys almost) govern there', he wrote about Bengal in 1788,

> without society and without sympathy with the natives . . . Animated with all the avarice of age and all the impetuosity of youth, they roll in one after another, wave after wave; and there is nothing before the eyes of the natives but an endless, hopeless prospect of new flights of birds of prey and passage.[17]

The Muslim historian Ghulam Hussain Khan Tabatabai (1727–1806), who also worked for the British in Bengal, concurred about the corruption and insularity of his bosses. 'No love, and no coalition can take root', he wrote in a history of India published in 1781, 'between the conquerors and the conquered.'[18] This hardly mattered to the British. As Haji Mustapha, a Creole convert to Islam who translated Tabatabai's book into English in 1786, pointed out in his introduction: 'The general turn of the English individuals in India seems to be a thorough contempt for the Indians (as a national body). It is taken to be no better than a dead stock that may be worked upon without much consideration, and at pleasure.'[19] Increasingly powerful in India, the British could afford to be more aggressive in China, where European traders, confined to the port of Canton, had long fantasized about the potentially huge inland market for their goods. Since they occupied rich agricultural lands in eastern India, the British were particularly keen to find buyers for their produce, especially opium, and they chafed at the arbitrary and opaque nature of China's imperial authority. Emboldened by their successes in India, the British travelled a much shorter distance between awe and contempt in confronting the rulers of China.

Though less extensive than the land of Islam, a unitary Chinese empire persisting over two millennia had made for a high degree of self-absorption. Tribute-bearing foreigners from places as far away as Burma allowed the Chinese to think of themselves as inhabitants of the 'Middle Kingdom'. Indeed, not even Islam could parallel the extraordinary longevity and vitality of Chinese Confucianism, which regulated everything from familial relations to political and ethical problems and had eager imitators in Korea, Japan and Vietnam.

In 1793, the British envoy Lord Macartney led a diplomatic mission to Beijing (Peking) with a letter from King George III asking Emperor Qianlong for a commerce treaty, more ports for British traders and ambassadorial presence at his court. Like Sir Thomas Roe before him, Macartney faced many threats to his dignity. His retinue was made to travel under a banner that said, in Chinese, 'Ambassador bearing tribute from the country of England'. Macartney also had to engage in a long and delicate diplomatic dance to avoid prostrating himself full-length in the ceremonial kowtow before the emperor. He bent one knee instead in the emperor's presence, and handed over various presents attesting to Britain's advanced technical and manufacturing skills, such as brass howitzers and astronomical instruments. The Chinese emperor, then a fit eighty-year-old, graciously asked after King George's health and offered Macartney some rice wine during a 'sumptuous' banquet, which struck the Englishman as possessing a 'calm dignity, that sober pomp of Asiatic greatness, which European refinements have not yet attained'.[20]

The British delegation was treated with bland courtesy for a few more days before being abruptly ushered out of the country with a reply from the Celestial Emperor that stated unequivocally that he had 'never valued ingenious articles' and had not 'the slightest need of England's manufactures'. It was right that 'men of the Western Ocean' should admire and want to study the culture of his empire. But he could not countenance an English ambassador who spoke and dressed so differently fitting into the 'Empire's ceremonial system'. And, the emperor added, it would be good if the English king could 'simply act in conformity with our wishes by strengthening your loyalty and swearing perpetual obedience'.[21]

The letter had been drafted well before Lord Macartney arrived in Beijing. The condescending tone reflected the Chinese elite's exalted sense of their country's pre-eminence, and their determination to protect the old political system in which rich families and landowners supplied well-schooled officials for the administration, and trade was conducted over land and sea with neighbours. The Chinese also knew of the growing power of the 'barbarians' in Asia, where the Europeans had taken a lead in maritime trade, setting up military posts and trading stations across India's coast and South-east Asia. 'It is said', Qianlong wrote to his Grand Minister, 'that the English have robbed and exploited the merchant ships of the other western ocean states so that the foreigners along the western ocean are terrified of their brutality.'[22] The emperor thought it best to keep such aggressive adventurers at bay.

The British persisted, sending another, less expensive embassy to the Qing court in 1816. This time, the Chinese absolutely insisted on the kowtow, and did not let the ambassador enter Beijing when he refused to ritually abase himself before the Chinese emperor.

But China's bluff was about to be called. Lord Macartney, who had been governor of Madras (Chennai) in British India, had shrewdly noted during his travels in China that though the country, 'an old, crazy, first rate man-of-war', could 'overawe' her 'neighbours merely by her bulk and appearance', it was prone to drift and be 'dashed to pieces on the shore'.[23] The nautical metaphors were apt. Explaining why China had dropped out of world history, Hegel had pointed to its indifference to maritime exploration. It would be from the sea that European powers would soon probe China's weaknesses and scratch its wounds. And, like the Mughals and the Ottomans, the Manchus would know the bitter consequences of ignoring the West's innovations of state-backed industry and commerce.

As the Chinese would come to do again in more recent times, they exported much more to Europe and America – mostly tea, silks and porcelains – than they imported, creating a severe balance-of-payments problem for the West which found its precious silver disappearing into Chinese hands. The British East India Company hit upon an alternative mode of payment once it increased its stranglehold over the fertile agricultural lands of eastern India. It was opium, which grew luxuriantly and could be cheaply processed into smokable paste, speedily shipped to southern China and sold through middlemen at Canton to the Chinese masses.

The export of opium exponentially increased revenues and quickly reduced Britain's trade deficit with China; mass Chinese intoxication became central to British foreign policy. But the easy availability of the drug quickly created a problem of addiction in the country. In 1800, the Chinese forbade the import and production of opium; in 1813, they banned smoking altogether.

Still, the British kept at it: by 1820, there was enough opium coming into China to keep a million people addicted, and the flow of silver had been reversed.[24] In the 1830s Emperor Daoguang, faced with a growing scarcity of silver, considered legalizing opium. But he had to contend with a vociferous anti-opium lobby. According to one of the petitioners to the emperor, opium was a dangerous conspiracy organized by red-haired Westerners, which had already 'seduced the nimble, warlike people of Java into the use of it, whereupon they were subdued, brought into subjection and their land taken possession of'. Another anti-opium campaigner claimed that 'in introducing opium into this country, the English purpose has been to weaken and enfeeble the central empire. If not early aroused to a sense of our danger, we shall find ourselves, before long, on the last step towards ruin.'[25]

The anti-opium lobby suggested that smokers be deterred with the death penalty, but the sheer number of smokers raised the spectre of mass executions. In 1838, Daoguang decided to stop the trafficking and consumption of opium altogether. China's war on drugs was conducted peacefully at first; Qing officials drew upon Confucian values of sobriety and obedience to persuade many addicts to renounce smoking, and Chinese middlemen to desist from the trade. The same moral appeal was also addressed to the Westerners, including a letter to Queen Victoria by Lin Zexu, the imperial commissioner at Canton.

Lin, an exemplary official in the Confucian tradition, had acquired a reputation for probity and competence in previous posts as governor of provinces in central China. Addressing the British potentate, he expressed amazement that traders would come to China from as far off as Britain 'for the purpose of making a great profit'.[26] He assumed naively that the British government was not aware of the immoral smugglers in Canton and would uphold the moral principles of Confucius just as vigorously as the Chinese emperor had. 'May you, O King,' he wrote, 'check your wicked and sift out your vicious people before they come to China.'[27] He urged the British monarch to eradicate the opium plant in Madras, Bombay, Patna and Benares and replace it with millet, barley and wheat.

With the Western traders, Lin took a tough line. When they resisted, their factories in Canton were blockaded until they yielded up their opium stocks, which were promptly flushed into the sea. Those who refused to sign bonds pledging not to indulge in opium trafficking were summarily expelled: it was then that a group of British traders first settled on the rocky island called Hong Kong.

The Chinese, however, underestimated the importance the trade in opium had assumed for the British economy. Nor did they know much about the boost of self-confidence the British had received after defeating Napoleon and becoming the paramount power in India – Lin's letter to Queen Victoria, for instance, was not even acknowledged.

In general, growing technological power and commercial success were making Westerners change their opinion of China. Far from being the apogee of enlightenment, as it had appeared to Voltaire and Leibniz, the country was now viewed as a backward place. Even to treat it like an equal, as an American diplomat put it, would be like 'the treatment of a child as it were an old man'.[28] Furthermore, in Britain's expanding economy of the early nineteenth century, 'free trade' seemed as much a universal good, to be enforced through military means, as 'democracy' was to appear in modern times.

A bevy of aggressive private merchants in Canton agitated for more markets in China after the relatively conservative East India Company lost its monopoly over trade in Asia in 1834. These businessmen and their lobbyists raised such an alarm about Chinese actions that the British government felt impelled to dispatch a punitive fleet to China. After arriving in June 1840, the ships blockaded Canton and sailed up China's north coast, finally threatening the city of Tianjin and beyond it the seat of the emperor himself in Beijing. Aware of their weak military, the Qing sued for peace, ceding Hong Kong to the British and agreeing to pay an indemnity of £6 million and to reopen Canton to British traders.

This wasn't enough for the British government. The fantasy of a big China market for British goods had grown unchecked in Britain. Prime Minister Lord Palmerston, an aggressive imperialist, raged that his representatives hadn't exacted more stringent terms from the Chinese after defeating them. He dispatched another fleet in 1841, which, after capturing Shanghai and blocking traffic on the lower Yangtze, threatened to assault the former capital city of Nanjing.

After suffering more military reverses the Chinese again capitulated and signed the humiliating Treaty of Nanjing in 1842, which opened five trade ports, including Shanghai, to foreigners and granted Hong Kong to the British in perpetuity. Writing to his business associates at the British firm Jardine, Matheson & Co. the Indian merchant Jamsetjee Jejeebhoy cautioned that the 'Chinese had enough from us upon this matter ... now keeping distance is far better than showing threat'.[29] The Chinese themselves remained perplexed by the apparently unappeasable greed of the British. As one of the emperor's representatives reasoned in a letter to the British:

> We ponder with veneration upon the Great Emperor's cherishing tenderness towards foreigners, and utmost justice in all his dealings. He thereby causes the whole world to participate in his favour, and to enjoy his protection, for the promotion of civilization – and the full enjoyment of lasting benefits. But the English foreigners have now for two years ... on account of the investigation in the opium traffic, discarded their obedience and been incessantly fighting ... what can possibly be their intention and the drift of their actions?[30]

The Emperor received a heavily edited account of the tough British negotiating style: 'Although the demands of the foreigners are indeed rapacious', his representative wrote, 'yet they are little more than a desire for ports and the privilege of trade. There are no dark schemes in them.'

This proved to be optimistic. Demanding compensation for the opium destroyed, the British asked for more indemnities, including ransom for those cities, such as Hangzhou, that they had not occupied. Other Western nations followed suit, notably the United States, which had maintained a presence in Canton since its own liberation from British rule. The Americans insisted that the Chinese allow Protestant missionaries to work in the treaty ports. The French asked for even broader rights for Catholics, completing the identification in Chinese eyes between the West and the proselytizing religion of Christianity.

The treaties gave Western powers the right to dictate vital aspects of China's commercial, social and foreign policies for the next century. As it turned out, even such craven surrender of Chinese sovereignty did not satisfy the free traders. The supposedly unlimited China market failed to materialize and the trade in opium, not mentioned in the treaties but implicitly accepted by all sides, remained the main Western commercial activity. By 1900, 10 per cent of the Chinese population smoked the drug; one third of those were addicts.[31]

The greater their frustrations around the Chinese market, the louder British businessmen clamoured for the relaxation of remaining restrictions on trade. In 1854, as the Qing faced the growing Taiping rebellion, British, French and American representatives demanded revisions to the Nanjing Treaty facilitating free access to all parts of China, unimpeded navigation of the Yangtze, their diplomatic presence in Beijing, the legalization of opium, and the regulation of Chinese labour emigration (during the lawlessness that prevailed at the end of the Opium War, Chinese men were kidnapped or deceived into travelling to places as far away as California and Cuba to supply local demands for cheap labour).

The Chinese naturally resisted these demands. However, using an allegedly illegal Qing search of a Hong Kong-registered ship called the *Arrow* as a pretext the British went to war again, joined this time by the French who, under Napoleon III, were keen to flex their muscles. In 1859, Lord Elgin, the son of the earl who had taken the marble friezes from the Parthenon to England, arrived at the head of a fleet that quickly captured Canton and moved north to Tianjin.

The hapless Chinese again offered to negotiate through the viceroy of Tianjin. But Elgin was determined to deal with the imperial court itself rather than its provincial governors. The emperor in Beijing yielded and sent his representatives to sign an agreement granting full access to the Yangtze, unimpeded travel inside China for those with passports, six more treaty ports, freedom for missionaries, a diplomatic presence in Beijing, and immunity from Chinese jurisdiction for foreigners. Elgin, with the French in tow, pressed for more. And he found the excuse to move on Beijing when, amid the chaos of war, his negotiators were arrested and executed by the Chinese.

Arriving first at the city's north-eastern outskirts as negotiations with the Chinese were under way, the French came upon the Yuan

Ming Yuan, the elegant Summer Palace, which Jesuit missionaries had designed for Emperor Qianlong, and promptly plundered it. For three days, French soldiers rampaged across the thirty-seven acres of pavilions, gardens and temples, barely believing their luck: 'to depict', one intoxicated looter wrote, 'all the splendours before our astonished eyes, I should need to dissolve specimens of all known precious stones in liquid gold for ink, and to dip it into a diamond pen tipped with the fantasies of an oriental poet.'[32]

When Elgin arrived, the French offered to split the loot, and the earl got the Chinese emperor's green jade baton. Elgin, who had helped quell the Indian Mutiny before coming to China, was a reluctant imperialist by the standards of his time. He considered the broad thrust of British policy in China to be 'stupid'. 'I hate the whole thing so much that I cannot trust myself to write about it', he wrote in his diary as British warships under his command bombed and killed 200 civilians in Canton.[33] But when he received news of European prisoners dying in Chinese custody, Elgin's remaining scruples vanished.

The Chinese had to be taught a severe lesson. The French excused themselves from this act of retribution, in which British troops torched the Summer Palace, before Elgin proceeded to sign the treaty that gave the British more indemnities, and another treaty port (in Tianjin) and legations for all Western powers in Beijing. The Summer Palace burnt for two days, covering Beijing with thick black smoke. The 'crackling and rushing noise', one English observer wrote, 'was appalling . . . the sun shining through the masses of smoke gave a sickly hue to every plant and tree, and the red flame gleaming on the faces of the troops engaged made them appear like demons glorying in the destruction of what they could not replace.'[34]

The Chinese were relatively slow to awaken to their perilous position in the world. The innovative steamships of the British had navigated far up the Yangtze, threatening inland Chinese cities, and the British quickly mobilized Indian soldiers against the Chinese. But this evidence of a globally resourced maritime power only prompted the Confucian scholar-official Wei Yuan, obviously deeply immersed in the Middle Kingdom, to remark in the light of these events that 'India is nearby and must not be considered [a] barren land on the periphery [of the world]'.[35] As late as 1897, two years after Japan had brutally exposed the military weakness of Qing China, Liang Qichao was arguing that 'China cannot be compared to India or Turkey'.[36] It took the cumulative effect of internal and external political shocks – the Taiping Rebellion, defeat by Japan in Korea, and the subsequent scramble for Chinese territory by European powers – to instil a new sense of the changing global topography among the Chinese elite.

By late 1898, when the failure of the so-called 'Hundred-Day' reforms at the Qing court seemed clear, China had finally begun to look, in Liang's view, as vulnerable to the West as Turkey and India, its predicament part of a global one caused by Western-style capitalism and imperialism. Soon Liang, forced into exile in Japan, was closely examining the situation in the Philippines, where the United States was fighting a popular insurgency, for parallels with China. The philosopher Yan Fu described an increasingly widespread Chinese view of the Opium War by the late 1890s:

> When the Westerners first came, bringing with them immoral things that did harm to people [i.e., opium], and took up arms against us, this was not only a source of pain to those of us who were informed; it was then and remains today a source of shame to the residents of their capital cities. At the time, China, which had enjoyed the protection of a series of sagacious rulers, and with its vast expanse of territories, was enjoying a regime of unprecedented political and cultural prosperity. And when we looked about the world, we thought there none nobler among the human race than we.[37]

Since the 1890s, the Opium War and the destruction of the Summer Palace have been carefully remembered in China as the most egregious of the humiliations the country suffered at the hands of the West in the nineteenth century. In an essay titled 'The Death Traffic' written in 1881, a youthful Rabindranath Tagore marvelled at how a 'whole nation, China, has been forced by Great Britain to accept the opium poison – simply for commercial greed'. Tagore was aware that his own grandfather Dwarkanath Tagore was one of the Indian businessmen who had become rich by shipping opium to China. 'In her helplessness', Tagore wrote, 'China pathetically declared: "I do not require any opium." But the British shopkeeper answered: "That's all nonsense. You must take it." '[38]

Explaining Europe's growing dominance over the world, the conservative Bengali writer Bhudev Mukhopadhyay mourned that 'this Chinese War remains a good example of the fact that virtue does not always triumph. In fact, victory often lies with the unrighteous.'[39] For many Indians this was also true of the Mutiny of 1857, which spelt the end of centuries-long Muslim rule over India.

Muslims had been the biggest losers as the British East India Company became the major military power in the subcontinent. It was the defeat of two Muslim rulers in central and south India that cleared the Company's path to unchallenged supremacy over India, and then the British moved quickly, annexing the hinterland piecemeal in open battle or through treaty, finally subduing the great Muslim-majority lands of the Punjab in 1848.

All through the first half of the nineteenth century, Muslim ruling classes in north India were either scornfully deposed by the British or emasculated by restrictions on their authority. The most egregious of these annexations occurred in 1856 in the province of Awadh, which since the late eighteenth century had been subordinate to British commercial and political interests, and had been seen, as the British governor-general put it, as a 'cherry which will drop into our mouths some day, it has long been ripening'.[40] Successive Shiite Muslim kings had made Lucknow the capital city of Awadh. It was famous for its distinctive architecture, which blended Persian with European forms, and for its culturally rich courts which attracted some of north India's best poets, artists, musicians and scholars. Wajid Ali Shah, Lucknow's last king, sang, danced and wrote poetry to a high standard, but to the British these accomplishments were just another sign of his unfitness to rule. Awadh's landowning aristocracy, which mostly supported Wajid Ali Shah, had long been apprehensive of the British intentions before the Europeans, no longer willing to wait for it to drop, finally plucked the cherry. Exiling the popular king to Calcutta, the British moved quickly to extract the steepest possible land revenues from landlords and peasants.

The realm of culture, too, was far from insulated from the larger social and economic changes unleashed by the British. In the decades leading up to the Mutiny, Lucknow had replaced Delhi as the premier city of north India. However Delhi had remained an intellectual and cultural centre for north Indian Muslims, its madrasas drawing the most talented men from the provinces. Loss of territory and influence had diminished the Mughal emperors in Delhi into figureheads as early as the mid-eighteenth century, but the British continued to give the Mughals generous pensions and allowed them to hold shows of pomp and ceremony periodically. Despite their infirmity, the emperors retained, in British eyes, the symbolic value of belonging to India's oldest and most prestigious ruling dynasty. *Mushairas*, public poetry recitals, attracted huge audiences, and the rivalry of the two greatest poets at the Mughal court, Zauq and Ghalib, fuelled the gossip in the city's alleys. A young poet called Altaf Husain Hali trekked miles from his province to attend Delhi's celebrated institutions of education, and to hang out with the poets and intellectuals whose 'meetings and assemblies', he later wrote, 'recalled the days of Akbar and Shah Jahan', culturally the most assured among Mughal emperors.[41]

However, this turned out to be, as Hali wrote, 'the last brilliant glow of learning in Delhi'. Passing through Delhi in 1838, the English diarist Emily Eden lamented the city's steady incorporation into a profit-minded empire. 'Such stupendous remains of power and wealth passed and passing away – and somehow I feel that we horrid English have just "gone and done it", merchandised it, revenued it and spoiled it all.'[42] As education and judicial institutions were secularized, the *ulema*, the Muslim clergy, found it difficult to find a livelihood for itself. The replacement of Persian by English as the official language also undermined the traditional cultural world of Indian Muslims. As Hali recalled:

> I'd been brought up in a society that believed that learning was based only on the knowledge of Arabic and Persian . . . nobody even thought about English education, and if people had any opinion about it all it was as a means of getting a government job, not of acquiring any kind of knowledge.[43]

But here, too, the Muslims' former subjects – Hindus – seemed to be favoured by the new rulers, and were quick to educate themselves in Western-style institutions and assume the lowly administrative positions assigned to them. The British were beginning to replace their economic and political regime of pure plunder, as had existed in Bengal, with monopoly interests in shipping, banking, insurance and trade, and administrative structures. They enlisted native collaborators, such as the middlemen who expedited the lucrative export of opium grown in India to China, but these tended to be Hindu, Sikh or Parsi rather than Muslim.

The British indifference to Indian society and culture that Edmund Burke and the Indian historian Ghulam Hussain Khan Tabatabai had noticed in the previous century was replaced by increased cultural and racial aggression. Lord Macaulay dismissed Indian learning as risibly worthless, enjoining the British in India to create 'a class of persons, Indian in blood and colour, but English in taste, in opinion, in morals, and in intellect'. Convinced of their superiority, the British sought to entrench it with profound social and cultural reforms wherever they could in India. Often run by Christian missionaries, British-style schools, colleges and universities in India were soon churning out faux-Englishmen of the kind Macaulay had hoped for.

Many Muslims spurned this modern education out of fear of deracination. They mostly watched helplessly as the British set up plantations, dug canals and laid roads, and turned India into a supplier of raw materials to, and exclusive market for, British industries. Artisan communities in north Indian towns, which tended to be Muslim, were pauperized as British manufactured goods flooded Indian bazaars. Gandhi, one of the most prominent defenders of the local artisan, was to later sum up the multifarious damage inflicted on India by British rule in his Declaration of Indian Independence in 1930:

> Village industries, such as hand spinning, have been destroyed ... and nothing has been substituted, as in other countries, for the crafts thus destroyed. Customs and currency have been so manipulated as to bring further burdens on the peasantry. British manufactured goods constitute the bulk of our imports. Customs duties betray partiality for British manufacturers, and revenue from them is not used to lessen the burden on the masses but for sustaining a highly extravagant

administration. Still more arbitrary has been the manipulation of the exchange which has resulted in millions being drained away from the country . . . All administrative talent is killed and the masses have to be satisfied with petty village offices and clerkships . . . the system of education has torn us from our moorings.

Elsewhere, these wrenching private and social makeovers were proving too traumatic for people accustomed to living by the light of custom and tradition. Unprotected by tariffs, which the British insisted on reducing, the nascent local industries of Egypt, Ottoman Turkey and Iran could not compete with the manufactured products imported from Europe. Not surprisingly, merchants, weavers and artisans in the bazaars of Cairo and Najaf, who perceived a direct threat from European businessmen and free traders, were at the forefront of anti-Western movements in the late nineteenth century.

India's most famous thinker of that century, Swami Vivekananda (1863–1902), articulated a widespread moral revulsion among Asians for their European masters:

Intoxicated by the heady wine of newly acquired power, fearsome like wild animals who see no difference between good and evil, slaves to women, insane in their lust, drenched in alcohol from head to foot, without any norms of ritual conduct, unclean, materialistic, dependent on material things, grabbing other people's land and wealth by hook or crook . . . the body their self, its appetites their only concern – such is the image of the western demon in Indian eyes.[44]

Westerners in Asia were increasingly seen as engaging in a deliberate assault on indigenous ways of life. Native frustration and grievances were inevitably articulated through religion, which, as Marx shrewdly pointed out, was much more than a belief system: it was a 'general theory of the world, its encyclopaedic compendium, its logic in a popular form, its spiritualistic *point d'honneur*, its enthusiasm, its moral sanction, its solemn complement, its universal source of consolation and justification'.[45] Native rage, quietly simmering, often erupted into violence: the Boxer Rising in China, the tribal disturbances in east-central India at the very end of the nineteenth century, the Mahdist revolt in Sudan, the Urabi revolt in Egypt in

1882 and the tobacco revolution in Iran in 1891 would signify the strength of unorganized anti-West xenophobia, often accompanied by a desperate desire to resurrect a fading or lost socio-cultural order.

The Indian Mutiny of 1857 was one such eruption. In the early nineteenth century, marginalized and embittered Muslims had begun to be receptive to the puritanical and scripturalist reformers of Islam – now known as Wahhabis – then growing dominant in Arabia. Claiming that India was *Dar al-Harb*, Muslim theologians and activists declared jihads in 1803 and again in 1826 against the British and their Indian collaborators. Overrunning parts of north-west India, the jihadists were finally suppressed in 1831 at the Battle of Balakot, which was to assume a tragic aura in South Asian Islamic lore comparable to the martyrdom of Imam Hussein at Karbala in AD 680.

The Mutiny was a bigger explosion than any of these scattered rebellions mounted by Indian Muslims against the British. It was sparked by rumours that new cartridges used by the British Indian army were greased with pork and beef. However, for many of India's old elite, the Mutiny had been simmering for years as the British peremptorily redrew the social, political and economic map of India. A full measure of this was provided by the Delhi newspaper *Delhi Urdu Akhbar*, whose editor, Maulvi Baqar, a member of the city's old elite, swiftly moved in 1857 from being an anodyne court-chronicler to a fiery anti-imperialist pamphleteer. 'In truth', he wrote, 'the English have been afflicted with divine wrath ... and their arrogance has brought them divine retribution.'[46] Baqar recalled for his readers the many crimes of the British – the broken treaties with local rulers, the siphoning off of profits to Britain – and how now the tables were being turned on them by Hindus and Muslims: 'They have taken countries and governments away from the owners on the charge of bad management and ostensibly to bring relief to their subjects. Today the same logic is reverted upon them to say that you could not administer the country.'[47] One of Awadh's dispossessed landlords offered the same vengeful logic to a British official, whom he had rescued from a furious mob:

> Sahib, your countrymen came into this country and drove out our King. You send your officers round the districts to examine the titles to

the estates. At one blow you took from me lands which from time immemorial had been in my family. I submitted. Suddenly misfortune fell upon you. The people of the land rose against you. You came to me whom you had despoiled. I have saved you. But now – now I march at the head of my retainers in Lucknow to try and drive you from the country.[48]

The mutineers did not spare British women and children. One of the many fiery proclamations for the general revolt set out a division of labour among Indians whose 'bounden duty' it was

> to come forward and put the English to death . . . some of them should kill them by firing guns . . . and with swords, arrows, daggers . . . some lift them up on spears . . . some should wrestle and break the enemy into pieces, some should strike them with cudgels, some slap them, some throw dust into their eyes, some should beat them with shoes . . . In short no one should spare any efforts, to destroy the enemy and reduce them to the greatest extremities.[49]

Though Hindus often led the mutineers, Muslims, especially those degraded by British rule, participated in large numbers, and the confused revolution coalesced briefly around the figure of the Mughal emperor in Delhi before it was brutally suppressed. Exhorted by public opinion back home and such venerated figures as Charles Dickens, the British in India exacted terrible reprisals as they dispersed the mutineers. Vengeful soldiers lashed tens of thousands of mutineers to the muzzles of cannons, and blew them to pieces; they left a trail of destruction across north India, bayoneting and burning their way through villages and towns.

Encamped outside Delhi, waiting for the city to fall, British soldiers dreamt of 'a nice little diamond or two' from the 'rich old niggers'.[50] They went on to indulge in an orgy of murder and looting of astonishing ferocity. 'Can I do anything,' Lord Elgin wondered as he read in China of the savage quelling of the Indian Mutiny, 'to prevent England from calling down on herself God's curse for brutalities committed on another feeble Oriental race? Or are all my exertions to result only in the extension of the area over which Englishmen are to exhibit how hollow and superficial are both their civilisation and Christianity?'[51]

Elgin answered his question by burning down the Chinese emperor's Summer Palace. As it turned out, the Qing Empire limped on for another half-century. But British rage and vandalism after the Mutiny made even the symbols of the Mughal Empire untenable. The formal end of Muslim power in India finally came when an English soldier executed the sons of the rebellious, and – as it turned out – last Mughal emperor, and left their corpses to rot in the streets of Delhi.

THE NEW GLOBAL HIERARCHY

A lack of unity and effective leaders doomed the Mutiny even though it had a broad mass base and the rebels vastly outnumbered the British. Writing of the mutineers in 1921, Abdul Halim Sharar, one of the first novelists in Urdu and chronicler of the fading magnificence of Lucknow, grieved that

> There was not a single man of valour among them who knew anything of the principles of war or who could combine the disunited forces and make them into an organized striking force. The British, on the other hand, who were fighting for their lives, stood their ground. Facing the greatest danger they repelled their assailants and proved themselves skilled in the latest arts of war.[52]

The gap between the British and their Indian opponents was more than just military. As Sharar wrote bitterly,

> It was impossible for the intelligence of these foreigners and their good planning and methodical ways not to prevail against the ignorance and self-effacement of India. At this time the world had assumed a new pattern of industrialized civilization, and this way was crying aloud to every nation. No one in India heard this proclamation and all were destroyed.[53]

However melodramatic, this was not an unrealistic assessment of European power. Helped by new technologies, superior information-gathering and attractive trade terms, Europeans were by the mid-nineteenth century challenging the Chinese, pushing Persia out of its sphere of influence in the Caucasus, invading North Africa, forcing the Ottomans to open up their markets, promoting Christianity in Indochina and eyeing a long-secluded Japan. Eight decades after Napoleon's invasion of Egypt, the British would successfully occupy that country.

These rapid advances are not explained by hoary Western accounts of Asian 'decline', 'stagnation', or 'Oriental Despotism', which many self-pitying Asians also embraced. As early as 1918, the Indian sociologist Benoy Kumar Sarkar dismissed what he identified as a scholarly 'Occidental' superstition about an energetic Europe outpacing a somnolent Asia. Sarkar warned against the historical 'dogma that naturally accrues to domineering and triumphant races'.[54] Contemporary scholarship validates his view by demonstrating that Asia remained economically and culturally dynamic in the eighteenth century. Europe's competitive edge was a product of its own clearly superior skills for 'industrialized civilization' or, more simply, organization – something that Asians would soon envy and seek to imitate – and the several advantages it had accumulated throughout the 1700s.

'The spirit of the military organization,' Tokutomi Sohō marvelled about Europe in 1887, 'does not stop with just the military.' Its influence was 'extended to all corners of society'.[55] As more than one Asian observer noted, European forms of political and military mobilization (conscript armies, efficient taxation, codified laws), financial innovations (capital-raising joint-stock companies) and information-rich public cultures of enquiry and debate fed upon each other to create a formidable and decisive advantage as Europe penetrated Asia. Individually, Europeans might be no more brave, innovative, sensitive or loyal than Asians, but as members of corporate groups, churches or governments, and as efficient users of scientific knowledge, they mustered more power than the wealthiest empires of Asia.

As Sharar pointed out, a large part of Europe's power consisted of its capacity to kill, which was enhanced by continuous and vicious wars among the region's small nations in the seventeenth century, a time when Asian countries knew relative peace. 'The only trouble with us,' Fukuzawa Yukichi, author, educator and prolific commentator on Japan's modernization, lamented in the 1870s, 'is that we have had too long a period of peace and no intercourse with outside. In the meantime, other countries, stimulated by occasional wars, have invented many new things such as steam trains, steam ships, big guns and small hand guns etc.'[56] Required to fight at sea as well as on land, and to protect their slave plantations in the Caribbean, the British, for instance, developed the world's most sophisticated naval technologies. Mirza Abu Talib, an Indian Muslim traveller to Europe in 1800, was among the first Asians to articulate the degree to which the Royal Navy was the key to British prosperity. For much of the nineteenth century, British ships and commercial companies would retain their early edge in international trade over their European rivals, as well as over Asian producers and traders.

There was also something else behind European dominance. Writing in 1855 to Arthur Gobineau (who first developed the theory of an 'Aryan' master race), Alexis de Tocqueville marvelled at how 'a few million men, who a few centuries ago, lived nearly shelterless in the forests and in the marshes of Europe will, within a hundred years, have transformed the globe and dominated the other races'.[57] Pondering the same phenomenon a year later, the Bengali writer Bhudev Mukhopadhyay reached some disquieting conclusions:

> The effort to conquer other people's lands is on the increase and becomes more intense with time among Europeans: there is a sharp edge to their thirst for material pleasures and it keeps getting sharper; these do not indicate any enhancements of moral standards or any prospect thereof ... It would be logical to conclude their descendants would also inherit their penchant for marauding ... If thus Europe does not need external control, who does?[58]

But there was to be no external control – at least not until the calamity of the First World War. It was as though the competitive energies unleashed by the American and French revolutions could not be contained within the West; they could only spread around the globe, propelling Europe's small nation-states into Asia's remotest regions – a standing reproach and unique threat to peoples who were neither modern nor had any means with which to achieve economic or diplomatic parity with Europe.

There had been other imperialisms in the past. Indeed, many victims of European conquests themselves belonged to powerful empires – Ottoman Turkey, Qing China. But modern European imperialism would be wholly unprecedented in creating a global hierarchy of economic, physical and cultural power through either outright conquest or 'informal' empires of free trade and unequal treaties. As Fukuzawa Yukichi observed in the 1870s:

> In commerce, the foreigners are rich and clever; the Japanese are poor and unused to the business. In courts of law, it so often happens that the Japanese people are condemned while the foreigners get around the law. In learning, we are obliged to learn from them. In finances, we must borrow capital from them. We would prefer to open our society to foreigners in gradual stages and move toward civilization at our own pace, but they insist on the principle of free trade and urge us to let them come into our island at once. In all things, in all projects, they take the lead and we are on the defensive. There hardly ever is an equal give and take.[59]

By 1900, a small white minority radiating out from Europe would come to control most of the world's land surface, imposing the imperatives of a commercial economy and international trade on Asia's mainly agrarian societies. Europeans backed by garrisons and gunboats could intervene in the affairs of any Asian country they wished to. They were free to transport millions of Asian labourers to far-off colonies (Indians to the Malay Peninsula, Chinese to Trinidad); exact the raw materials and commodities they needed for their industries from Asian economies; and flood local markets with their manufactured products. The peasant in his village and the market trader in his town were being forced to abandon a life defined by religion, family and tradition amid rumours of powerful white men with a strange god-on-a-cross who were reshaping the world – men who married moral aggressiveness with compact and coherent nation-states, the profit motive and superior weaponry, and made Asian societies seem lumberingly inept in every way, unable to match the power of Europe or unleash their own potential.

As European countries went from one easy conquest to another, leaving manifold social, economic and cultural disruptions in their wake, many Asian intellectuals would grow profoundly anxious about the fate of their societies. Many Muslims interpreted the loss of

42

their territories to Christian Europeans in India, Africa and Central Asia as God's punishment for their religious laxity. The sense of great and permanent crisis was profound even in places such as Japan and Turkey, which were not occupied or ruled directly by European powers. As Japan's great novelist Natsume Sōseki (1867–1916) described it:

> The civilization of the West has its origins within itself, while that of modern Japan has its origin outside the country. The new waves come one after another from the West . . . It is as if, before we can enjoy one dish on the table, or even know what it is, another new dish is set before us . . . We cannot help it; there is nothing else we can do.[60]

The great speed of change, and helplessness before it, was a common experience. The slightest Western contact with Asian lands inevitably sparked a drastic churning – usually for the worse. The Industrial Revolution and Europe's demand for raw materials for its manufacturing industries not only thwarted industrialization in Asia; it also forced traditionally self-sufficient peasants across Asia to become rubber-tappers, tin-miners, coffee-growers and tea-pickers. In Islamic societies, the imperative to match Western power and build a European-style centralized state created new classes of bureaucrats, technocrats, bankers, urban workers and intellectuals which threatened to undermine the old Islamic world of the guilds, the bazaars, caravanserai, the *ulema* and Sufi peers. Even the unalloyed boon of modern medicine in the rising West turned into something darkly ambiguous in Asia when it helped increase populations in the absence of corresponding economic growth, compounding the problem of poverty.

The cultural effects of Europe's primacy were no less dramatic. Civilization came to be represented by European forms of scientific and historical knowledge and ideas of morality, public order, crime and punishment, even styles of dress. Asians everywhere came up against Europe's new self-understanding in which it was everything Asia was not: non-despotic, increasingly urban and commercial, innovative and dynamic. Rabindranath Tagore wrote exasperatedly of

> Asia's being ever a defendant in Europe's court and ever taking her verdict as the last word, admitting that our only good is in rooting out

the three-fourths of our society along with their very foundation, and in replacing them with the English brick and mortar as planned out by English engineers.[61]

And Liang Qichao was not alone in worrying that such a dramatic change in his society's external circumstances fatally damaged inner lives and older notions of morality: 'I fear,' he confessed in 1901 during his most pro-Western phase, 'that mental training will gradually become more important, while moral training decays, that the materialist civilization of the West will invade China, the 400,000,000 people be led away and become as the birds and beasts.'[62]

For thinkers like Liang, Sōseki and Tagore, the challenges of the West were as much existential as geopolitical. What was good and bad about the old ways and the new ones proposed by the West? And was Europe's modern civilization truly 'universal' and 'liberal', as its defenders claimed, or did it discriminate against non-white races? Could one stay loyal to one's nation while importing ideas from the same Western countries that threatened that nation's existence and survival? And how was one to define the new concept of the nation?

Varying geopolitical conditions and religious and political traditions would determine Asian responses and their timings. Long sequestered, the Japanese were able to borrow the tool-kit of modernity earlier and more comprehensively than any other Asian country. Emulating Russia and their Muslim peers in Egypt, the Ottoman Turks tried to embrace European military and administrative techniques in an attempt to make themselves invulnerable to European power. The Chinese went on lamenting their 'backwardness' vis-à-vis Europe late into the twentieth century.

A number of highly intelligent men turned to a traditionalist worldview grounded in fealty to the moral prescriptions of Islam, Confucianism and Hinduism. Some of the most innovative Asians sought an enlightened synthesis between their religious traditions and the European Enlightenment. Islamic modernists, for instance, called for a selective borrowing of European science, politics and culture, insisting that the Koran was fully compatible with modernity.

But in whatever these Asians did they all affirmed the extraordinary dominance of the West in almost every aspect of human endeavour in the modern world. It was as though Asia's vast empires, its venerable traditions and time-honoured customs had no defence against Europe's purposive traders, missionaries, diplomats and soldiers. One by one, the Egyptians, the Chinese and the Indians revealed themselves as vulnerable, poorly fitted for a new modern world the West was making and which they had to join or perish. This is why the European subordination of Asia was not merely economic and political and military. It was also intellectual and moral and spiritual: a completely different kind of conquest than had been witnessed before, which left its victims resentful but also envious of their conquerors and, ultimately, eager to be initiated into the mysteries of their seemingly near-magical power.

TWO: THE STRANGE ODYSSEY OF JAMAL AL-DIN AL-AFGHANI

What brought on this era? What happened that other people, ignoring us completely while they changed and developed their machines, built, carried out plans, and moved in and out of our midst and we awoke to find every oil derrick a spike impaling the land?

Why did we end up Westoxified?

Let's go back to history.

Jalal Al-e Ahmad, Gharbzadegi *('Westoxification'), 1962*

AN INSIGNIFICANT MAN IN
ROUGH GARMENTS

In the early 1960s, a group of Iranian exiles in Paris often met at a café called Au Départ in Saint Germain. Most of them were political refugees from Iran, where in 1953 the American CIA and British MI6 had helped topple the elected government of Mohammad Mossadegh after the latter nationalized the Iranian oil industry. Among these angry figures was Ali Shariati (1933–77), later the primary intellectual guide of Iran's Islamic Revolution. 'Convicted of the crime of having afflicted the first lash at the pillaging West,' he lamented on the eighth anniversary of the Anglo-American coup, 'a people still remain in chains.'[1] Like his fellow exiles, Shariati had few aims in Paris other than to advance his political and intellectual training, and then to inform and educate his compatriots in turn. He translated Jean-Paul Sartre's *What Is Literature* and Frantz Fanon's *The Wretched of the Earth* into Persian. He wrote about Sun Yat-sen, the anti-French revolt in Algeria, and Gandhi and Nehru (whom he saw as India's Mossadeghs) in periodicals run by Iranian exiles (which were often smuggled back to Iran); he attended demonstrations against the brutal murder of Patrice Lumumba in the Congo. He also closely monitored the bloody uprising of June 1963 against the pro-Western regime in Iran, which first made a cleric named Ruhollah Khomeini politically prominent; and increasingly in their Saint-Germain haunts, he and his friends discussed an itinerant nineteenth-century activist and thinker called Jamal al-Din al-Afghani.

Early in 1892, in a letter to the Ottoman sultan Abdulhamid II, al-Afghani had articulated the fear that ruled his life and which now dominated Shariati's as well, that Western powers

> all have only one desire, that of making our land disappear up to our last trace. And in this there is no distinction to make between Russia, England, Germany, or France, especially if they perceive our weakness and our impotence to resist their designs. If, on the contrary, we are united, if the Muslims are a single man, we can then be of harm and of use and our voice will be heard.[2]

As a young student in 1955 in Mashhad, Shariati had written one of his very first articles about this relatively obscure figure. In Paris in the 1960s he turned again to al-Afghani after a long intellectual detour through Western secular ideologies of emancipation, and, as he wrote in 1970, Shariati was convinced that 'to understand him is tantamount to recognizing Islam and Muslims, and our present and future as well'.[3]

In Iran, Jamal al-Din al-Afghani is revered as the intellectual godfather of the Islamic Revolution, which Michel Foucault, visiting Tehran in 1979, called 'the first great insurrection' against the 'global systems' of the West.[4] More remarkably, left-wing secularists as well as Islamists, pan-Arabists and pan-Islamists in Muslim countries as disparate as Egypt, Turkey, India, Pakistan, Afghanistan and Malaysia regard al-Afghani as a path-breaking anti-imperialist leader and thinker. Compared to the two other great political and philosophical exiles of the nineteenth century, Karl Marx and Alexander Herzen, al-Afghani is barely known in the West today, even though his influence exceeds that of Herzen and, at least in its longevity, almost matches Marx's.

This is at least partly because there are gaping holes in his biography. Much of what he did and said during his journeys across the Muslim world has been lost to history. To reconstruct his intellectual trajectory, as the following pages attempt, is to explore the social and political tumult of the different countries he travelled through – the experiences that defined his worldview. In any case, a history of his ideas cannot depend, as is the case with many Western thinkers, on published texts setting out clear concepts and well-referenced biographies. Intellectual history in this case is the history of his arguments, which are not and could not be internally consistent with his world.

Certainly, there was scarcely a social or political tendency in Muslim lands – modernism, nationalism, pan-Islamism – that al-Afghani's catholic and vital sensibility did not either ignite or stoke. Nor was there a realm of political action – anti-imperialist conspiracy, education, journalism, constitutional reform – on which he did not leave the imprint of his ideas. Ali Shariati was only exaggerating a bit when he claimed that al-Afghani was 'the man who first raised the voice of awareness in the dormant East'.[5]

*

By his own admission, al-Afghani was an 'insignificant man, who has no high rank and who has not achieved exalted office'. Yet, as he warned, 'great deeds' were performed by men like himself, 'wandering and with rough garments, knowing cold and heat, bitter and sweet, and having traversed many mountains and deserts and experienced the ways of men'.[6] His deeds look greater in retrospect, especially when compared to those of the Muslim thinkers who preceded him.

Napoleon's invasion of Egypt had first demonstrated to many Muslims that some people of the West had discovered new sources of economic and military power, and could project it thousands of miles away from home. But long afterwards, many among the Islamic countries' ruling classes and intelligentsia kept fervently advocating assimilation to Western modes of life, and accommodation with rather than resistance to European power. They did not yet fear Europe as a profoundly disruptive force, one that would challenge Muslims' most strongly held conceptions about their place in the world. Though rattled by Napoleon's incursion, the Egyptian chronicler al-Jabarti found it easy to mock the French for their toilet habits. He did not enquire into French motives for coming to Egypt, and he met the ideas of the French Revolution that plunged Europe into turmoil – republicanism, social equality and mobility, the just and impartial state – with near-total incomprehension. Later observers of the West's innovations were more curious than anxious, especially as Egypt and the Ottoman Empire set about creating modern states and armies on the Western model.

Europe actually appeared to be a benign example to the great Egyptian scholar Rifa'a Badawi Rafi al-Tahtawi (1801–73), who spent five years in Paris from 1826 to 1831. Explicating the French Revolution and the French constitution, he provided Arabic speakers with their first full account of a political system in a Western country. 'The French people', he wrote admiringly, 'are equal before the law despite their differences in prestige, position, honor, and wealth.'[7] Similarly, during his many trips to Europe between 1850 and 1865, the Tunisian Khayr al-Din al-Tunisi became a devoted admirer of Voltaire, Condillac, Rousseau and Montesquieu, regretting only these philosophers' bitter attacks on religion. He noted the voluntary associations and organizational skills of Europeans: 'If people join with one another to achieve a joint end, it is possible for them to attain even the most difficult things.' One of the 'incredible examples' of this was British rule over India. 'The British government through an association of her merchants known as the India Company, acquired about three hundred millions, five hundred square metres of land with a population of over one hundred and eighty million persons.'[8]

Al-Tahtawi, Khayr al-Din and the Syrian educationist Butrus al-Bustani (1819–83) – whose dictionary, great encyclopaedia and periodicals helped create modern Arabic language and literature – were among the first officials, teachers and soldiers in the Muslim world convinced of the necessity of reform to offset internal decline and decay. In the late eighteenth and early nineteenth centuries, many intellectuals around the Ottoman court in Istanbul, too, had come to the same conclusion: that their social-political order had grown old and decrepit, and needed to be renewed by outside learning. These intellectuals did not relate, as al-Afghani was soon to do, their domestic conditions to the alarming shifts in international relations. They saw reform as largely a matter of adopting European knowledge and practical skills into their societies, and updating their militaries. Many European elites had already begun to regard Christianity and the white race as superior and unique. But the Turkish and Egyptian admirers of Montesquieu and Guizot, who initiated modernization under Western tutelage in the 1830s, had yet to become fully aware of Europe's new racial hierarchies; they hoped their Muslim societies would eventually become advanced enough to achieve parity with Europe. The Ottoman writer Namik Kemal was convinced in the 1860s that

> it took Europe two centuries to reach this condition and while they were the inventors in the paths to progress, we find all the means ready to hand . . . can there be any doubt that we, too, even if it takes us two centuries, can reach a stage where we would be counted as one of the most civilized countries?[9]

Remarkably, al-Afghani was already alert to the perils ahead for Muslim countries in the 1860s, when the European presence in Asia was still largely confined to India. He realized that history was working independently of the God of the Koran, and that the initiative had been seized by the restless, energetic peoples in the West who, erupting out of longstanding cultural and political backwaters, were discovering and exploring new worlds and subjugating with means never wielded in previous imperial expansions Muslim as well as other non-Western peoples.

The Awakening in India and Afghanistan

Facts about al-Afghani's early life are scarce and obscured by his claim, repeated in several countries, to have been a Sunni Muslim from Afghanistan. But it is clear now that he was born in 1838 in the village of Asadabad near Hamadan in north-west Persia, and educated in Tehran, the seminaries of great Shiite cities, mainly Najaf, and then in India. His early years in Persia coincided with the rise of Babism, a radical and messianic interpretation of Islamic traditions. Suppressed in Persia, many followers of Babism fled to Shiite cities in Ottoman-ruled Mesopotamia; they may have had some effect on al-Afghani's own bold and sometimes nearly heretical view of Islam, and his revolutionary messianism. But he also received an early grounding in the tradition of Persian Islamic philosophy, which, more open to innovation than its Sunni Arabic counterpart, clearly emboldened al-Afghani's revisionist Islam.

Shiite Islam had a more unorthodox tradition in Persia, which even as late as the nineteenth century produced a major Islamic philosopher, Mullah Hadi. Shiite Persia had preserved philosophical traditions that had long been moribund in Arabic-speaking lands, such as reconciling rationalist ideas with revealed religion. Trained in a heterodox tradition, al-Afghani was sooner able to speak of reform and change than his Sunni peers. But, as a Shiite, his appeal would have been limited among Sunnis, and he seems to have thought it prudent to claim Afghan ancestry in order to pass himself off as a Sunni Muslim in the countries that he wished to reform. He was also, if briefly, a Freemason in Egypt. Neither an unthinking Westernizer nor a devout traditionalist, al-Afghani seems to have been concerned most with the exigencies of anti-imperialist strategizing. He travelled to India in the late 1850s to continue his education, and spent a considerable part of the next decade there, in, among other places, Bombay (which had a large community of Persians) and Calcutta. It was during this time of fierce Indian assaults on the British and the latter's brutal backlash that his intellectual heritage of revolt from the Babis began to turn from a local into a global ideology of resistance.

Soon afterwards, al-Afghani entered documented history in a small but tantalizing role, appropriately enough in Afghanistan, which was then, as it has been recently, the treacherous crossroads for many different geopolitical ambitions. Secret British government reports from Kandahar and Kabul in 1868 describe al-Afghani as having arrived from India in 1866, a virulent anti-British agitator and likely Russian agent, a slender man with a pale complexion, open forehead, penetrating azure eyes and goatee, who drank tea constantly, was well-versed in geography and history, spoke Arabic, Turkish and Persian (the last language like a native of Persia), not visibly religious and with a European rather than Muslim lifestyle.[10]

Shortly after arriving in Kabul, al-Afghani became a counsellor to Afghanistan's amir, who was then involved in a complex civil war with his half-brother and was suspected by his powerful neighbours, the British in India, of conniving with Russia. The Afghans had proved perspicacious foes of the British. In 1839, the British in India tried to install a friendly ruler in Kabul. Afghan guerrilla fighters bided their time, and then assaulted a large British expeditionary force sent to the city, reducing it through successive attacks to just one man: a British army surgeon whose slumped figure on a horse, famously depicted in a Victorian painting titled *Remnants of An Army*, came to stand for the worst of British military disasters in the nineteenth century.

By the 1860s, the British were pressing Afghanistan again, and al-Afghani apparently saw an opportunity. In a history of Afghanistan he wrote in 1878, al-Afghani affirmed his faith in Afghan hatred of foreign usurpers: 'Nobility of soul leads them to choose a death of honor above a life of baseness under foreign rule.'[11] Here was al-Afghani's chance to pit the fiercely proud Afghans against the British. He advised the amir to consider collaborating with the Russians, by now the well-established rivals of the British in the region spanning the Ottoman Empire and Tibet. Among the reasons for preferring Russia over Britain that al-Afghani gave to an Afghan informant of the British was this: 'The English are thieves of unknown extraction, who have lately sprung up, and owe all that they have gained to their intrigues. The Russian state has existed since the time of Alexander the Great.'[12]

In any case, al-Afghani overplayed his hand. In 1868 the amir was defeated by his half-brother, Sher Ali, and lost his throne. Sher Ali struck a deal with the British and promptly expelled al-Afghani from Kabul, forcing him to look for another Muslim ruler to indoctrinate with the perils of British imperialism. Al-Afghani left Afghanistan with a particularly poor impression of Afghan leaders, whom he thought were unreliable and prone to collaborate with European powers (he later altered his impression when Sher Ali turned against his British patrons in 1878, sparking the second Anglo-Afghan War).

Imprisoned at the Bala Hisar fort in Kabul awaiting expulsion from the country, he composed in rhymed prose an ironic commentary on the misunderstandings he evoked in Afghanistan (and would soon evoke in many other countries):

> The English people believe me a Russian
> The Muslims think me a Zoroastrian
> The Sunnis think me a Shiite
> And the Shiite think me an enemy of Ali
> Some of the friends of the four companions have believed
>   me a Wahhabi
> Some of the virtuous Imamites have imagined me a Babi
> The theists have imagined me a materialist
> And the pious a sinner bereft of piety
> The learned have considered me an unknowing ignoramus
> And the believers have thought me an unbelieving sinner
> Neither does the unbeliever call me to him
> Nor the Muslim recognize me as his own
> Banished from the mosque and rejected by the temple
> I am perplexed as to whom I should depend on and whom
>   I should fight
> The rejection of one makes the friends firm against its opposite
> There is no way of escape for me to flee the grasp of one group
> There is no fixed abode for me to fight the other party
> Seated in Bala Hisar in Kabul, my hands tied and my legs
> Broken, I want to see what the Curtain of the Unknown will

Deign to reveal to me and what fate the turning of this malevolent
Firmament has in store for me.[13]

In the decades ahead, al-Afghani would frequently find himself on the
losing side. But still he would amplify, more eloquently and urgently
than any Muslim of his time, the manifold threats posed by the West
to the civilization built by Islam. And he would never cease to stress his
early experience of India, the only country with a large Muslim population to be occupied and partly administered by the British. In 1857
Maulvi Baqar, the editor of *Delhi Urdu Akhbar*, was already expressing an incipient religious anti-colonialism, using Hindu epics and
mythology as well as Koranic fables and Turkish history to describe an
Indian nation wholly different from and opposed to the British. Writing about the Mutiny in 1878, al-Afghani, too, claimed to have been
struck by the anti-British feeling shared across all social and religious
divisions in India. 'Their rancour and enmity [toward the British]', he
wrote, 'have attained such a pitch that there is not an Indian living who
does not pray for the advance of the Russians to the frontier of India.'

The political instruction al-Afghani drew from the Mutiny and its
particularly bitter aftermath served him well for the rest of his life.
Talking to an Afghan years later, he was still lamenting the weakness
of the mutineers and the ease with which the British had annexed
Awadh. He would compare the British to 'a dragon which had swallowed twenty million people, and drunk up the waters of the Ganges
and the Indus, but was still unsatiated and ready to devour the rest of
the world and to consume the waters of the Nile and the Oxus'.[14]

The violence of al-Afghani's language was provoked at least partly
by the destruction of a whole Muslim society and culture that he witnessed in post-Mutiny India. In Delhi the British had levelled large
parts of the city, and killed or expelled most of its Muslim inhabitants.
'When the angry lions entered the town,' Ghalib, the greatest poet of
the last Mughal court, wrote to a friend, 'they killed the helpless and
burned houses. Hordes of men and women, commoners and noble-
men, poured out of Delhi from the three gates and took shelter in the
small communities and tombs outside the city.'[15] 'The city,' Ghalib
lamented, 'has become a desert.'[16] The British did not allow Muslims

back into the city until 1859. 'The Muslims' houses remained so long empty . . . that the walls seemed to be made of grass,' Ghalib wrote.[17]

The forebears of Jawaharlal Nehru, who had been administrative officials at the Mughal court, were among those who fled British vindictive fury in Delhi in 1857. But the Nehrus, high-caste Hindus from Kashmir, did not suffer as much as elite Muslims such as their *munshi* (secretary), who, Nehru relates in his autobiography, saw his family financially ruined and then partly exterminated by English troops. And these weren't the only kind of losses. For Indian Muslims accustomed to ruling over India, the vicious quelling of the Mutiny was nothing less than a radical and comprehensive spiritual defeat.

It was the poets who evoked most eloquently the humiliation and deracination of their community. Akbar Illahabadi, who witnessed the Mutiny, versified a widespread bitterness: 'If you should pass that way you'll see my ravaged village / A Tommies' barracks standing by a ruined mosque.'[18] In another poem, Illahabadi described the painful sensation of adjusting to an entirely new world:

> The minstrel, and the music, and the melody have all changed. Our very sleep has changed; the tale we used to hear is no longer told. Spring comes with new adornments; the nightingales in the garden sing a different song. Nature's every effect has undergone a revolution. Another kind of rain falls from the sky; another kind of grain grows in the fields.[19]

Altaf Hussein Hali, a poet from the provinces, also evoked the fallen state of Muslims in his popular poem *Musaddas: The Flow and Ebb of Islam* (1879):

> If anyone sees the way our downfall passes all bound,
> The way that Islam, once fallen, does not rise again,
> He will never believe that the tide flows after every ebb,
> Once he sees the way our sea has gone out.[20]

In the early twentieth century, Hali's elegies would be routinely recited at political meetings of Muslim anti-colonialists, many of whom would later agitate for a new homeland – Pakistan – for Indian Muslims.

> When autumn has set in over the garden,
> Why speak of the springtime of flowers?

When shadows of adversity hang over the present,
Why harp on the pomp and glory of the past?
Yes, these are things to forget; but how can you with
The dawn forget the scene of the night before?
The assembly has just dispersed;
The smoke is still rising from the burnt candle;
The footprints on the sands of India still say
A graceful caravan has passed this way.[21]

The British tended to blame Muslims more than Hindus for the Mutiny, and after it they were more eager than ever to reduce the role of Muslims in public life. In a personal meeting with Randolph Churchill, the British Secretary of State for India in 1885, al-Afghani would confront him with reasons why Indian Muslims hated Britain: 'You destroyed the Empire of Delhi; secondly, because you give no salaries to the imams and muezzins and keepers of the mosques. And you have resigned the Wakf property and do not repair the sacred buildings.'[22] But when he first arrived in a humiliated country in the late 1850s, al-Afghani seems to have been more interested in absorbing the larger lessons from the victims of imperialism.

Indian Muslims, such as Sir Sayyid Ahmed Khan, an official in the East India Company during the Mutiny, had already begun to stress a Western-style education for Muslims, convinced that the mastery of science was the basis of success in the modern world. Asked by mutineers to leave the British and join the rebellion in 1857, Sir Sayyid gambled correctly. 'British sovereignty,' he replied, 'cannot be eliminated from India.'[23] (He went on to secure safe passage for a British district collector and his family, who were likely to be murdered by the mutineers.) Subsequently assisted by the British in his efforts to set up educational institutions, most famously at the north Indian town of Aligarh, Sir Sayyid advised his Muslim compatriots to profit from 'the style and art of Englishmen'.[24] His motto became 'Educate, Educate, Educate', and he had many supporters among Indian Muslims. Nazir Ahmed, a leading novelist and essayist in Urdu, claimed that

While all of us were spending time in useless disputation
The men of Europe leap into the void of God's creation.
Time was when their condition was more miserable than ours

But now the wealth of all the world rains down on them in showers.
Now God himself has moved to share his secrets with these nations
Because they have perceived the mode of Nature's operations.[25]

Al-Afghani would exhort his fellow Muslims similarly over the next decades. 'O, sons of the East,' he wrote in 1879, 'don't you know that the power of the westerners and their domination over you came about through their advance in learning and education, and your decline in those domains.'[26] At the same time, he would never cease to hate and distrust perfidious Albion – feelings developed during his time in India, and best summarized by the satirical poet Akbar Illahabadi:

> The Englishman can slander whom he will
> And fill your head with anything he pleases.
> He wields sharp weapons, Akbar. Best stand clear!
> He cuts up God himself into three pieces.[27]

In Egypt in 1878, when his account of British oppression in India was challenged, al-Afghani dismissed his critics as influenced by history books authored by English people, which, he claimed, 'are marked by the hands of English self-love, with the pens of conceit and the pencils of deception, and inescapably they do not relate the truth and do not report reality'.[28] Convinced that British accounts of India 'laid the snare of ambiguity and the trap of duplicity' for their readers, al-Afghani also never succumbed to the claims of imperial propagandists that the British were in India for the good of the Indians, and had built cities, railways and schools, and deposed tyrants like the king of Awadh, to this end. This was laughable, he claimed. Even if Indian rulers were oppressive and corrupt, their reach was very limited, and they spent their ill-gotten wealth in India. The British terrorized and exploited all Indians, and exported the spoils to Britain. As for their telegraph and railways, any Indian would say, he asserted, that they were built

only in order to drain the substance of our wealth and facilitate the means of trade for the inhabitants of the British Isles and extend their sphere of riches: other than this, what has brought us to poverty and need, our wealth exhausted, our riches ended, and many of us dead, consumed by hunger?[29]

Claiming to speak on behalf of Indians, al-Afghani sounds pre-sumptuous. But, writing his autobiography decades later, Jawaharlal Nehru was no less emphatic that the 'heralds of industrialism', rail-ways, telegraphs and the wireless, 'came to us primarily for the strengthening of British rule' – to the extent that, Nehru wrote, 'the railway, the life-giver, has always seemed to me like iron bands confin-ing and imprisoning India'.[30]

It appears – reliable information is lacking on this score – that after completing his education in British-ruled India in the early 1860s, al-Afghani went to Iran, and, probably, to Mecca, Baghdad and Istanbul. His little cameo in the Great Game in Afghanistan was only the first of many international intrigues al-Afghani involved himself in. But it set a pattern: the consistent thread through his activities from now on would be his fear and distrust of Western, particularly British, power and its native enablers in Muslim countries.

Certainly, India was already a subjugated country, and Afghanistan a backward little principality, its rulers petty feudatories compared to the rulers and intellectuals of the Ottoman Empire, to which al-Afghani next went in 1869. But here he was to witness how even the most powerful Muslim empire of its time, though not militarily threat-ened by the West, had slipped into dependence on it; and how the Ottomans in their attempt at self-renovation – by creating new admin-istrative structures, modern armies and efficient taxation – had set off a great internal tumult.

THE 'SICK MAN' OF EUROPE AND HIS DANGEROUS SELF-THERAPY

By late 1869, when al-Afghani arrived there, Istanbul was the largest city in the Muslim world and the political centre of both Arabs and Persians. Horse-drawn trams clattered through the western quarter, a mosaic of nationalities – Bulgarians, Circassians, Arabs, Greeks, Persians and Kazakhs – was on display at the Galata Bridge over the Golden Horn. Most of Istanbul's population was Christian, and parts of it – the western quarters of Pera and Galata – resembled, superficially at least, a more cosmopolitan version of Berlin or St Petersburg.

Europeans attracted by the possibility of easy money had poured into the city after 1838, when the Ottomans signed a free-trade agreement with Britain and loosened their control of the economy. Al-Afghani lived in the old city where Muslims in turbans and flowing robes still studied the Koran and Hadith. But elsewhere Turks wore the fez and the stambouline, a cut-away frock-coat, and an imperial decree issued in 1856 (a 'day of weeping and mourning for the people of Islam', according to some Turkish Muslims) had permitted church bells to be rung in the city for the first time since the Ottoman conquest of Constantinople in 1453.

Indeed, churches, palaces, hospitals, factories, schools and public gardens were advancing relentlessly to the shores of the Golden Horn and the Sea of Marmara, squeezing out traditional Muslim neighbourhoods. In 1867, Sultan Abdulaziz, who was determined to build palaces more magnificent than any in Europe, had returned from a grand tour of Paris, London and Vienna with big plans to make Istanbul appear more European. In 1869, the Prince of Wales visited the city. Attending the opera with him and the sultan, the British journalist William Howard Russell marvelled at the obvious wealth and glamour of the audience. 'It needed an effort to believe we were in Constantinople, so brilliant and Europeanized was the spectacle.'[31] The Westernizing Ottoman statesmen would have received this as a tremendous vindication of their efforts. But Europeanizing was an expensive business which exacted a high political as well as economic cost from the Ottomans.

European banks mushroomed, offering loans at extortionate interest rates. As the Ottomans sank steadily into debt, European power inexorably grew. Ambassadors of Britain, France, Russia and other European nations sailed into Istanbul on warships; Ottoman soldiers saluted them at every guard post they passed and they intervened with impunity in Ottoman affairs. Under the long-standing Ottoman *millet* system, religious communities were allowed a high degree of self-rule; they had their own legal courts, for instance, and collected their own taxes. But the Capitulations, a system of legal privileges granted to

foreigners in the Ottoman Empire, made leading European powers –
the French, Russians and British, in particular – the formal protectors
of ethnic minorities in the Ottoman Empire. Furthermore, the Capitulations made Europeans immune to litigation or trial in Muslim
courts, no matter how severe their crime.

A year before al-Afghani reached Istanbul, Ziya Pasha, one of the
discontented 'Young Ottomans' who began to protest against European influence in the 1860s, had written: 'We have remained mere
spectators while our commerce, our trades, and even our broken-
down huts have been given to the foreigners ... Soon it will not be
possible to make a living.'[32] Many Ottomans, accustomed to a sense
of superiority over 'infidels', were appalled by their apparent weakness before Europe, which they had long threatened. Sitting by Rumeli
Hisari, the fortress from which the Ottomans launched their capture
of Constantinople in the fifteenth century, the writer and statesman
Ahmed Vefik could only lament, 'Perhaps we are justly punished. We
were insolent and unjust in our dealings with foreign nations in our
day of power. Now in our adversity you trample us.'[33]

In Ottoman Turkey the dominion of the West was achieved not
through outright conquest, as had happened in India, but through
urgent borrowings of political, economic and cultural ideas from Europe. Nonetheless, as al-Afghani was to find out, the changes unleashed
upon ordinary Muslims were no less disorientating than they had
been in India.

Compared to its Safavid and Mughal peers, the Ottoman Empire
still looked intact and politically independent as the nineteenth century opened. Spread across three continents, from the Danube to the
Persian Gulf, and from Tripoli to Trebizond on the Black Sea, it was
the most cosmopolitan state in the world, with a light imprint in its
peripheries many of which were fully or partially autonomous. It had
proved over centuries to be a vast, sophisticated political organism,
capable of accommodating much ethnic and religious diversity and
adjudicating disputes between different regions and communities: the
millet system, promoting a degree of cultural and religious pluralism,
was exemplary in this regard in the pre-modern world. Contrary to
European perceptions of irreversible decline, which were shaped by

the Ottoman failure to capture Vienna in 1683, the empire had been flourishing politically, economically and culturally. Nevertheless, as European power expanded across the world, the empire's eighteenth-century rulers grew anxious about their ability to build a state strong enough to compete with its continental rivals. As Sultan Mustafa III (1757–74) put it in a quatrain shortly before his death:

The World is turning upside down, with no hope for better during
  our reign
Wicked fate has delivered the state into the hands of despicable men,
Our bureaucrats are villains who prowl through the streets of Istanbul,
We can do nothing but beg God for mercy.[34]

This was too melodramatic. But it is true that post-Enlightenment Europe had already embarked on its extraordinary ascent; and proximity to the continent made the Ottomans as eager and anxious as the Russians to do the right thing and join the European-led march of progress. Even Egypt, nominally an Ottoman province, had started a programme of rapid internal modernization after its encounter with Napoleon in 1798. As it turned out, one shock after another in the first half of the nineteenth century focused some of the brightest Ottoman minds on the imperative of reform.

Having become even more aggressive after its defeat of Napoleon in 1812, Russia carved out large chunks of the Ottoman Empire. Sultan Mahmud II (1808–39) had to countenance the nationalist rebellions of his Balkan Christian subjects, emboldened by their patrons in the West. The successful Greek insurgency, which was jointly enabled by European powers in 1829, encouraged more minorities within the Ottoman Empire to internationalize their grievances.

In the meantime, the Europeans nibbled away at Ottoman territory. In 1830 the French occupied Algeria, provoking nothing more than an official protest from Istanbul. Wahhabi fundamentalists, espousing a return to a bleakly puritanical Islam, overran parts of Arabia before being pushed back. Much of Muslim North Africa, including Egypt, was effectively independent of Ottoman control. Muhammad Ali, the insubordinate viceroy of Egypt, even dared threaten the Ottoman heartland itself in 1832 and 1839 and had to be deterred with the help of Russian and British forces. Things unravelled so quickly that only the fierce rivalry between Western powers and Russia and the fear of a wider European war seemed to protect the empire from demise. As the duke of Wellington proclaimed, 'The Ottoman Empire stands not for the benefit of the Turks but of Christian Europe.'[35] This was true in more ways than one: apart from a guarantee against European conflict, an unimpaired Ottoman Empire also offered a lucrative single market for European products, especially after trade treaties favourable to Europe reduced tariffs.

Military defeats made it imperative for the Ottomans to reform the army; however, that meant more buttressing and centralization of the civilian administration, which in turn made changes in the social and economic habits of the population imperative. Still, Sultan Mahmud II managed, often brutally, to force through a degree of centralization. As Muslim rulers in India had done, the Ottomans had tried to train their army in the European way in the late eighteenth century. Military and naval academies were set up and fiscal administration was reformed in order to pay for regular infantry. Now, the Ottoman ruling class instituted such further reforms as a conscript army, taxes, a trained bureaucracy (rather than court appointees) and modern education.

Sultan Mahmud's efforts to create a modern state were supplemented by his successor, Sultan Abdulmejid (1839–61), whose bureaucrats launched with great fanfare a reform programme called Tanzimat ('regulations'). Though prefaced with references to the Koran and the law of Sharia (a conciliatory gesture to the *ulema* and other conservative forces), the Tanzimat edict explicitly aimed to create a legal and administrative system along Western, and more specifically French, lines. It promised legal equality to minorities instead of assigning them to the *millet* system, sought to establish a secular university, and even allowed peasants to migrate from their villages. Modernizing reformers within the government centralized the administration, undermining the power of local notables and encouraging new secular ideas of Ottoman 'citizenship'. They set up a finance ministry and began to promote secular education.

The effects of the Tanzimat were soon visible. Journalism and literature received a boost; European lifestyles became highly sought after. Western-style private schools for the wealthy classes, which

Lord Macaulay might have approved of, were set up. Among the first such schools was the Lycée Imperial de Galataseray in Pera, the European quarter of Istanbul, which was reputedly more cosmopolitan than any comparable school in Western Europe or Russia. (These centres of secular education were to produce Turkey's educated elite.) A grand quasi-European palace, the Dolmabahçe, arose on the shores of the Bosporus, replacing the Topkapi, the traditional residence of the Sultan.

The pashas (officials) enforcing the Tanzimat, many of whom had been educated in Paris, were almost totally sold on the idea of Westernizing social, cultural and intellectual life in Turkey. They had little time for old pieties. As Fuad Pasha, one of the reform-minded and autocratic ministers of the Sublime Porte, the government of the Ottoman Empire, declared, 'Islam was for centuries, in its setting, a marvellous instrument of progress. Today it is a clock which has lost time and which must be made to catch up.'[36]

Personally suave in the European sense, the reformists could be ruthless in the preservation of their power and prerogatives as a modernizing class, rarely hesitating to ride roughshod over traditional elites. Indeed, reform for them was a means to securing their own position at the heights of Ottoman society. They partly aimed the Tanzimat at European opinion, hoping to persuade it of Turkey's claim to civilization (the modernizing Turks had some European fans: the positivist philosopher Auguste Comte decided that Turkey could be the right laboratory for his Religion of Humanity).

Certainly, the Ottomans succeeded in improving their international standing. Fighting alongside France and Britain against Russia in the Crimean War (1853–6), they were promoted to parity with the Christian powers. Ottoman desire to be part of the Concert of Europe, echoed today by the Turkish application to join the European Union, was fulfilled at the end of the war by the Treaty of Paris of 1856. Britain became an informal ally against the ever-present Russian threat; the Ottomans reciprocated by calling upon Indian Muslims to remain loyal to their British masters during the Mutiny.

But the multi-ethnic, multi-religious character of the Ottoman Empire did not cease to be an anachronism in the age of nationalism. The sultan ruled Armenian, Greek, Serbian, Bulgarian and Arab

Christians as well as Muslim Arabs and Kurds. Christians comprised 35 per cent of the Ottoman population, and seemed to invite Western interference in Ottoman affairs, which actually became more flagrant after the Treaty of Paris. Posing as protectors of Christian and Jewish minorities in Ottoman lands, and indulged by Turkish statesmen, European ambassadors in Istanbul were extraordinarily overbearing. Ottoman ministers decided on important matters only after close consultation with them, while foreigners accused of crimes against Ottoman subjects claimed the legal protection of consular courts.

In 1860 French troops stepped in to protect Christians in Lebanon, and the Ottomans had to appoint a Christian governor. Nationalists in the Balkans forced more concessions out of Istanbul. Meanwhile corruption persisted, helped by the growth of the bureaucracy. Most peasants were indifferent to their new freedom to migrate to the cities. Endowed with legal equality, non-Muslims preferred the jurisdiction of their own communities to that of the central government. Christian minorities such as Greeks and Bulgarians benefited from the new careers opened up by modernization, but Muslim Turks felt isolated: not surprisingly, European garb became an object of mockery among ordinary people. Westernization had its strongest opponents among the *ulema*, who saw the outgrowth of secular educational institutions and their un-Islamic teachings as a direct threat.

Muslims deeply resented the granting of apparently blasphemous legal equality to non-Muslims who not only remained exempt from military conscription but could also call upon their European Christian patrons to exert pressure upon the Ottoman state with impunity (even as Muslims remained without rights in Asian and African countries administered by European colonial powers). Looking back at European attitudes towards Turkey, Hüseyin Cahid, Turkey's most prominent journalist in the early twentieth century, explained why he and other Young Turks became such fervent nationalists and anti-imperialists:

> The Turk was a tyrant, an oppressor, he knew nothing of right and justice. The Turk had no conscience, he was hostile to civilization, he understood nothing, his heart was indifferent to human sentiments. Turkey was the legitimate and natural property of the civilized West that could exploit it as it pleased; its inhabitants were in the eyes of the

Europeans exploitable and only fit to be made to work as hard as possible. Yes, citizens, we Turks had to submit to all this, though our only fault was that our ancestors were hospitable to our guests. While we groaned under these calamities, when we turned at times to beg for mercy, our supplications, which showed that we had begun to recognize our honour and dignity, were met by new oppressions. Every time we raised our heads, we received a blow; every time we tried to stand erect we received a kick. Such was the lot of the Turks! While in their own countries their own citizens coveted the bread of their brothers and the poor started revolutions to secure a large part of the riches of the wealthy, we ourselves were not allowed to aspire to any part of the riches stolen from our country. While in their countries king and coachman are equal before the law, here an Ottoman vizier was inferior to a foreigner's servant. We were doing all we could to help any Westerner who came to our land; the income of all the taxes paid by this poor nation went to ensure his well-being. On his part, he had no regard for this country, paid no taxes, and found fault with our law courts. Sometimes, there were attacks on our citizens and our officials, attacks that made our blood boil. But we could do nothing.[37]

Young Turks such as Cahid emerged at the end of the nineteenth century to protest against the dire state of their country. But by the 1860s some young Ottoman intellectuals had also begun to fret about Istanbul's seemingly relentless capitulation to ever-aggressive demands from Europeans (or Franks, as they were called), and advocated a more democratic and constitutional regime. These were often bureaucrats in the Ottoman government who suspected the Tanzimat modernizers of being anti-Islamic as well as mindlessly pro-European. The most articulate figure in the secret group that came to be known as the Young Ottomans was Namik Kemal; he felt keenly the bewilderment of ordinary people who were left 'stranded, materially and spiritually' by Westernization.[38] Kemal also deplored the superficial and often tawdry Westernization preferred by the enforcers of the Tanzimat, which, according to him, consisted of no more than 'the establishment of theatres, frequenting ballrooms, being liberal about the infidelities of one's wife and using European toilets'.[39] Another Young Ottoman, Ziya Pasha, complained:

Islam, they say, is a stumbling block to the progress of the State;
This story was not known before and now it is the fashion.
Forgetting our religious loyalty in all our affairs
Following Frankish ideas is now the fashion.[40]

All in all, the top-down modernization during the Tanzimat years left an ambiguous legacy. It broadened the gap between elites and masses. Contrary to assumptions, the old Turkey did not disappear before the new, nor did religion lose its appeal. The rhetoric of equality released nationalist aspirations, and centralization from above provoked more defiant assertions of identity. No less importantly, deeper economic links with Europe brought about traumatic social changes. As the Young Ottomans pointed out repeatedly, manufactured goods from Europe that flooded into the Turkish economy, destroying local industries and trade associations and guilds, removed a central plank on which urban life was built.[41]

Turkey was now outlining a pattern soon to be visible in Egypt and Iran – the countries al-Afghani would go on to visit – and also elsewhere in Asia: that modernization shifted, often drastically, the locus of power within any society, and invited resistance from old elites who felt ignored or slighted. For instance, the reformist Ottomans who imposed a uniform wool hat, or fez, on all Ottoman government employees, regardless of their faith, provoked severe disaffection among tradition-minded elites, especially the *ulema*, as the fez, chosen for its resemblance to Western hats, was not the ideal headgear for the prostrations required during prayers. (It nevertheless was to become a symbol of Muslim identity outside Turkey.)

Indeed, one of the two most enduring consequences of modernization everywhere in the Asian world would be the rise to power of new secular and Westernizing groups, whether military officers or government bureaucrats and new professionals. The other would be the backlash from those ordinary citizens who were asked to pay taxes, the religious-social elites who saw their influence threatened by the Westernizers, and the minorities who, in the face of a centralizing authority, became aware of their separate ethnic or religious identity.

Unless the conditions were propitious – as in Japan with its ethnically uniform population and secular state, or in Russia under Peter the Great – modernization could unleash chaos and disunity. As it turned out, the Ottomans with their unwieldy territories, massive Christian populations and institutionalized *ulema* turned out to be extremely poorly equipped for rapid social and political reorganization along Western lines. So disruptive was the overall effect that in 1876 Sultan Abdulhamid would himself join the growing popular reaction against Westernization, and turn to pan-Islamism as a bulwark against Western encroachments upon the Muslim world.

Why did al-Afghani go to Istanbul in the late 1860s? Indian Muslims harassed by the British, and Muslim Tatars ill-treated by the Russians, were beginning to call for the Ottoman sultan to assume leadership of the Muslim world and declare jihad (holy war) on infidels. But pan-Islamism, of which Istanbul became the magnetic centre for Muslims in the last quarter of the nineteenth century, was no more than a rumour among exile circles in 1869 – Namik Kemal in 1872 was the first writer we know of to use the phrase 'Muslim Unity'.[42]

Istanbul was, however, famous as a centre of the protective modernization that al-Afghani would later urge upon fellow Muslims – a theme he stressed in his first recorded speech in Istanbul in 1870. The same year he arrived in Istanbul, a former grand vizier, Fuad Pasha, had written to the sultan to warn him that his empire 'is in danger. We must change all our institutions, political and military, and adopt the new laws and new appliances invented by the Europeans.'[43] But al-Afghani couldn't bring himself to advocate wholesale Westernization of the kind Istanbul, a city with a Christian majority, had become an exemplar of. In many ways he had more in common with the Young Ottomans, who argued for self-strengthening without blind imitation of the West, and who insisted that the Koran itself sanctioned many of the values – individual freedom and dignity, justice, the use of reason, even patriotism – touted by Turkish high officials as 'Western'.

The people who later gathered around al-Afghani in Egypt were Muslims marginalized and rendered insecure by modern reforms. A typical Young Ottoman like Ali Suavi, an *alim* or scholar and a representative of the traditionalist lower-middle class in Istanbul who resented being left behind by Tanzimat-style modernization, would have gravitated to al-Afghani. However, since the Young Ottoman group had been proscribed and its members exiled in 1867, two years before al-Afghani arrived in the city, he had very different collaborators in Turkey.

Al-Afghani met Ali Pasha, one of the most powerful of the Westernizing statesmen. His host was a leading reformist in the field of education, a Tanzimatist. As in Afghanistan, al-Afghani seems not to have had much trouble insinuating himself into the highest echelons of the ruling class. Within a few months of his arrival he was appointed to the Council of Education and invited to speak at the opening of Darülfünun-i Osmani, a new modern university, where the education minister was in attendance along with other top officials of the administration.

Al-Afghani knew the director of the university, a freethinker who was frequently attacked by conservative *ulema*. The modernizing Tanzimatists probably saw al-Afghani as a useful ally, a token *alim* with whom to defuse criticism of secular education by their own religious figures. Certainly, al-Afghani himself seemed sincerely committed to reviving Muslim power through modern education. Thanks to his Persian background of heterodox philosophy, al-Afghani was also more likely than the Sunni Ottoman *ulema* to recognize the importance of reason and science. In his first recorded speech at the secular-minded Darülfünun-i Osmani in 1870, al-Afghani lamented the ignorance bred by madrasas and 'dervish convents' among the Islamic people (*milla*) and their resulting subjugation by the scientific West:

> My brothers, Arise from the sleep of neglect. Know that the Islamic people [*milla*] were [once] the strongest in rank, the most valuable in worth . . . Later this people sank into ease and laziness . . . Some of the Islamic nations came under the domination of other nations. The clothes of abasement were put on them. The glorious *milla* was humiliated. All these things happened from lack of vigilance, laziness, working too little, and stupidity . . . Are we not going to take an example from the civilized nations? Let us cast a glance at the achievement of others. By effort they have achieved the final degree of knowledge and the peak of elevation. For us too all the means are ready, and there remains no obstacle to our progress. Only laziness, stupidity, and ignorance are obstacles to [our] advance.[44]

Al-Afghani's choice of words was instructive. 'Civilized nations' was a term of nineteenth-century politics, used by Western European statesmen to exalt their countries above all others. The terms used to define 'civilization' were exclusively European and Christian; the Tanzimatists had taken them on as a challenge in their bid to promote Turkey on the scale of evolution. Al-Afghani's own deployment of the term hinted at how far he had gone in his rejection of Muslim vanity and exceptionalism. It implied, dangerously, that Muslims were no longer the chosen people; their history was no longer congruent with God's plan. And madrasas were no longer up to the task of educating Muslims.

Clearly, the lessons from Afghanistan and India were crystallizing in al-Afghani's mind – mainly that Muslims could not return to the glorious imperial past. They had to look ahead and to catch up with the West; and it wasn't enough to confine the necessary modernization to the army, as the Ottomans and the Egyptians were then doing. The great Muslim adversary of the British in South India, Tipu Sultan, had deployed tactics learnt from French soldiers but still lost to the British. The rebel soldiers of the Mutiny belonged to a modern army of a European type. But, lacking central organization, they could conceive of no higher objective than restoring the hapless Mughal emperor to his throne in Delhi. As al-Afghani saw it, a much greater transformation – primarily in the mind – was needed.

But al-Afghani had arrived in the last phase of the Tanzimat, in the midst of a growing backlash against the modernizing reformers by the *ulema*. Whether he liked it or not, he was identified with the modernizers and exposed to the malignity of the conservatives; he was soon to feel the full force of their disapproval. In the course of another public lecture at the same university, the first of a planned series of fourteen such lectures, al-Afghani ventured to compare prophets to philosophers, coming down slightly on the side of the latter: 'The teachings of the philosopher are universal, and do not take into account the particularities of a given epoch, whereas those of a prophet are conditioned by the latter. That is why the prescriptions of the prophet vary.'[45]

This sounds innocuous to modern ears. But al-Afghani was proposing nothing less than that the Prophet Muhammad's Sharia was not immutable, that it was open to revision by philosophers. Many Muslim thinkers in Persia and India in previous centuries, and even in the Arab world before that, had accepted this principle; they believed that men of reason could forego the literal observance of prophecy, which was meant strictly for the uneducated masses. But the paranoid resisters of modernization in Turkey thought al-Afghani had come close to apostasy and deserved swift execution.

Al-Afghani was to go much further fifteen years later in his riposte to the French historian Ernest Renan, who believed that Islam made Muslims incapable of a scientific temperament. But the Tanzimatist reformers had handled the old *ulema* very cautiously; al-Afghani had broken their delicate protocol by connecting secular ideas to old controversies of dogma, and appeared to challenge the authority of the Prophet himself. Promoting secular disciplines of history, law, economics and philosophy, the new university was already a formidable rival to the traditional madrasas; now al-Afghani seemed to be questioning Islamic theology itself. In the storm of protests that followed, the director was sacked. The university itself was closed down after just a year of operation. Al-Afghani was removed from the Council of Education and his lecture series was cancelled. In early 1871, he was expelled from Istanbul; he had spent less than two years there.

One of the few possessions of al-Afghani extant today is a passport from Cairo's Iranian consulate for a trip to Istanbul, which he seems to have obtained soon after he arrived in Cairo in 1871. The planned trip to Istanbul did not happen. However, he was to return to the city at another, more difficult time, when his reputation was fixed as that of a widely feared and respected man, and the Ottoman Empire itself was beset with multiple challenges.

Nevertheless, his first stay in Istanbul was crucial in his self-education. Despite the setbacks, al-Afghani was learning how to make his views acceptable to a broader constituency than the ruling classes in Muslim countries. Many Muslim reformers in his time spoke of following the West, but it was not easy for most ordinary Muslims to follow the ways of infidel peoples whom they feared or hated or knew nothing about. Like the Young Ottomans, al-Afghani knew how to speak of new ideas and possibilities in the idiom of Islam, and make reform acceptable, even attractive, as a step to political independence and unity. (His disguise as a Sunni Muslim gave him a secret advantage.) In Egypt this intellectual flexibility, and his ability to retrofit the Koran for modernity, would help al-Afghani from the outset, even if it again invited the displeasure of the traditionalist *ulema*.

Al-Afghani arrived in Egypt when the country, like Ottoman Turkey, was reaching the limits of self-Europeanization. Political consciousness had been rapidly rising across the country, partly provoked by the Indian Mutiny, news of which had been relayed across Egypt by itinerant Indian merchants and pilgrims. In 1858, the British consul reported much local 'sympathy' for the mutineers. 'There is reason to suppose,' he added, 'that Indian and Persian partisans have done their best to increase, if not excite, that sympathy.'[46] In 1865, the region around the city of Asyut witnessed a major uprising by Egyptian disciples of an Indian Sufi who had fought the British during the Mutiny in 1857 and had then fled to Egypt; the khedive (viceroy) himself had to travel up the Nile with a military contingent to crush the revolt against his un-Islamic and pro-imperialist ways.

EGYPT: THE POLEMICIST EMERGES

Secluded from the disruptive advances of the West, and a relative cultural backwater compared to Mughal India or Persia, Egypt had been jolted into history by Napoleon's invasion in 1798. It had to modernize, but so much of what had been available to Europe in its modernization – the long building-up of scientific knowledge, technical skills, intellectual and political freedom – was lacking in Egypt. The result was greater economic and political dependence on the West, more efficient despotism, and increasingly frustrated and resentful upwardly mobile Egyptians.

Muhammad Ali (1769–1849), a renegade Ottoman soldier from Thrace who forced Istanbul to recognize his viceroyalty of Egypt, wished to build a formidable military and consolidate his own dictatorial power. To this end, he recruited soldiers from the French army, conferring on some of these mercenaries the title of Bey or Pasha ('The French *canaille* abroad is impressive,' Flaubert wrote to a friend from Egypt in 1849, 'and let me add – there is a lot of it.'[47]). He also wooed European potentates, showering them with such extravagant gifts as the Rameses II obelisk that now stands in Paris's Place de la Concorde and 'Cleopatra's Needle' on London's Embankment. Sycophantic before Europeans, he was ruthless with his Egyptian subjects. He confiscated the properties of old feudal grandees, and stripped Islamic institutions of their highly lucrative landholdings. Intervening heavy-handedly in traditional rural lives, he forced his peasants to focus on producing a single cash crop – cotton – for European factories, altering the fundamental pattern of what had been a strong and self-sufficient economy.

Egypt had become one of the main exporters of cotton to Britain and France by 1840, and the proceeds of this lucrative export economy enabled Muhammad Ali to build a professional conscript army and meritocratic bureaucracy. His radical reforms were continued by his dynastic successors, who chose to give themselves the title Khedive. Very soon, modernization in Egypt, which was cheer-led and sponsored by the West, was inducing vast and tumultuous changes.

Egyptian peasants, who had never previously left their villages, served in the armies that expanded Egyptian territory into the Sudan and defeated Wahhabi fundamentalists in Arabia as well as secessionists in Greece. Modern schools and factories were set up, producing teachers, bureaucrats and engineers; a few students even travelled to Europe. Egypt possessed telegraph and rail networks decades before Japan and China. The American Civil War, which disrupted exports from the American South, multiplied Egyptian revenues from cotton. An increasingly prosperous Cairo became the cultural as well as the financial capital of the Arab world, a status it was to retain into the mid-twentieth century.

The Egyptian capital was graced with European-style urban conveniences such as broad avenues, waterworks, gasworks, and even an opera house (where Verdi's *Aida* was premiered in December 1871). Like the Ottoman sultan, his nominal overlord (and petulant rival), Khedive Ismail (1830–95) had returned from the Paris Exposition in 1867 with a determination to make his capital resemble the magnificent city of the Second Empire. Accordingly, the compulsively polygamous khedive installed the rich – mainly European, Syrian and Sephardic Jewish businessmen – in Cairo's new western flank, relegating such unattractive sights as the poor to other designated areas. One result of his urban planning was that everywhere near the Nile arose eyesores, as Stanley Lane-Poole, the chronicler of Cairo, wrote: 'unsightly and ill-built palaces in which viceregal extravagance and ostentation have found an outlet'.[48]

Like Istanbul, Cairo attracted its share of foreign buccaneers. A new rail line from Alexandria, completed in 1858, shattered its previous isolation from the Mediterranean. In 1868, the British travel agent Thomas Cook extended the Grand Tour to Cairo, presenting it as an irresistible 'combination of ancient Orientalism with Parisian innovations'.[49] Over 200,000 Europeans lived in Cairo and Alexandria by the 1870s. The khedive himself fervently courted, and was in turn pampered by, European rulers: invited to tea with Queen Victoria at Balmoral, and greeted by the French emperor with greater pomp and ceremony than the Ottoman sultan had been in 1867. (He was less tolerant of Western art forms, sacking the Jewish writer James Sanua as court playwright when the latter attacked polygamy and mocked the British.) In 1869, the opening of the Suez Canal, attended by European royalty, seemed to confirm Egypt's arrival in the modern world. Austria's bemused Emperor Franz Joseph wrote to his wife about the khedive's ball, which several thousand people attended, including Indian maharajas, Levantine merchants, European diplomats, desert chieftains and 'very many vulgar people'.[50] 'My country is no longer in Africa,' Khedive Ismail is reported to have boasted; 'it is in Europe.'[51]

The Europeans were even less persuaded by the Egyptian claim to high civilization than they had been by the Ottoman regard for their sovereignty. British tourists exploring the country in the late 1870s were warned by their *Baedeker* guides that the Egyptians 'occupy a much lower grade in the scale of civilization than most of the western nations, and cupidity is one of their failings'.[52] 'I have been really amazed', the British traveller Lady Duff Gordon wrote about her compatriots in 1863, 'at several instances of English fanaticism this year. Why do people come to a Muslim country with such a bitter "hatred in their stomachs"?'[53] The answer was, at least partly, the Indian Mutiny of 1857, which had instilled a deep distrust, even violent loathing of Muslims and Islam among Britain's colonial elite.

Expatriate businessmen routinely had their Egyptian workers whipped. 'They [the British] try their hands on the Arabs', Lady Duff Gordon wrote, 'in order to be in good training' for India.[54]

Beholden to coarse Europeans, and personally dissolute, the khedive singularly failed to impress the vast majority of his own people. The Egyptian poet Salih Magdi expressed a widespread revulsion when he wrote:

> Your money is squandered on pimps and prostitutes
> Normal men take a woman for a wife
> He wants a million wives
> Normal men take a house for a living
> He takes ninety.
> Oh, Egyptians, there is disgrace all around.
> Awake, awake![55]

As the Ottomans were demonstrating, hitching one's fortunes to Europe carried unknown and potentially lethal costs. The revenues from cotton weren't enough to subsidize modernization, and the end of the American Civil War and the subsequent collapse of cotton prices damaged the Egyptian economy. Egypt by then was already heavily dependent on huge high-interest loans from European banks, which fervently encouraged Ismail's profligacy. While increasing Egypt's debt, which soon made the country subservient to European financiers (and brought European ministers into his cabinet in 1878), the khedive failed to build institutions that could accommodate the rising aspirations of the many newly educated and self-confident Egyptians. His European patrons had even less need for popular institutions. Arab landowners, bureaucrats and military officers pushing for deeper modernization found themselves thwarted, and came to begrudge their country's dependence on the West.

Cotton produced great private fortunes, but the link to the international economy put Egypt into a precarious position, subject to the frequent panics and depressions of remote markets. Western-made industrial goods flooded the Egyptian market, destroying not only the old crafts economy but also the social and cultural life of guilds. The Egyptian journalist and politician Ibrahim al-Muwaylihi, one of al-Afghani's disciples in Cairo, wrote angrily about the local merchant, who 'has been impoverished by a stagnant market and forced to cling for shelter to the hem of the foreigner, who can, if he pleases, ruin him or allow him to remain where he is.'[56]

Extortionate taxes imposed by the khedive also made life intolerable for many Egyptians outside the cities. Lady Duff Gordon, a rare European to have spent considerable time in the Egyptian countryside, reported a year after the opening of Suez Canal the exploitation of the *fellaheen* (peasants) that had made it possible: 'I cannot describe to you the misery here now – Every day some new tax. Now every beast, camel, cow, sheep, donkey, horse is made to pay. The fellaheen can no longer eat bread; they are now living on barley-meal mixed with water and raw green stuff, vetches etc.'[57] In addition to the country's nascent intelligentsia, the peasantry furnished ripe material for an insurrection. Until the revolts of the 1870s, British officials counted on the possibility that the Egyptian peasant was so beaten down that 'no amount of misery or oppression would provoke him to resistance'.[58]

In 1878, a time of serious political crisis, al-Afghani would be sighted in Alexandria, trying to stir up a crowd of peasants: 'Oh! You poor fellah! You break the heart of the earth in order to draw sustenance from it and support your family. Why do you not break the heart of your oppressor? Why do you not break the heart of those who eat the fruit of your labour?'[59]

This political activism was an extraordinary change for al-Afghani. When he first arrived in Cairo he was little more than an eager participant in the city's old culture of café discourses. The one unexpected result of the khedive's obsession with recreating Paris on the Nile was that the historical quarter, which dated back to the Fatimid era, was neglected rather than destroyed altogether. Here were the great mosques and shrines and madrasas, and the residences of wealthy merchants in which intricately carved wooden screens shielded the household's women from prying gazes from passers-by. 'By god,' an awestruck Flaubert had written in 1849,

> it is such a bewildering chaos of colours that your poor imagination is
> dazzled as though with continuous fireworks as you go about staring at
> minarets thick with white storks, at tired slaves stretched out in the sun

on house terraces ... with camel bells ringing in your ears and great herds of black goats bleating in the streets amid the horses and the donkeys and the pedlars.[60]

It was in this colourful chaos of the old city that al-Afghani lingered – the European parts of the town would have spoken to him and his disciples of everything that was going wrong in the country. Yet again he secured the patronage of a local dignitary, Riyad Pasha, a powerful politician he had met in Istanbul. Offered a job at the al-Azhar mosque, he declined, preferring to teach at home and in a café (though he accepted a stipend from Riyad Pasha). He focused on teaching rational sciences and reinterpreting old Islamic texts rather than insisting on rote memorizing.

He carried on from where he had left off in Istanbul, offering what conservative Muslims regarded as 'heretical' knowledge to his students. Certainly, he showed no excessive regard for Islamic beliefs. 'One of his peculiar excellencies,' the Syrian-Christian author and editor Adib Ishaq (1856–85) later recalled, 'is that he used to follow the movement of European knowledge and scientific discoveries and acquaint himself with what scientists discovered and what they had recently invented.'[61] He also taught Islamic classics that were not standard in Cairo at that time, such as Ibn Khaldun's philosophy of history, *Muqaddima* ('Introduction'). Al-Afghani's lessons in mathematics, philosophy and theology soon provoked the wrath of the conservative clergy – particularly the sheikhs of al-Azhar, then as now Egypt's leading theological centre. They denounced al-Afghani as an advocate of atheism. So virulent was the campaign against him that some of his students, including Saad Zaghlul (in many ways, the father of the modern Egyptian nation), had to conceal their association with him.

Undeterred, al-Afghani went on. He lived in the city's old Jewish quarter, which is near the old Turkish bazaar, now famous as Khan-ei-Khalili, and was often seen at the Matatiya Café in 'Attaba Square, drinking tea while smoking cigarettes and expounding his views on Ibn Sina and Nasir al-din Tusi, the thirteenth-century Persian philosopher.

This part of Cairo, a pit of disaffection, would produce Egypt's future nationalists, revolutionaries and intellectuals. It was here, in the summer of 1879, that the correspondent of *The Times* of London met al-Afghani, 'a mysterious being', he later reported, whose name had 'become recently familiar as attached to a considerable but unknown power in Egypt', and who

> had almost obtained the weight of a Median law among the lower and less educated classes ... There was certainly no striking originality in his views, nor did he give expression to that fanaticism with which he is credited. But certain well-defined ideas he possessed and he knew how to express them with force.[62]

The Times' correspondent went on to propose that a 'native opinion exists ... and is not to be entirely ignored'. This was a startlingly gracious acknowledgement given that the paper's reporting from Egypt leading up to its occupation by Britain was otherwise near hysterical, obsessed with the dangers from ostensibly fanatical Muslim mobs to European life and property. But the London paper was right about the influence of al-Afghani on the 'lower and less educated classes', which were indeed becoming discontented after decades of upper-class accommodation with the West.

But, apart from insurrections in the countryside, which were easily quelled, there was no organized opposition to the khedive and his European string-pullers. There was little information available about the outside world, and hardly any newspapers to articulate dissent or propose alternative ideas about political and economic life. Western-style schools had been opened, but their students had been trained in the old rote system of learning and didn't know what to make of chemistry and engineering. Eventually, the schools were able to reorient their students, thus fulfilling their original aim. But meanwhile the old centres of education such as al-Azhar had been impoverished. So, while a Westernized generation lacked all real knowledge of Islam and Egypt, students in the old school system knew nothing of modern life.

Adib Ishaq and the playwright later anointed as the 'Molière of Egypt', James Sanua (1839–1912), held cultural salons and organized educational societies in their own homes. Ahmad Urabi, who in 1881–2 led an army officers' revolt against the monarchy, attended these informal gatherings, as did many others lacking a modern education. When the gatherings were prohibited by the khedive, Sanua moved his activities to a Masonic lodge. Bringing news of the outside world to curious but isolated Egyptians, al-Afghani became similarly important to a generation of students.

On someone like Mohammed Abduh, born into a peasant family and narrowly trained to read Islamic texts, al-Afghani had a liberating effect. As Abduh, who later wrote a near-sycophantic biography of al-Afghani and also became one of the leading modernist thinkers of the Muslim world, described it:

> The Egyptians before 1877 in their public and private affairs put themselves completely under the will of the sovereign and his functionaries . . . None of them dared to hazard an opinion on the way in which their country was administered. They were far from knowing the state of other Muslim or European countries . . . Beside, who would have dared to show his opinion? Nobody, since one could, on the least word, be exiled from one's country or despoiled of his goods or even put to death. Amid this darkness arrived Jamal al-din.[63]

Abduh did not exaggerate entirely about the 'darkness'. More vividly than Ottoman Turkey, Egypt had revealed the severe limitations and problems of modernization within an international capitalist economy where the rules were made by European imperialists, and were usually rigged against latecomers. *The Times*' correspondent encountered al-Afghani towards the end of his time in Egypt. With European bondholders and moneylenders practically running the country, al-Afghani was becoming less discreet than before about the dangers of Western encroachment. For much of his time in the country he had been content to advise piecemeal reform. Most people who met him attested to the essentially non-traditional nature of his teachings; some even thought him irreligious. Certainly he mostly spoke about religion only to the extent he could apply it to practical and secular ends.

But late into his stay in Egypt, he became an active player in the country's political scene. He also became one of the progenitors of activist journalism in the Arab world, creating a public sphere that eventually staged the politicization of the Middle Eastern masses. In one of his newspaper sketches, James Sanua describes a café discourser modelled on al-Afghani, addressing his listeners as 'redeemers of their lands'.[64] His disciples were among the most active of those forming public opinion and a sense of nationality – two of them, Abdallah al-Nadim and Salim al-Naqqsh, coined the slogan 'Egypt for the Egyptians' that is still used today.

This nascent nationalism in Egypt was to steadily become part of a larger assertion of Arab identity vis-à-vis both the Ottomans, who increasingly privileged Turks and the Turkish language, and Europe. Islam had originated in Arab lands and also achieved its classical glory there. But for centuries its real flowering had happened elsewhere, most recently in Persia, India and Turkey. Arabs were acutely conscious of their lowly position in Muslim countries as well as the larger modern world in general. The late nineteenth-century assertions of Arab identity that tried to alleviate feelings of inferiority were led by non-Muslim Arabs, such as the Syrian Christian and Jewish associates of al-Afghani, who set up the first Arabic independent newspapers. This is how Beirut, Alexandria and Damascus, where many Christian Arabs lived, became centres of modern Arab journalism and literature. Soon Muslims joined in, but they emphasized regaining the old glory of Islam as well as purifying and reviving Arabic as a language of modern communication. In 1871, al-Afghani had arrived in Egypt precisely as this intellectual and political ferment began; he quickly became its central figure.

Egypt's most famous newspaper, *al-Ahram*, had been set up in 1875 without any input from al-Afghani. However, by 1879 almost all of Egypt's newspapers were being run by al-Afghani's disciples. The demands of European financiers in Egypt had shaken up the staid world of establishment newspapers that had, as Abduh wrote, 'only published facts of no importance'.[65] 'An irresistible desire pushed people to subscribe, with a force more powerful than despotism' to the new lively papers. 'With time, the newspapers touched on political and social questions concerning foreign countries and then set boldly to dealing with the question of Egyptian finances, which embarrassed the government.'[66]

In 1877 James Sanua established, with al-Afghani's help, a satirical journal, *Abu-Naddara Zarqa* ('The Man With Blue Spectacles'). Containing conversations, short plays and essays, it denounced Ottoman-Egyptians as well as European 'infidels' looting the Muslim

country – Sanua, though Jewish, was not above invoking Islamic rhetoric against European imperialists. The journal, which was the first to
use colloquial Arabic rather than the formal language of scholarship,
lasted all of two months before being shut down by the authorities.
Sanua himself was banished to Paris in 1878, where he resumed
publishing his journal (thousands of copies were smuggled back into
Egypt and were read eagerly even in remote villages, until the
magazine's closure in 1910). Undeterred, al-Afghani encouraged his
Levantine Christian disciple Adib Ishaq to make another attempt:
Misr ('Egypt') appeared in 1877 in Cairo (before relocating to Alexandria) and was an immediate success.

Ishaq launched a sustained attack in the paper on Egypt's monarchy and its foreign backers. He criticized the preference given to
expatriates in government jobs; he mocked the European habit of
proclaiming liberty and equality at home and blocking constitutional
reform abroad. He objected most strongly to the legal privileges
enjoyed by Europeans under the Capitulations:

> Being pardoned for obvious misdeeds has encouraged them to rebel, so
> that they have acted violently and caused as much mischief as they wished,
> to the extent that not a day goes by but we hear that such-and-such Ital-
> ian or Maltese stabbed an Egyptian national with a dagger. The wounded
> victim is carried to the hospital, whereas the assailant is delivered to the
> consulate, and put in a luxurious room where he eats gourmet meals.[67]

As Lady Duff Gordon bitterly recorded, 'What chokes me is to hear
English people talk of the stick being "the only way to manage Arabs"
as if anyone could doubt that it is the easiest way to manage any
people where it can be used with impunity.'[68]

All through the late 1870s Egypt and Turkey hurtled towards a political and financial crisis. The Congress of Berlin, which followed the
Russo-Turkish War of 1877–8, deprived the Ottomans of most of
their Balkan provinces, and revealed that only Western powers could
guarantee the integrity and security of the Empire, which still technic-
ally ruled Egypt. Al-Afghani, like many Egyptians, had joined the
Freemasons to hold political discussions – as in Persia, Freemasonry,
which guaranteed a degree of secrecy, compensated for the lack of

social and political organizations in Egypt. He took the opportunity to break cover and emerge as a bold thinker in the public eye. He was reading widely, often translations of European works, and *Misr* became a platform for some of al-Afghani's own reading-based speculations, some published under his own name, others under a pseudonym. His study of the French historian François Guizot, who credited civilization to solidarity and reason and saw Protestantism as the decisive event in European history, confirmed al-Afghani in his convictions that the Islamic world needed a Reformation, preferably with himself as the new Luther.

European interventions in Egyptian politics also spurred al-Afghani's explicitly political writing. He was in close contact with Egyptian nationalists, many of whom were patrons and allies of the army officers under Colonel Urabi who were briefly to take over the Egyptian government in 1880. He had also developed friendly relations with the son of Khedive Islamil, Crown Prince Tawfiq, through his Masonic lodge. He gave speeches and wrote articles directly exhorting Egyptians to remember their glorious classical past and awaken to their political plight. As the Second Afghan War erupted in the autumn of 1878, he published an article praising the anti-imperialism of the Afghans, whom he had criticized previously as 'unreliable', and he hailed the unity between Hindus and Muslims during the Indian Mutiny in 1857.

In an essay published in early 1879 called 'The True Reason for Man's Happiness', al-Afghani denounced British claims to have civilized India by introducing such benefits of modernity as railways, canals and schools. In his defence of India, al-Afghani was ecumenical, praising Hindus as well as Muslims. Echoing Edmund Burke, who had asserted that Indians were 'people for ages civilized and cultivated – cultivated by all the arts of polished life, whilst we were yet in the woods', al-Afghani dismissively asked why the English 'who suffered for long ages and wandered in wild and barbaric valleys' should presume to speak of the 'deficiency' of the glorious 'sons of Brahma and Mahadev, the founders of human sharias and the establishers of civilized laws'.[69]

Al-Afghani went on to argue that the British improved transport and communication in order to drain India's wealth to England and facilitate trade for British merchants. Western-style schools, he argued, were meant merely to turn Indians into English-speaking cogs of the British administration. This was a sophisticated idea for its time, when Indian nationalists had barely begun to formulate it. Al-Afghani's experience of imperialism in India seems to have been deepened by his prolonged exposure to Egypt, where the presence of a few emblems of modernity – railways, commercial crops – had failed to generate a sustainable economy while stifling old cottage industries. But he was no less critical of fellow Muslims. Reviewing Butrus Bustani's Arabic encyclopaedia in *Misr* in 1879, he wrote: 'O, sons of the East, don't you know that the power of the Westerners and their domination over you came about through their advance in learning and education, and your decline in those domains?'[70] Moving quickly across a vast intellectual realm, al-Afghani tried to diagnose the reasons for Muslim backwardness.

Chief among them, according to him, was despotism. In an article titled 'Despotic Government', he praised republican and constitutional forms of government, and called for the strengthening of the parliamentary system in Egypt. He attacked the Ottoman sultans for imposing their own backward-looking interpretation of Islam, and preventing the acquisition of new learning, which allowed Europeans to get ahead of, and then subjugate, Muslims. In his only recorded speech in Alexandria later in 1879, he identified his audience as descendants of the innovative ancient Egyptians, Phoenicians and Chaldeans who had made major breakthroughs in engineering and mathematics, and who had taught writing, agriculture and philosophy to the Greeks.

Al-Afghani then wondered about the backwardness of Asian peoples who had once created great civilizations. He explained that the West had come to dominate the East because of the latter's two basic evils of fanaticism and political tyranny. The only thing that would help Muslims, he insisted, was 'zeal', which was possessed only by people who 'know that their honour is in their race, their power is only in their community [*umma*] and their glory is only in their fatherland'.

This was the language of the Young Ottomans. Namik Kemal had been among the first Muslims to think of organizing anti-imperialist

Muslims around the principle of *watan* (nation), and al-Afghani seems to have adopted this early discourse of nationalism for his own purposes. He said he hoped his listeners would establish a national political party and strive for parliamentary rule in Egypt, dispensing altogether with foreigners.

He also pointed out some potential hurdles. 'No doubt you know,' he said, 'that that national party has no power or permanence as long as the people of the country have no common language, developed with good style.'[71] He returned to this subject in a later article warning against Muslim adoption of foreign languages, sounding more and more like the cultural nationalists of Europe who were even then building national languages and literatures:

There is no happiness except through nationality and no nationality except through language ... A people without unity, and a people without literature are a people without language. A people without history are a people without glory, and a people will lack history if authorities do not rise among them, to protect and revivify the memory of their historical heroes so that they may follow and emulate. All this depends on a national [*watani*] education which begins with the fatherland [*watan*], the environment of which is the fatherland, and the end of which is the fatherland.

In the same speech at Alexandria, al-Afghani also stressed the importance of women's rights. He declared it

impossible to emerge from stupidity, from the prison of humiliation and distress, and from the depths of darkness and ignominy as long as women are deprived of rights and ignorant of their duties, for they are the mothers from whom will come elementary education and primary morality ... I think that when a woman's education is neglected, then even if all the males of a nation are learned and high-minded, still the nation is able to survive in its acquired stage only for that generation. When they disappear, their children, who have the character and educational deficiencies of their mothers, betray them, and their nation returns to the state of ignorance and distress.[72]

There is little evidence apart from these speeches and articles that al-Afghani played a direct role in any of the complex intrigues – the revolt by nationalist army officers, or the appointment of Colonel Urabi to the khedive's government – that were overtaking Egyptian politics in the late 1870s. However, he had spoken casually to Mohammed Abduh of assassinating the then khedive, revealing a preference for violent solutions that was to grow stronger as he grew more embittered with Muslim rulers. When Crown Prince Tawfiq became khedive in June 1879, al-Afghani sent his congratulations and urged the new ruler of Egypt to expel foreigners from the government. Publicly, he kept up his anti-imperialist rhetoric even as the new khedive, supported by European powers, cracked down on dissenters (and abandoned Egypt's treasury to European accountants).

A French journalist, Ernest Vauquelin, wrote the following eyewitness account of an al-Afghani lecture:

> One evening in the Hasan mosque in Cairo, before an audience of four thousand people, he gave a powerful speech in which he denounced with a deep prophetic sense three years before the event [the British occupation of Egypt] the ultimate purpose of British policy on the banks of the Nile. He also showed at the same time the Khedive Tawfiq was compelled to serve – consciously or not – British ambitions, and ended his speech by a war-cry against the foreigner and by a call for a revolution to save the independence of Egypt and establish liberty.[73]

These speeches were always likely to get al-Afghani into trouble; and European consuls had been tracking him for some time. Writing to his superiors in London, the British consul in Cairo, Frank Lascelles, reported that al-Afghani

> is a man of considerable capacity and of great power as an orator, and he was gradually obtaining an amount of influence over his hearers which threatened to become dangerous. Last year [1878] he took an active part in stirring up ill feeling against the Europeans, and more especially the English, of whom he seems to entertain a profound hatred.[74]

Rumours that al-Afghani wanted to overthrow the regime and install a liberal government prejudiced the new khedive's mind against him; British pressure did the rest. The correspondent of *The Times*, who had previously described al-Afghani's influence in Cairo, now reported his expulsion in late August 1879, amplifying Tawfiq's alleged belief (contrary to al-Afghani's) that 'Egyptian regeneration must come from the West'. The correspondent did admit that the expulsion 'may not seem consonant with English ideals as to the free expression of opinion', but added that the 'peculiar circumstances of the country must be considered'.[75] Arrested in Cairo, al-Afghani was denied food for two days in Suez, and his few possessions were taken from him by the police before he was expelled to India. A revolt led by Colonel Urabi was easily put down in 1882. That same year, the British ferociously bombarded Alexandria and began their long occupation of Egypt.

Thus ended al-Afghani's first – and only – stay in Egypt. His peremptory departure on political grounds confirmed his reputation, in British eyes at least, as an agitator, but it belied his more lasting intellectual influence on a broad range of Egyptian thinkers and activists. Wilfrid Scawen Blunt, the English poet and Arabophile who later befriended al-Afghani, was in Egypt in late 1880 when he came across a very liberal-minded and modern-sounding sheikh from al-Azhar. Enquiring further into this new and welcome trend in Egyptian Islam, he learnt that, as the sheikh put it, 'the true originator' of the liberal religious reform movement among the *ulema* of Cairo was, strangely enough, not an Arab, nor an Egyptian, nor an Ottoman, but a certain 'wild man of genius' who 'preached the necessity of reconsidering the whole Islamic position, and, instead of clinging to the past, of making an onward intellectual movement in harmony with modern knowledge'.[76] The sheikh from al-Azhar also reported that al-Afghani's 'intimate acquaintance with the Koran and the traditions enabled him to show that, if rightly interpreted and checked the one by the other, the law of Islam was capable of the most liberal developments and that hardly any beneficial change was in reality opposed to it'.

Al-Afghani himself began to develop a more hardline and less liberal approach to Western imperialism and its native allies after his experience of Egypt. It was setbacks everywhere in the countries he knew best that pushed him towards it. The Ottomans' own credit bubble had burst in 1875, with the Treasury defaulting on interest payments to European bankers. The following year in Istanbul, Egyptian-style bankruptcy through foreign debt encouraged reformers to try to introduce a new liberal constitution; but the new sultan,

Abdulhamid II, abrogated it and, as future despots in Muslim countries were to do, he used the modernized structures of the Ottoman state, including a centralized police and spy system, to establish a repressive despotism in full view of his Western patrons.

A similar demand for a constitution emerged in Egypt among disaffected men like Colonel Urabi. Supported by small landowners and young *ulema* like Abduh, Urabi scored some temporary successes, becoming a minister in the khedive's cabinet. But the final outcome was never in doubt once Urabi started asking for an end to European interference in Egyptian affairs. Visiting Cairo in January 1850, Gustave Flaubert had commented 'it seems to be almost impossible that within a short time England won't become mistress of Egypt'.[77] In India, monitored closely by the British authorities, al-Afghani probably derived no satisfaction at seeing his own predictions, no less acute than Flaubert's, come true. In the previous year – 1881 – the French had occupied Tunisia in much the same fashion as the British now took Egypt, despite the Tunisian elite's desperate attempt at modernization.

BEYOND SELF-STRENGTHENING: THE ORIGINS OF PAN-ISLAMISM AND NATIONALISM

In the late 1870s, while he was still in Egypt, al-Afghani wrote to Sultan Abdulhamid describing his pain and outrage over the humiliation of Muslim countries by Western powers:

> When I considered the condition of the Islamic people [*milla*] it rent the shirt of my patience and I was overcome by fearful thoughts and visions from every side. Like a fearfully obsessed man day and night, from beginning to end, I have thought of this affair and have made the means of reform and salvation of this *milla* my profession and incantation.[78]

Al-Afghani requested that the Ottoman sultan use his power and prestige as caliph to launch a pan-Islamic front against the West, offering to be his representative in India, Afghanistan and Central Asia. His expulsion from Egypt and the defeat of liberal hopes there seem to have convinced al-Afghani of the need for a new tack. He would still experiment with different modes of resistance, often seeking to exploit European rivalries, but he would now advocate nationalisms, religious-based rather than ethnic or secular, in different Muslim countries, and would also deploy such potent invocations as pan-Islamism and holy war.

Al-Afghani was not alone in moving on from piecemeal reforms and constitutionalism to stressing the need for a strong Islamic centre that could beat back the encroaching West. In the last quarter of the nineteenth century the tone was changing all across the Muslim world as it took stock of its own helplessness against an increasingly aggressive West. Modernization, it was clear, hadn't secured the Ottomans against infidels; on the contrary, it had made them more dependent. Nor had it saved Egypt from buckling to British pressure – indeed, its globalized economy had made Egypt a subservient client state.

The failure of these first attempts at reform under European auspices created resentful new alliances between landowners, small entrepreneurs and bazaar merchants, creating a new sense of regional identity. It also first pushed many Muslim thinkers to ideas of nationalism that had emerged from the rivalries of nineteenth-century Europe.

Post-Revolutionary France had vividly demonstrated how the impersonal institutions of the state that overruled older and parochial identities and loyalties could bind a country's citizenry into a resilient unit. One after another, European nations had followed this model, partly to protect themselves against French imperial ambitions. Japan had already become the first country in Asia to attempt a national consolidation. Muslim thinkers, too, were increasingly attracted to the idea that an efficiently organized society could harness its cumulative social power well enough through a nation-state – one that could hold its own against other such national mobilizations.

The big problem which all Asian leaders in diverse societies would face lay in finding a way of unifying disparate populations around shared ideals and goals. Was there a common Egyptian or Turkish identity that transcended all other religious and ethnic identities? It was hard to see, but for the moment the spirit of negative nationalism – of opposition to foreign aggressors under a shared banner – seemed to suffice.

Moreover, nationalism could blend easily with, and even complement, pan-Islamism, as it did in al-Afghani's ideas; the contradictions
between the two would emerge only in the twentieth century. The idea
of a strong Caliph bubbled up in such far-off places as India and Indonesia, where Muslims considered themselves oppressed by Europeans
and hankered for their own universal civilization. It had its critics,
such as the pro-British educationist Sir Sayyid Ahmed Khan, who
claimed that 'the Turkish *khalifa*'s sovereignty does not extend over
us. We are residents of India and subjects of the British government.'[79]
But its emotional appeal was great.

The ruling classes of Istanbul finally noticed Muslims' rising international awareness during the 1870s. The Young Ottoman Namik
Kemal ironically described the Ottoman public's new-found interest
in the Muslims of Xinjiang: 'Twenty years ago, the fact that there
were Muslims in Kashgar was not known. Now, public opinion tries
to obtain union with them. This inclination resembles an overpower-
ing flood which will not be stopped by any obstacle in its way.'[80]

The Ottomans heeded the distant calls from Muslims partly because
of their own bitter experience of transnational solidarities. The Ottomans had witnessed, and suffered from, Russian-inspired pan-Slavism
in the Balkans and the rise of ethnic and religious solidarities elsewhere
in Europe. As Namik Kemal pointed out, 'Against this kind of European
union, we are obliged to secure our own country's political and military
union.'[81] Sultan Abdulhamid, who faced both financial implosion and
military defeat, was only too happy to revive the moribund post of the
caliph. Reform had run its course; the dalliance with Europe's values
was over. It was the turn of Islam to serve as a ruling ideology.

Abdulhamid took his universal leadership of Muslims, which to
Western eyes seemed like a version of the papacy, very seriously, building, for instance, a railway for pilgrims to Medina in Arabia. He
needed an ideological justification for his despotism, and some kind
of leverage over European powers who ruled millions of restless Muslims in colonized countries; pan-Islamism served him well on both
counts. Very quickly, Muslims around the world embraced the idea
that what could now save Islam was a strengthened pan-Islam centred
in Istanbul, with the only surviving great Muslim power, the Ottoman
sultan, as the caliph or *khalifa*.

Meanwhile, European expansion provoked violent backlashes from Islamic peoples who had so far been untouched by the West or those, like the Wahhabis, who completely rejected their native modernizing rulers. In the Sudan in the 1870s, a charismatic leader calling himself the Mahdi emerged at the head of a millenarian movement to beat back not only the Egyptian khedive but also his British allies. Scoring one brilliant victory after another, he promised to Islamize the entire world.

Al-Afghani later claimed, probably falsely, to know the Mahdi. Like many Muslims around the world, he was electrified by this previously unknown Sudanese's exploits against British forces in the early 1880s, particularly his long siege of the Anglo-Egyptian garrison in Khartoum which ended with its massacre in 1885. Indeed, the Sudanese Mahdi seemed to many Muslims a better candidate for the post of caliph than the Ottoman sultan himself.

It is not clear what al-Afghani thought in the 1870s of this ferocious warrior who promised instant revolution to Muslims, but by the time he completed his second stint in India in 1882, he had clearly and vehemently turned against the kind of accommodation to Western power and tutelage that many Muslim elites had previously advocated. Though no more devout than before, al-Afghani adopted the guise of an orthodox Muslim, an uncompromising defender of Islam against Western encroachments. In 1883, soon after leaving India, he claimed in a French newspaper that

All Muslims await the Mahdi and consider his coming as an absolute necessity . . . The Indian Muslims, in particular, in view of their infinite sufferings and the cruel torments they undergo under English domination, await him with the greatest impatience . . . Does England hope to stifle the voice of the Mahdi, the most awesome of all voices since its power is even greater than the voice of the Holy War, which issues from all Muslim mouths? . . . Does she think herself able to stifle this voice before making itself heard in all the East from Mount Himalaya to Dawlaghir, from north to south, speaking to the Muslims of Afghanistan, of Sind and of India.[82]

In India from 1879 to late 1882, al-Afghani visited Karachi and Bombay but spent most of his time in Hyderabad and Calcutta. Tailed everywhere he went by British spies, he kept his distance from political activism. Nevertheless, he refined his ideas in a series of published articles. Many of these were directed against Sir Sayyid Ahmed Khan, the foremost Muslim leader in India, who had, since the British suppression of the Mutiny, led a campaign to make Indian Muslims useful and trustworthy again to their foreign rulers. Khan thought that Indian Muslims had lagged behind Hindus in taking up the opportunities of modern education. He set up the Aligarh College in north India to close this evident gap between the two communities.

Al-Afghani couldn't have agreed more with Khan's belief in educating the Muslim community. As he himself wrote in an Indian periodical, 'With a thousand regrets I say that the Muslims of India have carried their orthodoxy, nay, their fanaticism to such an evil extreme that they turn away with distaste and disgust from sciences and arts and industries.'[83] Berating the insular Indian *ulema* in another article, al-Afghani wrote:

> Why do you not raise your eyes from those defective books and why do you not cast your glance on this wide world . . . You spend no thought on this question of great importance, incumbent on every intelligent man, which is: What is the cause of the poverty, indigence, helplessness, and distress of the Muslims, and is there a cure for this important phenomenon and great misfortune or not?[84]

As al-Afghani saw it, Khan emphatically did not have that cure. On the contrary: al-Afghani regarded him as a deluded and parochial Westernizer, who was blind to the fate of his co-religionists elsewhere and the *mala fide* intentions of the British in Muslim lands. Khan was a very dangerous man, al-Afghani asserted in a Calcutta-based periodical, who aimed 'to weaken the faith of the Muslims, to serve the ends of the aliens, and to mould the Muslims in their ways and beliefs'.[85]

This was unfair. Khan took a pragmatic attitude, and in the early twentieth century his college in Aligarh was to produce some of the most influential leaders of the Indian Muslim community. And he was no more pro-British than many Hindu reformists of the nineteenth century, such as the grandfather of Rabindranath Tagore. Yet al-Afghani was at least partly right. Khan regarded Muslim participation in the Mutiny as an appalling folly, and even claimed that most

Muslims had stayed loyal to the British. Visiting Europe in 1869, he wrote a series of letters home, stating that the English were justified in seeing Indians as 'imbecile brutes'. 'What I have seen,' Sir Sayyid warbled, 'and seen daily, is utterly beyond the imagination of a native of India . . . all good things, spiritual and worldly, which should be found in man, have been bestowed by the Almighty on Europe, and especially on England.'[86] Passing Sicily, he wondered about the lack of enduring monuments built by Muslims during their long presence there. In 1876, he claimed, 'The British rule in India is the most wonderful phenomenon the world has seen.'[87]

Sir Sayyid's sycophancy had its Indian critics. The poet Akbar Illahabadi (1846–1921) had this to say to Anglophone Muslims like him:

Give up your literature, say I; forget your history
Break all your ties with shaykh and mosque – it could not matter less.
Go off to school. Life's short. Best not worry overmuch.
Eat English bread, and push your pen, and swell with happiness.[88]

Illahabadi thought that the Muslims supporting Sir Sayyid's Aligarh College, though well-meaning, were essentially flunkeys of the British.

What our respected Sayyid says is good.
Akbar agrees that it is sound and fair.
But most of those who head this modern school
Neither believe in God, nor yet in prayer.
They *say* they do, but it is plain to see
What *they* believe in is the powers that be.[89]

He saw Western-style education as a particularly insidious form of colonialism. 'We of the East break our opponents' heads / They of the West change their opponents' nature / The guns have gone, and now come the professors.'[90] And he bitterly denounced the uprooting of young Muslims from their tradition:

We do not learn the things we ought to learn –
And lose what was already in our keeping;
Bereft of knowledge, plunged in heedlessness,
Alas, we are not only blind but sleeping.[91]

Al-Afghani did not disagree. In article after article published in

Indian periodicals he attacked Khan's efforts to create local func-
tionaries for the British by promoting Western-style education and
government jobs for Muslims. 'Why should', he wrote, deploying
words to be used often against Westernizing despots in Muslim countries, 'someone who destroys the life spirit of a people be called their
well-wisher; why should a person who works for the decline of his
faith be considered a sage? What ignorance is this?'[92]

Visiting India in the mid-1880s, Wilfrid Blunt came across many
Indian Muslims attracted by al-Afghani's assaults on Khan. Nothing,
however, enraged them and their hero more than Khan's preaching of
a new materialist Islam that took human beings to be the judge of all
things. Al-Afghani, who was not known for religious fundamentalism, encouraged and welcomed reinterpretations of Islamic texts.
Both he and his most influential disciple, Mohammed Abduh, hoped
to restore a weakened Muslim *umma* by portraying Islam as a rational
religion, contrasting such an 'authentic Islam' with one corrupted and
far removed from its glorious origins, and regrettably manifest in
much of the Muslim world's recent history and practices. But al-
Afghani stuck close to his belief in a transcendent god and rejection
of creeds that took 'the world or man [as] being a fit object of worship'. In his longest published work, 'Refutation of the Materialists',
a riposte to Sir Sayyid's view of Islam, al-Afghani took on everyone,
from Democritus to Darwin, who exalted man and explained the
world as self-created. As he saw it, attacking religion risked undermining the moral basis of society altogether and weakened the bonds
that held communities together – precisely the weakening that had
plunged Muslims everywhere into crisis.

Increasingly, al-Afghani veered towards armed struggle and violent
resistance to the West. He was clearly emboldened by the Mahdi's
successes in Sudan. In his long letter to the Ottoman sultan in 1879,
written shortly before he arrived in India, al-Afghani had proposed
himself as a roving revolutionary who could arouse and unify Muslims
across Central Asia and India and provoke a clash between the Russian and British Empires, fulfilling the sultan's pan-Islamic programme.
It was full of lines such as these: 'I wish after the completion of the
Indian affair to go to Afghanistan and invite the people of that land,

who like a wild lion have no fear of bloodshed and do not admit hesitation in war, especially holy war, to a religious struggle and a national endeavor.'[93] Abdulhamid's response to him is not known. The sultan's pan-Islamism was less adventurous and more opportunistic; he also had a clearer sense of invincible European power than al-Afghani did. But he may have taken note of the latter's intellectual and political passion – he was to try to make al-Afghani serve his purposes a decade later.

Interestingly, al-Afghani did not speak of pan-Islamism to the Indian Muslim intelligentsia, which was growing conscious of its echoes around the Muslim world; he seemed aware that India's large non-Muslim population could also be harnessed to his anti-imperialist cause. This was shrewd. As it turned out, Sir Sayyid Ahmed Khan's political influence over Indian Muslims would fade, and the more vigorous campaign in support of the Ottoman caliphate would come in the early 1920s in the form of a countrywide agitation – the first major mass movement of Muslim India – backed by the great Hindu leader, Mahatma Gandhi. As Akbar Illahabadi would write, explaining the joint campaign for the caliphate by Gandhi and the Indian Muslim leader Maulana Muhammad Ali: 'Maulana has not blundered, nor has Gandhi hatched conspiracies / What blows them on the same course is the gale of Western policies.'[94] Al-Afghani may have anticipated this nationalist moment by stressing the need for Hindu-Muslim unity in India. In the same vein, he also argued that linguistic ties were more profound than religious ones (a lesson Pakistan was to learn when the Bengali-speaking Muslims in East Pakistan seceded to form Bangladesh in 1971).

Whereas in Egypt he had invoked the country's pre-Islamic greatness, in India he hailed the discoveries of science and mathematics by Hindus of the classical age. Speaking in Calcutta to a largely Muslim audience, he pointed to the presence of young students, and confessed to be

> happy to see such offspring of India, since they are the offshoots of that India that was the cradle of humanity. Human values spread out from India to the whole world. These youths are from the very land where the meridian circle was first determined. They are from the same realm

that first understood the zodiac. Everyone knows that the determination of those two circles is impossible until perfection in geometry is
achieved. Thus we can say that Indians were the inventors of arithmetic
and geometry. Note how Indian numerals were transferred from here
to the Arabs, and from there to Europe ... [The Indians] reached the
highest level in philosophic thought.

Invoking the religious and legal texts of Classical India, the Vedas and
the Shastras, al-Afghani added that 'these youths are also the sons of
a land that was the source of all the laws and rules of the world'.[95]

In the century ahead, India's Hindu nationalists would frequently
make similar assertions about India's scientific and philosophical
heritage. Certainly, al-Afghani knew how to tailor his message. But he
was consistent in his anti-colonialism, according to which Muslims in
India, as in other countries, should awaken and join other Muslim and
non-Muslim peoples in a united front against the British. At the same
time, Islam for Muslims ought to remain the main source of strength
and values; they should not be deluded by Sir Sayyid Ahmed Khan's
pro-British agenda. And neither Hindus nor Muslims should turn
their backs on their traditions. As Akbar Illahabadi exhorted himself:
'Akbar, in all the verse you write / Make this your theme repeatedly /
Muslim, take up your rosary / And Brahman, wear your sacred
thread.'[96] India had originally alerted al-Afghani to the advantages of
Western science and knowledge; India also served as a warning against
those advocating drastic, total Westernization.

THE EUROPEAN INTERLUDE

After a brief stopover in London, during which he met Wilfrid Blunt
and contributed an anti-British article to a newspaper run by a Lebanese Greek Catholic disciple, al-Afghani arrived in Paris in January
1883, shortly after Britain had suppressed the uprising in Egypt and
occupied the country. The French capital was then, as it had been for
much of the nineteenth century, a Mecca for various political mal-
contents. Among the host of exiles from North Africa there was
al-Afghani's old disciple from Egypt, James Sanua. He heralded

al-Afghani's arrival in Paris with a lithographed drawing of the latter in his magazine, *Abu Nadarra Zarqa*. Al-Afghani began writing for Sanua immediately.

Shortly before leaving India for Europe, al-Afghani was interrogated by the British authorities in Calcutta, and briefly placed under house arrest. The harassment, together with the apparent prostrations of Muslims like Sir Sayyid Ahmed Khan before the British, seems to have embittered him. Explaining why he went to Paris after India, he wrote to his old patron Riyad Pasha in Egypt that he wanted to be in

> lands whose inhabitants enjoy sound minds, attentive ears, and sympathetic hearts to whom I can recount how a human being is treated in the East. Thus will be extinguished the fire that so many sufferings have lit in me and my body will be freed from the burden of sufferings that have broken my heart.[97]

After a long spell in *Dar al-Harb*, al-Afghani now intended to give priority to Muslim self-strengthening against the West above the issue of internal reform. A measure of this new defensive mood could be found in one of his first articles in an Arabic periodical in Paris, an open letter to its editor, a Lebanese Maronite disciple of al-Afghani's, admonishing him for excessive criticism of 'Easterners', who were suffering at the hands of foreign imperialists, and of the Ottoman Empire, which was the only protector of Muslims worldwide. Only internal unity among Easterners, he asserted, could stop them from becoming prey to foreigners. Likewise Ottomans should remain united behind their potentate. Al-Afghani would look for and find supporters in both France and the Ottoman Empire for such views.

His articles praising the Ottoman sultan as a potential unifier of Islam were received particularly gratefully by his old Egyptian disciples and colleagues who had gone into exile in Beirut after the British occupation of Egypt. Mohammed Abduh, among others, wrote to lavishly praise his role in the awakening of Egypt. A few months later Abduh joined him in Paris and together they founded a secret society of Muslims dedicated to the unification and reform of Islam.

Funded by a wealthy Tunisian political reformer and other well-off sympathizers, and assisted by such volunteers as Qasim Amin (1863–1908), the Alexandria-born advocate of women's rights, al-Afghani and Abduh started a magazine called *al-'Urwa al-wuthqa* (literally, 'The Firmest Bond') for free distribution in the Muslim world. Published from a small room near the Place de la Madeleine, its eighteen issues dealt with the ravages of British imperialism, the need for Muslim unity and cultural pride, and the correct reinterpretation of Islamic principles. Though prevented from circulating in European-controlled countries, the magazine in its samizdat incarnations became hugely influential across the Muslim world and beyond. The opening issue of *al-'Urwa al-wuthqa* addressed itself to 'easterners in general, and Muslims in particular', claiming that the magazine would serve them by explaining the causes of their decline and offering a remedy. It went on to assert that European imperialists had finally been exposed and that long-oppressed Muslims were now beginning to be aware of the need for unity against the foreigners occupying their lands.

The exhortatory note makes the magazine sound like the *Communist Manifesto*. But it is hard to underestimate its importance as the first international periodical to call explicitly for the revival of Islamic solidarity in the face of the encroaching West. Nothing like it had ever existed in Arabic, or in any of the other languages of the Islamic world. Having invented liberal journalism in Egypt, al-Afghani and Abduh were now inaugurating a tradition of radical polemic which explicitly rejected the previous Muslim programme of internal reform and national consolidation. As Abduh explained in an interview with the *Pall Mall Gazette* before the British occupation of Egypt:

> We wished to break down the tyranny of our rulers; we complained of
> the Turks to the foreigners; we wished to improve ourselves politically,
> and to advance as the nations of Europe have advanced on the path of
> liberty. Now we know that there are worse evils than despotism and
> worse enemies than the Turks.[98]

It was *al-'Urwa al-wuthqa* that first offered, in Abduh's prose, an interpretation of jihad as an individual rather than a communal duty – an obligation to keep Muslim lands under Muslim control which was binding on all Muslims, not just their rulers. Both Abduh and al-Afghani worked hard to find messages in the Koran that could fit their political programme of awakening the Muslim masses; they also dispatched copies of the periodical as far as Tripoli and the Malay

Peninsula. The Syrian writer Rashid Rida wrote of how, when he read the articles in *al-'Urwa al-wuthqa* of 'the call to pan-Islamism, the return of glory, power and prestige to Islam, the recovery of what it used to possess, and the liberation of its people from foreign domination', he was 'so impressed that I entered into a new phase of my life'.[99] Rida, mentored later by Mohammed Abduh, was to continue al-Afghani's work through *al-Manar* ('Beacon'), a major periodical which combined an anti-imperialist programme with the revival of Islam between 1898 and 1935; it would spread al-Afghani's reputation deep into Central Asia and further east to the Muslims of China and the Malay Peninsula.

The wide circulation of al-Afghani's writings brought him the unwelcome attention of the British Foreign Office in London. One of Britain's spies in Hyderabad sent a letter claiming that James Sanua's magazine was 'not fit to be allowed into India' and was 'even less suitable for Egypt'. The letter included a translated article in the magazine, a report from Egypt under British occupation: 'Power is in the hands of the Europeans who have purchased us through traitors and today we are led by them like donkeys.' The article ended with a eulogy to al-Afghani, pleading with him to 'send us his lucubrations which inspire a new soul into us since they open our hearts to national honour and patriotism and incite us to unfurl the standard of liberty'.[100]

The alarmed British authorities asked the French police to enquire into al-Afghani's activities. They received a less than reassuring report, which noted the anti-British agitator's close association with James Sanua. Al-Afghani 'passes as very well-educated', the report said, 'and although he expresses himself in French with difficulty, he commands eight languages'. It confirmed that 'his habitual conduct and his morality do not give rise to any unfavourable remark', though 'he receives many visits and appears to be in comfortable circumstances'.[101]

This was partly true. In Paris, al-Afghani seems to have savoured the raffish cosmopolitanism of political exiles. Visiting al-Afghani and Abduh at their offices in a garret on the rue de Seize, Wilfrid Blunt found a 'very curious party of strangers who quite filled the room – a Russian lady, an American philanthropist, and two young Bengalis

who announced themselves as Theosophists, come, they said to consult the great Sheykh'.[102]

The Indian visitors were keen to learn about the Mahdi, then the
kind of minatory figure to Westerners that Osama bin Laden was to
become later. Previously reticent about the Sudanese, al-Afghani now
hailed him as the harbinger of a worldwide Muslim revolt against the
West: 'Another serious victory of the Mahdi', he wrote in a French
newspaper, 'would have as a fatal consequence not only the provo-
cation of an insurrection in the Islamic countries under Turkish
domination, as well as in Baluchistan, Afghanistan, Sind, India,
Bukhara, Kokand, Khiva – but also lead to troubles in Tripoli, Tunis,
Algeria, and as far as Morocco.'[103]

With this religious-political messianic strain fully established in
al-Afghani's thought, he underwent a sartorial makeover. While
previously he had usually dressed in flowing robes and turban, al-
Afghani now switched to stiff white collars, necktie and coat. He
invited the attentions of an attractive German woman. He had a brief
affair with her – the only recorded romantic intimacy in his life – but
left her letters unread. He provoked, too, the curiosity of European
intellectuals, most prominently Ernest Renan.

Renan met al-Afghani in March 1883 through an Arab exile in Paris
who often contributed to the magazine *Journal des Débats*. 'Few
people', Renan later wrote, 'have produced on me a more vivid impression.' Their conversation led Renan to write and deliver a lecture
titled 'Islam and Science' at the Sorbonne. Al-Afghani responded to it
with a long article; Renan wrote a rejoinder. It was the first major
public debate between a Muslim and a European intellectual, and it
prefigured many later Western discussions about Islam in the modern
world.

In the article that opened this debate, Renan eulogized Hellenism
and denounced Islam as the begetter of despotism and terrorism. He
invoked the racial hierarchy in which rationality, empiricism, indus-
triousness, self-discipline and adaptability defined Western man, and
their near-total absence defined the people he dominated. 'The liberals
who defend Islam do not know it,' he asserted in his article. 'Islam
is ... the reign of a dogma, it constitutes the heaviest chains which

have ever shackled humanity.'[104] Renan attacked Islam in terms similar to those he and other European freethinkers deployed against Catholicism: with its claims to supernatural revelation, it was an affront to reason, and a violent persecutor of free thought. He also stridently identified progress as the unique achievement and prerogative of the white race and Christianity, arguing that Islam and modern science were incompatible. He explained away Arab achievements in philosophy and sciences as the work of near-apostates who had rebelled against Islam and borrowed heavily from the Greeks and Persians.

Al-Afghani refuted the racialist argument easily by pointing to Persian Islamic philosophers who were Muslim and worked in Arabic. Then he went further than any modern Islamic thinker by agreeing with Renan's view of religion's intellectual failings, though he objected to Islam being singled out in this regard. All religions, he said, began with manifesting intolerance towards reason and science, and only slowly broke free of these prejudices. Islam was behind Christianity by many centuries in the long curve of learning. It had 'tried to stifle science and stop its progress', but it had been and could still be made compatible with the traditions of intellectual enquiry. It was important to believe it could, otherwise 'hundreds of millions of men would thus be condemned to live in barbarism and ignorance'.[105]

Renan began his rejoinder patronizingly: 'There is nothing more instructive than studying the ideas of an enlightened Asiatic in their original and sincere form.' He insisted that intelligent Muslims, like al-Afghani, were those 'entirely divorced from the prejudices of Islam', who, furthermore, came from places like Persia and India, 'where the Aryan spirit lives still so energetically under the superficial layer of official Islam'. Still, he conceded some ground to al-Afghani: 'Galileo was,' he admitted, 'no better treated by Catholicism than Averroes by Islam.'[106]

This is where the debate ended. Interestingly, Abduh declined to translate al-Afghani's response to Renan. He did not want any criticism of Islam to circulate among the devout. 'We cut off the head of religion only with the sword of religion,' Abduh explained to al-Afghani, and the latter does not seem to have disagreed. For both Abduh and al-Afghani at this time, Islam, however inadequate, was the only source of ethics and stimulus for political mobilization. And al-Afghani also presciently saw that a totally secular society – the dream of nineteenth-century rationalism – was doomed to remain a fantasy in the West as well as in the Muslim world. As he concluded in his response to Renan:

> The masses do not like reason, the teachings of which are understood only by a few select minds. Science, however fine it may be, cannot completely satisfy humanity's thirst for the ideal, or the desire to soar in dark and distant regions that philosophers and scholars can neither see nor explore.[107]

There were many such responses to Renan from Muslim intellectuals. The one from the Young Ottoman Namik Kemal became best known but it was mainly defensive in nature, upholding Arab scientific and philosophical accomplishments and attacking the West, whereas al-Afghani admitted the currently deficient state of Islamic learning.

This exchange proved yet again al-Afghani's intellectual flexibility, his ability to interpret Islam, and also to project himself, in new contexts. During his debate with Renan, he argued that the original teachings of Islam were in accordance with modern rationalism but since then Muslim societies had become internally weak and intolerant; they needed a Martin Luther to reconcile themselves with the modern world.

That Islam needed a Reformation, with himself as Luther, was gradually becoming a favourite theme of al-Afghani. In the meantime, he was ready to settle for a strong ruler who could unite Muslims against the West. One of the likely candidates was Sultan Abdulhamid, whom al-Afghani carefully praised in his articles. The other was the Mahdi. Writing for left-wing French papers, al-Afghani invoked the likelihood of a Russo-Franco-Ottoman attack on the British, which, he claimed, could be followed by a massive worldwide uprising of Muslims. The Mahdi was a crucial figure in his plan to alarm the British, which was not purely fantastical. During his time in Paris he was involved in various intrigues, including one proposal, advanced by Wilfrid Blunt, to persuade the Mahdi to cease his attacks on the British in exchange for Egypt's independence.

Al-Afghani's centrality to this scheme depended on his exaggerated claims of influence over the Mahdi. They persuaded at least some people. He was believed to be an efficient mediator by high-ranking British officials, and in July 1885, he even went to London, on Blunt's invitation, to meet with Randolph Churchill, the Secretary of State for India. Blunt warned Churchill beforehand that his house guest al-Afghani 'is in the black book . . . of everyone here, and is an enemy of England'. 'But,' he added, 'if he was not he would be of no use to us.'[108] Al-Afghani bluntly informed Churchill that Indian Muslims hated Britain more than they hated its great rival in the Great Game, Russia. Still, Britain could redeem itself by leaving Egypt and entering into an 'alliance with Islam, with the Afghans, the Persians, the Turks, the Egyptians, the Arabs . . . The Mullahs would preach a jihad to join you against the Russians.'[109]

Nothing came of these implausible and overreaching plans (they foreshadow the Anglo-American anti-Russian jihad in Afghanistan by nearly a century). The Mahdi disappointed by abruptly dying in 1885, and the opportunistic al-Afghani would soon enjoin the Russians to ally themselves with Muslims against the British. After three futile months of scheming with the British, al-Afghani had to leave Blunt's home in London after a loud quarrel with two of his Muslim friends. 'Jamal al-din', Blunt later wrote,

> was a man of genius whose teaching exercised an influence hardly to be overrated on the Mohammedan reform movement of the last thirty years. I feel highly honoured at his having lived three months under my roof in England; but he was a wild man, wholly Asiatic and not easily tamed to European ways.[110]

Certainly, Europe and the placid pleasures of exile were not for al-Afghani. It was also around this time that he parted ways with Abduh. The reasons were never stated, but they were apparent in their respective political journeys, which would take them to very different places.

For nearly two decades, al-Afghani had not returned to his homeland; he hadn't even kept in touch with his family until he was living in Paris. In 1886, he travelled to Persia, spending several months in the port city of Bushehr. He was a famous man by then. And, yet again changing his persona to meet new circumstances, he now stressed his Persian ancestry. His hosts in Persia were powerful men of the court, merchants and landowners, and even budding activists like Mirza Nasrallah Isfahani, later known as Malik al-Mutakallimin, a progressive member of the *ulema*, who would become one of the leaders of Persia's constitutional revolution in 1906.

Malik al-Mutakallimin had just been exiled from India by the British; he found a fatherly figure in al-Afghani, who discoursed at length on pan-Islamism. Other members of the Persian intelligentsia attached themselves to al-Afghani, and some of them were to constitute his inner circle during his exile in Istanbul in the 1890s. Even Shah Naser al-Din had heard of him, and invited him to Tehran. On their first meeting al-Afghani told the shah that he was like a 'sharp sword' in the ruler's hands and asked him not to keep it idle. The aggressive words seem to have alienated the conservative shah, who was already disturbed by news of al-Afghani's political speeches and writings; he quietly banished the potential troublemaker from Persia.

Al-Afghani then went on to Moscow. The British were closely monitoring his movements at this time, and the British ambassador to Russia expressed his concern to the Russian foreign minister about the man who had 'launched the most violent attacks on Her Majesty's Government', and who was trying to 'promote disaffection in India'.[111] This was correct, and al-Afghani himself made no secret of his intentions of provoking Russia's tsar into action against British influence in the Muslim world. In July 1887, the *Moscow Gazette*, a newspaper edited by Mikhail Nikiforovich Katkov, a well-known conservative nationalist and al-Afghani's host in Moscow, claimed that 'his object in visiting Russia was to make himself practically acquainted with a country on which 60,000,000 Indian Muslims place sole reliance, and which they hope will afford them protection and emancipate them from the detested English yoke'.[112]

Unfortunately, Katkov died soon after al-Afghani's arrival. But the latter continued to lobby for influence at the tsar's court. In an interview given to *Novoe Vremya*, al-Afghani expressed surprise at Russian willingness to let Britain define the Russian–Afghan border. He confessed he was worried about British influence in Afghanistan; the British, he said, always crept into countries as advisers before becoming their masters. This could also, he added, be proved true in Persia, where the shah was beginning to make major concessions to the British at the expense of Russia.

In Moscow, al-Afghani met with likely co-conspirators, including Dalip Singh, the colourful son of the last Sikh king of Punjab, who felt militantly aggrieved by his treatment by the British. Together the two plotted a Russo-British war that would lead not only to the liberation of India but also to the extirpation of European presence in all Eastern lands. More evidence of al-Afghani's ecumenical approach to anti-imperialism came from the Russian-born Muslim Abdurreshid Ibrahim, who was then at the beginning of a remarkable career in international activism. He observed al-Afghani in dialogue with a Russian *alim* in St Petersburg, and later reported that al-Afghani shocked the Russian when in response to a question of Islamic jurisprudence (*fiqh*), he laughed and said, 'Haven't you stopped being concerned with questions of *fiqh*? You will drown in a sea of contradictions.'[113]

Impatient of abstract theorizing, al-Afghani was now a political activist above all, with Islam as his major, though by no means only, instrument. Abdurreshid Ibrahim described how, unable to secure an audience with the tsar of Russia, al-Afghani appeared at the opera house in his robes and turban and took a box near the tsar. Not long after the curtain lifted on a scene, he rose from his seat. Facing Mecca, he loudly announced, 'I intend to say the evening prayer, Allah o Akbar!'

All eyes turned to al-Afghani as he began his recitation. A Russian general entered their box, demanding to know what al-Afghani had in mind. Nervously, Ibrahim asked him to wait until his companion had finished. As a puzzled tsar and his family watched, al-Afghani went on with his prayers. When he rose he told the general to inform the tsar that, 'I have a time with God which has no room for King or Prophet.'[114] To Ibrahim, who was terrified of being executed on the spot, al-Afghani claimed that he had brought the word of Islam to the tsar, the empress and the ministers of Russia.

Although apparently impressed by this instance of Muslim devotion – enough at any rate to not immediately arrest al-Afghani and Ibrahim – the tsar failed to advance any anti-British conspiracies. This might have been the end of the line for al-Afghani. Budding revolutionaries usually have one shot at success. Al-Afghani had had several, but he had nothing to show for his efforts except a wide net-work of friends, sympathizers and fellow conspirators across three continents. His greatest political victory, however, was still to come, and it would be achieved in Persia, the country of his birth.

APOTHEOSIS IN PERSIA

Apparently influenced by al-Afghani's networking in Russia, the shah of Persia overcame his dislike enough to invite him again to Tehran. The shah may have also wanted to put an end to al-Afghani's loud strictures against rising British influence in his country. He offered the activist a sinecure of sorts – the editorship of a newspaper – but the first article al-Afghani submitted strongly denounced European influ-ence over the Muslim world. According to the French ambassador in Tehran, the shah was appalled to read in al-Afghani's article that the 'blood of infidels must run in order that the number of Muslims should grow and their influence increase in the world, etc. etc.'[115] This was probably an exaggeration as al-Afghani never used such language in his printed articles. In any case, the shah soon realized that inviting al-Afghani to Persia was a serious mistake, for Persia was fertile ground for an anti-imperialist Muslim agitator like al-Afghani – and popular opinion there was more favourable to him than it had been in Egypt.

Persia had suffered little from Western encroachments, unlike its Ottoman neighbour and Egypt. This was partly because the country had no capital-generating item of export such as cotton with which to invite foreign investment or improve its infrastructure. Consequently, there weren't enough resources to build a national army and adminis-tration, or to embark on extravagant public works. Guilds still organized life in cities and towns; social and economic arrangements hadn't been disrupted by a Western-style economy emphasizing for-eign trade and individual property rights. Unchallenged by Western modernity, Islam retained its moral appeal, cultural prestige and cohe-sive force, and was capable of turning into the political weapon al-Afghani now wanted it to be.

Like the Ottoman sultan and the Egyptian khedive, the shah of Persia had also gone on expensive Grand Tours of Europe. He wrote admiringly of what he saw (a Moscow ballet, as well as things for which there were no words in Persian, such as 'tunnel', which he translated as 'hole in the mountain'). He sent a few students to Paris, and allowed Christian missionaries to set up schools in Persia. But he carefully refrained from following the Egyptians and Turks in undertaking extensive reforms at home. Like many other despots, he was interested in modernization only in so far as it strengthened his apparatus of surveillance and control, and made him look enlightened to foreign investors.

Visiting Persia in 1880, two Japanese diplomats took a sceptical view of the shah's modernization. 'If a ruler is striving hard only for a fair outside appearance without making the foundation secure, then the fate of the Empire is likely to hang in the balance.'[116] By the time he invited al-Afghani back to Tehran, the shah's failure to consider any liberalization had begun to alienate young Persian intellectuals who wanted reform. The rival powers competing for influence over Persia – Britain and Russia – had grown more aggressive. They dominated Persia's foreign trade; the British in particular transported opium grown in Isfahan to lucrative markets in China and used Persian territory for their overland telegraphic link to India.

The shah and his dealings with foreigners were widely distrusted. The influx of infidels into the economy had provoked the conservative clergy. Generally, the power of Shiite clerics in Persia was greater than that of the Sunni *ulema* in Egypt. Meanwhile, Britain was driving hard bargains, and Russia pressed its own claims. In lieu of foreign trade, the shah had begun to grant concessions to European businessmen, expecting to share in the profits of new railways, oil discoveries and state lotteries.

In 1872, the shah had granted a complete construction monopoly in railways, roads, factories, dams and mines to a British citizen, Baron Reuter (founder of the Reuters news agency). Even the die-hard imperialist Lord Curzon later described the sale as 'the most complete surrender of the entire resources of a kingdom into foreign hands that has ever been dreamed of much less accomplished in history'.[117] Russian protests sank the arrangement; but Reuter got other favourable deals, and the shah persisted in selling concessions to Europeans in order to fund his massive fiscal deficit.

*

This was, of course, how the khedive in Egypt had made his country dependent on European finance and eventually vulnerable to British occupation; innocuous traders from the West were usually followed by predatory soldiers. As al-Afghani, who had learnt the lessons of imperialism in several Muslim countries, warned in a letter addressed to the Persian authorities, the foreign enemies of Persia had entered the country under

> various deceitful pretexts. One under the name of the Police Chief [Count Monteforte], another under the pretext of being the Director of the Customs [Monsieur Kitabgi], one calling himself instructor [Russian officers], another saying he is a priest [Dr Torrence and American missionaries], another under the excuse of hiring the mines [English Mining Company], another of establishing a bank [Imperial Bank of Persia], and another under the plea of having the monopoly of tobacco trade [Major Talbot] are taking away the resources of the country and in time they will take possession of the country itself, when it will be the beginning of your misfortunes.[118]

Al-Afghani broke with the shah almost immediately after reaching Persia, taking refuge in a shrine outside Tehran. From this sanctuary he kept up a barrage of speeches warning Persians of the imminent sale of their country: 'Before you become the slaves of the foreigners like the natives of India you must find a remedy.'[119] He acquired his most fervent supporters among Shiite nationalist intellectuals excited by his ideas, especially that the principles of Islam contained all the conditions necessary for bringing about democracy and the rule of law. Their battle cry was what today would be called 'Islamic Democracy', which they believed al-Afghani echoed in his speeches. As it turned out, al-Afghani's campaign received the support of not only reform-minded nationalist intellectuals, or anti-foreign bazaar merchants, but also the conservative *ulema* (who in Egypt and Turkey had tended to distrust him).

After seven months the shah finally got fed up with al-Afghani's agitprop; his soldiers violated the sanctity of the shrine where al-Afghani was hiding, arrested him and forced him into a gruelling mid-winter march across the border into Ottoman-ruled Mesopotamia. A humiliated al-Afghani became even more vociferous in his exile;

and now events conspired to give him, at last, a leading role in a major mass movement against foreign predators and their native enablers.

In 1891, the shah granted a tobacco concession to a British businessman, effectively empowering him to monopolize the purchase, sale and export of an agricultural crop universally popular among Persians. Al-Afghani pointed out, to a loud approving chorus, that tobacco growers would be at the mercy of infidels, who would also destroy the livelihood of small dealers while contaminating the smokes of strict Shiites. Secret societies set up by him in Tehran – a political innovation in Persia – sent out anonymous letters to officials and distributed leaflets and placards calling upon Persians to revolt. The language of these writings was strikingly similar to those of his speeches to the *fellaheen* in Egypt:

> These few pounds of tobacco, which were produced with labor and which a few men with trouble used to export in order to obtain a piece of bread have been coveted and they have been granted to the infidels and forbidden to the followers of the prophet. Oh great human beings, don't you know yourselves? When are you going to wake up?[120]

The Persians responded by erupting in angry protests in major cities in the spring of 1891. They were helped by the invention of the telegraph and the secret societies with their leaflets and placards; the mass demonstrations seem to have been as carefully co-ordinated as they would be in Khomeini's cassette-tape-aided revolution in 1978–9, and women participated in large numbers.

Al-Afghani wrote furious letters to leading Shiite clerics who were then resident in the shrine cities of Mesopotamia, asking them to shed their political indifference and move against the shah. One of his letters to Mirza Hasan Shirazi, a much-respected Shiite cleric, violently denouncing the shah as well as Russian and British influence over the country was widely distributed in Persia and Europe. Patiently, al-Afghani initiated the apolitical cleric into the 'structural adjustments' enforced by Western financiers in poor countries:

> What shall cause thee to understand what is the Bank? It means the complete handing over of the reins of government to the enemy of Islam, the enslaving of the people to that enemy, the surrendering ... of all dominion and authority into the hands of the foreign foe.[121]

Shirazi seems to have absorbed al-Afghani's lessons. A few months later, while al-Afghani was in London, having escaped via Basra, Shirazi wrote his very first letter on political matters to the shah, denouncing foreign control of Muslim peoples through banks and commercial concessions. The shah, desperate to keep the *ulema* on his side, sent various intermediaries to plead with Shirazi. The latter not only did not relent; he issued a fatwa, effectively making it un-Islamic to smoke until the monopoly was withdrawn. The ban was astoundingly successful to the extent that even the shah's palace became smoke-free. Finally, the shah capitulated to the alliance between intellectuals, clergy and merchants, and cancelled the concession.

Al-Afghani had done much to bring about this victorious axis, which was to endure and would shape Iran's history (Mohammad Mossadegh first developed his fateful distrust of foreign companies as a precocious nine-year-old in 1891). It was al-Afghani's finest moment, and he let everyone know it. Much to the anger of the shah, he kept giving public speeches in London and publishing articles in the British press, calling upon the Shiite *ulema* to depose the corrupt and heedless regime in Tehran. Many of these articles were addressed to British readers, reproaching them for their government's support of the despotic shah. Among the furious tracts there were insights that remain strikingly relevant today. Writing in the *Contemporary Review*, he explained why Muslims came to dislike the West as well as the despots it propped up in their countries:

> However *bizarre* it may seem, it is nevertheless a fact, that after each visit of the Shah to Europe, he has increased in tyranny over his people. Probably this may be more or less due to his receptions . . . in Europe. The result is that the masses of Persia . . . attributed their increased suffering to European influences, and hence their dislike of Europeans became yet more intense, at the very moment when a rapprochement might easily have been effected.[122]

Al-Afghani deplored the British press for presenting Iranian protestors as religious fanatics when in fact they expressed a genuine desire for reform and a legal code. He pointed to biased reports by the Reuters news agency (owned, of course, by a British subject who still had banking and mining rights in Iran). He again called for the British to leave Egypt and India in order to reduce Muslim hostility to them, and to cease their support to the Persian shah. He continued to call for the shah to be overthrown. The Iranians protested repeatedly to the British about al-Afghani's writings; London claimed helplessness. In an interview with the *Pall Mall Gazette* in December 1891, al-Afghani described the Persians as more disposed to progress and reform than other Asians, and stressed his own likely role as a catalyst for change in Muslim countries. 'The true spirit of the Koran,' he claimed, 'is in perfect accordance with modern liberties . . . A learned Mussulman well acquainted with the liberal principles of Europe, can easily convey them to his people with the authority of the Koran, without the difficulties which surrounded Luther.'[123]

IN A GOLDEN CAGE: AL-AFGHANI'S LAST DAYS IN ISTANBUL

Al-Afghani had scarcely been more powerful as an agitator. But he was also reaching the end of his influence. His decision to accept a flattering invitation to counsel the Ottoman Sultan Abdulhamid II and go to Istanbul would effectively remove him from the political scene he had hoped to alter.

In the summer of 1892 al-Afghani arrived in Istanbul, surprising his Ottoman hosts with his meagre luggage. He was installed in one of the sultan's large guesthouses in Yildiz, the palace complex Abdulhamid had built for himself on the banks of the Bosporus, and put on a monthly retainer. The Ottoman sultan had long distrusted al-Afghani, whom he thought was trying to stoke Arab disaffection with the Ottoman Empire. But Abdulhamid was also fascinated by the itinerant activist, and keen to employ him for his own purposes. He hoped that he could enlist al-Afghani as a propagandist for an Ottoman caliphate and also control him by keeping him in Istanbul.

The reforms of the Tanzimat had long been stymied; they were widely perceived, and not just by the conservative *ulema*, to have encouraged non-Muslim secessionists while doing little for Muslims. The sultan had greatly increased his power, using a fully modern network of spies, informers and a police force proficient in torture. He was obsessed with the example of Japan, which was increasingly achieving parity with European powers in Asia. Risibly paranoid (he was worried, for instance, that the emperor of Japan might convert to Islam and pose a political challenge to him), Abdulhamid was eager to win the support of Muslims worldwide. He had invited various Islamic grandees from India and Syria to adorn his court and boost his claim as caliph, but he needed relatively independent figures like al-Afghani by his side too.

He turned out to have calculated well. Al-Afghani himself did not much like or trust the sultan, but he was ready to use the ruler's prestige, if that's what it took, to rouse Muslims. And he may have been flattered to be asked to advise the most important Muslim ruler in the world, who now hoped to extend his realm of sovereignty. After all, al-Afghani had been looking for such an official boost to pan-Islamism for a long time.

The sultan gave al-Afghani an audience soon after the latter reached Istanbul. Witnesses to their meeting were taken aback by the wandering agitator's free and bold manner with the sovereign of all Muslims. Abdulhamid's hospitality extended to offering al-Afghani marriage with a court concubine. The peripatetic thinker's refusal was philosophically phrased: 'Man in this world is like a traveler – naked, afraid, surrounded by obstacles on all sides, and fighting to free himself of them and to be liberated. What would happen if you burdened this traveler?'[124]

In lieu of a female companion, al-Afghani gathered around himself his usual multinational retinue of fans and students. A Syrian student, Abd al-Qadir al-Maghribi, who like many Muslim thinkers credited his intellectual and emotional growth to the periodical al-Afghani and Mohammed Abduh had published from Paris, now became his ardent follower; al-Maghribi later compiled his recollections of al-Afghani in a book. And Afghanistan's foremost writer and thinker, Mahmud Tarzi (1865–1933), began his political education during the seven months he spent with al-Afghani and his disciples in Istanbul.

The Ottoman capital was also full of Persian exiles, including some radical freethinkers who advocated the renunciation of Islam. But even they found al-Afghani's pan-Islamism compelling, embracing the belief that Muslim unity against the West took priority over internal reform.

One of these freethinking Persians, the poet Shaikh Ahmad Ruhi, inscribed on his seal the words, 'I am the propagandist of the Unity of Islam.'[125]

The Egyptian nationalist leader Saad Zaghlul visited al-Afghani in Istanbul, as did the young Rashid Rida, disciple of Abduh and later inspiration for the Muslim Brotherhood. Abduh himself remained aloof. Convinced that confrontation with European imperialists was futile, he had started on a journey that would take him back to Egypt and collaboration with the British.

Al-Afghani gave talks, faithfully recorded by his disciples, in which he, like all isolated political exiles, greatly exaggerated his role in world events. He claimed intimacy with the tsar of Russia and the Mahdi; he boasted he had spurned the shah of Iran's overtures. He shared some brilliant historical insights, such as that the innumerable wars in Europe in the centuries following Luther had helped hone the organizational skills of many European countries, which in the long term had led to modern civilization. He often returned to his favourite themes. Muslim mimicry of European ways, he argued, would expose them to European rule: 'this is an imitation that by its nature will drag us into admiration for foreigners; and being content with their domination over us.'[126] The imperatives for reform and science were contained in the Koran, which was perfectly compatible with modern science, politics and economics. He stressed a clear and modern reading of the Koran; no traditionalist interpretation of the holy text, he seemed to argue, should stand in the way of Muslim unity.

He rejected the Shiite–Sunni schism in Islam, blaming it on selfish rulers who used wars to keep their populations ignorant. He spoke, too, of the necessity of constitutional reforms, which were then being stressed by reformers and political activists in all the Muslim lands ruled by despots and European colonialists. More surprisingly, he spoke of the essential unity of the great monotheistic religions, underlining the fact that what he opposed of the West was not Christian values but its imperialism.

However, unwritten rules prohibited him from any explicit political activity, like summoning the Iranians to revolt against their shah. The Iranian diplomats in Istanbul insisted on police surveillance of al-Afghani. The sultan also forbade him from publishing anything. It was only in 1894 that al-Afghani wrote to the Shiite *ulema*, requesting the clerics support the sultan's claim to be caliph. And he found himself more and more isolated within the Ottoman city.

The Iranian government kept lodging one strong protest after another against al-Afghani's presence in Istanbul. The obsessively secretive sultan's spies also kept an eye on him and his followers. There were enough conservatives at the imperial court wary of al-Afghani and his freewheeling ways with Islam. They became more suspicious when Egypt's new khedive came to Istanbul and expressed a wish to see him (the request was denied).

Rumours circulated around the capital about al-Afghani's lack of religion, and, more implausibly, his beer-drinking and frequenting of disreputable taverns. Abdurreshid Ibrahim, who had witnessed al-Afghani's Islamic ostentations before the tsar in St Petersburg, now saw him in Istanbul rejecting the requests of a devout Muslim who wanted to break up his usual gathering for prayers. In 1895 al-Afghani tried to leave Istanbul by securing a British passport. His old enemies bluntly refused to help him out.

His vision of the world grew darker. In 1896 he dramatically summed up the Muslim condition:

> The Islamic states today are unfortunately pillaged and their property stolen; their territory is occupied by foreigners and their wealth in the possession of others. There is no day in which foreigners do not grab a part of the Islamic lands, and there is no night in which foreigners do not make a group of Muslims obey their rule. They disgrace the Muslims and dissipate their pride. No longer is the command of [the Muslims] obeyed or their word heeded. [The foreigners] chain up the Muslims, put around their necks a yoke of servitude, debase them, humiliate their lineage, and they do not mention their name but with insult. Sometimes they call them savages and sometimes regard them as hard-hearted and cruel and finally consider them insane animals. What a disaster! What an affliction! What kind of situation is this? What kind of adversity is this? England has occupied Egypt, the Sudan and the great Indian Peninsula which are large parts of the Islamic states; the French have taken possession of Morocco, Tunisia and Algeria; the Netherlands have become a despotic ruler of Java and the Oceanic islands; Russia has captured West

Turkistan, the large cities of Transoxiana, Caucasia and Daghestan; China has taken East Turkistan. Not more than a few Islamic countries, which are also in great danger, have remained independent.

Out of fear of the Europeans and Westerners they [the Muslims] cannot sleep at night and have no peace in the daytime. The foreigners' influence has affected [even] their blood vessels to the extent that they shudder with fear when they hear the words of Russia and England; they become stupefied with dread when they hear the words of France and Germany. This is the same nation which used to take poll-tax from great kings and to whom the leaders paid tribute voluntarily with the utmost humility, [but] today [the Muslims] have come to the point where the whole world lost hope about their existence [because] they are bitterly oppressed in their own homes. The foreigners are forever frightening these helpless people by tricks and making them unhappy by deceit and ruining their lives. [On the other hand], the Muslims neither have legs to run away nor have they hands to fight. Their kings humble themselves before the non-Muslim kings in order to live a few days longer. The subjects of the [Muslim] kings take refuge in different houses here and there, hoping to have peace of mind. Oh! Oh! What an immense tragedy! What a great catastrophe has fallen [on us]! What a situation has arisen! Where is that power and dignity? What happened to that omnipotence and greatness? Where did that magnificence and glory go? What is the cause of this measureless decline? What is the reason for this poverty and helplessness? Is it possible to doubt God's promise? God forbid! Is it possible to lose hope of God's mercy? God protect us! What should be done then? Where can we find the cause? Where can we look for the reason and whom should we ask? [There is no answer to these questions] except to say that: 'God changes not what is in a people, until they change what is in themselves.'[127]

Imprisoned in Kabul in 1868, al-Afghani had written, 'I want to see what the Curtain of the Unknown will deign to reveal to me and what fate the turning of this malevolent firmament has in store for me.' Wilfrid Blunt, who visited Istanbul in December 1895, reported that the sultan no longer received al-Afghani. His position finally became untenable after one of his Persian disciples, Mirza Reza Kermani, assassinated the shah in 1896, just as the latter was about to celebrate his fiftieth year in power, at the shrine outside Tehran that al-Afghani had made his base in 1889. Explaining his action to Iranian interrogators, Kermani deployed some al-Afghanian rhetoric:

> When a king has ruled for fifty years and still receives false reports and does not ascertain the truth, and when after so many years of ruling the fruit of his tree are such good-for-nothing aristocratic bastards and thugs, plaguing the lives of Muslims at large, then such a tree ought to be cut down so it won't yield such fruits again. When a fish rots, it rots from its head.[128]

The Persians immediately pointed to al-Afghani as the assassination's instigator. Certainly al-Afghani's hatred of the shah was pathological. A month before the assassination, a Persian follower of al-Afghani in Istanbul had found him furiously pacing his room and crying out, 'There is no salvation except in killing, no way out except in killing!' Furthermore, the shah's assassin had spent much time with al-Afghani in Istanbul during the previous year. Interrogated by the Persian police, Kermani cited al-Afghani's harsh expulsion by the shah in 1891 as his prime motivation.

Al-Afghani in turn disclaimed all connection with the assassin, asserting his innocence in several interviews with European journalists, including a German who met him in Istanbul. Al-Afghani's own dwelling was simple, the German reporter said, but he spent much of his time at a large salon with European furnishings, surrounded by Muslims of many different nationalities. His black eyes were as sharp as ever, but also full now of bitterness: 'I have striven, and still strive,' al-Afghani told the German, 'for a reform movement in the rotten Orient, where I would like to substitute law for arbitrariness, justice for tyranny, and toleration for fanaticism.'[129]

The Persian government now pressed even harder for his extradition. Briefly imprisoned by the sultan, al-Afghani would have stewed for some more years in obscurity and bitterness had a lifetime of smoking not caught up with him. In late 1896, he was diagnosed with cancer of the jaw – news greeted with great exultation among Persian diplomatic circles. 'There is no more hope for him,' the Persian ambassador in Istanbul reported back to Tehran. 'Surgeons have cut off one side of his chin along with its teeth and he will soon die.'[130]

Al-Afghani spent a few painful months before dying, still only fifty-nine, on 9 March 1897, with only his Christian servant beside him, another of the expiring century's political exiles to perish in obscurity, far away from home and relatives and friends, his self-appointed tasks unfulfilled, bitterness eating away at him as ruthlessly as the cancer that had consumed half his jaw. His grave was left unmarked. It would not be disturbed for almost a half century. During this time, ordinary people rather than despots would eagerly absorb his ideas. Then, in yet another pendulum swing of fortune usual with political exiles, he would be famous again, revered by a new generation of politicized Muslims who had taken to heart his favourite Koranic injunction: 'God does not change the condition of a people until they change their own condition.'

THE LONG AFTERMATH

In 1924, with Turkey embarked on its most ambitious modernization programme following the death of the Ottoman Empire, an American millionaire and Arabophile called Charles Crane, who was 'searching the world for a really great Moslem', heard of al-Afghani from Sultan Abdulhamid, then living in exile in San Remo. As Crane, who later served as a diplomat for Woodrow Wilson's government, described in his memoir, he looked for al-Afghani's remains a long time in the cemeteries of Istanbul. Then one day a distinguished-looking Muslim man in a green turban appeared before him, offering to take him to the right cemetery in Istanbul.

'There is no mark on the grave of al-Afghani,' the man said, 'but I know its place by the line from two trees which I noted when I first found it.' According to Crane, 'we found the two trees and on taking our bearings came to the little plot of ground, absolutely flat and unmarked, where this man, one of the most distinguished Moslems that ever lived, was buried.'[131]

Based on this identification of al-Afghani's grave by the turbaned Turk, Crane built a monument on the spot. In 1944, the Afghan government disinterred the body; an Afghan minister flew with al-Afghani's apparent remains to Karachi, and then took them on a train to Peshawar, and from there to Kabul by road. Awestruck crowds lined the streets everywhere the cortège passed through – Karachi, Lahore, Peshawar and Jalalabad. In a ceremony attended by Afghanistan's leaders and Kabul's foreign diplomats, al-Afghani was reburied in the grounds of Kabul University. Potentates and poets vied to hail the Muslim leader as Afghanistan's most distinguished son (carefully avoiding Tehran's objections that al-Afghani was actually Persian by birth). The British, the Americans and the Russians laid wreaths on the grave. The German ambassador gave a Nazi salute.

The tomb of al-Afghani (if it is indeed his) still lies in Kabul University, overshadowed by a black marble plinth, and the ironies of the Western reverence for this greatest of modern Muslim activists continue to accumulate. In October 2002, almost a year after the Taliban were driven from power by the United States, the tomb, damaged by Afghanistan's endless wars, received an unexpected visitor: Robert Finn, the then American ambassador to Afghanistan, who pledged a donation of $25,000 to help restore it. Speaking on the occasion, he said:

> This is, in a sense, a double tribute by my country. In doing so we honor the memory of an Afghan and Muslim intellectual giant of the 19th century: a scholar, journalist, political thinker, advisor to kings and a revolutionary who inspired Muslims from Egypt to India. This was a man steeped in the learning of the Qur'an who called for freedom, reason and scientific inquiry. He was a learned man, a skilled writer and debater, he had the moral courage of strong convictions, criticizing the West for its materialism but not shying away from criticizing the Muslim rulers of the day and what he saw as self-destructive tendencies in his own religion . . . This donation is also a recognition that the day will come when Afghanistan will again produce great leaders and thinkers that will shake the world and inspire hope and reform.[132]

After a long delay, the mausoleum's repairs were finally completed in early 2010. But now the black monument radiates a particularly bleak historical irony as the most recent armed missionaries for Western 'values' meet their nemesis in the Pashtun tribes al-Afghani celebrated for their anti-foreign intransigence; and Afghanistan proves yet again to be the graveyard of empires.

*

There was much wishful thinking in the American ambassador's speech (quite apart from the claim, long disproved, that al-Afghani was from Afghanistan). The tribute made the man in the tomb sound like the moderate and liberal Muslim much sought-after in contemporary Europe and America after 9/11 – the kind who might help his co-religionists reach a reasonable *modus vivendi* with the modern West. The mercurial and brilliant al-Afghani was anything but this bland figment of sanguine imagination.

In the late nineteenth century many Muslims were to develop their sense of a world out of touch with God, of a glorious history gone terribly wrong, and the related suspicion that their failure to adhere to a 'true' path of Islam was to blame for their political setbacks. These have since become recurring notes in the modern history of Muslim countries. It was al-Afghani's unique achievement to sense and amplify this predicament more keenly than anyone before him, from places – the central parts of the Muslim world – where it was most acutely felt.

He was not a systematic thinker, and seems to have developed his ideas on the run; he was consistent only in his anti-imperialism, for which cause he accumulated a variety of resources. He advocated both nationalism and pan-Islamism; he lamented the intolerance of Islam; he evoked its great glories in the past; he called for Muslim unity; he also asked Muslims to work with Hindus, Christians and Jews, and did so himself. He admired Western achievements in science; but he claimed that rationality was intrinsic to Islam. In the end, one may be left with an impression of a tremendous energy and enthusiasm rather than thoughtfulness: a vitality that could not be fruitfully directed.

Yet al-Afghani was among the first to insist that Muslims discard their passive and resigned ways before the overwhelming power of Western nations. He recognized the key to that power – science, education, military power – and was convinced that Muslims, too, could acquire it. He never ceased to quote the Koranic verse, 'God does not change the condition of a people until they change their own condition.' And if Muslim peoples moved within a century from being subjects of history to its makers, this was in no small measure due to al-Afghani's continuous exhortations and endeavours across three continents, and their subsequent amplification by his influential followers. It is impossible to imagine, for instance, that the recent protests and revolutions in the Arab world would have been possible without the intellectual and political foundation laid by al-Afghani's assimilation of Western ideas and his rethinking of Muslim traditions.

He was among the new lay educated men, the first people from outside the traditionalist world of Islamic scholarship to reckon with the apparently fallen state of Muslims: the predecessor of India's Muhammad Iqbal as well as Egypt's Sayyid Qutb and Saudi Arabia's Osama bin Laden. His devised solutions also anticipated the two main and interconnected Muslim responses to the West in the modern era: modernism, which sought to strengthen a revealed religion against the challenge of Western knowledge and power, and Islamism, which attempted to reshape the West-dominated world itself according to a utopian and revolutionary understanding of Islam.

Of the two, we have become more familiar in recent years with the second, and in many countries al-Afghani is seen as the founder of modern political Islam along with his main disciple and collaborator Mohammed Abduh, whose own disciples consisted of the Muslim world's foremost leaders in the early twentieth century. This doesn't seem on the face of it an entirely accurate claim to make for a man whose own relationship with Islam bordered on the instrumental. Furthermore Abduh, who, appointed Grand Mufti by the British occupiers of Egypt, went on to develop his own rationalist and flexibly contemporary interpretation of the Koran, had many Westernized disciples who went on to serve in important political and administrative positions in Egypt. The most famous of them, Saad Zaghlul, also a follower of al-Afghani, led the mass nationalist movement against the British after the First World War under the banner of 'Wafd', a broad-based coalition of young professionals and the working class. The idea that Islam offered a solid basis for anti-Western solidarity was developed further by such Turkish cultural nationalists as the poet Ziya Gökalp (1876–1924), who, though a secularist himself, famously wrote, 'The minarets are our bayonets, the domes our helmets, the mosques our barracks and the faithful our army.'

Another set of al-Afghani's and Abduh's followers, however, became proponents of a puritanical movement called Salafism, which spread across the Muslim world as far as Malaysia and Java; they are also part of al-Afghani's mixed legacy. The movement, which stressed a model of virtue and conduct associated with the Salaf, Islam's righteous forefathers, would assume different forms everywhere, but it had certain shared traits. In the beginning, the Salafists espoused an Arab-centric and sternly Sharia-minded Islam as a bulwark against European powers and their native enablers, whom they saw as corrupt and overly Westernized. They had a vision of Islam as a motor of socio-economic and political change; and they were unafraid to use the tools of modernity – the press, political organizations – to propagate their ideas. Their leader was Rashid Rida, who initially revered both Abduh and al-Afghani, and who then distanced himself from Abduh as the latter became an official cleric under British auspices and an advocate of Muslim co-operation with European imperialism. Expounding the more conservative pan-Islamist ideas of al-Afghani, Rida would later become the inspiration for the Islamic fundamentalist group Ikhwan al-Muslimun (Muslim Brotherhood), which was founded in 1928, and spawned in turn a host of similar movements across Asia and Africa. Speaking in 1930, Rida stressed that the *umma* needed 'an independent renewal like that of Japan to promote our economic, military, and political interests and develop our agricultural, industrial, and commercial wealth'. It definitely did not need the 'imitation of Western Civilization' that Turkey and Egypt had disastrously attempted.[133]

Representing a small political tendency initially – Rida played no part in Egypt's 1919 anti-British uprising – the strain of Salafi Islam would grow stronger underground in the second half of the twentieth century as one modernizing despot after another launched brutal crackdowns on Islamist groups. The ideology travelled elsewhere, most fatefully to Afghanistan, where in the person of Ayman al-Zawahiri, a co-conspirator in the assassination of Egyptian president Anwar Sadat, it married Arabia's even more austere Wahhabi Islam, embodied by Osama bin Laden. Brought together in Afghanistan, Islamist refugees from Westernized and despotic regimes in Egypt, Tunisia, Syria and Algeria began to plot the overthrow of pro-West and Westernizing governments; they also began to target these regimes' main Western patrons, the United States and Europe, translating al-Afghani's internationalist anti-imperialism and often romantic Islamic revivalism into the language of global jihad.

Al-Afghani's potent revolutionary formula of Islamic unity and anti-Westernism was also adopted elsewhere.

> Colonialism has partitioned our homeland and has turned the Moslems into separate peoples . . . The only means that we possess to unite the Moslem nation, to liberate its lands from the grip of the colonialists and to topple the agent governments of colonialism is to seek to establish our Islamic government. The efforts of this government will be crowned with success when we become able to destroy the heads of treason, the idols, the human images and the false gods who disseminate injustice and corruption on earth.[134]

This could be al-Afghani in one of his more Islamic moods. It is actually Ayatollah Khomeini. Al-Afghani may have slightly resembled the kind of Muslim ally the United States sought in the immediate aftermath of 9/11 – this is what the American ambassador seemed to imply at his speech in Kabul in 2002. In fact, he was the first major Islamic thinker to use the concepts 'Islam' and 'the West' as violently opposed binaries.[135] In many other ways, he was ahead of his time, participating in popular movements, speaking of Muslim unity and rebellion when political awareness among Muslim masses was still underdeveloped. His Islamic anti-imperialism can be seen now to have inaugurated a tradition of political activists and revolutionaries that culminated, more than a century later, in a major assault on the very capital of Western modernity.

Unlike bin Laden, another peripatetic observer of Muslim infirmity, al-Afghani was no preacher of terrorist violence. Witnessing the insidious influence of European bondholders in Egypt and tobacco traders in Iran, he recognized early how the power of the West did not just rest on military force and could not be resisted by military means alone. He warned presciently against any Muslim ruling class's accommodation with, or blind allegiance to, Western geopolitical and economic interests. His failure to make the Muslim potentates of his time heed his warnings gave him, towards the end of his life, the bitterness of the spurned prophet: 'The entire Oriental world,' he told the German journalist who visited him in Istanbul, 'is so entirely rotten and incapable of hearing the truth and following it that I should wish for a flood or an earthquake to devour and bury it.'

Decades later, Muslim leaders such as Mehdi Bazargan (1907–95), the Islamic Republic of Iran's first prime minister, would fault al-Afghani for investing his political energies in ruling elites rather than ordinary people. Al-Afghani himself seems to have realized his mistake. In his last years he seemed to draw great solace from the ideal of mass democracy. In probably the last letter he wrote (to a Persian disciple), he grieved that he wouldn't live long enough to witness the imminent awakening of the East. He lamented the fact that he had wasted the seed of his ideas 'in the salt and sterile soil' of kingly sovereignty:

> For what I sowed in that soil never grew, and what I planted in that brackish earth perished away. During all this time none of my well-intentioned counsels sank in the ears of the rulers of the East whose selfishness and ignorance prevented them from accepting my words . . . Would that I had sown all the seed of my ideas in the receptive ground of the people's thoughts![136]

Trapped by Sultan Abdulhamid in Istanbul, al-Afghani finally admitted that the kind of political mobilization he was looking for was not going to be led by despots, enlightened or not. More drastic, and popular, revolutions from below were needed; and they needed to shatter the bases as well as the superstructures of oppression. As he put it, 'the stream of renovation flows quickly towards the East. Strive so far as you can to destroy the foundations of this despotism, not to pluck up and cast out its individual agents.'[137]

The Arab Spring has finally brought popular mass movements to the Middle East. But what if the individual agents of despotism, periodically cast out, keep returning in new incarnations? And what if the foundations of despotism remain untouched? What if external intervention and internal weakness cancel out the gains of mass nationalist mobilizations, and pro-Western despots either linger long or periodically emerge to power? A measure of the magnitude of al-Afghani's self-appointed task is that the problems he dealt with remain as dauntingly intransigent as ever, and their ramifications now extend not only to the Muslim countries he travelled through but also to the rest of the world.

THREE: LIANG QICHAO'S CHINA AND THE FATE OF ASIA

Europe thinks she has conquered all these young men who now wear her garments. But they hate her. They are waiting for what the common people call her 'secrets'.

A Chinese intellectual in André Malraux,
The Temptation of the West *(1926)*

THE ENVIABLE BUT INIMITABLE RISE
OF JAPAN

In 1889, while al-Afghani was stirring up anti-foreign agitation in Persia, an Ottoman frigate called the *Ertuğrul* set sail for Japan on a goodwill mission. On board were some senior Ottoman military and civilian officials. It travelled for nine months, passing many ports in South and South-east Asia. Myths about the Ottoman Empire had long been in circulation in East Asia, and large numbers of Muslims turned out wherever the ship docked to witness the 'man-of-war of the great Padishah of Stamboul'.[1] Though slightly decrepit, the frigate seemed living proof of the potency of the last great Muslim ruler, the Ottoman sultan.

It also attested to the growing fascination with Japan among peoples suffering from what the Japanese journalist Tokutomi Sohō, writing three years previously, had described as an 'unbearable situation':

> The present-day world is one in which the civilized people tyrannically destroy savage peoples ... The European countries stand at the very pinnacle of violence and base themselves on the doctrine of force. India, alas, has been destroyed. Burma will be next. The remaining countries will be independent in name only. What is the outlook for Persia! For China? For Korea?[2]

The outlook for Japan at least was clearer. The country, after a brief period of tutelage to the West, was breaking free of its masters, whereas the Ottomans, the Egyptian and Persians, while trying to modernize themselves, had slipped into a profound political and economic dependence on Western powers. The Ottoman frigate's mission was evidence of how Asians everywhere were beginning to be transfixed by the amazingly rapid and unique rise of Japan.

The Ottoman officials were received by the Japanese political elite, including the prime minister and the emperor; they were taken to military parades and given tours of factories. Eager to match the West, and making good progress, the Japanese were prone to look down upon their poor Asian cousins. In 1885, Fukuzawa Yukichi had proposed that since Asian countries were hopelessly backward and weak, Japan should 'escape Asia' and cast its lot in with 'the civilized nations of the West'.[3] This was the dominant mood of the Japanese elite at that time.

Still, there were some dissenting voices, too, about the real intentions of the 'civilized nations of the West' in Asia, and the Ottomans, a curious sight in Japan, managed to provoke some nascent fellow-feeling – the first pangs of what would later turn into full-blown pan-Asianism. Welcoming their Ottoman guests, Japan's highest-circulation newspaper, *Nichi Nichi Shinbun*, expressed sympathy for a country that Europeans had subjected to

> blatant outrages . . . The unjust and overbearing system of extraterritoriality was first practiced on them. Their country has yet to be able to escape from those shackles. Europe then extended these practices to the other countries of the East. Our country, too, suffers from this disgrace. The Turks are Asians like us . . . And so, they've come to us and communicated their friendship.[4]

When on its return journey the *Ertuğrul* collided with a reef and sank, killing more than four hundred Turks on board, a wave of sympathy moved across Japan. Many Japanese donated generously to a fund set up for the survivors, and religious services for the dead were held across the country. Two Japanese warships took the remaining sixty-six Turks all the way to the Sea of Marmara. Sultan Abdulhamid himself received the Japanese naval officers in Istanbul and pinned medals on them.

Japan's reputation continued to rise in Istanbul throughout the 1890s and the next decade, especially after Japan achieved what the Ottomans had for decades tried unsuccessfully to do: a military pact with Great Britain in 1902, signalling its arrival as an equal in the Europe-ordained system of international relations. Abdulhamid, keen on stoking pan-Islamism, was disconcerted by the Japanese emperor's rising status in Asia. Advised by al-Afghani, he politely declined a proposal from the Japanese emperor to send Muslim preachers to Japan. But he was also intrigued by how the Japanese had remained loyal to their emperor while modernizing. In 1897, shortly after al-Afghani's death, the sultan's mouthpiece newspaper, published from Yildiz, editorialized that

> The [Japanese] government, adorned with great intelligence and ideological firmness in progress, has implemented and promoted European [methods] of commerce and industry in its own country, and has turned the whole of Japan into a factory of progress, thanks to many [educational institutions]; it has attempted to secure and develop Japan's capacity for advancement by using means to serve the needs of the society such as benevolent institutions, railways, and in short, innumerable modes of civilization.[5]

The Young Turks who raged against the Ottoman Empire's inability to achieve parity with Western powers, and blamed their oldfangled monarchy for it, drew a different lesson from Japan's alliance with Great Britain and its subsequent victory over Russia in 1905. 'We should take note of Japan,' the exiled Ahmed Riza wrote in 1905 in Paris, 'a nation not separating patriotic public spirit and the good of the homeland from its life is surely such that [though] sustaining wounds, setting out against any type of danger that threatens its existence, it certainly preserves its national independence. The Japanese successes ... are a product of this patriotic zeal.'[6]

For the Young Turks, soon to assume power and build a nation-state on the ruins of the Ottoman Empire, Japan provided clear inspiration. These envious outside observers of Japan's progress did not see the extreme violence of the country's makeover. Nor did they notice the trends towards conformity, militarism and racism that were later to make Japan an ominously successful rival to Europe's imperialist nations – by 1942 Japan would occupy or dominate a broad swathe of the Asian mainland, from the Aleutian Islands in the north-east to the borders of India, after booting out almost all the previous European masters in between. For many Asians in the late nineteenth century, the proof of Japan's success lay in the extent to which it could demand equality with the West; and, here, the evidence was simply overwhelming for people who had tried to do the same and had failed miserably.

*

Its previous seclusion made Japan's transformation between the years 1868 and 1895 particularly astonishing. The Ottomans had been nervously aware of Europe's great intellectual ferment – the Enlightenment, the French Revolution – all through the eighteenth century. But the Japanese learnt of the French and American revolutions only in 1808, after closely questioning the few Dutch traders who had been allowed, following the expulsion of all foreigners from Japan, to retain an outpost at Deshima, a small island off Nagasaki.

In the 1840s, the British began to impose the first of many settlements designed to make China as dependent as India on a 'free trade' regime defined by Western powers. But even the news of their great neighbours' woes travelled late to Japan. In 1844 the Dutch monarch addressed a formal proposal to the Japanese shogun, praising the universal virtues of free trade and gently pointing to China's humiliation as an example of countries that had tried to buck the 'irresistible' worldwide trend. He received a brusque reply from the Japanese asking him not to bother writing again.[7]

Japan's remarkably self-contained world was, however, nearing its end. The British, ensconced in India and coastal China, had long eyed Japan; British ships often sailed menacingly up the latter's coast. But it was left to a new Western power, the United States, to force the issue.

Having completed its conquest of California in 1844, the United States looked across the Pacific for new business opportunities. In 1853, Commodore Matthew Perry sailed into Tokyo (then called Edo) Bay with four men-of-war, and handed over a letter for the Japanese emperor from the American president which began with the ominous words, 'You know that the United States of America now extend from sea to sea.'[8] Denied an audience with the emperor, Perry retreated with subtle threats to return with more firepower if the Japanese did not agree to open their ports to American trade. They refused. He did as he said; and the Japanese succumbed.

During the long period of national isolation, many Japanese had studied with the Dutch traders and sailors based in Deshima; they turned out to be well informed about the strengths of Western barbarians – enough at any rate to know that resistance would be futile until Japan was internally strong. Much to the resentment of

Japanese nobles and the samurai, the Americans were granted trading rights and consular representation. Soon the British, Russians and Dutch were demanding the same for themselves.

The capitulation to foreign barbarians and the repeated violation of Japan's long-preserved sovereignty incited great hostility, and eventually a full-scale rebellion, against the shogun. Meanwhile, the Americans pressed for more privileges, such as extraterritorial jurisdiction, and received them from an increasingly hapless old regime. Eventually, the shogunate collapsed under the strain of simultaneously appeasing foreigners and placating domestic xenophobia, and the Meiji Restoration began.

The westward expansion of America, and the rivalries of European powers, had abruptly begun to shape Japan's politics. Japan looked as abject before Western soldiers, diplomats and traders as the Egyptians, Turks, Indians and Chinese had been. But what happened next broke radically with the pattern of dependence set by other Asian countries.

A generation of educated Japanese, some exposed to Western societies, came to occupy powerful positions in the Meiji Restoration. They recognized the futility of unfocused xenophobia, shrewdly analysed their own weaknesses vis-à-vis the West as scientific and technical backwardness, and urgently set about organizing Japan into a modern nation-state.

To this end, the emperor was brought out of seclusion and exalted as a symbol of the new religion of patriotism with its own shrines and priests. Buddhism was denounced, and Shinto, an assortment of beliefs and rituals, turned into a state religion, yet another glue to use for nation-building. Students were sent abroad; Japanese delegations, many of which included Japan's future leaders and thinkers such as Fukuzawa Yukichi, travelled to the West. Foreign experts were welcomed in every realm, from education to the military. Western dress and hairstyles were adopted and Christian missionaries tolerated. The series of painstaking efforts culminated in a constitution in 1889 that, though exalting the emperor to divine status, tried to follow Western models in other details.

In apprenticing Japan to the West, the Meiji statesmen were lucky to face fewer obstacles than their modernizing Ottoman or Egyptian peers had to deal with (and which the Chinese were yet to experience). Their powers of organization were helped by the fact that Japan, a small country, had an ethnically homogenous population. Groups such as the samurai and wealthy merchants did not resist modernization in the way that traditional elites in the Muslim world did. Indeed, the power of the supplanted elite, the samurai, could be redeployed in the task of national consolidation.

Japan's economy had remained strong. So-called 'Dutch' learning – useful Western knowledge – was circulating in Japan well before Commodore Perry's arrival. A strong local tradition of banker-merchants and an efficient tax-collection system meant that the Japanese economy was not crippled by foreign loans of the kind that banished Egypt, the first non-Western country to modernize, to the ranks of permanent losers in the international economy.

Moreover, the Meiji state never lost sight of its main objective: to radically revise the terms of Japan's relationship with the West. If this meant accepting the superiority of Western civilization, as Fukuzawa Yukichi and others advocated, it seemed a small price to pay for national regeneration and admission to the exclusive club of powerful Western nation-states. For this to happen, however, the unequal treaties imposed on Japan by force of arms had to be revised. Japanese diplomats kept pleading, especially with the British who, of all the Western powers present in Japan, most vehemently opposed the withdrawal of their special concessions. The Japanese even resorted to flattery, presenting themselves as Anglophiles and the 'civilized' equivalent of the British in the East. Finally, after one failed attempt in 1886, which incited a backlash from patriotic Japanese, Japan persuaded the British in 1894 to agree to terminate extraterritorial rights in five years' time.

That same year Japan went to war with China. The cause was Korea, which both countries sought to dominate. It was the first test of Japan's modernity, and also, as Tokutomi Sohō frankly put it, a golden opportunity for Japan to 'build the foundation for national expansion in the Far East ... to take her place alongside the other great expansionist powers in the world'.[9] The brisk rout of Chinese naval and land forces not only resoundingly proved the sturdiness of

Japan's military and its industrial and infrastructural base. It also showed that, as Sohō put it, 'civilization is not a monopoly of the white man'.

Overtaxed Japanese peasants had already paid a huge price for Japan's modernization along Western lines, a process inherently brutal for the weakest everywhere. It was now the turn of the Chinese. The 'real birthday of New Japan', the writer Lafcadio Hearn, then living in Japan, wrote, 'began with the conquest of China'.[10] Tokutomi Sohō hailed a 'new epoch in Japanese history'. White men had regarded the Japanese, Sohō complained, as 'close to monkeys'.[11] Now

> We are no longer ashamed to stand before the world as Japanese . . .
> Before we did not know ourselves, and the world did not yet know us.
> But now that we have tested our strength, we know ourselves and we
> are known by the world. Moreover, we *know* that we are known by the
> world.[12]

Closely following the practices of 'civilized' nations, Japan forced China to pay a huge indemnity, to open riverside towns deep in the hinterland as treaty ports, and to cede the island of Taiwan (then called Formosa). As part of the Treaty of Shimonoseki, Japan even appropriated a bit of mainland China, the Liaotung Peninsula, before Russia, France and Germany prevailed upon the country to be less punitive and hand it back.

The return of the Liaotung Peninsula under Western pressure provoked more discontent among Japanese patriots (exacerbated when Russia forced the Qing emperor to lease Port Arthur (now Dalian) on the peninsula to the Russian navy, which caused a rift with Japan that led to the Russo-Japanese War in 1904). There was no question now of Japan remaining subordinate to Western powers on its own territories. The treaties were revoked, and in 1902, nearly half a century after the Ottoman Empire first tried to climb on to the international stage on the back of the greatest European power, the Japanese concluded an alliance with the British Empire.

Tokutomi Sohō, already Japan's most respected journalist, was on a ship en route to the Japanese military base at Port Arthur when he learnt of the Treaty of Shimonoseki. Sohō had long been convinced that Japan, a small country with few resources of its own for modernization, had to expand its territories, a 'matter of the greatest urgency', and for that she had to 'develop a policy to motivate our people to embark upon great adventures abroad' and 'solve the problem of national expansion without delay'. Now – April 1895 – it seemed possible. The news put him in a buoyant mood.

It was the first time he had left Japan. In Port Arthur, he later recalled,

> spring had just arrived. The great willows were budding; the flowers of North China were at the height of their fragrance. Fields stretched out before the eye; a spring breeze was blowing. As I travelled about and realized that this was our new territory, I felt a truly great thrill and satisfaction.[13]

Sohō's joys of new ownership died quickly as he received news of Japan being forced to give up the territory by Western countries. 'Disdaining', he later wrote, 'to remain for another moment on land that had been retroceded to another power, I returned home on the first ship I could find.'

Sohō took a handful of gravel back to Japan to remind him of the pain and humiliation he had suffered. It was clear that, as he lamented, 'the most progressive, developed, civilized, and powerful nation in the Orient still cannot escape the scorn of the white people'. And, having been 'baptized into the gospel of power',[14] as he wrote bitterly, Sohō, the champion of individual rights and freedoms, would now become a loud advocate of Japan's imperialist expansion in Asia, which, he hoped, would 'break the worldwide monopoly and destroy the special rights of the white races, eliminate the special sphere of influence and the worldwide tyranny of the white races'.[15]

The return of Japan's spoils of war under Western pressure was no consolation to many Chinese; the damage to their self-esteem had already been done. The question for them was whether it would spur any meaningful attempt at self-strengthening in China.

Shortly after China's defeat in early 1895, Japanese troops stopped and searched a Chinese steamer in the North China Sea. Such infringements of China's sovereignty had become routine then, but by one of the strange accidents of history there were among the many students on board a twenty-two-year-old called Liang Qichao and his mentor, Kang Youwei, then aged thirty-seven, both travelling to Beijing to sit the imperial examinations for China's civil service.

Liang was to become China's first iconic modern intellectual. His lucid and prolific writings, touching on all major concerns in his own time and anticipating many in the future, inspired several generations of thinkers including the much younger Mao Zedong. A restless intellectual seeker, Liang combined his Chinese classical learning with a great sensitivity to Western ideas and trends. And his life, and its many intellectual phases, manifested more profound dilemmas than many other Chinese thinkers, bolder but shallower than Liang, faced. It would be woven tightly through all major events and movements in China over the next three decades.

The exams selected the men of 'virtue' whom Confucian classics called upon to be responsible for the social order. Success in them was the passport to status and prestige in China. There were more men passing them than there were government jobs, but Liang and Kang could still look forward to membership of an elite culture, and good jobs in teaching or business if not necessarily high positions with the government. However, they had other things on their minds than personal advancement.

Hailing from scholar-gentry families near Canton (Guangzhou) in Guangdong, the Chinese province most exposed to Western aggression, they were both patriotically concerned about the fate of China, and seethed at its ignorance and helplessness in the face of the Western challenge. Early in the nineteenth century, Indian intellectuals had begun to receive – and transform – the ideas of Rousseau, Hume, Bentham, Kant and Hegel; by the middle of the century, they were following the fortunes of Mazzini and Garibaldi. But most Chinese in the nineteenth century did not know of the existence of Western countries, let alone of their internal revolutions.

China came into contact with the West only at the port of Canton, which, closely regulated and strictly commercial, was never likely to turn into the transmitter of Western knowledge that Deshima became for the Japanese. A large part of the problem was that for too long

China had, Liang wrote in 1902, 'looked on its country as the world', and regarded the rest as barbarians.[16] Liang himself first learnt about China's lowly position in the world when in the spring of 1890 he came across books in Chinese on the West in Beijing.

In 1879, Kang Youwei had been similarly surprised while visiting Hong Kong. Awestruck by the British-run city's efficiency and cleanliness, he realized that educated Chinese like himself ought not to look down upon foreigners as barbarians. Further reading in Western books convinced him that the Chinese status quo was unsustainable, and, after a brief flirtation with Buddhism, Kang resolved to rejuvenate the social ideals of Confucianism.

Liang was one of the bright young students Kang had gathered around himself in a Confucian temple in Canton to both prepare for the imperial examinations and to reinterpret the Confucian canon as a call to social and educational change. Kang had already spent a decade importuning the Qing court in Beijing with letters and memos about the urgency of reforms. Experiencing Japanese arrogance on board his ship to Beijing now hardened his conviction, and loosened his tongue. At the risk of *lèse-majesté*, Kang now told his fellow students that China had degenerated so much that it resembled Turkey, another once-confident and now-feeble country carefully maintained in its infirmity by exploitative foreigners.

This, if anything, was an optimistic diagnosis. The European ambassadors in Istanbul may have been intolerably interfering in Turkey's domestic affairs, but they exercised none of the brute force that their counterparts in Beijing did. The Ottoman sultan never had to scurry into hiding to escape their wrath; Istanbul was not besieged, nor its grandest imperial palace burnt to the ground.

From the late 1830s (just as the Tanzimat reforms were being set in motion in Istanbul), to the Second World War, China was bullied and humiliated on a vast scale. And it was more shocking for the Chinese because they had lived with the illusion of power and self-sufficiency for much longer than the Ottomans. 'Our country's civilization', Liang Qichao pointed out in 1902, 'is the oldest in the world. Three thousand years ago, Europeans were living like beasts in the field, while our civilization, its characteristics pronounced, was already equivalent to theirs of the middle ages.'[17]

This wasn't just some cultural defensiveness. China could trace its culture back 4,000 years, and political unity to the third century BC. If the Han and Tang dynasties had supervised the writing of China's historical classics and its greatest poetry, the Song had built a network of roads and canals across China. China led the world in science and arts, and in the development of a sophisticated government bureaucracy selected through competitive examinations. Recruiting its bureaucrats from a provincial gentry that was schooled in Confucian classics, the Chinese imperial state relied less on coercion than on the loyalty of local elites across China.

As in Islamic countries, a literary culture and a morality derived from canonical texts gave Chinese civilization an extraordinary coherence, and made it the most influential cultural model for neighbours such as Japan, Korea and Vietnam. Western travellers, many of them Jesuit missionaries, brought back highly coloured descriptions of self-possessed, sophisticated and ethical followers of Confucius, turning such Enlightenment philosophers as Voltaire and Leibniz into ardent Sinophiles and nascent European consumers into connoisseurs of all things Chinese.

Contrary to the general picture of the decline of Asia and the rise of the West, the Chinese economy was buoyant in the eighteenth century, developing its own local variations and with trade links across Southeast Asia. Silk, porcelain and tea from China continued to be in great demand in Europe (and in the American colonies) even though in 1760 the Chinese confined all Western traders to the port city of Canton. Tribute-paying neighbours as near as Burma, Nepal and Vietnam (and as far away as Java) upheld Beijing's solipsistic view that the Chinese emperor, presiding over the central kingdom of the world, had the right to rule 'all under heaven'. The Qing Empire, founded by nomadic warriors from north-east China, or Manchuria, in 1644, was still expanding its territory in the eighteenth century. The last great Manchu emperor, Qianlong, personally supervised the annexation of Xinjiang and parts of Mongolia, and the pacification of Tibet.

The Manchus were foreigners, but they hadn't radically disrupted

China's traditional socio-political order, which, unparalleled any-where in the world, had been perfected over centuries by several imperial dynasties using the teachings of the sixth-century BC sage Confucius. Far more long-lasting than Islam, Confucianism had underpinned Chinese government and society for two millennia; its values of *ren*, *yi*, *xiao* and *zhong*, imperfectly translated as 'benevolence', 'propriety', 'filial piety' and 'loyalty', prescribed the correct modes of behaviour and action in both private and political life.

As the Mongols had done before them with Muslim countries, the Manchus did not impose their ways upon the conquered population of Han Chinese. Rather, they tried to persuade the latter that they were not uncouth upstarts from the north. They upheld Confucianism as the source of social and personal values, with the Kangxi and Qian-long emperors presiding over a major reinterpretation of Confucian classics. Confucian ideas intermingled with and were often overlaid by other Chinese religious traditions. But they remained the basis for the imperial examinations that led so many Chinese to seek service with the state's vast bureaucracy, and they had long contributed to China's extraordinary political unity and ideological consensus.

China's population expanded rapidly during Qianlong's long reign, putting pressure on the land. Towards the end of his reign, a series of local rebellions and economic crises revealed that all was not well with the Qing Empire. Corruption among Manchu nobles had grown, and partly in response, revolts, often of a millenarian cast, erupted across north China. There were more such shocks to come in the nine-teenth century, especially the Taiping rebellion, which was led by an eccentric sect fired by Christian millenarianism. But the panoply of omnipotence was carefully maintained throughout these crises: China remained the universe, with everyone else on its insignificant periphery. The illusion could not survive.

Even before the Opium War, Western powers had begun to nibble at the edges of the Qing Empire, annexing the territories that the Man-chus had brought into the tributary system. Beginning in 1824, after many hard battles the British subdued Burma, and made it a province of their Indian empire in 1897. In 1862, while the Qing were busy fighting the Taiping rebels, France overran southern Vietnam; it invaded the north of the country in 1874, and then, in 1883, announced the old kingdom of Annam in central Vietnam to be its protectorate. The Chinese resisted, and in the war that ensued the French destroyed much of the Chinese navy.

As in the Ottoman Empire, military losses to Western powers made Chinese bureaucrats call for urgent 'self-strengthening'. Contrary to the Western caricature of the 'Confucian' mentality that was not amenable to modernization, the Chinese were quick to learn the lesson from their defeats. Two years after witnessing the total defencelessness of Chinese coastal cities during the First Opium War, Lin Zexu, the former imperial commissioner at Canton, wrote a private letter to a friend underlining the need for adopting modern weapons technology. 'Ships, guns, and a water force are absolutely indispensable. Even if the rebellious barbarians had fled and returned beyond the seas, these things would still have to be urgently planned for, in order to work out the permanent defence of our sea frontiers.'[18]

Another Chinese scholar-official, Li Hongzhang, who led one of the victorious Qing armies against the Taiping rebels, managed to persuade the conservative court to set up factories and dockyards for the production of modern weapons and ships, regulate relations with foreign powers, open legations in the capitals of Europe, America and Japan, and send students abroad. Li also helped set up the country's first coal mines, telegraph networks and railway tracks in the 1870s.

China's infant industries faced the same kind of insuperable hurdles that free-trading Britain had imposed on Egypt and Ottoman Turkey; they could not compete with European, American and Japanese manufacturers. Unlike countries directly occupied by European powers, this was the situation of the 'semi-colony' in which, as Liang Qichao pointed out in 1896, 'a hundred times more than Western soldiers, Western commerce weakens China'.[19] Still, with Li Hongzhang's help, a modicum of industrial manufacturing soon became visible with the country's first cotton mills and iron works.

British businessmen, who wished to prop up the ailing Manchus as much as they could, were eager to help. Dining with some of them in Hong Kong in 1889, Rudyard Kipling did not think a modernized China was a good idea. He deplored the men who were doing their best to 'force upon the great Empire all the stimulants of the

West – railways, tramlines, and so forth. What will happen when China really wakes up?'[20] Kipling was right to worry; but this China still lay a century ahead. For now, as the Ottomans had learnt, piece-meal modernization was revealed as inadequate – in 1884 the French took only an hour to destroy the Chinese navy's arsenal in Fuzhou that Li Hongzhang had helped set up.

The smallest move to imitate their Western adversaries provoked a backlash from the most powerful conservative forces in the country, the scholar-gentry, who worried about the loss of their judicial and moral authority over citizens exposed to European modes of thinking and action. In a country as large and old as China, the shock of the West did not really travel deeply enough to begin to force change until the last decade of the century. The intellectual world of the scholar-gentry, defined by strict adherence to Confucian values and absolute loyalty to the emperor, remained more or less unimpaired. Self-made young men in the provinces, such as Sun Yat-sen, had begun to dream of the overthrow of the Manchus, but for much of the scholar-gentry there was no question of even slightly modifying the imperial system which was presided over by the politically reactionary and fiscally profligate Dowager Empress Cixi, who spent nearly the entire national treasury on building a new Summer Palace.

China, which had entered the nineteenth century with a favourable balance of trade, was running massive foreign debts at the end of it. Up to a quarter of government revenue went into paying foreign debts and indemnities. Foreigners administered virtual mini-colonies within sixteen cities: as in Ottoman Turkey and Egypt, they were protected from the local police and courts even for the gravest crimes.

The harsh lessons of the international system could no longer be kept at bay, not after neighbouring Japan, which most Chinese saw as inferior, trounced China in battle in 1895. At the Chinese port city of Weihaiwei, the Japanese, creeping up overland from the rear, turned China's own guns on the Chinese fleet in the bay. As Japan secured the choicest spoils of war in the subsequent Treaty of Shimonoseki with China, imperialists elsewhere were further emboldened. The Western scramble for Africa and South-east Asia was already under way. Qing China seemed an even easier picking.

Britain forced China to lease it Weihaiwei and the New Territories north of the island of Hong Kong. France established a base on Hainan Island and mining rights across China's southern provinces. Germany occupied part of Shandong province. Even Italy, a latecomer to Chinese affairs and expansionism in general, demanded territory (although it was successfully rebuffed). The United States did not participate in this dismemberment of the Middle Kingdom, the slicing of the Chinese melon as it came to be called. But, reaching the limits of their own westward expansion and urgently seeking foreign markets, the Americans announced in 1900 an 'Open Door' policy that cannily reserved the profits of an informal empire of free trade for foreigners while leaving the costs and responsibilities of governance to the Chinese.

THE FIRST IMPULSES OF REFORM

By 15 April 1895, when the terms of the treaty with Japan were announced, Liang Qichao had reached Beijing with Kang Youwei and hundreds of other candidates to compete for the two hundred available degrees. The news, which spread rapidly from the coastal cities to the hinterland, wounded the Chinese in a way that the Opium War had not. 'Previously young Chinese people paid no attention to current events,' a provincial reader of newspapers later recalled, 'but now we were shaken ... Most educated people, who had never before discussed national affairs, wanted to discuss them: why are others stronger than we are, and why are we weaker?'[21] It was brutally clear that two decades of 'self-strengthening' reforms undertaken by the Qing – the building of arsenals and railways – had amounted to nothing. For the first time, China was being forced to give up an entire province, Taiwan, to a foreign power, in addition to paying the largest indemnity ever and renouncing suzerainty over Korea, its last major tributary state.

Enraged by China's abasement, an activist called Sun Yat-sen organized an uprising in Guangzhou with the help of money raised from overseas Chinese communities. His plot was discovered and the uprising aborted by the Qing authorities. Sun was forced to flee to Japan, and then on to London, where he was to meet many other nationalists and radicals from India, Egypt and Ireland.

Kang, who had also witnessed the shaming defeat of China by France in 1884, wasn't about to try something as extreme as overthrowing the Qing Empire. Still, the extreme humiliation inflicted by Japan, a country which, gallingly, had received its high civilization from China, forced Kang to do something unprecedented in the history of politics in Qing China. He organized a meeting of the examinees, the young men aspiring to be the country's next elite, and petitioned the emperor, the young and weak Guangxu who was in thrall to the dowager empress, his aunt, to reject the treaty.

The drama of this is easily missed. As a humble aspirant to the civil service, Kang had no *locus standi*; and his long petition, which called for the total transformation of the economic and educational systems, aimed at nothing less than a revolution from above – a Tanzimat-style shake-up of institutions. Extraordinarily, his petition reached the emperor, who read it and forwarded a copy to the dowager empress. Nothing came of it, and conservative elements at the court eventually forced Kang out of Beijing. But he had set a precedent by organizing a meeting and authoring a mass petition in a place where such things were unheard of; he had initiated nothing less than what Liang later described as the first mass movement in Chinese history.[22]

Kang now threw himself into propaganda and organization work, establishing study-societies for the edification of the scholar-gentry across China with names like 'Society for the Study of National Strength'. Often helped by politically congenial local governors, these voluntary organizations set up libraries, schools and publishing projects that aimed to make the Chinese 'people', a hitherto unheard-of category, more responsive to the emperor, and active participants in public life.

Liang, who had laboriously made copies of the long petition submitted to the emperor, was freshly energized. Visiting Shanghai in 1890 – the same year he met Kang Youwei in Canton – Liang had come across an outline of world geography and translations of European books. His horizons expanded even more when in 1894 he acted as the Chinese secretary to a British missionary, who translated a then popular book, a booster-ish history of Europe's progress.

The next year Liang became the secretary of the Beijing branch of a study-society, and started a newspaper with the help of private donations. When imperial censors closed it down, he went to Shanghai and started another paper in 1896 called *Xiwu Bao* ('Chinese Progress'). It lasted for a mere two years. However, it was read widely for its articles on the urgency of industrialization and modern education, many of them authored by Liang himself, and it made Liang the most influential journalist in China.

Nearly two decades had passed since the press became, with al-Afghani's help, an instrument for aspiring modernizers in the Arab world. Nearly a century before, a public sphere for debate and discussion had opened up in India. China was starting relatively late, and Liang tried to make up for lost time. In article after article, he stressed the urgency of political reform, which he held to be more important than technological change; the key to this reform was the abolition of the old imperial examinations and the establishment of a nation-wide school system that created confidently patriotic citizens for the New China. For,

> If there is no moral culture in the schools, no teaching of patriotism, students will as a result only become infected with the evil ways of the lower order of Westerners and will no longer know they have their own country ... The virtuous man, then, will become an employee of the foreigners in order to seek his livelihood; the degenerate man will become, further, a traitorous Chinese in order to subvert the foundations of his country ... In the state of disrepair to Chinese armaments, we see one road to weakness; in the stagnation of culture, a hundred roads.[23]

Calling for a severe modification of existing institutions, Liang was not blind to the appeal of Confucianism, or that of the traditional structure of Chinese society and state in which the individual was loyal to his family and an elite of scholar-officials mediated between the imperial court and the population. He still hoped to rouse the scholar-gentry first to the tasks of nation-building. Addressing scholars in Hunan in 1896, he said, 'Now you gentlemen, who wear the scholar's robes and read the writings of the sages, must find out whose fault it is that our country has become so crippled, our race so weak, our religion so feeble.'[24] In fact, he was as loyal as Kang at first to the ruling Qing order; the idea of overthrowing it, which had already energized Sun Yat-sen, did not feature in his political plans for the future. But his intellectual trajectory, though initially hewing close to Kang's, was showing signs of divergence.

As Liang began to see, China's old system of monarchy had become a force for the status quo and intellectual and political conformity; it was capable now of nothing more than maintaining the ruling dynasty in power. The state needed popular consent from those it ruled, and only a well-educated and politically conscious citizenry could create the kind of collective dynamism and national solidarity essential to China's survival in the dog-eat-dog world of international geopolitics.

Never explicitly named, ideas of popular sovereignty and national-ism bubbled beneath the surface of Liang's writings for *Xiwu Bao*, and his teachings at a reformist school in Hunan (where he went in 1897 after leaving *Xiwu Bao* over a disagreement with its manager). In the beginning, Liang phrased them through invocations of Chinese tradition: 'Mencius says that the people are to be held in honour, the people's affairs may not be neglected. The governments of present-day Western states come near to conformity with this principle, but China alas, is cut off from the teachings of Mencius.'[25]

Liang was beginning to realize that, however admirable in itself, the old Chinese order was not capable of generating the organizational and industrial power needed for survival in a ruthless international system dominated by the nation-states of the West. Though educated traditionally, he had already begun to drift away from the narrow world of Chinese scholarship and imperial service. And he was to move far from the ideas of his great teacher and mentor. Kang saw himself as a Confucian sage with a moral mission to rejuvenate China. With this outcome in mind, he didn't hesitate to reformulate Confu-cianism itself. Liang would follow a different path for much of his life before returning to some of the ideals of his youth.

In retrospect, and especially from the outside, Confucianism seems like an abstract philosophy or a set of beliefs imposed upon the Chin-ese people by the state – something easily and voluntarily discarded. But its roots in China were deep and it provided by general consensus the religious and ideological underpinning of China's political order. It upheld the principle of kingship; the only political community it envisaged was the universal empire, ignoring the city-state and the nation-state that were central to the Western tradition. And it prescribed the duties of the state as the maintenance of Confucian moral teachings, rather than political and economic expansion.

So for Kang, as for many other reformers of the late Qing period, Confucian teaching was beyond reproach. Even Liang, who would depart radically from his mentor, did not cease to see himself as an embodiment of a unique repository of cultural ideals and beliefs – one that defined China as much, if not more, than Christianity defined the West. Confucianism's extraordinary continuity partly ensured this reverence. The social and ethical norms it prescribed for both the ruler and the ruled seemed essential to maintaining order. Peasant uprisings in the past had challenged the Confucian system and its main representatives, the scholar-gentry, but they could be explained away as revolts against Chinese rulers and imperial bureaucrats who had betrayed Confucian teachings.

Still, the new external threat posed by Western capitalism and Christianity was not explained away so easily. Indeed, as these pressures intensified by the 1850s, many imperial bureaucrats defensively put forward an extremely conservative view of Confucian belief and practice: one that preserved their moral and judicial authority. (A similar hardening of religious and ethical belief-systems was also under way in India, Ceylon (Sri Lanka) and the Muslim world.)

This is why both Kang and Liang were nothing less than radical in their demand for political innovation and public participation in government. In their milieu, the mastery of Confucian classics and success in traditional exams were what brought power and respect to the literati. It was their task to uphold the dictates of Confucian morality, which emphasized a hierarchical society held together by mutual moral obligations. This elite with its highly developed sense of social responsibility, refined manners and etiquette provided the natural leaders of communities in villages and towns across China. Confucian teaching provided the content, for instance, of the civil service examination: the so-called 'eight-legged essay', which had decided the outcome of the examinations for centuries, was to be written on one of the themes from the canonical Confucian writings, the 'Four Books'.

Such formalist education was clearly ill suited to the modern age, and the Confucian stress on private morality was not up to the task of creating the public-spiritedness needed for a new nation. Writing in 1895, the writer and translator Yan Fu described the differences between China and the West as stark:

> China values the Three [family] Bonds most highly, while the Western-
> ers give precedence to equality. China cherishes relatives, while
> Westerners esteem the worthy. China governs the realm through filial
> piety, while Westerners govern the realm with impartiality. China val-
> ues the sovereign, while Westerners esteem the people. China prizes the
> one Way, while Westerners prefer diversity ... In learning, Chinese
> praise breadth of wisdom, while Westerners rely on human strength.[26]

It was clear to Kang that China could survive only by absorbing some of the virtues of the West. At the same time, Confucianism had to be maintained in some form in order to preserve the political and social basis of China. In other words, Confucianism had to be rein-vented in order to save it.

Similar anxieties had afflicted many of the scholar-gentry as the pressures from the West exposed the fragility of the Qing Empire, and there was a large enough audience for Kang by the end of the nine-teenth century. Still, how was one to break with something so revered and rooted in Chinese soil as Confucianism? How was one to reinter-pret something so symbolic of order and continuity as a philosophy of social change?

Kang was like the conservative reformers in the Muslim world for whom the verities of Islam could not be fundamentally challenged, or even like Gandhi, who saw Indian traditions as a perfectly adequate resource for a new nation. They all faced the task of having to gener-ate a new set of values that ensured survival in the modern era while respecting time-honoured traditions – of appearing loyal to their nation while borrowing some of the secrets of the West's progress.

Fortunately, in the intellectual free-for-all that characterized this moment of transition to new ideas of nation and people, the scope for radical interpretation of tradition was great. Confucianism, in par-ticular, had been marked by competing schools of thought. Reviving an old controversy among Confucian scholars, Kang attacked the pre-

146

vailing school of Confucianism as fake, claiming that the authentic teachings of Confucius were contained in the New Text School that had been dominant during the former Han dynasty.

Kang set out his ideas in two books, which Liang described as a 'volcanic eruption' and an 'earthquake' in the world of Confucian literati.[27] Kang, Liang later said, was the 'Martin Luther' of Confucianism. But Kang saw himself as entering something more than a scholastic or theological dispute with other Confucianists. As with Gandhi and the *Bhagavadgītā*, and al-Afghani and the Koran, Kang was aiming to make political reform and mass mobilization a central concern of Confucius himself, in order to make his ideas relevant to China's present and future and give sanction to the reformist aspiration for scientific and social progress. Thus, in Kang's reading of the Confucian classics, emancipation of women, mass education and popular elections came to appear central concerns of the sixth-century BC sage.

Kang was to go even further, offering a utopian vision of an inevitable universal moral community, where egoism and the habit of making hierarchies would vanish, and which would realize the Confucian idea of *ren* (benevolence). But this would lie in the future, after the Chinese nation had pulled itself together. For now, Kang was content to emphasize the need for institutional reform within China, for the country, as he saw it, faced a challenge from the West that was not only political but also cultural and religious. The West not only endangered the Chinese state; it also threatened Confucianism. This anxiety motivated all his campaigns for a nationwide school system or a constitutional monarchy or military academies. Perhaps influenced by the exalting of Shintoism as a state religion in Japan, Kang would even propose that Confucianism be made a state religion to combat the effect of Christianity, with local shrines turned into temples to the 'important sage'.

By the 1890s, many voluntary organizations in coastal China were propagating the religion they called 'Confucianism', and Kang converted many scholar-gentry to Western political values by making them seem part of Confucian traditions. The challenge he posed to the traditional political order with his arsenal of traditional political theory was to prove momentous; it was the beginning of a new radical phase in China's history, in which all the old verities would be questioned and overturned.

Certainly there was a range of reformist ideas thrown up by the intellectual ferment of China in the 1890s. While Liang was publishing his periodical in Shanghai, Yan Fu was bringing out a popular newspaper and magazine from Tianjin, where he was president of the naval academy. Yan, who had studied in England for two years, was among the handful of Chinese to have experienced the West at first hand. His translations of Herbert Spencer, John Stuart Mill, Adam Smith and T. H. Huxley first introduced many Chinese thinkers, including Liang, to contemporary Western philosophers and, most importantly, to the quasi-Darwinian explanation of history as the survival of the fittest.

Like many intellectuals in Asia, Yan awoke with a shock to the threat from Western imperialists. 'They will enslave us and hinder the development of our spirit and body,' he wrote in 1895. 'The brown and black races constantly waver between life and death, why not the 400 million Yellows?' Like many of his Asian peers, Yan Fu became a Social Darwinist, obsessed with the question of how China could accumulate enough wealth and power to survive. As he wrote, 'Races compete with races, and form groups and states, so that these groups and states can compete with each other. The weak will be eaten by the strong, the stupid will be enslaved by the clever ... Unlike other animals, humans fight with armies, rather than with teeth and claws.'[28] 'It is', he added, 'the struggle for existence which leads to natural selection and the survival of the fittest – and hence, within the human realm, to the greatest realization of human capacities.'[29]

Yan believed that the West had mastered the art of channelling individual energy and dynamism into national strength. In Britain and France people thought of themselves as active citizens of a dynamic nation-state rather than, as was the case in China, as subjects of an empire built upon old rituals. Like people in the West, Yan Fu asserted, the Chinese people had to learn to 'live together, communicate with and rely on each other, and establish laws and institutions, rites and rituals for that purpose ... We must find a way to make everyone take the nation as his own.'[30] Yan's ideas, which seemed at odds with Confucian notions of cosmic harmony, and helped introduce such words as 'nation' and 'modern' into the Chinese vocabulary in the 1890s, would not encounter much resistance among several generations of Chinese intellectuals, including, most prominently, Liang Qichao. In fact, they were quickly embraced, for they perfectly described the precarious situation China found itself in.

Compared to Yan Fu, a figure like Tan Sitong was a traditionalist philosopher. As a young man in Beijing in 1895, Tan, the idealistic son of a high official, sought out Kang Youwei. Kang was then in Canton, and it was his chief assistant Liang who introduced and converted Tan to Kang's worldview, besides introducing him to Buddhism. Tan, one of the most original minds of his generation, went further than his mentors, advocating republicanism rather than a reformed monarchy, and nationalism in place of loyalty to the Manchus. Not unlike Gandhi, Tan posited the need for constant moral action and awareness, expanding the Confucian notion of the good as something that combined sensitivity to social ethics in the present and future with a personal struggle for self-perfection.

For a few weeks at least, this was not all theorizing in the sad teahouses of Beijing. In early 1898, the dowager empress allowed the twenty-three-year-old Guangxu to rule properly as emperor, and suddenly Kang's and Liang's many study-societies, newspapers, schools and behind-the-scenes discussions with reformers at the imperial court seemed to bear fruit. The newly empowered emperor, who had already noted one petition by Kang in 1895, turned to him for help with reform. Kang responded with several spirited essays, including one on the success of Meiji Japan, and another on the helplessness of India under British rule. 'Reform and be strengthened,' he wrote, 'guard the old and die.'[31]

Kang was invited to the Forbidden City. An extraordinary five-hour-long meeting with the emperor ensued. It was followed in June by a barrage of imperial edicts ordering bold reforms in almost every realm, from local administration and international cultural exchange to the beautification of Beijing. For about a hundred days, Kang, Liang and Tan Sitong became as powerful as any group of like-minded intellectuals elsewhere had been since the French Revolution.

A decree made Liang, who had yet to pass the imperial examinations, the director of the translation bureau. More surprisingly, his news-paper *Xiwu Bao* was turned into an official organ. Liang and Tan accompanied Kang to meetings with the emperor at his palace where they dropped all ritual and ceremony, planning reforms while loung-ing side by side.

But Kang and Liang had overplayed their hand. The pace of change was too swift; such radical moves as the abolishment of the eight-legged essay aroused strong opposition. It alarmed and alienated the old guard within the imperial court who were still loyal to the dow-ager empress in retirement at the Summer Palace. Persuaded by them that the emperor would move against her next, the dowager empress, who was not averse to some moderate reform, took it upon herself to squash her little nephew.

An unsuccessful pre-emptive coup against her, spearheaded by Tan Sitong, only expedited her moves. On 21 September 1898, 103 days after the first imperial decree, she announced that the emperor had been struck down by a serious illness (in fact he had been imprisoned on a small island in the imperial gardens) and that she was again tak-ing over the administration of the empire. In addition to cancelling most of the reform edicts, she also issued orders for the arrest of Kang, Liang and Tan, among other reformist intellectuals. Kang had left Bei-jing a day earlier for Shanghai, from where he was able to escape to Hong Kong. Liang, who was still within the city walls, managed to find refuge in the Japanese legation. Tan joined him there, but only to say goodbye.

Liang pleaded with Tan to go with him to Japan, but Tan only said, in words to be commemorated by several Chinese generations, that China would never renew itself until men were prepared to die for it. He left the legation building and was immediately arrested. He and six other associates of Liang, including Kang's younger brother, were sentenced to death. The declaration was read out from the gates of the Forbidden City. The condemned were taken in a cart to Caishikou market where many of the scholars visiting Beijing to take the civil service exams often stayed. A bowl of rice wine was offered to them outside a tea-house. A large crowd watched as the bowl was broken. The men were then made to kneel on the ground and were swiftly beheaded.

The graves of Kang Youwei's family were desecrated on the orders of the dowager empress. As rewards for his own arrest and execution were announced, Liang fled, with Japanese help, to Tianjin, from where he sailed to a long and eventful exile in Japan. He was only twenty-five. Thus ended China's opportunity to enact the kind of top-down modernization that Turkey and Egypt had attempted. Revolution became as inevitable as it had become in countries elsewhere in Asia.

JAPAN AND THE PERILS OF EXILE

Announcing a reward for Liang's capture, the *Peking Gazette* referred to him as a 'little animal with short legs, riding on the back of a wolf'.[32] The image was meant to mock his intellectual dependence on Kang, but it was inaccurate. Liang, politically more pragmatic than his mentor, had already begun to move away from Kang.

Always hungry for knowledge – he had begun to study Japanese while still on board the ship that took him to Japan – he quickly started a newspaper, funded largely by Chinese merchants in Yokohama, and began to transmit new ideas as soon as he had absorbed them from Japanese books to an audience that now consisted of students as well as the scholar-gentry. Many of the students he had taught at Hunan moved to Japan to be with him. Liang put them up in his own living quarters until they were housed in a school he started in 1899 with the financial assistance of Chinese merchants.

In Japan, while Kang travelled to India and the West, Liang was to come into his own as China's most famous intellectual, dealing, above all, with the problem of nationalism – given special urgency by his view of a world order defined by Social Darwinism. Writing in Japan in 1901, he bleakly concluded that

> All men in the world must struggle to survive. In the struggle for survival, there are superior and inferior. If there are superior and inferior, then there must be success and failure. He who, being inferior, fails, must see his rights and privileges completely absorbed by the one who is superior and who triumphs. This, then, is the principle behind the extinction of nations.[33]

The Chinese intelligentsia were now divided between reformists like Kang and Liang and anti-Manchu revolutionaries represented by Sun Yat-sen. But Liang's writings often transcended the differences, making them appealing to readers on a broad ideological spectrum in China. As Hu Shi, a liberal thinker and a bitter critic of Liang acknowledged (in a tone reminiscent of Mohammed Abduh's tribute to al-Afghani): 'He attracted our abundantly curious minds, pointed out an unknown world, and summoned us to make our own exploration.'[34]

Liang was helped a great deal by his setting. For educated Chinese, Japan was as much the centre of culture and education as Paris was for Westernized Russians and London for Indian colonials; thousands of Chinese students would travel there after 1900, and return to assume leadership positions at home. The Japanese had absorbed many Western ideas since the Meiji Restoration, and it was the first experience of modernity for many Chinese, such as Liang, forcing almost all of them to re-evaluate their previous notions about the world. Words like 'democracy', 'revolution', 'capitalism' and 'communism' were to make their way into the Chinese language via Japanese.

The Sinocentric worldview had been smashed to pieces by Western intrusions in China; and Liang would take it upon himself to describe harsh political realities that China had to come to terms with.

> Because of our self-satisfaction and our inertia, the blindly cherished old ways have come down more than three thousand years to our day. Organization of the race, of the nation, of society, our customs, rites, arts and sciences, thought, morality, laws, religion, all are still, with no accretions, what they were three thousand years ago.[35]

This was an exaggeration, but made understandable by the scale of the challenges Liang felt himself confronted with. China was one of the oldest states in the world. But did its citizens see it as a nation? Could they shed their Confucian emphasis on self-cultivation enough to feel notions of civic solidarity? Indeed, could the state's institutions be overhauled enough to cope with the challenges of international politics? And could a modern Chinese nation come into being without destroying China's proud cultural identity? Liang posed these large and complex questions without offering any clear-cut answers. Nevertheless, he phrased them more forcefully than all the other Chinese intellectuals. He had already sown the seeds of post-Qing China with his newspapers, schools and study-societies which radiated the urgency of change to the most secluded of Chinese scholar-gentry. His writings, smuggled back into the Chinese mainland from Japan, would now inspire the next generation of thinkers and activists.

However, first Liang had to negotiate his way through the tangled politics of both his Japanese hosts and the groups of Chinese expatriates in Japan. The Japan he travelled to in 1898 was still far from being the confident imperial power it would become after its defeat of Russia and annexation of Korea in 1910. Then it followed the precedent set by other imperialist powers in wanting its own share of the Chinese booty after war; in 1900, Japan was to participate in the Allied powers' attempt to quell the Boxer Rising.

However, Japan feared the division of China in the same way that European powers dreaded the disintegration of the Ottoman Empire: the sick men of Asia were better alive than dead, for they held chaos at bay, and could also be bullied at will. Japanese statesmen closely followed the Hundred Days' Reform, attracted by the prospect of a reformed Manchu ruling dynasty doing a better job of keeping China from total collapse. They appreciated the conservatism of Kang and Liang, who did not wish to depose the emperor. Ito Hirobumi, thrice prime minister of Japan and the main maker of the Meiji constitution, was in China when the dowager empress cracked down on the reformists; he quietly instructed Japanese diplomats to ensure the safety of Kang and Liang. When Kang Youwei reached Tokyo via Hong Kong in November 1898, he was treated as the head of a government-in-exile, and taken to meet the most powerful statesmen in Japan.

Kang and Liang received even greater support through unofficial channels. Despite an authoritarian political system, Japan possessed strikingly diverse intellectual currents. Its emergence as a major world power had brought it face to face with the racialist underpinnings of the international system – despite its successes, it was still regarded as a 'yellow peril' by Western powers, and in 1898 the United States had announced its presence in Japan's neighbourhood by wresting the

Philippines from the doddering Spanish Empire (for the same reason Japan had removed Korea from the Chinese sphere of influence – because it was there to be taken).

Like any rising power, Japan was also developing an awareness of its 'national interest' that lay far beyond its physical borders. Toku-tomi Sohō summed it up: 'The countries of the Far East falling prey to the great powers of Europe is something that our nation will not stand for . . . We have the duty to maintain peace in East Asia.'[36] In 1885 Fukuzawa Yukichi had a responsive audience when he called for Japan to 'escape' Asia and join the West. But now the fear of a racially tinged Western imperialism pushed a wide range of Japanese intellectuals and politicians into fresh considerations of Japan's cultural identity, and, by extension, its old links with China and the rest of Asia.

This was the beginning of pan-Asianism, a major strand in Japan's self-image and actions for the next half-century. For many Japanese the idea that Asian countries had grown weak, and exposed themselves to humiliation and exploitation by the West, was an undeniably solid basis for a pan-Asian identity; as was the demand for racial equality, which the Japanese were to struggle to enshrine as a principle in international relations. There was strength in numbers, and in the notion that Japan, being the first country to modernize itself, could force recognition of Asian dignity from Western powers. By virtue of its successful empowerment, Japan might even lead a crusade to free Asia from its European masters.

From the very beginning the advocates of pan-Asianism in Japan belonged to a broad ideological spectrum. Among them could be found, for instance, a figure such as Nagai Ryūtarō (1881–1944), a devout Christian who championed many liberal causes such as universal suffrage and women's rights, spoke admiringly of socialism and also sought to raise the alarm against what he called 'the white peril'. 'If one race assumes the right to appropriate all the wealth,' he asked, 'why should not all the other races feel ill-used and protest? If the yellow races are oppressed by the white races, and have to revolt to avoid congestion and maintain existence, whose fault is it but that of the oppressor?'[37] Indeed, many of the self-appointed sentinels of Japan's prestige saw themselves as guarding Asian values in general against the 'white peril'. According to Sohō, Japan, rather than the West, was best placed to 'create true universal equality and progress'.[38] Some of these pan-Asianists were militarists who thought China and Korea ought to be ruled by Japan. Others were more sensitive to the interests of their neighbours, and hospitable to political refugees from China, Korea and South-east Asia. Liberal nationalists, who wished to modernize Japan in order to make it the equal of the West, felt obliged to strengthen China against foreign imperialists. More far-seeing and ambitious pan-Asianists saw Japan as the future imperial conqueror and leader of Asia. Their ranks would also include such idealists as Ōkuwa Shūmei, Japan's leading scholar of Indian and Islamic cultures, who was converted to pan-Asianism in 1913 after reading a book about India's dire state under the British.

As Japan grew more powerful, there would develop a contradiction between its imperative to expand and dominate and the pan-Asianist desire to express solidarity with other Asian countries. Organizations such as the Kyujitai, the Amur River Society (popularly known as the Black Dragons) and the Genyosha (Great Ocean Society) would become increasingly militant and powerful advocates of Japan's rights in Asia. But, initially at least, political differences among pan-Asianists did not matter much; many of the pan-Asianists, emerging at a time of transition, were looking for a new aim in life. The Meiji reforms had unleashed a whole class of political and intellectual adventurers, often former samurai, who saw themselves as nobly selfless idealists. These rootless men, who dreamed of saving China from itself, worked as pressure groups and lobbyists. They often attached themselves to the Chinese and South-east Asian nationalists who were beginning to arrive in Japan towards the end of the nineteenth century, and who had been forced into new ways of defining their identity and affirming their dignity by successive humiliations by the West – as members of nascent nations, races, classes, or such supra-national entities as pan-Islam and pan-Asia.

One such Japanese idealist was Miyazaki Torazō (1871–1922), a professional pan-Asianist and revolutionary, who tried to stir up an anti-Qing movement in China as early as 1891 and then later that decade smuggled guns to anti-American guerrillas in the Philippines. He decided he had found his saviour of China when he met Sun

Yat-sen in 1897. Thus Sun, who had already engineered a failed revolt in China, was installed in Japan, well-connected within the expatriate community of Chinese merchants and students, when Liang arrived there in the autumn of 1898, followed shortly afterwards by Kang Youwei. There were already many Chinese students in Yokohama, and the respective followers of these men soon began to join them in Japan. Their Japanese patrons tried to bring them together on a common platform of Chinese regeneration, encouraging them with money and advice to fuse their groups into a single party in exile. But they ran into the kind of internecine discord commonly found among nineteenth-century political expatriates, including the followers of Marx as well as of Herzen.

Unlike Kang and Liang, Sun came from a family of farmers in Guangzhou. Poverty forced his brother to emigrate; he went to Hawaii, and Sun joined him there in his early teens. Educated at missionary schools, Sun spoke English fluently and wrote classical Chinese badly. Dressed in Western-style clothes and financially beholden to overseas Chinese, Sun was as far away as possible from the traditional world of the Confucian gentry Kang and Liang belonged to. Well-travelled in the West, Sun also had a sharp eye for China's infirmities. In 1894, when a bold petition from Sun to the imperial court was rejected, he was convinced that China needed to overthrow the Manchu monarchy and turn itself into a republic. This belief in itself would have caused problems with the royalist Kang. Nevertheless, Sun, a master improviser, was eager to join with Kang and Liang. As it turned out, Kang couldn't abide Sun, regarding him as a worthless, boorish adventurer. Rebuffed, Sun, who was a convert to Christianity, came to regard Kang's attempt to interpret Confucianism in the light of modern conditions as a meaningless academic exercise.

Kang's uncompromising elitism also made him unpopular with the Japanese, who were already made nervous by Chinese protests over the presence of Sun, Liang and Kang in their country – the dowager empress had described them as China's three greatest criminals. The pressures on Kang mounted, and in the summer of 1899 he left for Canada, where he formed, with the help of overseas Chinese, the 'Society to Protect the Emperor'. Liang was left to deal with Sun and the former students who had flocked to his side from China.

The Japanese now tried to bring Sun and Liang together; and a degree of co-operation was established, especially over money. Liang was also more sympathetic to Sun's anti-monarchy stance than he could freely express at the time. But just when the two seemed to be co-operating more closely in late 1899, Liang was ordered by Kang to travel to Hawaii and America on a fund-raising tour.

Liang complied; Kang was still his revered teacher in the Confucian tradition. But Japan had begun to emancipate him, as it was to do for two generations of Chinese thinkers. He had begun to read and think more widely. Dependent until then on Yan Fu's translations, he expanded his knowledge of Hobbes, Spinoza, Rousseau and Greek philosophers, and even wrote biographical studies of Cromwell, Cavour and Mazzini. His knowledge of the world outside China broadened.

Qingyi Bao ('Journal of Pure Critique'), the newspaper he started soon after arriving in Japan, carried reports on the Philippine resistance to the United States, and Britain's difficulties with the Boers in South Africa. The modern competition for territory and resources began to preoccupy Liang above all, whether he was writing about the unification of Italy or the French subjugation of Vietnam. In Japan he also met many revolutionary thinkers and activists from India, Indonesia, Vietnam and the Philippines; many of these had flocked to Japan after its defeat of Russia in 1905. Liang was in Japan in April 1907 when some Japanese socialists, Indians, Filipinos and Vietnamese formed the Asian Solidarity group in Tokyo, and he may not have disagreed much with another Chinese exile in Japan, Zhang Taiyan (1869–1936, also known as Zhang Binglin), the scholar of Buddhism, who, summing up the prevailing sentiments of cultural pride, political resentment and self-pity among Asian refugees, claimed in the society's manifesto that

> Asian countries . . . rarely invaded one another and treated each other respectfully with the Confucian virtue of benevolence. About 100 years ago, the Europeans moved east and Asia's power diminished day by day. Not only was their political and military power totally lacking, but people also felt inferior. Their scholarship deteriorated and people only strove after material interests.[39]

Liu Shipei, an anarchist and one of the society's members, was clear about what needed to be done. 'Today's world is a world of brute force', he wrote in his article 'On the Recent Trends in Asia', 'and the territory of Asia is a ground upon which the white race uses its brute force. We must eliminate their involvement in Asia.'[40] Ou Jujia, an associate of Liang Qichao, exhorted the Chinese people to learn from the Filipinos who, though stateless, had put up a strong fight against the Americans. The condition of the Philippines impressed itself particularly forcefully on Chinese émigrés in Japan. Ma Junqu, another intellectual in Liang's circle, hailed José Rizal, the anti-imperialist poet who had been executed by the Spanish in 1896, as the quintessential Asian patriot. Liang himself saw the Filipinos as 'pioneers of independence for Asia', who, if successful, he wrote in 1899, would 'bring to two the number of new states in the Eastern Pacific' (one being Japan, the other the Philippines) which could then form 'a united Asian force that could resist the thrust of Europe's drift eastward'.[41]

Zhang Taiyan wrote about his friendship with Indian revolutionaries living in exile in Tokyo, and his own distress at learning about India's abysmal condition under British rule. He attended a commemorative meeting for Shivaji, the seventeenth-century Indian rebel king who had harassed the Mughal Empire, convinced that the king's guerrilla tactics would be needed to drive the British out of India. Chinese commentators also followed the Boer War (1899–1902), seeing it as another struggle of a weak people for freedom from the West. When the United States brutally suppressed the anti-imperialist revolt in the Philippines, another Chinese exile in Japan, Tang Tiaoding, mournfully described the events, concluding with a denunciation of 'white people's histories':

> They provide plenty of indisputable evidence on the extent of the primitive customs and ignorance of the native people, as proof of why these people deserve to be conquered. This type of praise [for themselves] and condemnation [of others] is done with an eye towards the final judgment of history. Egypt, Poland, Cuba, India, South Africa, all these regions: just read the books on the history of their perishing! . . . I had often felt that the situation demanded that these countries could not but perish . . . But now I know that these books were all written by

white people, where truth and falsehood are confused . . . I know one thing for sure: if you seek the truth about the Philippines in the history books of the Spaniards, you would not doubt for a moment that the country is ignorant and vile, and you would only wonder why it had not perished sooner . . . Learned people of my country! Are there any of you who are getting ready to write our history? Do not let white children, laughing behind our backs and clapping their hands with glee, take up their pens and paper [to write our history for us]![42]

Liang was certainly not going to allow the white children's version of Asian history to prevail. He published, often with his own introduction, the histories of what were described in China as 'lost' (*wangguo*) countries. In 1901, as Western powers imposed yet another treaty on the Chinese in the wake of the Boxer Rising, he wrote an angry summing-up of the manifold ways in which the West subjugated weaker countries; caustically titled 'On the New Rules for Destroying Countries', it could just as easily have been written by al-Afghani. Liang described the endless subtle ways in which European merchants and mine-owners had progressively infiltrated and undermined many societies and cultures. The essay detailed these methods, which included cajoling countries into spiralling debt (Egypt), territorial partition (Poland), exploiting internal divisions (India), or simply overwhelming adversaries with military superiority (the Philippines and the Transvaal). 'To those who claim', Liang wrote, 'that opening mining, railroad, and concessionary rights to foreigners is not harmful to the sovereignty of the whole, I advise you to read the history of the Boer War.'[43]

Liang concluded that the power of the European powers and the United States had 'increased relative to the power of those whom they have attacked in the modern competition among peoples'.[44] Soon he began to move from his idea of a Chinese people to the idea of the state as the essential unit, the defender of the people. As he saw it, the Boers, a strong people saddled with a weak state, had nevertheless been pushed back by the British.

A few years before Lenin identified imperialism as the last stage of capitalism, Liang described how the West's unprecedented economic expansion had led it organically to the conquest of Asia. By tying imperialism to individual economic interests, Western countries had given it a popular base among their own populations. It wasn't just motivated by the political ambitions of rulers; it claimed a degree of consent from the ruled.

This made modern imperialism very different from the expansionism of tyrants like Alexander the Great or Genghis Khan, and posed a unique danger to peace.

> The motivating force [of modern international competition] stems from the citizenry's struggle for survival which is irrepressible according to the laws of natural selection and survival of the fittest. Therefore the current international competitions are not something which only concerns the state, they concern the entire population. In the present-day international struggles in which the whole citizenry participate (and compete) for their very lives and properties, people are united as if they have one mind. The international competitions of the past, which were the concerns of the rulers and their ministers, would subside after a period. But the current international struggle will last forever because it is constantly a matter of concern for the life and property of the people. How dangerous this is! How will we, who bear the brunt of this international struggle, stave it off?[45]

India, in particular, was a horror story about a 'lost country' that had failed miserably in the international struggle: 'small capitalists' from Britain had taken over an entire continent by training Indians to be soldiers; Indians enforced British policies at the expense of their own compatriots. China was in danger of repeating that experience because her people had developed no sense of a corporate interest or national solidarity – the basis of European power and prosperity.

One reason for this was that the country's neighbours were so vastly inferior that the Chinese people had felt themselves to be the whole world. The conceit, once shared by Liang himself, could no longer be maintained in an international system where China had to either recognize the reality of conflict and competition with other societies or sink. For, 'In the world there is only power – there is no other force. That the strong always rule the weak is in truth the first great universal rule of nature. Hence, if we wish to attain liberty, there is no other road: we can only seek first to be strong.'[46]

THE BOXER RISING: MORE LESSONS
FROM DEFEAT

Events in China confirmed and sharpened Liang's anxiety. While he was fund-raising among the Chinese community in Hawaii in the spring of 1900, the Boxer Rising broke out. Led by a shamanistic secret society devoted to traditional martial arts, the revolt was directed against foreigners, especially missionaries, who, deep in China's interior, were seen to be undermining and insulting Chinese beliefs and practices. As spontaneous as the Indian Mutiny of 1857, the Rising attracted a motley crowd of disgruntled Chinese including peasants and decommissioned soldiers, smugglers, and even some officials and gentry.

The Boxer Rising revealed the resourcefulness of ordinary people's resistance as well as the depth of popular resentment of the foreign presence in China, and of the pressures it put on local officials. Few Chinese people ever saw a white man, but their lives were deeply affected by the new facts created by foreigners in China: the subjection to global economic cycles, for instance, which threw people out of work.

A country whose standard of living was superior to Europe's before 1800 had steadily become through the nineteenth century a helpless giant before Western missionaries, businessmen, diplomats and soldiers. Foreign debts and indemnities placed a crippling burden on the national exchequer. The government had to borrow heavily for the smallest attempt at modernization; even the railway, a symbol of progress everywhere else, only served to push China deeper into debt while opening up large parts of China's interior to foreign troops.

The Boxers reflected a long-simmering public rage by tearing up railway tracks. When Boxer attacks on Westerners and Chinese converts to Christianity spread to Beijing in June 1900, Western powers protested to the dowager empress, who calculated that she could use the Boxers against the Westerners and rid China of them altogether. The decision reflected a total ignorance of the real balance of power in the world. Her opportunistic declaration of war while the foreign legation was under siege by the Boxers was soon matched by a military mobilization against her by all the major world powers. Twenty thousand troops drawn from several countries, including Japan, marched to Beijing to relieve the siege and loot the city.

Among the British contingent was a north Indian solider, Gadhadar Singh, who felt sympathetic to the anti-Western cause of the Boxers even though he believed that their bad tactics had 'blanketed their entire country and polity in dust'. His first sight of China was the landscape near Beijing, of famished Chinese with skeletal bodies in abandoned or destroyed villages, over whose broken buildings flew the flags of China's joint despoilers – France, Russia and Japan. River waters had become a 'cocktail of blood, flesh, bones and fat'. Singh particularly blamed the Russian and French soldiers for the mass killings, arson and rape inflicted on the Chinese. Some of the soldiers tortured their victims purely for fun. 'All these sportsmen', Singh noted, 'belonged to what were called "civilized nations".'[47]

'Even hearts of stone', Singh wrote, 'would have melted and felt compassion.' 'It was not necessary for my heart to be moved by pity', he added, 'because I had come to fight against the Chinese. But . . . I felt an emotion that was born not out of duty but in the mind.' Trying to understand his sympathy for the Chinese, Singh realized it was because the Chinese were Buddhist, like many Indians, and therefore 'neighbours and fellow residents of Asia'.[48]

Not many soldiers experienced such tender regard for the Chinese. Dispatching a German punitive force to China in 1900, the kaiser had exhorted them to be as brutal with the 'heathen culture' as Attila the Hun, so that 'no Chinaman will ever again dare to even squint at a German!' The French writer Pierre Loti witnessed the devastation inflicted by Western troops on the capital city: 'Little grey bricks – this is the sole material of which Beijing was built; a city of small, low houses decorated with a lacework of gilded wood; a city of which only a mass of curious debris is left, after fire and shell have crumbled away its flimsy materials.'[49]

Re-living her escape from the barbarian-besieged capital in 1860, the dowager empress fled Beijing disguised in the blue costume of a peasant. Her representatives signed another agreement with Western powers that, among other penalties, imposed an indemnity almost twice the size of the government's annual revenues. They promised to build monuments to the Christian missionaries murdered by the Boxers and, while accepting restrictions on the size of their military, had to countenance an increased foreign military presence on Chinese soil.

Chastened by this turn of events even the dowager empress now contemplated some radical reforms. She began slowly, but by the time she died in 1908 she had taken enough steps to ensure the construction of a modern state. Soon after Japan's defeat of Russia in 1905, she abolished the traditional examinations for the civil service that had served as the backbone of the imperial state for over a millennium. In their place, the Qing court established modern schools with a Western curriculum and sent Chinese students abroad, to Europe and the United States as well as to Japan. The news, reaching the then fiery nationalist Aurobindo Ghose (1872–1950) in distant India provoked him to rapturous praise for an apparently rising neighbour:

> China has been educating, training and arming herself with a speed of which the outside world has a very meagre conception. She has sent out a Commission of Observation to the West and decided to develop constitutional Government within the next ten years. She has pushed forward the work of revolutionising her system of education.[50]

Thousands of young Chinese were thus first introduced to modern sciences, engineering, medicine, law, economics, education and military skills. In his inland province of Hunan, the sixteen-year-old Mao Zedong (1893–1976)was one of the first students at a school imparting what was called the 'New Knowledge'. The teenaged Mao read about the American and French revolutions and Rousseau and Washington, and he learnt about the full scale of China's degradation at the hands of the West from a teacher who had studied in Japan. Decades later, he recalled to the American writer Edgar Snow that

> I began to have a certain amount of political consciousness, especially after I read a pamphlet telling of the dismemberment of China. I remember even now that this pamphlet opened with the sentence: 'Alas, China will be subjugated!' It told of Japan's occupation of Korea and Taiwan, of the loss of suzerainty in Indo-China, Burma and elsewhere.

After I read this I felt depressed about the future of my country and began to realize that it was the duty of the people to help save it.[51]

Among other reforms, the army was modernized. A new, professional elite of army men soon emerged, particularly under Yuan Shikai (1859–1916), a general in the old Qing army. The military academy established by Yuan south of Beijing initially trained, among others, the future Nationalist leader – and Mao's rival – Chiang Kai-shek (1888–1975). A glamorous militarist strain appeared in Chinese urban life which had so far conferred prestige on silk-robed Confucian gentlemen with a gift for poetry and calligraphy. Voluntary organizations dedicated to modernizing and strengthening China sprang up in both China and the Chinese diaspora.

The reforms also had consequences not obvious to the Qing reformists. Students who had become deeply politicized by their stay in Japan returned to form enduring anti-Qing alliances with like-minded graduates of the new schools and military academies. Many of these were radical nationalists in the European Social Darwinist style, borrowing from the examples of Germany and Japan to posit a Han 'national essence' against alien Manchus.

For the radical nationalists, Manchu or 'foreign' rule over China constituted a greater evil than Western imperialists. The most famous of them, an eighteen-year-old student from Sichuan called Zou Rong, published a tract titled 'The Revolutionary Army' in 1903, which denounced Han Chinese habits of mental slavery and argued for redemption through a bloody extirpation of the Manchus. Anticipating Frantz Fanon's views of the emancipatory quality of revolutionary violence, Zou wrote that

> Revolution is a universal rule of evolution. Revolution is a universal principle of the world. Revolution is the essence of the struggle for survival or destruction in a time of transition. Revolution submits to heaven and responds to men's needs. Revolution rejects what is corrupt and keeps the good. Revolution is the advance from barbarism to civilization. Revolution turns slaves into masters.[52]

In the same year, Zhang Taiyan, the classical scholar and a close colleague of Zou Rong, wrote an open letter to Kang Youwei ridiculing him for his continuing support of the Manchu emperor, a 'despicable little wretch who cannot so much as tell the difference between a bean and a noodle'. He also mocked Kang for expressing the fear that revolution in China would lead to terrible bloodletting, dictatorship and foreign invasions: 'Can a constitutional system,' he asked, 'ever be achieved without bloodshed?'[53] Zhang claimed that violence in the cause of racial-ethnic revenge was as morally justified as revolution for human rights: 'As for those peoples who, following the model of the devilish [American president] McKinley, engaged in expansionism under the pretext of helping others, we should make it a principle to kill them without pardon.'[54]

Zhang also attacked Kang Youwei's praise for Indian literature and philosophy. 'Indians', he wrote, 'have generally not cared if their national territory is lost or if their race declines . . . Chinese determination is stronger than the Indian, and we can foresee that Chinese accomplishments will certainly surpass those of the Indians.'[55] Zhang was imprisoned for his remarks about the emperor. In jail, where he embarked on a life-changing study of Buddhism, he wrote more rousing missives:

> With our people and our culture in their proper places, I must seek to irradiate their splendour. My will has not yet achieved its end. I am still shackled by the enemy state. Others will follow me to renew the golden flame. If our nation's antiquity and our people's historical record should come to an end in my hands, and the continuance of China's broad and magnificent scholarship be severed, this will be my crime to bear.[56]

From Hawaii, Liang Qichao followed the news of China's greatest humiliation yet, and the last of his old beliefs began to die. In a letter to Kang, he denounced 'the slavish mentality' of the Chinese people.[57] In this bleak world that China found herself in, where 'battle is the mother of all progress', Confucius could no longer be the sole guide.[58] Nor could constitutional monarchy be the right system for a people who desperately needed to be educated and mobilized around a strong nation-state.

The status quo was intolerable since a self-perpetuating autocratic system treated the Chinese people as slaves, making them indifferent to the public good. In his famous series of essays, 'Discourses on the

New People', Liang argued that nothing less than a total destruction of the Manchu regime could save China. 'I have thought and thought again', he wrote, 'about the popularly accepted system in China today; there is almost not a single aspect of it which ought not to be destroyed and swept away, root and branch.' Invoking Social Darwinism again, Liang warned, 'when a race cannot meet the exigencies of the times, it cannot endure'.[59] Freedom was the absolute necessity for China, he wrote, invoking Patrick Henry's famous words, 'Give me Liberty or give me Death.'

Liang was moving close to a break with Kang Youwei, who still believed that a wise and paternalistic monarchy could launch China into modernity. Kang had tried to stoke an armed revolt during the Boxer Rising. Failure forced him to seek refuge in Penang, where he quarrelled with Sun Yat-sen; he then moved to India in December 1901. He spent a year in the Himalayan resort of Darjeeling, during which he finished his treatise called *Book of the Great Community*, which offered a utopian vision of a post-nationalist harmony. Like many Chinese thinkers of his period, Kang turned out to be less a nationalist than a utopian internationalist. As he saw it, a universal moral community of the future would transcend all distinctions of race, ethnicity and language, and would even dissolve the family – a vision that would be resurrected in China under Mao Zedong.

PAN-ASIANISM: THE PLEASURES OF COSMOPOLITANISM

While Kang moved to India, many more Asians gravitated to Japan. Muslim intellectuals in Egypt, Persia and Turkey had long been fascinated by Japan, as were their Chinese and Indian counterparts. In the early years of the twentieth century, Tokyo became a Mecca for nationalists from all over Asia, the centre of an expanded Asian public sphere – a process quickened by Japan's victory over Russia in 1905. Beyond Tokyo, globe-trotting literati from almost every colonial society – Sinhalese Buddhists, Islamic modernists, Hindu revivalists – were to create melting-pots of intellectual culture in such far-flung places as Chicago, Berlin, Johannesburg and Yokohama. These broadened horizons of enquiry, reflection and polemic and committed many men and women to a restless nomadism, to ceaseless exploration and analysis of self and the world.

Western-style schools and colleges in urban centres, often on the coast (such as Calcutta and Canton), and journalism and print media created secular spaces where the newly educated elites learnt a new vocabulary of self-awareness and analysis. Many of them travelled to the West and within Asia, making physical and intellectual journeys wholly unavailable to their ancestors, and which only indentured labourers, lascars and ayahs – the service class of empire – had undertaken so far. The need for vocational training took Gandhi to London, Lu Xun to Japan, and Sun Yat-sen to Honolulu. Here, in the centres of empire, they were safe from the malevolence of the colonial police. Yet their incandescent words, printed in small-circulation magazines or carried home by individual travellers, could spread like wildfire. A Vietnamese nationalist, Dang Thai Mai, described the effect at home of his compatriots abroad:

> Liaison between the various patriots and the people, the country's youth at home, was never severed. Once in a while, from some remote base, from Siam, China, or Japan, a 'rootless' individual would furtively return. In the midst of the night a shadow from afar would step into the house, cautiously assess the mood of relatives and friends, and remain on the lookout for the omnipresent informers of the enemy authorities. He would be around only a night, an instant, with whispered stories of perilous existence, of bravery among those not yet dead, those never willing to accept defeat. Sometime there would be a letter, or a book from distant shores, providing a bit of information on 'world conditions', or describing the courageous spirit of revolutionaries from other countries. A new vista was spread before the inquiring eyes of the young people.[60]

Far from home, 'rootless' Asians often also had their most crucial self-education. China's foremost modern writer, Lu Xun, first felt a political panic when, as a student in Japan during its war with Russia in 1905, he saw a picture of a Chinese crowd apathetically witnessing the execution of an alleged Chinese spy by the Japanese. 'Physically, they were as strong and healthy as anyone could ask,' he later wrote, 'but their expressions revealed all too clearly that spiritually they were calloused and numb.'[61] Abandoning his studies in medicine, Lu Xun soon began a hectic career of literary and moral exhortation.

The advance of imperialism everywhere forced Asian elites into anxious sideways glances as well as urgent self-appraisals. Very quickly in the early twentieth century, a transnational intellectual network grew, bringing Asian intellectuals into dialogue with each other. In the more remote past, the Indian reformer Ram Mohun Roy, who died in Bristol in 1833, had written feelingly about the fate of Italian and Spanish revolutionaries in the 1810s, and supported the Irish against the British. And there was something weirdly modern about the career of Jamal al-din al-Afghani, born in a small Iranian town but subsequently resident in Delhi, Kabul, Istanbul, Cairo, Tehran, London, Moscow and Paris. By 1901, it seemed in the nature of things that Kang Youwei should write about the urgency of Chinese reform in the Indian hill station of Darjeeling – as did the fact the Russian-born Muslim intellectual Abdurreshid Ibrahim discussed the fate of the Mongolian and Tibetan peoples with the spiritual leader of Mongolia's Buddhists.

Ibrahim, author of a famous book *The House of Islam*, which recorded his travels among and exhortations to Muslims in Siberia, Manchuria, Japan, Korea, China, South-east Asia, India, Arabia and Istanbul, was one of those itinerant cosmopolitans to whom national issues and identities – such as the fate of Muslims in Russia – were becoming increasingly important. But they also overlapped with larger solidarities, such as pan-Asianism, pan-Islamism and pan-Arabism. It was the 'opposition among Asian peoples', Ibrahim wrote in the prospectus of the society he established in Japan in 1909, Ajia Gikai (The Society for the Asian Cause), 'that enabled Western powers to invade the East. Without being aware of this defect, and putting an end to internal opposition, Asian peoples will have no future.'[62]

Born in Siberia, and educated partly in Medina, Ibrahim had met al-Afghani in St Petersburg and Istanbul in the 1890s, and had witnessed the latter's frantic attempts to catch the eye of the Russian tsar during an opera performance. By 1909, he was the best-known pan-Islamic intellectual, surpassing even his peripatetic master in the amount of travel he did. Driven into exile by the persecution of

Muslims in Russia, he visited Japan in 1909, and was immediately invited into the highest political circles. He became a close associate of the militant group the Black Dragons, which was already backing Sun Yat-sen and other nationalist movements in Asia. Writing in the journal *Gaiko Jiho* ('Foreign Affairs'), Ibrahim claimed that 'as a whole, Asians are disgusted by Europeans' and that 'bringing about the union of Asian countries to stand up to Europe is our legitimate means of self-defense'.[63]

Together with the Egyptian nationalist army officer Ahmad Fadzli Beg, who was exiled to Tokyo by the British rulers of Egypt, and the Indian émigré Maulvi Barakatullah, a teacher of Urdu at Tokyo University, Ibrahim started an English-language paper, *Islamic Fraternity*. He also translated *Asia in Danger*, a pamphlet by Hasan U. Hatano (1882–1936), an important Japanese pan-Asianist who converted to Islam along with his wife and her father and adopted a Muslim name. Carrying photos of beheadings and massacres conducted by Westerners in Asia, it was widely distributed in the Muslim world.

Assisted by the Black Dragons, Ibrahim travelled to Istanbul in 1909, spreading the prescient message through the Muslim communities in China and in British and Dutch colonies that Japan would be their saviour. (Later, during the First World War, he would raise an 'Asian Battalion' from Russian prisoners of war in German captivity; it was sent to fight the British in Mesopotamia.)

The Vietnamese Phan Boi Chau (1867–1940) was another exile to shrewdly harness nationalist and internationalist sentiments in Japan. Born into a scholar-gentry family quite like Liang Qichao's, Phan would have become a government official in the Confucian manner had he not been radicalized by successive French attacks on Annam. His denunciations of French rule contained a familiar mix of bewilderment, anger and shame:

> Since France gained their protectorate they have taken over everything, even the power of life or death. The life of 10,000 'Annamese' is worth less than one French dog; the prestige of 100 mandarins is less than that of one French female. How is it that those blue-eyed, yellow-bearded people, who are not our fathers or elder brothers, can squat on our heads, defecate on us?[64]

Like many others, Phan was thrilled by Japan's victory over Russia in 1905. 'Our minds', he wrote, 'may now contemplate a new, exquisite world.' Later that same year he travelled to Japan, passing through Chinese political circles in Hong Kong and Shanghai. At the turn of the century, the first generation of Vietnamese nationalists like him had been riveted by the efforts of Kang Youwei and Liang Qichao. Liang's writings were widely available across Vietnam. Reaching Japan, Phan Boi Chau immediately sought out Liang and held many conversations with him about international affairs. Liang spoke of the French railway in Yunnan province as 'cancers in China's stomach', but advised the Vietnamese not to seek assistance from Japan until he had awakened his own people to the challenges of the international system.[65] Inspired by Liang, Phan feverishly began writing what became the *History of the Loss of Vietnam*. Serialized by Liang in his newspaper and then published as a book, it would be read in the remotest villages of Vietnam, and become a seminal text for such second-generation Vietnamese anti-colonialists as Ho Chi Minh.

LIANG AND DEMOCRACY IN AMERICA

While Kang was in India, moving into the private dream world that would increasingly make him politically irrelevant, Liang travelled to Canada and the United States for a fund-raising tour. This major trip outside Asia proved to be a turning point in his intellectual career.

He travelled from the west coast and back again, passing through Vancouver, Ottawa, Montana, Boston, New York, Washington, New Orleans, Pittsburgh, Chicago, Seattle, Los Angeles and San Francisco. Since the great emigration to the American West in the 1860s and 1870s, more than 100,000 Chinese had settled in America, working as laundrymen and restaurateurs in remote railroad and mining towns as well as living in the crammed Chinatowns of New York and San Francisco. A handful of Chinese students had also arrived at Harvard and Yale on American scholarships.

The United States was then completing its major transition from a frontier society to a European-style industrial economy, and had a fast-developing sense of its imperial destiny. In 1902, a year before

Liang arrived in America, Woodrow Wilson had published his five-volume *History of the American People*. Describing the Philippines as 'new frontiers', Wilson, then president of Princeton University, frankly acknowledged the growing American thirst for foreign markets: markets 'to which diplomacy, and if need be power, must make an open way'. 'Since trade ignores national boundaries and the manufacturer insists on having the world as a market,' Wilson explained, 'the flag of his nation must follow him, and the doors of the nation which are closed must be battered down.'[66] Following this precept of economic imperialism, the United States had already expelled Spain from its Caribbean backyard and flexed its muscles in East Asia, and since the nineteenth century, American missionaries in China, mostly Protestant, had reflected the growing national confidence as they propagated the American way of life as much as Christianity.

America's interest in China, led by businessmen, had also begun to peak, reflected in its announcement of the 'Open Door' policy which protected American stakes in the potentially great China market. One result of this was that Liang found his tour heralded by American newspapers everywhere he went. He was received by the banker and industrialist J. P. Morgan, the Secretary of State John Hay, who told Liang that China would be a great power one day, and finally by President Theodore Roosevelt himself at the White House.

In his prose, which was a model of simplicity and directness, Liang proved to be a sharp and confident observer of the American scene, impressed but not overawed, and surprisingly insightful given that he had never been to the West before. He noted things both big and small: the extension, with Roosevelt's big navy, of the Monroe Doctrine to the world, as well as New York traffic, American libraries and the condition of Italian and Jewish immigrants ('their clothing is shabby, their appearance wretched', he wrote).

The United States he travelled to was a country of extreme inequality: '70 percent', Liang reported in scandalized tones, 'of the entire national wealth of America is in the hands of 200,000 rich people ... How strange, how bizarre!' The tenements in New York horrified him. Commenting on the death rates in them, he quoted the Tang dynasty poet Du Fu: 'Crimson mansions reek of wine and meat while on the road lie frozen bones. Rich and poor but a foot apart; sorrows too hard to relate.'[67] The political corruption exceeded anything described in Henry Adams' novel *Democracy* published two decades previously. And Liang began to lose his faith in people's rights as the cure-all to autocracy as his indictment of American democracy grew.

As he saw it, corporate interests played an insidious role in American politics. Frequent elections made for policy short-sightedness and cheap populism. People entering democratic politics tended to be third-rate; far too many American presidents had been mediocre and uninspiring. The best aspects of American democracy were to be found at the local level – the political institutions of states, towns and counties – and these were too particular to America to be adapted to China's circumstances. Democracy itself was best built from the bottom up over a long period. It couldn't be imposed through revolution, as the fragility of democracy in France and Latin America had proved. And even in America, the liberal democratic state had been achieved with much coercion, and now, as America assumed its place in the world, it faced the danger of overcentralization. Also, imperialism was becoming more acceptable in America, as its financial and industrial power grew.

During Liang's tour of America, President Roosevelt told a crowd in San Francisco that 'before I came to the Pacific slope, I was an expansionist, and after having been here I fail to understand how any man . . . can be anything but an expansionist'. Liang was struck by Roosevelt's directness. 'What was his point', he worried, 'in talking about "role" and "purpose" when he said, "playing a great role on the world's stage" and "carrying out our great purpose"? I hope my countrymen will ponder this.'[68]

Liang was in America, too, when the United States manipulated its way into control of Panama and its crucial canal. Reading newspaper accounts, Liang was reminded of how the British had compromised Egypt's independence over the Suez Canal. Remarking on the Monroe Doctrine, he said the original meaning – 'the Americas belong to the people of the Americas' – had become transformed into 'the Americas belong to the people of the United States'. 'And who knows,' he added, 'if this will not continue to change, day after day from now on, into "the world belongs to the United States".'[69] Indeed, the large modern business corporations of America threatened to dominate the entire world. Imperialism together with financial and industrial expansion constituted a 'giant monster', far beyond the imagination of a Napoleon or Alexander, which would soon cross the Pacific to prey upon a weak China.[70]

Liang's disillusionment with democracy deepened as he came face to face with the ever-present threats to Chinese dignity in an America that also treated its black population atrociously. 'The American Declaration of Independence says', he wrote, 'that people are born free and equal. Are blacks alone not people? Alas, I now understand what is called "civilization" these days.'[71] Liang was particularly appalled by the practice of lynching: 'Had I only been told about this and not been to America myself I would not have believed that such cruel and inhuman acts could be performed in broad daylight in the twentieth century.'[72]

While Liang was in America, a Chinese consular official in San Francisco committed suicide after being insulted by the police. This brought home to Liang a long-standing national humiliation – what the Indian sociologist Benoy Kumar Sarkar called the 'crime of colour' routinely committed against Chinese immigrants in America:

> The ballot was forbidden to Chinese living in America. Schools were closed against them. They were not allowed to give evidence on the witness stand even in cases affecting their own property. They suffered open torture in public places and residential quarters. In normal times it was 'mob-law' that governed their person and property. The dictates of American demagogues created a veritable reign of terror for them.[73]

Huang Zunxian, who had been the Chinese consul-general in San Francisco from 1882 to 1885 and was a fine poet, had written bitterly about the general ill-treatment of Chinese immigrants, and the pain of Chinese forced overseas by poverty.

> Alas! What crimes have our people committed,
> That they suffer this calamity in our nation's fortunes?
> Five thousand years since the Yellow Emperor,
> Our country today is exceedingly weak.
>
> . . .

Great China and the race of Han
Have now become a joke to other races.
We are not as simple as the black slaves,
Numb and confused wherever they may be.
Grave, dignified, I arrive with my dragon banners,
Knock on the customs gate, hesitant, doubtful.
Even if we emptied the water of four oceans,
It would be hard to wash this shame clean.[74]

Liang felt keenly this ignominy. But he was discouraged to find that Chinese expatriate communities in America, though subject to racial discrimination and abuse, did not support his grand vision of a self-empowering Chinese people at home. In the midst of a democratic country with freedom of speech, the Chinese-Americans preferred clannish ways; they clung to tradition, and produced criminal gangs and mafia dons rather than representative parties and leaders. 'The Chinese', he wrote, 'have a village mentality, not a national mentality ... Developed to excess, it is a major obstacle to nation building.'[75]

It was no longer possible for Liang to conclude that the Chinese were held back only by their autocratic system from becoming self-aware and nationalistic individuals. 'Who says America is a nation freely formed by all the people? I see only a few great men who imposed it on them. Since this is true even of Americans who are so used to self-government, others should certainly take warning.'[76]

The democracy and freedom that a revolution promised in China could only cause chaos rather than a nation-state capable of standing up to Western power. 'With countrymen such as these, is it possible to practice the electoral system? ... Freedom, constitutionalism, and republicanism, are all terms that mean government by the majority. But the overwhelming majority of the Chinese people are like those in San Francisco.'[77] Preparing to leave for Japan in October 1903, Liang wrote:

No more am I dizzy with vain imaginings; no longer will I tell a tale of pretty dreams. In a word, the Chinese people must for now accept authoritarian rule; they cannot enjoy freedom ... those born in the thundering tempests of today, forged and molded by iron and fire – *they* will be my citizens, twenty or thirty, or fifty years hence. *Then* we will give them Rousseau to read, and speak to them of Washington.[78]

This wasn't a sudden change of mind on Liang's part. The success of Meiji Japan, where he lived, had proved that an authoritarian state could be more effective than liberal democratic institutions in building a modern nation. As European countries moved to embrace protectionist economic policies, and built stronger states, many intellectuals in East Asia had begun to change their minds. By the late 1890s, Tokutomi Sohō, initially a liberal reformist, believed that individual rights were being discarded by Western nations themselves; he questioned the worth of 'representative government and party cabinets'.[79] It was almost inevitable that Liang would be influenced by the growing intellectual preference among Japanese for the statism embodied by Bismarck's Germany.

By now Liang was reading and speaking a great deal about the Japanese theorist Kato Hiroyuki, one of the many Japanese thinkers who believed that only enlightened despotism could bring about progressive change and ensure national survival against the challenge from the West. According to Hiroyuki, a republican system hadn't worked out even in the countries of its origin. France had suffered much violence after its revolution and still lacked a stable political structure. The United States, despite its British heritage, still discriminated against its ethnic and racial minorities, particularly blacks and Chinese, and Native Americans. It was still a barbarous country, artistically and intellectually; and, with all its love of liberty, it had been compelled to expand the power of the federal government to fit into its international role.

If greater centralization for the sake of military preparedness was the fate of even such a country as the United States, which had made such a fetish of federalism in the past, what was a country like China to do? As Liang saw it, China wasn't faced with a choice of political systems. Such were its circumstances – a weak and ineffectual government, and a poorly educated and ethnically diverse population in a large country – that an autocracy was a necessity. A democratic republic would quickly lead to war between the military and the people, between lower and upper classes, one province and another; and revolutions would occur frequently, sapping the strength and dedication to the common good the Chinese nation needed to deal with external threats.

Besides, as Liang's justification went on, autocracy was of many kinds. It could be responsive to the needs of the people, devoted to marshalling national strength and providing impartial justice. To be sure, Emperor Guangxu wasn't the enlightened despot Liang had in mind; nor did any other candidate present himself. But Liang wanted above all to forestall the possibility of a republican revolution, such as the one that Sun Yat-sen agitated for, for in Liang's view it could only lead to anarchy and chaos, and finally to the creation of a new tyranny. The fundamental change Liang sought – a centralized state that forged the Chinese people into a united citizenry – could only be achieved under a benign autocracy.

THE TEMPTATIONS OF AUTOCRACY AND REVOLUTION

Like many other Muslim intellectuals, al-Afghani had flirted with similar notions to Liang's of a unified resistance to the West, and sought his enlightened despot in Istanbul and Tehran. But this was the first time such arguments had been made by an anti-Qing Chinese thinker; they were to have a long history in the twentieth century and beyond.

Liang Qichao was soon vindicated in his suspicion of the chaos of republican democracy, not so much by the incapacity of the Chinese people as by the incompetence and intellectual overreaching of his rivals, Sun Yat-sen and his Revolutionary Alliance of republicans. After 1905 Liang had lost the battle for influence over Chinese expatriates to Sun, who gave Chinese nationalism a racial 'Han' tinge, turning it into an explicitly anti-Manchu sentiment. Even Phan Boi Chau, Liang's Vietnamese protégé, had begun to spend more time strategizing about Vietnamese and Asian freedom with Sun than with his earliest guru. The most articulate of the anti-Manchuists was the classical scholar Zhang Taiyan, who had been jailed for three years in China for insulting the emperor. The revolutionaries also spoke about socialism, without specifying what they meant by it – nationalization of land or public ownership of industry. Stressing the urgency of Western-style revolution in China, Sun's journal *Min Bao* became more widely read than Liang's periodicals.

Liang himself flirted briefly with anti-Manchuism. But, like Kang Youwei, he never ceased to be aware of the necessity of a broad anti-imperialist front that included China's many ethnic minorities. In this he remained within the mainstream of Chinese nationalism (anti-Manchuism itself became redundant after the collapse of the Qing dynasty in 1911). In his debates with Sun's revolutionaries, Liang continued to uphold the importance of 'broad nationalism', as opposed to what he called 'narrow nationalism'. He also criticized socialist ideas as inapplicable to China, which did not need the nationalization of land so much as nationalization of capital.

According to his original view, socialism had its roots in the terrible class inequalities and conflicts created by the laissez-faire policies followed in Western Europe after the Industrial Revolution. China had experienced no such polarization or clashes. What it needed was industrial production through capitalist methods carefully regulated by the state. This was how China could withstand the great power of American economic imperialism and hold its own in the international jungle. A megalomaniacal businessman like Cecil Rhodes could do whatever he liked in southern Africa because his government backed him. Accordingly, 'the economic policy I advocate is primarily to encourage and protect capitalists so that they can do their best to engage in external competition. To this policy all other considerations are subordinate.'[80] If this meant holding down workers' wages and rent, so be it. Far from endorsing Adam Smith's economic liberalism, Liang was arguing that in the age of imperialism, which was driven by the power of state-backed business enterprises, China had to accumulate the same kind of resources so as to hold its own internationally, for nation-states everywhere were acting with a unified will, trying to bring the flow of goods and people as much as possible under their control.

Setting economic – and moral – priorities that the 'capitalist' heirs of Mao Zedong may well have remembered, Liang maintained that 'Encouragement of capital is the foremost consideration; protection of labor is the second consideration.'[81] And his version of capitalism included a strong social welfare component, in which the state regulated private enterprises to prevent class tensions, economic exploitation and social conflict.

*

The revolution itself, when it fortuitously came in 1911 and over-threw the Manchu dynasty (and made Sun Yat-sen the first president of the Chinese Republic for all of six weeks), was not, however, the direct result of anything the exiles in Japan said or did. It coalesced through sporadic internal uprisings. And the utter chaos that followed the overthrow of the Manchus confirmed the most pessimistic of Liang's conclusions about revolution. It also revealed the great dis-tance between the stirring emotional ideal of nationalism – whether embodied by the Chinese people or, more parochially, the Han people – and the political reality of China.

The republic generated great enthusiasm at first, despite the polit-ical skulduggery that led to Sun Yat-sen ceding his office to Yuan Shikai, the old general who had the strongest army behind him. Polit-ical parties sprouted overnight to contest the first free elections, scheduled for 1912. Liberated from censorship, newspapers finally came into their own. Those Chinese who lived in cities cut off their queues, embraced Western dress and manners, and flew the newly designed national flag from their homes.

Liang at first kept his distance from the revolution, and then yielded to Yuan Shikai's blandishments, becoming his Minister of Justice and then his financial adviser. The unstable Yuan was not quite the enlight-ened despot Liang may have been looking for. In yet another affirmation that in transitional societies, power lay with men from the barracks, Yuan became president of the Chinese Republic, and then stamped out any lingering trace of opposition to himself. When in China's first free elections Sun's Nationalist Party (Guomindang) emerged as the winner, it was allegedly Yuan's agents who assassi-nated the prime minister-elect. Yuan then forced Sun into exile, banned the Guomindang and attempted to revive Confucianism as a ruling ideology, a venture in which he was assisted by Kang Youwei.

Yuan had inherited severe financial problems and a weakened administration from the Qing court. Revolution hadn't stopped the foreign powers from exacting tariff revenues and salt taxes from China. Yuan added to these debts by taking big loans from foreign banks and governments. In a pattern familiar by now from Egypt, Iran and Turkey, the European and Japanese lenders were soon running Yuan's economic policy, and foreigners were appointed as officials in the Chinese government. The loan money ran out, and then Yuan was forced to sell railway and mining concessions to his creditors.

Imperialism also had a fresh new face in China: Japan, which had hugely increased its commercial interests in China in recent years, and signed far-reaching agreements with Britain and France. (It would enter the First World War on the Allied powers' side.) In line with the country's role as a budding imperialist, the Japanese authorities had made life harder for some of the foreign pan-Asianists. Phan Boi Chau was expelled after Japan signed a pact with France, agreeing not to host anti-French activists on its soil. British pressure finally led to the closure of Abdurreshid Ibrahim's paper *Islamic Fraternity*.

A generation of Chinese had been educated in Japan by now, and pan-Asianism for many in the country's elite meant giving assistance to China. Nevertheless, sensing an opportunity in China's disarray, Japan pressed successfully for more territorial and commercial concessions from China in 1915, including recognition of Japan's control over Shandong, which it had seized from Germany the previous year. These were Japan's infamously punitive 'Twenty-One Demands' which came printed on stationery tactfully bearing a watermark of dreadnoughts and machine guns. Yuan succumbed, much to the horror of ordinary Chinese. In fact he had little choice, given Chinese indebtedness to Japan. The following year, he tried to declare himself the emperor of China, and to proclaim a new dynasty, before ferocious opposition, including from the military, forced him to back down.

Yuan died in 1916 before he could further damage his country, and with his death even the semblance of a government disappeared; most of China shattered into innumerable fiefdoms of warlords and bandits. Much of China would remain exposed to the vagaries of warlordism until 1927 – a situation made familiar to contemporary readers in pre-Taliban Afghanistan where arms from abroad flooded the country, old elites struck deals with military strongmen, and ordinary people suffered from arbitrary taxes and confiscations of property. Mao Zedong's native province of Hunan was particularly ravaged by rival warlords, and the bitter lessons of chaos and misrule would haunt future generations of Chinese.

*

The age of imperial dynasties was coming to an end everywhere, it seemed, but the future now seemed more clouded than before. China was not alone in failing to build a viable new democratic state soon after the shattering of the old one. Turkey and Iran were also suffering this fate, and were soon to witness the rise of autocratic governments. As in these countries, the modernization of the military in China had shifted the locus of power internally and elevated men trained in modern military academies: strongmen who could bind other men to ideas of discipline, zeal and self-sacrifice. Far from being vested in mastery of the Confucian classics, power would now flow from the barrel of the gun, as Mao Zedong, who observed the brutalities of the warlord era in his home province, noted in 1927. The chaos unleashed by this warlord period would be invoked late into the contemporary era to justify authoritarian governments.

Liang Qichao himself was not to remain untainted by Yuan's failures. As a teacher in exile in Japan he had been greatly revered. Some of his own protégés had risen to powerful positions in republican China and were engaged in the factional struggles that ravaged the country. Liang, who had already begun to aim his message more towards powerful officials than to students, sided with them, and rose to ministerial posts in the new government in Beijing.

He negotiated toughly with his former hosts, the Japanese, over their unreasonable demands. He also successfully advocated China's entry into the First World War in 1917; he calculated that to emerge on the winning side was the best way to insert China into the international system, cancel the unequal treaties that still bound her, and recover the Shandong peninsula from the Japanese. As part of Liang's deal with the Allied powers, Chinese workers and students, among them the first generation of Communist leaders such as Zhou Enlai and Deng Xiaoping travelled to France to work and study there.

Nevertheless, Liang's political career had proved to be disastrous. Returning to China after fifteen years, he had thrown himself into the tumult of the post-Qing state only to find himself utterly compromised by politically expedient associations with corrupt and violent warlords. One of the many wild pendulum swings of political fortune in post-Yuan China finally dispossessed him, and forced him to retire from active involvement in the political scene. A younger generation would now come to the fore, building on the foundation provided by his ideas.

The revolution of 1911 was a cruel failure in many ways, but it succeeded thoroughly in devastating old assumptions. Gone for ever was the sacredness of imperial dynasties, the millennia-strong prestige of the gentry and of classical learning. By destroying the old, the revolution created a new political and intellectual space in which young Chinese, radicalized by the brutal disappointments of 1911, now became visible.

The spectacle of total social and political fragmentation forced even a liberal thinker like Yan Fu to concede that Confucianism as a state religion might prove a cohesive force. But the days when a possibility like this could be realized were drawing to a close. Disillusioned with politics, young Chinese spoke of the necessity of a 'New Culture', a revolution in the mind which would preclude obeisance to the old ways. Consciousness-raising was deemed more important than party politics.

In 1912–13, the Bloomsbury writer G. Lowes Dickinson met some officials of the revolutionary government and was 'astonished' by their readiness for a complete Westernization:

> They are doing all they can to sweep away the old China, root and branch, and build up there a reproduction of America. There is nothing, I think, which they would not alter if they could, from the streets of Canton to the family system, and the costume of a policeman to the national religion.[82]

In the province of Hunan, a twenty-four-year-old Mao Zedong was moving swiftly away from his earlier reverence for Chinese tradition:

> I used to worry that our China would be destroyed, but now I know that is not so. Through the establishment of a new political system, and a change in the national character, the German states became the German Reich ... The only question is how the changes should be carried out. I believe that there must be a complete transformation, like matter that takes form after destruction, or like the infant born out of its mother's womb ... In every century, various nationalities have launched various kinds of great revolutions, periodically cleansing

the old and infusing it with the new, all of which are great changes involving life and death, formation and demise. The demise of the universe is similar . . . I very much look forward to its destruction, because from the demise of the old universe will come a new universe, and will it not be better than the old universe?[83]

In 1915, the establishment of the magazine *New Youth* had given the new radicals a resonant voice. These were students educated in Japan or the West, or in the Western schools hurriedly set up in the first phase of Qing reforms. Appalled by Yuan's attempt at a Confucian coup, they flinched from China's old traditions of Confucianism, Buddhism and Taoism. Indeed, they scorned the past with startling vehemence, describing it as the dead weight that held China down. In what seems now a parody of uncompromising Confucian moralism, *New Youth* identified Confucianism with the discredited monarchy, and called for a wholesale and uncritical adoption of Western values of science and democracy. The heroes of this new intelligentsia were Mr Science and Mr Democracy, who together signified the vitality of the West. The formula was coined by Chen Duxiu, the founder of *New Youth* as well as of, five years later, the Communist Party of China, who, in a letter to a friend in 1916, confessed to

the hopelessness of our catching up with European and American civilizations. Most of our people are lethargic and do not know that not only our morality, politics, and technology but even common commodities for daily use are all unfit for struggle and are going to be eliminated in the process of natural selection.[84]

As the Chinese radicals understood them, the concept of democracy referred mainly to freedom from traditional restraints, and science was a method to achieve progress and discard the 'superstitious' aspects of the traditional past, such as the hierarchical relationships of parents–children, rulers–subjects and husbands–wives enjoined by Confucianism. Democracy could release the creative individuality of the Chinese people that Confucianism had suppressed. Nationalism became another holy notion, because, as Chen Duxiu put it,

Looking at conditions in China, our people are still in the age of scattered sand. We have to follow the times, and nationalism has truly become the best means by which the Chinese can save themselves. To use this doctrine, the Chinese must first understand what it means . . . contemporary nationalisms refer to democratic nations, not nations of enslaved people.[85]

Liang's questioning of China's tradition, his scepticism about its ability to adapt to the harsh world of competition, was now the basis of a radical new despair and hopefulness. The young men shared none of the old reformist beliefs in evolution, gradual or rapid. Nothing would change without urgent and drastic effort.

What was needed was a revolution in the consciousness – a veritable New Culture – of a people whose intellectual state was a kind of 'syphilis', in the harsh judgement of a young Japanese-educated man called Zhou Shuren, soon to be known as Lu Xun.[86] One of Lu Xun's most celebrated short stories, published in 1919, would describe a madman who imagines cannibalism as the basis of China's old society and morality. In his fevered imagination, what the Confucian classics prescribe as 'filial piety' turns into an exhortation to 'eat people'.

Recoiling from warlordism and imperialism, the New Culture Movement would chart China's path into the modern world, even as it dealt with the questions first phrased by Liang Qichao. And the intellectual and social energies released by it would find their consummation in the May Fourth Movement in 1919. China's humiliation by the Western Powers at the Paris Peace Conference would bring young intellectuals together with factory workers and clerks, making the revolution of 1911 look like the product of small, isolated and ineffectual elites.

The American eagle strides the heavens soaring.
With half of the globe clutched in his claw.
Although the Chinese arrived later,
Couldn't you leave them a little space?
      Huang Zunxian, Chinese consul-general in
                   San Francisco in the 1880s

Those who live ... away from the East, have now got to recognize that Europe has completely lost her former moral prestige in Asia. She is no longer regarded as the champion throughout the world of fair dealing and the exponent of high principle, but rather as an upholder of Western race supremacy, and the exploiter of those outside her own borders.
                                 Rabindranath Tagore, 1921

THE UNITED STATES AND ITS
PROMISES OF SELF-DETERMINATION

In 1918 Liang Qichao sailed to France as one of China's unofficial representatives at the Paris Peace Conference which was to decide the shape of the post-war world. His list of demands was long but clear and fair: in return for the Chinese labour and raw materials that had been supplied to the Allies during the war, there would be an end to the unequal treaties, the cancellation of the Boxer indemnity, and the abolition of extraterritorial jurisdiction and other special concessions made to foreigners under duress. China would, Liang hoped, finally take its place in the international comity of sovereign nation-states – part of a new world order that seemed likely to rise from the ruins of the Austro-Hungarian, German, Ottoman and Russian empires.

Liang knew that like-minded representatives of other Asian countries were pressing for a similar outcome at Paris, especially after President Woodrow Wilson made plain his regard for weaker countries and the principle of national self-determination. The United States had emerged from the war as the world's greatest financial power, and these Asians hoped to persuade the American president to use his new influence to restore self-rule in countries dominated by European powers.

For much of the nineteenth century, the United States had been isolationist in its foreign policy, and protectionist in its economic; and its footprint was light in Asia and Africa. The war, which had enfeebled the economies of the major imperialist powers – Britain, Germany, Russia and France – and further discredited their regimes, had endowed America with both power and moral prestige.

Wilson, who barely had a foreign policy outside the Americas before war broke out in Europe in 1914, was not slow to realize the implications of European turmoil for the United States; he fleshed out a new and noble American sense of mission while still hoping to keep his country out of the European War. 'We are provincials no longer,' he famously declared in his second inaugural address in January 1917.[1] In speeches addressed to 'the peoples of the countries now at war' he burnished his credentials as the right kind of mediator to negotiate what he called a 'peace without victory'.[2] When his peace overtures failed, he joined the Allied side against Germany in April 1917, still confident 'that we are chosen, and prominently chosen, to show the way to the nations of the world how they shall walk in the paths of liberty'.[3] Later, he would propose a much more unusual and high-minded plan for enduring peace: replacing militarist regimes with democracies.

The United States of course had lost whatever leverage it had as an impartial mediator by declaring war against Germany. Nevertheless, Wilson pressed ahead with his scheme for a democratic international order, which he hoped would be cemented by a League of Nations. Speaking to the US Congress in January 1918, he revealed his most ambitious project yet: a fourteen-point manifesto for the new world that the United States was fighting for. Secret diplomacy was to have no place in the Wilson-ordained planet, where free trade, popular government, freedom of the seas, the reduction of armaments, the rights of small nations, and an association of nations to keep the peace were to be the new articles of faith.

Wilson's Fourteen Points would have been lofty ideals at any time (God, as the French prime minister Clemenceau joked, had only ten). They were particularly unrealistic during a global war that would soon end with Britain, France and Japan adding to their possessions in the Middle East, Africa and East Asia.

Nevertheless, disseminated to a worldwide audience Wilson's rousing speeches leading up to the Paris Peace Conference earned him, as John Maynard Keynes later recorded, 'a prestige and a moral influence throughout the world unequalled in history'.[4] Emboldened by him, nationalist leaders in Egypt, India and Ottoman Turkey joined Sinn Féin in Ireland in a serious challenge to established European authority.

In Egypt, Saad Zaghlul, Jamal al-din al-Afghani's old protégé, organized a new political party called Wafd in preparation for the Paris conference. Western-style nationalist idealism had always had a more secure hold in Egypt, al-Afghani's main theatre of operations, than anywhere else in the Muslim world. The abortive movement led by Colonel Urabi in the late 1870s, aimed against European dominance over Egypt's ruling class, had been the first such anti-colonialist upsurge anywhere in Asia. As one of the few Muslim peoples to be occupied and administered by a European power, many Egyptians, especially an emergent class of educated professionals, naturally developed a strong nationalist feeling. Since occupying Egypt in 1882, the British had boosted the country's agricultural capacity, building dams, canals and telegraph links. The population grew exponentially in most towns and Cairo was transformed by new public works between 1895 and 1907. But the basic contradiction that al-Afghani had witnessed never disappeared: Egypt's damaging dependence on the world economy as a supplier of raw materials, and a tutelary regime with an entrenched elite that blocked all upward mobility for the new classes being created by socio-economic development.

These restless Egyptians, or *effendis*, as they were called, longed for an independent and egalitarian Egypt; but they also had to rouse the working classes and the peasantry against the foreign elites and their local allies. They realized that both strength and legitimacy would have to stem from a mass movement. The Russo-Japanese War gave a big boost to Egyptian nationalists such as Mustafa Kamil, author of a laudatory book on Japan, *The Rising Sun*, and founder of the Nationalist Party in 1907. Kamil and his supporters aimed at fulfilling Urabi's aim of winning independence; and their efforts to mobilize popular anger against the foreigners briefly succeeded in 1906, when the British unjustly hanged four peasants in what came to be known as the Dinshawai incident.

Soon after war erupted in 1914, the British had declared Egypt a protectorate of the British Empire, formalizing the 1882 invasion and temporary occupation of the country. Zaghlul denounced the protectorate as illegal and hoped to enlist President Wilson on his side. Following al-Afghani's praise of Egyptian antiquity, he pointed to the sheer injustice of Egypt being denied its rightful place among nations. 'No people more than the Egyptian people', he wrote in a telegram to Wilson, 'has felt strongly the joyous emotion of the birth of a new era which, thanks to your virile action, is soon going to impose itself upon the universe.'[5]

Similar hopes bubbled up among the Muslims of Ottoman Turkey and their supporters worldwide. Before the First World War, the European powers had increased their assaults on the Ottoman Empire. In 1908 the Young Turks had forced Sultan Abdulhamid II to restore the constitution he had suspended in 1876, but this only intensified European suspicions that 'the sick man of Europe' was on his deathbed.

The Italians seized Libya in 1911, following a military conflict in which a young Salonica-born Ottoman officer called Mustafa Kemal first made his mark. The itinerant thinker Abdurreshid Ibrahim ignored his advanced age to travel to the battlefront, and he deployed his extensive network of contacts in the Muslim world in support of the Ottomans. It was during this war that an aeroplane dropped a bomb for the first time in history. The experience of this new form of warfare, along with that of more conventional Italian brutalities, shocked many Muslims. Shortly before being captured and executed by the Italians, the military leader of the Libyan resistance, 'Umar al-Mukhtar, wrote: 'They are excusable, those who cannot believe all of what is said and written about the Italian atrocities. It is actually difficult to believe that in the world there are men who behave in this unbelievable manner, but it is unfortunately only too real.'[6]

In British-ruled India, the ageing poet Akbar Illahabadi expressed a widespread sense of rage and helplessness when he wrote:

> Neither we possess licenses for weapons
> Nor have the strength to go and fight the enemies of the Turks
> But we do curse them from the core of our hearts
> That God may spike the Italian guns.[7]

In Lahore, the young poet Muhammad Iqbal, fresh from his readings of al-Afghani, began his journey to fame and future reputation as philosopher-founder of Pakistan by reciting a poem in a public assembly about the impunity with which the Italians had despoiled Ottoman territory. Addressed to God, the most famous lines of *Shikwa* ('Complaint') were:

> There are other nations besides us;
> There are sinners amongst them,
> Humble people and others swollen by pride,
> Slothful, careless or clever.
> Many there are who are weary of your name.
> But you bestow grace on their habitations,
> And your thunderbolts strike only our dwellings.[8]

To add to Ottoman woes, Austria-Hungary had fully annexed the Ottoman territory of Bosnia-Herzegovina in 1913. Allied with

Germany, Ottoman Turkey then entered the First World War on the eventual losing side, its secular leaders now deploying pan-Islamism in the hope of rousing Muslims worldwide against Western powers. Though surrounded by Allied forces on all sides, its armies performed creditably in various theatres of the war, including Gallipoli and Kut al-Amara in Mesopotamia. However, harassed by Armenian nationalists in the east of Anatolia, the Turks ruthlessly deported hundreds of thousands of Armenians in 1915, an act that later invited accusations of genocide. By 1918 the Turks were in retreat, utterly exhausted and fragmented by relentless Allied assaults. The Ottoman Empire steadily lost control of its Arab territories; and former Greek, Arab, Armenian and Kurdish subjects divided up parts of the empire among themselves. The Greeks, in particular, claimed Western Anatolia for themselves.

The success and failure of the Ottoman Empire in the war had a confusing intellectual import for many Muslims. There was pride at a major Muslim state fighting so many of Asia's enemies and alongside the other Central powers as an equal, but also anxiety about the Ottomans' own colonial role. For instance, the prospect of the Ottoman Turks defeating the British and reconquering Egypt, which seemed likely on two occasions during the war, did not appeal to Egyptian nationalists.

However, many secular Ottoman nationalists hoped the American president would secure them a just peace. They saw Wilson's plan for self-determination as favouring their cause of a Muslim-majority state in Anatolia – they were prepared to lose the Arab-majority provinces. The feminist writer Halide Edip, later Atatürk's close associate, was among those who signed a telegram addressed to President Wilson, asking him to protect the Ottoman Empire from expansionist European powers.

Inspired by Wilson's rhetoric, anti-Japanese nationalist leaders in Korea wrote their own Declaration of Independence and planned to send a delegation to Paris. Denied exit visas by the Japanese authorities, the Korean nationalists asked their expatriate colleagues to represent them; one, General Pak, living in poverty in China, began his long journey to Paris by walking along the tracks of the Trans-Siberian Railway. Expectations were even higher in India where the British, with the help of moderate Indian nationalists, had enlisted over a million soldiers and labourers to the Allied war effort in Europe and the Middle East (the great majority of those who died in the terrible siege of Kut al-Amara were Indians). The British promised, albeit vaguely, self-rule in return for Indian support; the American president seemed to stand as guarantor for them.

Touring the United States in 1916, Rabindranath Tagore had delivered strong denunciations of what he called the new god of the 'Nation (with a capital N)'. He had also attacked Western imperialism in Asia. 'There is', he wrote to Romain Rolland in early 1919, 'hardly a corner in the vast continent of Asia where men have come to feel any real love for Europe.'[9] Nevertheless, Tagore now hoped that the United States was 'rich enough not to concern itself in the greedy exploitation of weaker countries'.[10] Impressed by the American president, Tagore planned to dedicate one of his books to him. Moreover, stirred by Wilson's wartime speeches, Hindu and Muslim leaders of the Indian National Congress jointly demanded to send their delegates – a rising figure called Mohandas Gandhi among them – to represent India at the Paris Peace Conference.

In China, the news agency Reuters had already prepared a public opinion sympathetic to the Allied cause which had looked kindly upon the dispatch of 200,000 Chinese labourers to the European front. Wilson's speeches in favour of self-determination aroused extraordinary interest: in Beijing students gathered in front of the American embassy chanting 'Long Live President Wilson!' and holding placards that called for the world to be made 'safe for democracy'. Though racked by civil war, China wished to project a clear image of proud national sovereignty. It sent some of its most articulate diplomats to ensure that the country's sovereignty was respected by the victorious Allied powers, particularly Japan, which with Britain's blessing had seized German-held territory in the Shandong peninsula.

In the event, the Chinese delegation was excluded from the table of the major powers (at which Japan was present), and was relegated to the ranks of Greece and Siam (Thailand). This was not a good sign for a China determined to use the conference as the sign of its arrival as an equal and sovereign power. Its protests were ignored, and eventually the big decisions were all taken by the United States, France and Britain. Nevertheless, the excitement in China was great; and it was felt not only by Kang Youwei, who fantasized that the American president's plan for a League of Nations was fulfilling his own vision of a moral community, but also by Mao Zedong, then living in a provincial small city and gradually being radicalized by *New Youth*. Wilson's speeches were bound into a bestselling book in China; his 'Fourteen Points' could be recited by heart by many nationalists by the time the Paris conference opened. Having been instrumental in making China a party to the war, Liang Qichao probably took the largest burden of expectations to the peace conference, which turned out to be the harshest lesson yet in Western realpolitik for Asian intellectuals and activists.

LIBERAL INTERNATIONALISM OR LIBERAL IMPERIALISM?

Liang was at least part of an official delegation certain of representation at the conference, unlike many others – the Iranians, the Syrians and the Armenians – who tried to have their voices heard and were completely rebuffed. Reduced to trudging alongside the Trans-Siberian Railway, the Korean General Pak arrived too late for the talks; besides, the Korean case was squashed by the Japanese, who also killed thousands of protestors in Seoul in March 1919.

Among the many people denied representation was the Vietnamese Ho Chi Minh, then known as Nguyen Ai Quoc. Ho was an indigent menial worker in Paris in 1919 when President Woodrow Wilson arrived in the city with a plan to make the world 'safe for democracy'. Invoking their ideals of liberty, equality and fraternity, the French authorities in Vietnam had rounded up some 100,000 peasants and artisans and shipped them to the battlefields of France. In return, France was to consider self-rule for their country at some unspecified point in the future.

Ho had no faith in these promises. He was disgusted by France's practice of using poor Vietnamese as cannon fodder in its own pursuit of power and glory.

They perished in the poetic desert of the Balkans, wondering whether the mother country intended to install herself as favourite in the Turk's harem: why else should they have been sent here to be hacked up? Others, on the banks of the Marne or in the mud of Champagne, were heroically getting slaughtered so that the commanders' laurels might be sprinkled with their blood, and the field marshals' batons carved from their bones.[11]

Distrustful of French colonials, Ho found Wilson's advocacy of national self-determination thrilling. In Paris, he sought a personal audience with the president, carefully quoting from the United States' Declaration of Independence in his petition. The Vietnamese nationalist even rented a morning suit for the occasion.

As it turned out, Ho got nowhere near Wilson, or any other Western leader. His failed mission appeared to confirm what would become the *ur*-text of many anti-colonial activists and thinkers – Lenin's *Imperialism: The Highest Stage of Capitalism*. Written in 1916, this pamphlet had asserted that President Wilson was as unlikely to restore Indochina to the Vietnamese as he was to withdraw American troops from Panama. The United States, Lenin claimed, was as much of an imperialist power as Britain or Japan, greedy for resources, territory and markets, part of a capitalist world system of oppression and plunder whose inherent instability had caused the Great War.

The idea that European fighting for the spoils of Asia had led to the Great War was commonplace among many Asian thinkers. As the war intensified in 1915, Miyazaki Torazō, the Japanese pan-Asianist and Sun Yat-sen's doughty supporter, had described how Europeans 'swooped down on Asia like wolves and jackals, and the only thing that prevented them from using all their might was their fear of destroying the mutual balance of power within Europe – even if, ironically, the present upheaval is entirely the result of this [very breakdown].' Peace, Miyazaki predicted, would bring no respite to Asians. 'It is easy to see', he wrote, 'that the starving tigers [of Europe] will turn around on their heels and fight over scraps of meat in the Orient.'[12]

Lenin, however, didn't confine himself to rhetoric. Soon after coming to power in 1917, he exposed the secret agreement between France, Britain and Tsarist Russia to parcel out the Middle East (among other booties of the imperialist war). Lenin also voluntarily renounced the special concessions Russia enjoyed in China along with other Western powers and Japan. Lenin's actions were seen by many Asians, as Benoy Kumar Sarkar wrote, as nothing less than 'an extraordinary and incredibly supermanic promulgation of a new international morality'. The Soviet leader had pre-empted Wilson in calling for national self-determination. 'The new gospel', Sarkar wrote, 'of the political emancipation and sovereignty of all peoples is so world-sweeping or universal in its scope and so radical or fundamental in its Messianic good will that the Bolsheviks have already won the highest encomium in Chinese estimation.'[13]

Lenin went even further and declared that the ethnic nationalities of Russia's old Tsarist Empire would be autonomous, and would even have the right to secede. Lenin, who followed events in China and India closely, was keenly aware of the importance to Russia of an Asia liberated from European imperialists. As he put it, 'the outcome of the struggle depends in the last resort on the fact that Russia, India, China, etc., constitute the vast majority of mankind'. 'He who wants the victory of socialism,' Stalin confirmed, 'must not forget about the East.'[14]

Soon after the October Revolution, Lenin and Stalin called upon the peoples of the East to overthrow the imperialist 'robbers and enslavers'.[15] In 1920, the Bolsheviks organized the Congress of the Peoples of the East in Baku. Very soon, the Comintern was helping establish communist parties in different parts of Asia, and Soviet advisers were to help train Chinese Nationalists as well as Communists. Its unequivocally anti-imperialist stance was to make the Soviet Union attractive to many Korean, Persian, Indian, Egyptian and Chinese activists. Connecting the fate of Asian anti-imperialists with that of the Soviet Union, Sarkar made a prophecy of great shrewdness and accuracy when he wrote in 1921 that

> China's voice in the political conferences of nations would rise higher and higher as long as there is at least one nation on earth to preach and practice this creed of liberation of subject races from the domination by aliens; and this independently of the consideration as to the amount of progress that the anti-propertyism of Bolshevik economics is likely to achieve among the masses and intelligentsia of Eastern Asia.[16]

This new ideology of emancipation would begin to influence most Asians only in the 1920s. In 1919, Marxism was being studied and debated in many Asian cities and towns where European traders and missionaries had set up Western-style educational institutions, but the

Russian Revolution and its anti-imperialist attitudes were still not much known to educated natives. The press in most countries promoted Wilson and his message since foreign news in places like India and China was provided by Western news agencies. The most influential of these was Reuters, al-Afghani's old bugbear, which portrayed the Bolshevists as a highly destructive infestation. But Lenin's actions were telling, and they alarmed many in the West. It is likely that Wilson would not have upped the rhetorical ante in January 1918 if the Bolsheviks had not withdrawn Russia from the war and called upon workers and soldiers to cease fighting and become revolutionaries.

In asserting that America was fighting for a better world, President Wilson was trying to undercut Bolshevik claims that the war was a struggle among imperialist powers, with the victorious elites likely to share the spoils. He aimed to influence those Americans and Europeans who, growing tired of the endless war, appeared dangerously susceptible to Bolshevik propaganda. It was almost inadvertently that his message reached a much bigger and more receptive audience in the colonized world.

The United States was a relatively unknown player in international relations. It was, as Wilson himself stressed during his presidential campaign in 1912, full of 'expanding' industries, which 'will burst their jackets if they cannot find a free outlet to the markets of the world'.[17] Nevertheless, as Sarkar wrote in 1919, the United States 'has not yet had the time and "preparedness" enough to display excessive land hunger or market-quest, or zeal for the exploitation of weaker peoples in extra-American territories'.[18] America's record in Latin America – Wilson's imposition, for instance, of military protectorates upon Haiti and Nicaragua – was mostly unexamined by Asians. And there were very few Asians as well-informed as Sarkar, who was convinced that American 'crimes' against immigrants of Chinese and Japanese descent gave 'the same stimulus to vindictive will and intelligence as the steady annihilation of enslaved and semi-subject races by the dominant European powers and the notorious postulate of the "white man's burden" that pervades the intellectuals, journalists, university circles and "upper ten thousands" of Eur-America.'[19]

Indeed, Wilson, who presided over a serious erosion of civil liberties during the war at home, was no stranger to moral compromises in foreign policy. He supported, for instance, China's militarist president Yuan Shikai against Sun Yat-sen in 1913 in the hope that the dictator in Beijing, however brutal, would not close America's 'Open Door' to China. His anti-imperialism rested on a fine distinction that colonized peoples could not recognize. He regarded European imperialism as a matter of physical occupation of far-off lands and spheres of influence, and deplored it as such. Proposing the Open Door, he did not see that free trade, the third of his Fourteen Points, could be seen as equally oppressive by economically disadvantaged peoples. As the experience of countries from Egypt to China had testified, loans and foreign ownership of Asia's mines, factories and railways, and the presence of foreign troops to guard these European-held assets, amounted to a no less coercive and humiliating imperialism. China's sovereignty, for instance, was deeply compromised by its profound indebtedness to Japan, which stationed its troops in Manchuria as well as Shandong.

Asians and Africans accustomed to stonewalling colonial officials were naturally attracted by the generous promises of the American president. Even such die-hard sceptics as the editors of the radical magazine *New Youth*, Li Dazhao and Chen Duxiu, believed that Wilson was set to boldly redraw the rules of the international game. However, this was based on a profound misunderstanding of Wilson's background and motivations. For Woodrow Wilson was, in many ways, an unlikely hero in the alleys of Cairo, Delhi and Canton. Piously Presbyterian, and a helpless Anglophile (he had courted his wife with quotes from Bagehot and Burke), he had hoped that the United States in the Philippines and Puerto Rico would follow the British tradition of instructing 'less civilized' peoples into law and order.[20] 'After all, they are children and we are men in these deep matters of government and justice.'[21] A Southerner, Wilson also shared the reflexive racism of many of his class and generation (and many jokes about 'darkies').

Ho Chi Minh would not have bothered with renting a morning suit had he known that the cerebral Wilson believed as much as his temperamentally bellicose rival Theodore Roosevelt in America's responsibility to share the white man's burden, just as Kipling had exhorted. In January 1917 Wilson argued that America should stay out of the war in order, as he said in a cabinet meeting, 'to keep the white race strong against the yellow – Japan for instance'.[22] As he told his secretary of state Robert Lansing, Wilson believed that 'white civilization and its domination of the planet rested largely on our ability to keep this country intact'.[23]

Though apparently all-encompassing, Wilson's rhetoric about self-determination was aimed at the European peoples – Poles, Romanians, Czechs, Serbians – that were part of the German, Austro-Hungarian and Ottoman empires. Concerned with setting up the League of Nations, which he hoped would provide a framework for collective security and enduring peace in Europe, Wilson had little interest in persuading Britain and France to renounce their colonial possessions in Asia and Africa. Not that this was in any event possible. Wilson had his chance when in the spring of 1917 he first heard of the secret treaties that outlined how Britain, France, Japan and Italy would share whole empires among themselves after the war. He could have made American intervention in the war contingent upon the Allied powers cancelling their squalid arrangements. Instead, he pretended that the treaties did not exist, and even tried to prevent news of them being published in the United States after the Bolsheviks exposed them to the world.

MAKING THE WORLD UNSAFE FOR DEMOCRACY

When he travelled to Europe in 1919, President Wilson hoped that he would be able to appeal directly to people over the heads of their leaders; he was further deceived into believing this by ecstatic crowds in France and Italy that credited him with hastening the end of a deeply unloved war. In Paris he confronted hardened and cynical imperialists in the form of Britain's prime minister Lloyd George and Clemenceau of France. After several internecine wars in past centuries, the European imperial powers had settled on balance-of-power politics. Their representatives in Paris hoped to restore the equilibrium that the Great War had disrupted by suitably diminishing Germany's military and economic power, and Wilson accepted their demands in the hope that whatever old and new problems arose in the international order would be solved by his cherished League of Nations.

Mao Zedong, who in 1919 was a twenty-five-year-old of modest means and great intellectual curiosity, caught President Wilson's haplessness in Paris perfectly in a journal he edited in the hinterland province of Hunan:

> Wilson in Paris was like an ant on a hot skillet. He didn't know what to do. He was surrounded by thieves like Clemenceau, Lloyd George, Makino, and Orlando. He heard nothing except accounts of receiving certain amounts of territory and of reparations worth so much in gold. He did nothing except to attend various kinds of meetings where he could not speak his mind. One day a Reuters telegram read, 'President Wilson has finally agreed with Clemenceau's view that Germany not be admitted to the League of Nations.' When I saw the words 'finally agreed', I felt sorry for him for a long time. Poor Wilson![24]

Mao also lamented the failure of India and Korea: 'so much for national self-determination,' he wrote. 'I think it's really shameless!' Wilson's failures were more extensive, of course. Defeated over Germany, which France and Britain sought to utterly humiliate, Wilson barely put up a fight when it came to the rights of non-European peoples, many of whom did not get a hearing at the conference.

Even the Japanese, who arrived at the conference with a proper imperialist pedigree, were scornfully disregarded. They were seated at the far end of the long table, facing the representatives of Guatemala and Ecuador. But it wasn't the physical distance from where the Great Powers huddled that prompted Clemenceau to complain of not being able to hear the Japanese delegate Makino Nobuaki – and the terrible fate of being trapped with 'ugly' Japanese in a city full of attractive blonde women.[25] Discussions about the Pacific – an important arena of rivalry between Japan and Western powers – descended into racist jokes about cannibalism from Australian prime minister Billy Hughes and references to 'niggers' from Lloyd George. This raillery did not portend well for the most important item on the Japanese agenda: the enshrinement of the equality of nations – racial equality – in the League of Nations' constitution. The Japanese hoped that this would make the Californian government, for instance, permit Japanese immigration and unsegregated schools, and force the French in Indochina to remove unfair restrictions on Japanese imports.

The Japanese proposal not only appeared to undermine decades of anti-Asian legislation in the United States; it also threatened the 'White Australia' policy of that nation and was generally regarded by the Great Powers as a trigger to uncontrolled immigration by barbarians. The Japanese tried to draw attention to the apparently liberal claims made by the constitutions of the Great Powers. However, confronted with the American principle that 'all men are created equal', Lord Balfour, soon to be famous for his work on Palestine, flatly asserted his disbelief that 'a man of Central Africa was created equal to a European'.[26] In the end, Makino put the racial equality issue to a vote – and won. But President Wilson, in an act remembered for decades by Japanese nationalists, ruled that the majority vote was annulled by the fact that there were some strong objectors to the clause.

Wilson feared alienating the British and their Australian allies. To a large extent, Anglophilia blinded Wilson and his advisers (mostly members of the east coast's 'WASP' elite) to the anti-colonial passion in Asia and Africa. The American secretary of state fully backed British rule over Egypt. Allen Welsh Dulles, a future Cold-War warrior who was then a state department official, suggested that Egyptian demands 'should not even be acknowledged'.[27] The British ensured that the petitions sent to President Wilson in Paris were filed away into obscurity; they also informed Wilson that Rabindranath Tagore was a dangerous revolutionary (the poet did not get permission for his dedication).

In Persia, which had been occupied by Britain and Russia during the war, a deeply divided and fractious government sent an official diplomatic delegation to Paris. But the British ensured it did not get a seat. Indian and Korean nationalists didn't even get anywhere near Paris. India was represented by a delegation handpicked by the British, including the maharaja of the north-western kingdom of Bikaner. In 1900, this Indian potentate had travelled to China on behalf of the British to quell the Boxer Rising. He arrived too late to kill any Chinese. As soon as the European war broke out in 1914 he offered his services to India's rulers, claiming that he was 'ready to go anywhere in any capacity for the privilege of serving my Emperor'.[28] Nearly 80,000 Indian soldiers were to die fighting in the Middle East and Europe. The maharaja himself had an uneventful little war – just a skirmish near the Suez Canal in 1915 – before retreating to attend to his sick daughter in India. Delegated to the Paris Peace Conference, he became a striking figure at the discussions with his ferociously curled moustache and jewel-studded red turban, insisting on showing the leaders present the tiger tattooed on his arm (Clemenceau was impressed enough to undertake a shooting trip to Bikaner in 1920, from which he emerged with possibly the only positive short-term result of the Paris Peace Conference: two dead tigers).

In Paris, the maharaja fought most intensely to preserve the privileges of semi-autonomous kingdoms like Bikaner, and the British were only too happy to let him shoot his tigers in peace while holding out some suitably vague prospect of self-government for India. As Mao Zedong wrote, 'India has earned herself a clown' but 'the demands of the Indian people have not been granted'.[29] The Egyptians suffered a deeper humiliation. In March 1919, the British arrested Saad Zaghlul and deported him to Malta, provoking a great wave of public protests in Egypt – what later came to be known as the 1919 Revolution. Egyptians went on strike, students at the al-Azhar mosque built barricades, and Egyptian women threw off their hijabs to create picket lines and exhort the crowds. Such was the hatred of the British that mobs routinely murdered their soldiers. Faced with nationwide revolt, the British relented and allowed Zaghlul to proceed to Paris.

But while Zaghlul was honing his English-speaking skills on the journey, the British managed to persuade the Americans that Bolsheviks had joined Islamic fanatics in fuelling serious unrest in Egypt. Indeed, they presented Zaghlul and his nephew to the Americans as 'Lenin and Trotsky'. Zaghlul was still on his way from Marseilles to Paris when President Wilson moved to recognize the permanent British protectorate over Egypt. The Egyptian journalist Muhammad Haykal expressed a widespread outrage and anger when he wrote later:

> Here was the man of the Fourteen Points, among them the right to self-determination, denying the Egyptian people its right to self-determination . . . And doing all that before the delegation on behalf of the Egyptian people had arrived in Paris to defend its claim, and before President Wilson had heard one word from them. Is this not the ugliest of treacheries?[30]

Egypt remained volatile, and in 1922 the British were forced to concede it a degree of self-rule.

In Iran, which was still under military occupation by the British, Lord Curzon, now Britain's foreign secretary, saw an opportunity to create yet another buffer for his cherished Indian empire. In 1919, Curzon helped foil Iranian representation at the Paris Conference and drew up an Anglo-Persian agreement almost entirely destructive of Iranian sovereignty. (Mohammad Mossadegh, confined to Switzerland by the war, wept when he heard about the proposed agreement, and almost decided to make Europe his permanent home.) As it turned out, Curzon, who had already stoked Indian nationalism with his proposed partition of Bengal in 1905, had yet again misjudged the mood of the natives. The agreement with the British was widely denounced by Iranians; pro-British members of the Iranian parliament were physically attacked. Facing widespread opposition, Curzon grew more obdurate. 'These people have got to be taught', he wrote, 'at whatever cost to them that they cannot get on without us. I don't at all mind their noses being rubbed in the dust.'[31] Curzon's tactics did not work. Iranian anger finally sank the Anglo-Persian agreement in 1920; it also inaugurated an enduringly hostile perception of Britain in Iran. (In 1978, the shah of Iran thought he had damned Ayatollah Khomeini permanently by calling him a British agent in a newspaper article. The result was the first mass protests against him and his rule and the eventual collapse of his dynasty.)

The ways in which the year 1919 changed the world were manifold. In Indonesia, the nationalist group Sarekat Islam, which was founded after the Russo-Japanese War but had remained a toothless entity, began to transform itself into a mass-membership party, demanding complete independence from the Dutch. Ho Chi Minh found a sympathetic audience among the French Communists, and he officially joined the Communist Party in 1921. 'It was patriotism, not Communism,' Ho later recalled, 'which had prompted me to believe in Lenin.'[32]

In India, where nearly 10 million Indians died in the global influenza epidemic of 1918–19, the British reneged on their promise of self-rule and resumed the repressive policies introduced during wartime. But the massacre by troops of 400 demonstrators in Amritsar in April 1919 accelerated the transformation of the Indian National Congress from a gentlemen's debating club into a mass-based political party and the emergence of Gandhi as its leader. As Tagore wrote to the viceroy of India when he returned his knighthood in protest against the killings: 'Considering that such treatment has been meted out to a population disarmed and resourceless, by a power which has the most terribly efficient organization for destruction of human lives, we must strongly assert that it can claim no political expediency, far less moral justification.'[33] Tagore would later write in the *Manchester Guardian* of how Asians like himself who 'believed with all our simple faith that even if we rebelled against foreign rule we should have the sympathy of the West', were nursing a delusion.[34]

The Wilsonian moment, the twenty-nine-year-old Jawaharlal Nehru wrote, 'has passed and for ourselves it is again the distant hope that must inspire us, not the immediate breathless looking for the deliverance'.[35] The Wilsonian moment did not pass without bringing more cruel disappointment to the Ottoman Turks too. 'It is not Islam that shuns the Europeans,' al-Afghani's protégé Rashid Rida had written as European pressures on Muslim countries multiplied before the First World War, 'but the Europeans who force Islam to give them a wide berth. Harmony between them is not an impossibility, but the way to reach it requires the exercise of a large mind.'[36] In the event, a large mind was not forthcoming from Western leaders, and especially not from Lloyd George, who thought the Turks were 'a human cancer, a creeping agony in the flesh of the lands which they misgoverned, rotting every fibre of life', and who felt that the West had the right to administer victor's justice to the Ottomans.[37]

The Allied powers approved Greece's spurious claim to Western Anatolia on the grounds that Turkish Muslims were not fit and proper people to rule multi-ethnic and multi-religious societies. Then in 1920, British and French troops occupied Istanbul in a bid to forestall the Turkish national movement for independence. The humiliation spurred hatred and distrust for Western powers across the Muslim world. Pan-Islamism briefly revived; even Mustafa Kemal, soon to be known as the hard-line secularist Atatürk, organized a pan-Islamic conference in Ankara and solicited the support of Ahmad al-Sharif al-Sanusi, then famous as a heroic Muslim fighter against Italian colonialists in Libya. If America, the journal *Izmir'e Dogru* claimed, was 'keeping quiet in the face of this horrendous event, then the only solution for the Turks is to ask for help from the Muslim world with all its powers and capacity'.[38] In 1923, Ahmed Riza, a long-standing Ottoman exile in Paris, authored a famous tract, *La Faillite morale de la politique occidentale en Orient*, arguing that anti-Westernism in the Muslim world was largely created by Western policies towards it.

Some of the non-Ottoman Muslims most outraged by the shabby treatment of Ottoman Turkey were in India, where they would soon join forces with Gandhi in the Khilafat campaign – an attempt to coerce Britain into a more lenient attitude towards Turkey. As it turned out, the Turks needed such assistance only up to a point.

Miraculously, Mustafa Kemal, the hero of Ottoman battles against Italy, emerged out of the shambles of the First World War to win back Anatolian territories lost to the Greeks and expel all other foreign troops from Turkish soil. In 1923, a peace treaty with Western powers defined the boundaries of the new Turkish nation-state; it also cancelled all the privileges enjoyed by the West in the country. Hailed as the 'sword of Islam' in India, Atatürk showed that Wilsonian rights of self-determination or justice in the international system would not be something that Western powers could be persuaded to concede; they had to be fought for and preserved with military force. For the West, Mustafa Kemal told an interviewer in 1923, was 'an entity that, seeing us as an inferior society, has exerted its best efforts to encompass our destruction'.[39] Moreover, mass religious and political ideologies like pan-Islamism could be an effective means to the ends of true sovereignty and freedom from foreign interference – Mustafa Kemal used the rhetoric of communism as deftly as that of Islam when it suited his nationalist objectives. It is hard to exaggerate the impact of Atatürk's success on opinion across Asia – the greatest victory of the East since the Battle of Tsushima. 'The truth', Muhammad Iqbal wrote, 'is that among the Muslim nations of today, Turkey alone has shaken off its dogmatic slumber, and attained to self-consciousness.'[40]

In China this lesson would soon be learnt by young communists. The twenty-year-old poet Qu Qiubai, a student of Buddhism who later became a crucial contact in Moscow for the fledgling Chinese Communist Party (CCP), was not alone in feeling 'the sharp pain of imperialistic oppression', which liberated him from the illusions of 'impractical democratic reforms'.[41] Certainly, the post-1919 sense of betrayal was felt most acutely among Asians by millions of Chinese who, unlike the Indians, the Ottomans, the Egyptians and the Koreans, were adequately represented at the conference and felt entitled to a sympathetic hearing by virtue of their contribution to the Allied effort. After all, hundreds of thousands of Chinese workers had stepped into the positions vacated by dead and wounded European soldiers during the war. Liang Qichao had argued for China's entry into the war precisely to guarantee favourable treatment of it by the Allies.

The Chinese delegation argued eloquently that Shandong was wholly Chinese, and had been taken by Germany by force; it was the birthplace of Confucius and the 'cradle' of Chinese civilization. President Wilson was personally sympathetic to Chinese claims on Japanese-occupied Shandong, but he could not persuade Lloyd George and Clemenceau to rescind their wartime promises to Japan that it could hold on to the colony. Besides, both Britain and France had their own interests in China, obtained through force, to maintain. By selling munitions to the Allies and expanding its economic reach into Asian markets, Japan had emerged from the war as much of a great power in the Pacific as the United States was in the Atlantic. Its appeal for racial equality had already received a snub and Wilson, who wanted Japan to join the League of Nations, could not risk annoying the country further.

The blatant cynicism enraged even the American senator William Borah, who asserted that the failure to return Shandong to China would 'dishonor and degrade any people', and mocked Woodrow Wilson's pious hopes for a post-imperial world order: 'Naked, hideous and revolting, it looms up before us as a monster from the cruel and shameless world which all had hoped and prayed was forever behind us.'[42] From Paris Liang Qichao informed his Chinese readers about China's defeat over Shandong. 'Japan,' he reported, 'had left no stone unturned.'[43] But he also blamed the Chinese delegation, and cautioned that the principle 'might is right' 'hold[s] sway today as ever' and that weak nations who take literally such 'catch-phrases of the strong' as 'justice and humanity' will be 'quickly disillusioned'. 'The only one she [China] could count upon is herself,' he concluded, 'and her own undefeatable spirit and courage.'[44]

So it would be. News of China's failure in May 1919 brought enraged students out on the streets of Beijing, denouncing the American president as a liar. Demonstrations and strikes erupted across China, an explosion of intellectual and political energy that, later described as the May Fourth Movement, reverberated through the following decades.

The May Fourth Movement began with a single incident: a demonstration by some 3,000 students on 4 May 1919 at Beijing's Gate of Heavenly Peace, which overlooks Tiananmen Square. Holding flags with slogans in English and French as well as Chinese, the students demanded that the Chinese government reject any treaty that failed to recognize China's sovereignty over Shandong. The demonstrators turned restless as they passed through the Legation Quarter. Some assaulted the nearby house of a Chinese minister perceived as pro-Japanese, and, though the minister escaped narrowly, the Chinese ambassador to Japan was badly beaten.

The students were arrested, sparking more demonstrations and strikes in their support across Chinese cities, most notably in Shanghai, the intellectual and political centre for young Chinese. In June, workers and merchants joined the protests, initiating a successful series of anti-Japanese boycotts. Even in remote Singapore, the Chinese community erupted into demonstrations and riots, abruptly revealing the strength of anti-colonial sentiment in the city. Later that month, the new alliance of students, workers and merchants seemed to have won when the Chinese delegation to the Paris conference, overturning instructions from its superiors in Beijing, refused to endorse the Versailles Treaty.

Nothing much seemed to change. Japan, targeted by massive Chinese boycotts and protests, did not give up Shandong until 1923. Warlordism in China was to get worse. Still, the political significance of the May Fourth Movement was immense. It mobilized a new generation which spoke a completely different language from that of its predecessors. In contrast to Liang Qichao and Kang Youwei, this generation was educated in schools and universities following a Western-style curriculum. It felt much less need to carry the burden of tradition; it spoke to a broader constituency of newly educated Chinese. Nearly three decades after the first efforts of elite reformists around Kang

Youwei, China now plunged into mass politics. The initiative lay with the 'people', rather than with the literati, officials, warlords or professional politicians.

Still hopelessly aspiring to restore the monarchy with Confucian underpinnings, Kang Youwei nevertheless admitted that if any 'real public opinion or real people's rights have been seen in China in the eight years', it was due to the 'students' actions'.[45] The Chinese worker-students who had gone to France during the war had not been as unlucky as Vietnamese and Indian soldiers. Still, they returned to China radicalized by their harsh exposure to Europe. Deng Xiaoping later recalled the 'sufferings of life and the humiliations brought upon [us] by . . . the running dogs of capitalists'.[46]

> Upon arrival in France, I learned from those students studying on a work-study program who had come to France earlier that two years after World War I, labor was no longer as badly needed as in the wartime . . . and it was hard to find jobs. Since wages were low, it was impossible to support study through work. Our later experiences proved that one could hardly live on the wages, let alone go to school for study. Thus, all those dreams of 'saving the country by industrial development,' 'learning some skills,' etc., came to nothing.[47]

There was more politicization to come. Unlike the wheeler-dealer politicians and the warlords, the new activists were to be motivated by long-term causes and organized by modern political groups, whether the Nationalists or the Communists. As Mao later put it, the 'whole of the Chinese revolutionary movement found its origin in the action of young students and intellectuals who had been awakened'.[48]

Liang's telegrams from Paris to China had kept a large public at home informed of the goings-on at the conference. He also amplified its growing sense of betrayal. Writing in the *Manchester Guardian* about the humiliation of China, Liang said, 'No well-informed man can have any doubt that it will profoundly modify the history of the Asiatic continent, if not the whole world.'[49] 'China's only crime' had been 'her weakness and her belief in international justice after the war. If, driven to desperation she attempts something hopeless, those who have helped to decide her fate cannot escape a part of the responsibility.'[50]

Little did Liang know that he was describing the onset of a hard-line political ideology in China. In July 1919, Russian revolutionaries, sensing an opportunity in the Western betrayal, unilaterally renounced their country's unequal treaties with China, declaring that

> if the Chinese nation desires to become free like the Russian people, and to escape the destiny prescribed for it at Versailles in order to transform it into a second Korea or a second India, it should understand that its only allies and brothers in the struggle for liberty are the Russian worker and peasant and the Red Army of Russia.[51]

In less than two years, the Chinese Communist Party would be formed in Shanghai, gathering disaffected young radicals and giving them a clear cause and a set of ideas free of the baggage of the past. Mao Zedong was among the young Chinese who stumbled out of the events of 1919 into an absolute scepticism of Western motives and policies and a broader awareness of the political possibilities available to subjugated peoples. About to formally commit himself to communism in 1919, Mao wrote:

> I venture to make a singular assertion: one day, the reform of the Chinese people will be more profound than that of any other people, and the society of the Chinese people will be more radiant than that of any other people. The great union of the Chinese people will be achieved earlier than that of any other people. Gentlemen! Gentlemen! We must all exert ourselves! We must all advance with the utmost strength! Our golden age, our age of glory and splendor, lies before us![52]

The discrediting of President Wilson, Nehru wrote, had raised 'the spectre of communism' over Asia. Like Ho Chi Minh, Mao was finding that only communism could help bring true sovereignty to China. He wrote to his friends in France to say he was through with all other ideas and was devoting himself to the 'Russian Revolution'. The idea of revolution re-emerged in China after the failure of 1911, this time with a sharper target – Western imperialism – in sight. And this idea of revolution now had an essential international dimension.

Asians imbued with ideas of self-government and self-determination had already developed close links with similarly motivated activists elsewhere. In the years following the First World War, transnational movements and co-operation between different nationalist groups would flourish in a world increasingly seen as interdependent; where, as the French poet and essayist Paul Valéry wrote, 'there are no more questions that can be settled by being settled at one point'.[53] Pan-Islamism would connect the Dutch East Indies to North Africa as agents of the Soviet-established Comintern began to assist 'bourgeois' Chinese nationalists as well as communists in China, India, Iran and Turkey. Berlin (where the office of the Comintern was based) attracted thousands of anti-colonial activists from all over the world, including the first leaders of Asian communism: Tan Malaka from the Dutch East Indies and India's M. N. Roy. In 1920, Indonesia's influential communist party – Perserikatan Kommunist di India (PKI) – was established under the auspices of the Comintern; the next year its founders travelled to Shanghai to witness the official birth of the Chinese Communist Party, and moved on to Moscow for the First Congress of the Workers of the East. After 1925, Shanghai and Canton would become the Asian hubs of this transnational network; Ho Chi Minh would publish articles by Rashid Rida in his magazine *Le Paria* and travel to Moscow to meet with Russian, Chinese and Indian revolutionaries.

THE DECLINE OF THE WEST?

Liang Qichao himself was starting on another intellectual journey in 1919, back to his Confucian past; there would be no more dramatic detours until his death in 1929. Making Paris his base, Liang journeyed all over Western Europe, later publishing his impressions and reflections in a book titled *Impressions of Travels in Europe*. Melancholy and foreboding tinged everything as his trip progressed. The war, he would later write presciently, 'is not yet the whole story of a new world history. It is but a mediating passage that connects the past and the future.'[54] In cold, fogbound London, where he attended a garden party at Buckingham Palace, the sun was 'like blood'.[55] The whole continent cowered 'beneath the leaden skies of autumn'.[56] In Rheims, he saw the ruins of the great Gothic cathedral, bombed three times and half-destroyed by German artillery. In the Belgian town of Louvain, German troops had slaughtered hundreds of civilians and destroyed its famous university library.

Liang was aware of the history of gratuitous Western vandalism in his own country and other parts of Asia. He knew that during the Boer War the British had brought the term 'concentration camp' into common parlance. But such atrocities had never seemed, as they did now, a prelude to barbarities on the European mainland. The question occurred to Liang, and to many other Asian intellectuals, whether, as Tagore put it, 'the poison that civilized Europe had pushed down the gullet of such a great country like China has severely impaired its own forever', and whether 'the torch of European civilization was not meant for showing light, but to set fire'.[57]

Five years before the war erupted, Aurobindo Ghose claimed that the civilization of 'vaunting, aggressive, dominant Europe' was under 'a sentence of death', awaiting 'annihilation'.[58] 'The scientific, rationalistic, industrial, pseudo-democratic civilisation of the West,' he was now convinced, 'is now in process of dissolution.'[59] Muhammad Iqbal, who had spent three rewarding years as a student in Europe in the first decade of the twentieth century, now wrote of it in the satirical tradition of Illahabadi:

> The West develops wonderful new skills
> In this as in so many other fields
> Its submarines are crocodiles
> Its bombers rain destruction from the skies
> Its gasses so obscure the sky
> They blind the sun's world-seeing eye.
> Dispatch this old fool to the West
> To learn the art of killing fast – and best.[60]

On his previous trips to the West Liang, like Tagore and Iqbal, had been a qualified admirer. During this longest sojourn there, he began to develop grave doubts about the civilization that had so blithely thrown away the fruits of progress and rationalism and sunk into barbarism. The 'materialist' West had managed to subdue nature through science and technology and created a Darwinian universe of conflict between individuals, classes and nations. But to what effect? Its materialistic people, constantly desiring ever-new things and constantly being frustrated, were worn out by war, were afflicted with insecurity, and were as far from happiness as ever.

Having embraced Social Darwinism in his youth, Liang now

rejected it violently, describing the 'evil consequences' – the worship of money and power, the rise of militarism and imperialism – of its application to the 'study of human society': 'The great European war', he wrote, 'nearly wiped out human civilization; although its causes were very many, it must be said that the Darwinian theory had a very great influence.'[61]

Liang was alert to the new post-war intellectual mood on the continent, which was one of severe self-questioning and scepticism about the great progress vaunted in the previous century. Europe suddenly appeared mortal to its greatest thinkers and artists. The works of Thomas Mann, T. S. Eliot, Hermann Broch and Robert Musil expressed a suspicion that Europe's nineteenth-century dynamism had turned malign and uncontrollable, a period of hectic global change suddenly unleashing a war no one knew how to end. Liberal democracy, long tainted in the East by association with Western imperialism, now looked feeble within the West itself, compromised by the rapacity and selfishness of ruling elites. Science appeared to have been complicit in the uncontrollable and mindless slaughter of the First World War, which mocked every notion of rationality and utilitarianism. The novels of Hermann Hesse seemed to say that attachment to science and technology was another aspect of the overly materialistic and soul-destroying worldview that Europe had evolved.

As Liang wrote, 'the European people have had a big dream about the omnipotence of science. Now they are talking about its bankruptcy. This is then a great turning point in the change of modern thought.'[62] This was also the beginning of the profoundest self-appraisal Liang had undertaken so far. It was to bring him steadily back to a more traditionalist point of view, for after the disaster of the Great War, Confucius and Mencius, with their stress on a moral order, no longer seemed so inadequate before their Western peers. And the science that radicals of the New Culture movement advocated was no longer the omnipotent solution to problems of social welfare. Liang poured scorn over their naïve hopes and uncritical admiration for the West:

> Those who praised the omnipotence of science had hoped previously that, as soon as science succeeded, the golden age would appear forthwith. Now science is successful indeed; material progress in the West in the last

one hundred years had greatly surpassed the achievements of the three thousand years prior to this period. Yet we human beings have not secured happiness; on the contrary, science gives us catastrophes. We are like travellers losing their way in the desert. They see a big black shadow ahead and desperately run to it, thinking that it may lead them somewhere. But after running a long way, they no longer see the shadow and fall into the slough of despond. What is that shadow? It is this 'Mr. Science'.[63]

There was wisdom yet in the old learning, especially in the Confucian ideal of *ren*, which taught harmony and compromise and was superior to Western competitiveness. After all:

Material life is merely a means for the maintenance of spiritual life; it should never be taken as a substitute for the object which it serves ... In European nations today, the tendency is to regard life solely as material development with the result that, no matter how plausible the contrivances, the malady only becomes worse ... Our problem is, under the conditions of this unprecedented scientific progress, how can the Confucian ideal of equilibrium be applied so that every man may live a balanced life.[64]

As Liang asserted in his new defensive mood, 'of the methods of relieving spiritual famine, I recognize the Eastern – Chinese and Indian – to be, in comparison, the best. Eastern learning has spirit as its departure; Western learning has matter as its point of departure.'[65] The Westerners were doomed to be slaves of the body; the greatest philosophy of the East – Buddhism – taught release. Indeed, in Liang's view, the East had something to offer to the West: 'On the far shore of this great ocean millions of people are bewailing the bankruptcy of material civilization and crying out most piteously for help, waiting for us to come to their salvation.'[66] Liang may have identified the beginning, in the post-1918 period, of a Western obsession with poorly understood Eastern philosophies and religions. 'The European's current fondness for the study of Lao Tse,' he claimed, 'is in reaction to social Darwinism.'[67]

'European imperialism, which does not disdain to raise the absurd cry of the Yellow Peril,' Kakuzo Okakura had written in 1906, 'fails to realize that Asia may also awaken to the cruel sense of the White Disaster.'[68] In the wake of the First World War and the Paris Peace Conference, many thinkers and activists in the East began to reconsider their earlier captivation with Western political ideals. Modernization still seemed absolutely imperative, but it did not seem the same as Westernization, or to demand a comprehensive rejection of tradition or an equally complete imitation of the West. Freshly minted ideologies like revolutionary communism and Islamic fundamentalism, which promised to sweep away the debris of the past and initiate a fresh beginning, began to look attractive. And, most fatefully, liberal democracy did not seem necessary to national self-strengthening.

Among others, Liang's old mentor Yan Fu, the promoter of liberal individualism, began to think that the struggle for national wealth and power had profound moral consequences too. 'As I have grown older ... I have come to feel that Western progress during the last three hundred years has only led to selfishness, slaughter, corruption and shamelessness.'[69] Putting the learning of the past in the service of China's nascent modernity, the neo-traditionalists were encouraged by such disillusioned Western philosophers as Bertrand Russell, who, after a wildly successful lecture tour of China in the post May-Fourth era, asserted: 'The distinctive merit of our civilization, I should say, is the scientific method; the distinctive merit of the Chinese is a just conception of life.'[70] Russell was appalled by both Soviet communism and Europe's destructive war. Beguiled by traditional China, he claimed that 'those who value wisdom or beauty, or even the simple enjoyment of life, will find more of these things in China than in the distraught and turbulent West'.[71]

Even Sun Yat-sen, disenchanted by lack of support from the West, had begun to speak out against Western materialism and economic imperialism, upholding Chinese tradition as a basis for nationalism. Reformulating the Three People's principles, the basic text of the Nationalists, in Japan in 1924, Sun deplored the young men 'wholly intoxicated' by the New Culture, and insisted on the 'traditional virtues': 'loyalty and filial piety, then humanity and love, faithfulness and duty, harmony and peace'.[72] Upholding the 'Kingly Way' of the East, Sun denounced the Western civilization of 'scientific materialism':

Such a civilization, when applied to society, will mean the cult of force, with aeroplanes, bombs, and cannons as its outstanding features ... Therefore, European civilization is nothing but the rule of Might. The rule of Might has always been looked down upon by the Orient. There is another kind of civilization superior to the rule of Might. The fundamental characteristics of this civilization are benevolence, justice and morality: This civilization makes people respect, not fear, it. Such a civilization is, in the language of the Ancients, the rule of Right or the Kingly Way. One may say, therefore, that Oriental civilization is one of the rules of Right. Since the development of European materialistic civilization and the cult of Might, the morality of the world has been on the decline. Even in Asia, morality in several countries has degenerated.[73]

Liang Shuming (1893–1988), a scholar educated at Western-style schools and a specialist on Indian philosophy, published *Eastern and Western Cultures and their Philosophies* (1921) which dissected the material civilization of the West as severely as Liang Qichao had, upholding Buddhism and then Confucianism. According to Liang Shuming, the West had achieved economic growth by successfully conquering nature, but it had also cut itself off from a wider conception of humanity that Confucianism still vouchsafed. It was essential that Westerners embrace a social ethic and a higher notion of spirituality. Here, China, despite its material backwardness, could still offer a great deal to the world. As he put it, 'the fundamental spirit of Chinese culture is the harmony and moderation of ideas and desires'.[74]

Liang Shuming's book became very popular, inviting the scorn of the radical writers. Lu Xun may have been responding to it in his short story 'Kong Yiji', in which Kong (Confucius's surname), a failed scholar, petty thief and scrounger, considers himself to be a civilized gentleman. In Lu Xun's more famous 'The True Story of Ah Q', the eponymous character, another no-hoper, regards every beating he receives as a personal spiritual triumph. Undeterred by such mockery, Liang Shuming went on to set up a utopian rural community along Confucian lines in Shandong, where in 1937 he met and exchanged ideas with Mao Zedong.

Another thinker who sided with Liang Qichao's critique of modern civilization was Zhang Junmai (1886–1969). Zhang had accompanied

Liang to Europe in 1919, and stayed on to study at Jena University in Germany. He returned to China in 1923 to give a stern lecture at Tsinghua against the blind belief in science. As Zhang saw it, science could not determine the rules for a moral or just life which Confucius had made his primary task.

A furious debate erupted between Liang Qichao and like-minded intellectuals and the New Culture radicals who were already convinced that Marxism was the answer to both the crisis of the West and the disorder of China. Like Liang, the more overtly Confucian and Buddhist thinkers remained faithful to the imperative of China's survival in the modern world, and tried to make their quasi-religious ideals useful to progressives and conservatives alike. For instance, the reformist monk Tanxu (1890–1947) tried to give to Chinese Buddhism a this-worldly orientation by making monasteries, schools and lay societies sensitive to the poor and uneducated in China.

But this was not enough for the radicals of the New Culture. The debate made it clear that no Chinese thinker could any more conceive of a domestic order, in the way Kang Youwei could in 1895, without conceiving of China in a global order, and without entering very large and fraught debates about past and present ideologies offering salvation to humanity.

Writing on behalf of the New Culture, the Columbia-educated Hu Shi, a disciple of the educationist John Dewey and one of the more liberal of the 'total Westernizers', mocked as nonsense the notion that a weak and passive China, which was in thrall to its physical and political environment, could ever satisfy the spiritual cravings of its people. Chen Duxiu, secretary-general of the newly founded Chinese Communist Party, was equally contemptuous. But the science v. metaphysics controversy, which was part of a larger uncertainty about the place of China in the world, was only the prelude to the storm provoked when on 12 April 1924 Rabindranath Tagore arrived in Shanghai for a lecture tour of China arranged by Liang Qichao and Zhang Junmai. Tagore's journey to both China and Japan would presage, too, other, more violent storms yet to come – those that would for ever alter the map of Asia.

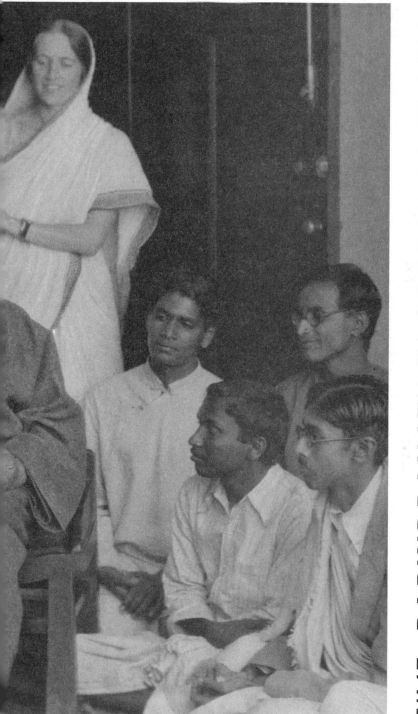

FIVE: RABINDRANATH TAGORE IN EAST ASIA, THE MAN FROM THE LOST COUNTRY

Our old brother [India], 'affectionate and missing' for more than a thousand years is now coming to call on his little brother [China]. We, the two brothers, have both gone through so many miseries that our hair has gone grey and when we gaze at each other after drying our tears we still seem to be sleeping and dreaming. The sight of our old brother suddenly brings to our minds all the bitterness we have gone through for all these years.

Liang Qichao, welcoming Tagore to China in 1924

I read his [Tagore's] essay on the Soviet Union in which he described himself as 'I am an Indian under the British rule'; he knew himself well. Perhaps, if our poets and others had not made him a living fairy he would not have been so confused, and the [Chinese] youths would not have been so alienated. What bad luck now!

Lu Xun remembering Tagore's visit in 1933

For many Chinese in the late nineteenth and early twentieth centuries, India was the prototypical 'lost' country, one whose internal weakness, exploited by foreign invaders, had forced it into a state of subjugation that was morally and psychologically shameful, as well as politically and economically catastrophic. For ordinary Chinese, there were visible symbols of this Indian self-subjection in their own midst: Parsi businessmen from Bombay who acted as middlemen in the British opium trade with China; Indian soldiers who helped the British quell the Boxer Rising; and Sikh policemen in treaty ports like Shanghai, whom their British masters periodically unleashed on Chinese crowds. In 1904, a popular Tokyo-based Chinese journal *Jiangsu* published a short story describing a dreamlike journey into the future by a feckless Chinese literatus named Huang Shibiao (literally, 'Representative of Yellow Elites') and a mythical old man. Walking down the streets of Shanghai, they see a group of marching people led by a white man.

> Shibiao looked closely at these people, and they all had faces black as coal. They were wearing a piece of red cloth around their heads like a tall hat; around their waists, they wore a belt holding wood clubs. Shibiao asked the old man: are these Indians? The old man said, yes, the English use them as police . . . Shibiao asked, why do they not use an Indian as the chief of police? The old man answered: who ever heard of that! Indians are people of a lost country; they are no more than slaves.[1]

Later in this dreamlike sequence, Shibiao sees a yellow-skinned man in a red Sikh-style turban; he turns out to be Chinese. The dream then quickly turns into a nightmare as Shibiao notices that everyone on the streets is wearing red turbans and that English is being taught in schools from textbooks designed by Christian missionaries. The story ends with Shibiao feeling profoundly disturbed by this vision of China subjected to India's fate.

India, conquered and then mentally colonized, was also a cautionary tale for al-Afghani. But from the perspective of China, where despite its weaknesses a political-moral order based on Confucianism had endured, India seemed dangerously out of touch with its own cultural heritage. Indian philosophy and literature – which only Brahmans in possession of Sanskrit could read – had been a closed book to a majority of Indians; it was the European discovery, and translation into English and German, of Indian texts that introduced a new Western-educated generation of Indian intellectuals to their cultural heritage.

As the Chinese saw it, foreigners had ruled the country continuously since the Mughals established their empire in the sixteenth century; there was no native ruling class capable of unifying the country. The most progressive elements seemed to be members of the Hindu castes that had faithfully served the imperial Muslim court and then turned into officials of the British as the latter expanded their administrative structures across the subcontinent.

Rabindranath Tagore's family, connected to the British East India Company right from the settling of Calcutta in 1690, was a prominent beneficiary of the British economic and cultural reshaping of India. His grandfather was the first big local businessman of British India, and socialized with Queen Victoria and other notables on his trips to Europe; his elder brother was the first Indian to be admitted by the British into the Indian Civil Service (ICS).

Born in 1861, four years after the Indian Mutiny and the establishment of new Western-style universities in Calcutta, Madras and Bombay, Tagore was part of a new Indian intelligentsia – one that was exposed to a range of Western thought and was also influenced by the 'social reform' movements initiated by such men as Ram Mohun Roy (1774–1833), often called the 'father of modern India'. Roy founded the Brahmo Sabha, a reformist society aimed at purging Hinduism of such evils as widow-burning and bringing it closer to a monotheistic religion like Christianity. Tagore's father, Debendranath, adopted and then elaborated Roy's syncretism in the organization Brahmo Samaj.

Just as many of China's modern thinkers emerged from the regions near Canton and Shanghai, the parts of the country most exposed to the West, so the Bengalis of India's eastern coast came to be natural leaders of what was later called the 'Indian Renaissance'. Tagore himself grew up in a culturally confident and creative family, and was exposed early to European society and culture. This meant that he never partook of the strident anti-Westernism that began to overwhelm many of his Bengali compatriots in the latter half of the nineteenth century.

Writing as late as 1921, when the tide of Indian nationalism was rising fast, he protested that 'if, in the spirit of national vainglory, we shout from our house-tops that the West has produced nothing that has an infinite value for man, then we only create a serious cause of doubt about the worth of any product in the Eastern mind.'[2] He would later develop serious differences with Gandhi over what he saw as the xenophobic aspect of the anti-colonial movement. At the same time, Tagore could never be part of 'Young Bengal', a group of Western-educated Bengalis who sought to escape Asia and join Europe just as fervently as the Ottoman Tanzimatists and the Meiji intellectuals in Japan had. Committed to a larger vision of the divine in man, and the essential unity of mankind, Tagore became in fact one of the clearest observers and strongest critics of India's Europeanization.

In nineteenth-century India, movements dedicated to reforming Hinduism and restoring its lost glory had grown very rapidly, part of the same larger trend mentioned previously of religious-political assertion in Muslim, Buddhist and Confucian societies. The inspiration and rhetoric of these neo-Hindu movements might have seemed archaic but, though often born out of a sense of racial humiliation, they were largely inspired by the ideas of progress and development that British Utilitarians and Christian missionaries aggressively promoted in India. The social reformer Dayananda Saraswati (1824–83), for instance, exhorted Indians to return to the Vedas, which contained, according to him, all of modern science; and echoed British missionary denunciations of such 'Hindu superstitions' as idol-worship and the caste system.

This 'modernization' of Indian religion under semi-European auspices was to release new political and social movements across India, many of them militantly opposed to British rule and dedicated to recovering national dignity. One emblematic figure of this ambiguous Europeanization of Indian culture was Bankim Chandra Chatterji (1838–94), an official in the British government in Bengal, who moved in his lifetime from Young Bengal-style uncritical adoration of the West to being the first icon of Hindu nationalism.

Bengalis were 'drunk with the wine of European civilization', Aurobindo Ghose complained in 1908, no doubt thinking of his own upbringing in a fanatically Anglophile Bengali family.[3] Saddled with the middle name 'Ackroyd', and banished to English public schools in the 1880s, Aurobindo acquired his knowledge of Indian languages and literature from European Orientalist scholars, and returned home in the early 1890s a bitter critic of the British and their Bengali imitators. As he saw it, 'the movements of the nineteenth century in India were European movements' which

> adopted the machinery and motives of Europe, the appeal to the rights
> of humanity or the equality of social status and an impossible dead level
> which Nature has always refused to allow. Mingled with these false
> gospels was a strain of hatred and bitterness, which showed itself in the
> condemnation of Brahminical priestcraft, the hostility to Hinduism and
> the ignorant breaking away from the hallowed traditions of the past.[4]

Such was the Bengali infatuation with Europe, Aurobindo claimed, that India as a whole 'was in danger of losing its soul by an insensate surrender to the aberrations of European materialism'. But it was also Bengalis who in the second half of the nineteenth century articulated an overwhelmingly negative view of the materialistic West, even as they grudgingly admired and sought to emulate some of its practical skills. For Swami Vivekananda (1863–1902), the earliest and most famous of Indian spiritual leaders, Europeans were the children of Virochana, the great demon of Indian mythology, who believed that the human self was nothing but the material body and its grosser cravings. 'For this civilization,' Vivekananda wrote of the West, 'the sword was the means [for the attainment of given ends], heroism the aid, and enjoyment of life in this world and the next the only end.'[5]

Vivekananda, who visited Europe and America often in his short life, saw Western societies and politics as controlled by the rich and powerful, and quite akin in their class stratifications to the Indian caste system: 'Your rich people are Brahmans,' he told his English friends on his last visit to Britain, 'and your poor people are Sudras.'[6] For Bhudev Mukhopadhyay, perhaps the most comprehensive nineteenth-century Bengali critic of the West, the innate human capacity for love had stopped, in Europe, at the door of the nation-state – it was the end-point of Europe's history and its endless conflicts. This faculty of love had latched on to such strange objects as money and an excessive concern for property rights – an extreme individualism that relieved human beings of their usual obligations to society and combined with machinery and the quest for markets and monopolies to lead to endless wars and conquests and violence. What was most galling for Mukhopadhyay was that the European never seemed to experience any contradiction between his selfish needs and the demands of morality. 'Whatever is to their interest,' Mukhopadhyay wrote about Europeans, 'they find consistent with their sense of what is right at all times, failing to understand how their happiness cannot be the source of universal bliss.'[7]

Aurobindo Ghose, too, raged against the English middle class that, unlike previous ruling classes, cloaked their imperialism in noble proclamations and intentions. England, he claimed, had conquered Ireland using the old methods of 'cynical treachery' and 'ruthless massacre' and then ruled it with the principle 'might is right'. But in the age of democratic nationalism, imperialism needed deeper self-justifications:

> The idea that despotism of any kind was an offence against humanity, had crystallised into an instinctive feeling, and modern morality and sentiment revolted against the enslavement of nation by nation, of class by class or of man by man. Imperialism had to justify itself to this modern sentiment and could only do so by pretending to be a trustee of liberty, commissioned from on high to civilise the uncivilised and train the untrained until the time had come when the benevolent conqueror had done his work and could unselfishly retire. Such were the professions with which England justified her usurpation of the heritage of the Moghul and dazzled us into acquiescence in servitude by the splendour of her uprightness and generosity. Such was the pretence with which she veiled her annexation of Egypt. These Pharisaic pretensions were especially necessary to British Imperialism because in England the Puritanic middle class had risen to power and imparted to the English temperament a sanctimonious self-righteousness which refused to indulge in injustice and selfish spoliation except under a cloak of virtue, benevolence and unselfish altruism.[8]

For Aurobindo, Indians who believed European claims to such superior values as democracy and liberalism were deluding themselves.

For the British themselves considered such ideals 'unsuitable to a sub-ject nation where the despotic supremacy of the white man has to be maintained, as it was gained, at the cost of all principles and all mor-ality'. Infused with a fierce new pride in India by his Oriental education, Aurobindo steadily turned into a militant nationalist, convinced that 'there can be no European respect for Asiatics, no sympathy between them except the "sympathy" of the master for the slave, no peace except that which is won and maintained by the Asiatic sword'.[9]

Like Aurobindo, Tagore was greatly influenced by the Orientalist scholarship that endowed India with a classical past. And he absorbed some of the Bengali suspicion of the modern West. In 1881, early in his career, he proclaimed his political distance from his businessman grandfather, a crucial intermediary in the opium trade. But his own intellectual and spiritual journey from a conservative aristocratic background and Western-style education took him to a very different place from that of his Bengali compatriots.

His long sojourn in the Bengali countryside between 1891 and 1901 was crucial in this regard. Proximity to lives in Indian villages helped distinguish his worldview from that of the middle-class intel-lectuals in Calcutta. It unleashed a love of natural landscapes, a regard for the everyday, the domestic and the fragmentary, as well as an insight into the plight of the rural poor. He remained convinced for the rest of his life of the moral superiority of pre-industrial civilization over the mechanized modern one; he became certain, too, that India's self-regeneration had to begin in its villages.

In 1901, he founded an experimental school in rural south-western Bengal. Santiniketan, as it was called, would expand into an inter-national university, and train some of India's leading artists and thinkers (including the filmmaker Satyajit Ray and the economist Amartya Sen). That same year, in an essay titled 'Eastern and Western Civilization', Tagore first developed his thesis of a dichotomy between rural harmony and urban aggressiveness, village-centred society and the nation-state. The East prescribed modes of social harmony and spiritual liberation. On the other hand, the West, he argued, was dedi-cated to strengthening national sovereignty and political freedom. 'Scientific rather than human', it was

overrunning the whole world, like some prolific weed . . . It is carnivo-
rous and cannibalistic in its tendencies, it feeds upon the resources of
other peoples and tries to swallow their whole future . . . It is powerful
because it concentrates all its forces upon one purpose, like a millionaire acquiring money at the cost of his soul.[10]

The imperialist wars in South Africa and the suppression of the
Boxer Rising, both involving Indian soldiers, had confirmed Tagore's
scepticism. On 31 December 1900, he completed a poem titled 'Sunset
of the Century': 'The century's sun has set in blooded clouds. / There
rings in the carnival of violence / from weapon to weapon, the mad
music of death.'[11] Tagore concluded the poem by scorning such imperialist poets as Rudyard Kipling, who had exhorted America to take up
the white man's burden in the Philippines: 'Awakening fear, the poet-
mobs howl round / A chant of quarrelling curs on the burning-ground.'

From 1905 to 1908 Tagore was very attracted to the Swadeshi Movement, led by young Bengali firebrands who boycotted British goods and
aimed at economic self-sufficiency. It was after the widespread protests
against Lord Curzon's partition of Bengal in 1905 that he composed
the two songs that subsequently became the national anthems of India
and Bangladesh. Like most Asian intellectuals, Tagore rejoiced in
Japan's victory over Russia in 1905, taking his pupils at Santiniketan
on an impromptu victory parade. But already in 1902, three years
before that landmark event in the political awakening of Asia, he was
hoping it would steer clear of mindless imitation of the West:

The harder turns our conflict with the foreigner, the greater grows our
eagerness to understand and attain ourselves. We can see that this is not
our case alone. The conflict with Europe is waking up all civilized Asia.
Asia today is set to realizing herself consciously, and thence with vigour.
She has understood, know thyself – that is the road to freedom. In
imitating others is destruction.[12]

Tagore saw no reason for Asians to believe that the 'building up of
a nation on the European pattern is the only type of civilization and
the only goal of man'.[13] After a brief fascination with the Swadeshi
militants, he recoiled from the militant Indian nationalism inspired
by thinkers like Chatterji, especially the series of assassinations and

terrorist attacks by young Bengali nationalists in the first decade of the twentieth century. He explored the middle-class fascination with violent politics in such novels as *Gora* (1910) and *Ghare Baire* ('Home and the World', 1916). But from 1917 he conducted a systematic critique of nationalism in his essays and speeches. The nation-state, he told audiences in America that year, 'is a machinery of commerce and politics turn[ing] out neatly compressed bales of humanity'.[14] 'When this idea of the Nation, which has met with universal acceptance in the present day, tries to pass off the cult of selfishness as a moral duty ... it not only commits depredations but attacks the very vitals of humanity.'[15] Like Kang Youwei, he formulated a non-nationalist ideal of Asian cosmopolitanism early in his life, and never departed from it. 'India has never had a real sense of nationalism ... it is my conviction that my countrymen will truly gain their India by fighting against the education which teaches that a country is greater than the ideals of humanity.'[16]

Tagore wasn't the only Indian with serious apprehensions about the trajectory of modern European civilization and its over-eager followers in the East. Travelling from London to South Africa in November 1909, the forty-year-old Gandhi feverishly wrote, in nine days, a stirring anti-modern manifesto titled *Hind Swaraj* that summed up many prevailing intellectual arguments against the West, and also anticipated many others still to come. Like Tagore, with whom he had a long and mutually enriching friendship, Gandhi in 1909 was engaged in a polemical battle with his radical and revolutionary peers who saw salvation in the wholesale imitation of Western-style state and society. Many of these were Hindu nationalists, the ideological children of Bankim Chandra Chatterji and later part of a religious-cultural movement that derived inspiration from the Fascist parties of Italy and Germany, and which aimed to unite India through a monolithic Hindu nationalism derived from the joint British-Indian reinvention of Hinduism in the nineteenth century. Gandhi saw that these nationalists would merely replace one set of deluded rulers in India with another: 'English rule', he wrote in *Hind Swaraj*, 'without the Englishman.'

Gandhi's own ideas were rooted in a wide experience of a freshly globalized world. Born in 1869 in a backwater Indian town, he came of age on a continent pathetically subject to the West, intellectually as well as materially. Dignity, even survival, for many uprooted Asians seemed to lie in careful imitation of their Western conquerors. Gandhi, brought out of his semi-rural setting and given a Western-style education, initially attempted to become more English than the English. He studied law in London and, on his return to India in 1891, tried to set up first as a lawyer, then as a schoolteacher. But a series of racial humiliations during the following decade awakened him to his real position in the world.

Moving to South Africa in 1893 to work for an Indian trading firm, he was exposed to the dramatic transformation wrought by the tools of Western modernity: printing presses, steamships, railways and machine guns. In Africa and Asia, a large part of the world's population was being incorporated into, and made subject to the demands of, the international capitalist economy. Gandhi keenly registered the moral and psychological effects of this worldwide destruction of old ways and lives and the ascendancy of Western cultural, political and economic norms.

As Gandhi wrote later in *Satyagraha in South Africa*, 'the nations which do not increase their material wants are doomed to destruction. It is in pursuance of these principles that western nations have settled in South Africa and subdued the numerically overwhelmingly superior races of Africa.'[17] Lenin and Rosa Luxemburg implicated capitalism in imperialism; and Gandhi, too, believed that colonial economic policies, enabled by native Indians, were meant to benefit foreign investors, and actually impoverished the mass of India's population. But he went further, implicating the whole of modern civilization and its obsession with economic growth and political sovereignty (the latter inevitably achieved through violence).

Gandhi eagerly acknowledged the many benefits of Western modernity, such as civil liberties, the liberation of women and the rule of law. Yet he saw these as inadequate without a broader conception of spiritual freedom and social harmony. He was of course not alone. By the early twentieth century, modern Chinese and Muslim intellectuals like al-Afghani and Liang Qichao were also turning away from Europe's universalist ideals of the Enlightenment – which they saw as a moral cover for unjust racial hierarchies – to seek strength and dignity in a revamped Islam and Confucianism. The same year that Gandhi wrote *Hind Swaraj*, Aurobindo Ghose sardonically wondered:

> Is this then the end of the long march of human civilisation, his spiritual suicide, this quiet petrifaction of the soul into matter? Was the successful business-man that grand culmination of manhood toward which evolution was striving? After all, if the scientific view is correct, why not? An evolution that started with the protoplasm and flowered in the orang-utan and the chimpanzee, may well rest satisfied with having created hat, coat and trousers, the British Aristocrat, the American capitalist and the Parisian Apache. For these, I believe, are the chief triumphs of the European enlightenment to which we bow our heads.[18]

However, the terms of Gandhi's critique, as set out in *Hind Swaraj*, were remarkably original. He claimed that modern civilization had introduced a whole new and deeply ominous conception of life, overturning all previous notions of politics, religion, ethics, science and economics. According to him, the Industrial Revolution, by turning human labour into a source of power, profit and capital, had made economic prosperity the central goal of politics, enthroning machinery over men and relegating religion and ethics to irrelevance. As Gandhi saw it, Western political philosophy obediently validated the world of industrial capitalism. If liberalism vindicated the preoccupation with economic growth at home, liberal imperialism abroad made British rule over India appear beneficial for Indians – a view many Indians themselves subscribed to. Europeans who saw civilization as their unique possession denigrated the traditional virtues of Indians – simplicity, patience, otherworldliness – as backwardness.

Gandhi never ceased trying to overturn these prejudices of Western modernity. Early in his political career, he began wearing the minimal garb of an Indian peasant and rejected all outward signs of being a modern intellectual or politician. True civilization, he insisted, was about moral self-knowledge and spiritual strength rather than bodily well-being, material comforts, or great art and architecture. He upheld the self-sufficient rural community over the heavily armed and centralized nation-state, cottage industries over big factories, and manual labour over machines. He also encouraged his political activists, *satyagrahis*, to feel empathy for their political opponents and to abjure violence against the British. For, whatever their claims to civilization, the British, too, were victims of the immemorial forces of human greed and violence that had received an unprecedented moral sanction in the political, scientific and economic systems of the modern world. *Satyagraha* might awaken in them, too, an awareness of the profound evil of industrial civilization.

Like Tagore, Gandhi opposed violence and rejected nationalism and its embodiment, the bureaucratic, institutionalized, militarized state – it was what in 1948 angered and provoked his assassin, a Hindu nationalist agitating for an aggressively armed, independent India. Both made national regeneration incumbent upon individual regeneration. Until it was cut short by Tagore's death in 1941, the two pursued a rich conversation covering their disagreements as well as shared preoccupations. But in 1909 when he wrote *Hind Swaraj*, Gandhi was still an unknown figure outside South Africa; his book did not attract attention until a decade later. Tagore was by far the more famous and influential Indian.

Soon after receiving the Nobel Prize for Literature in 1913, Tagore had become an international literary celebrity and spokesperson for the East. This was a unique privilege for him in many ways in a world where few, if any, voices from Asia were heard. As Lu Xun pointed out in 1927, 'Let us see which are the mute nations. Can we hear the voice of Egypt? Can we hear the voice of Annam and Korea? Except Tagore what other voice of India can we hear?'[19] Tagore's long white beard and intense gaze made him appear like some kind of prophet from the East. Receiving the Nobel Prize for Literature in 1968, the Japanese novelist Yasunari Kawabata recalled

> the features and appearance of this sage-like poet, with his long bushy hair, long moustache and beard, standing tall in loose-flowing Indian garments, and with deep, piercing eyes. His white hair flowed softly down both sides of his forehead; the tufts of hair under the temples also were like two beards and linking up with the hair on his cheeks, continued into his beard, so that he gave an impression, to the boy that I was then, of some ancient Oriental wizard.[20]

Packed lecture-halls awaited Tagore around the world, from Japan to Argentina. President Herbert Hoover received him at the White

House when he visited the United States in 1930, and the *New York Times* ran twenty-one reports on the Indian poet, including two interviews. This enthusiasm seems especially remarkable given the sort of prophecy from the East that Tagore would deliver to his Western hosts: that their modern civilization, built upon the cult of money and power, was inherently destructive and needed to be tempered by the spiritual wisdom of the East. But when, travelling in the East, he expressed his doubts about Western civilization and exhorted Asians not to abandon their traditional culture, he ran into fierce opposition.

By 1916 when he first arrived in Japan, Tagore had long been an admirer of the country. Japan's victory over Russia in 1905 had prompted him to write a verse contrasting the transmission of Buddhism from India to Japan with the need to learn new techniques from the Japanese:

> Wearing saffron robes, the Masters of religion [dharma]
> Went to your country to teach.
> Today we come to your door as disciples,
> To learn the teachings of action [karma].[21]

On his first visit, Tagore seemed assured of an audience for his advocacy of inter-Asian co-operation. Many important Japanese nationalists had dabbled in pan-Asianism. Kakuzo Okakura (1862–1913), one of Japan's leading nationalist intellectuals, was already known to Tagore. He had begun his 1903 book, *The Ideals of the East*, with the resonant declaration that 'Asia is one. The Himalayas divide, only to accentuate, two mighty civilizations, the Chinese with its communism of Confucius, and the Indian with its individualism of the Vedas.' Okakura claimed that, 'Arab chivalry, Persian poetry, Chinese ethics and Indian thought, all speak of a single Asiatic peace, in which there grew up a common life, bearing in different regions different characteristic blossoms, but nowhere capable of a hard and fast dividing line.'[22]

Okakura had been alerted to Japan's cultural heritage by his American teacher Ernest Fenollosa, an art historian and philosopher who believed that it was Asia's destiny to spiritualize the modern West. Just as Western Oriental scholarship about India informed Tagore's views of Asia and the West, so did Fenollosa's Japanophilia suffuse Okakura's idealized notion of Asian unity. He had spent a year in India in 1901–2, staying for some of this time in the Tagore family's mansion in Calcutta, where he drafted *The Ideals of the East* and influenced a host of Indian artists. Tagore subsequently received a stream of Japanese visitors sent by Okakura at his rural retreat in Santiniketan; and Okakura himself revisited India in 1911 on his way to Boston, where he was now a curator at the Museum of Fine Arts. Okakura was to become a major influence on such varied figures as Frank Lloyd Wright, T. S. Eliot, Wallace Stevens, Ezra Pound and even Martin Heidegger. In Tagore, however, he found a fellow traveller, someone also prone to uphold Asia's oneness and investigate the moral claims of the West. 'The guilty conscience of the West', Okakura wrote, 'has often conjured up the spectre of a Yellow Peril, let the tranquil gaze of the East turn itself on the White Disaster.'[23] Tagore concurred, at least partly. Like Gandhi, both men proclaimed their Asianness by partly rejecting Western dress. Okakura dressed in a dhoti while visiting the Ajanta caves in India; Tagore was to wear a Taoist hat in China. Both writers also sought to establish a cultural basis for Asia as a whole, stressing old maritime links, arts, and such shared legacies as Buddhism in India, China and Japan.

Advocating the essential oneness of humanity, Tagore once compared the two journeys of Buddhism and opium to the East:

> When the Lord Buddha realised humanity in a grand synthesis of unity, his message went forth to China as a draught from the fountain of immortality. But when the modern empire-seeking merchant, moved by his greed, refused allegiance to this truth of unity, he had no qualms in sending to China the deadly opium poison.[24]

Again and again in his writings, Tagore returned to the metaphor of modern civilization as a machine: 'The sole fulfillment of a machine is in achievement of result, which in its pursuit of success despises moral compunctions as foolishly out of place.'[25] Japan, Tagore wrote, could further the 'experiments . . . by which the East will change the aspects of modern civilization, infusing life in it where it is a machine, substituting the human heart for cold expediency'.

A more militant kind of Indian had made Japan his home before Tagore's arrival in 1916. These Indians were part of the foreign communities that had flocked to Japan to learn the secrets of its modernization. Along with New York and London, Tokyo was part of an international network of 'India Houses', where activists and self-styled revolutionaries exiled from India gathered. An Indian Muslim, Maulavi Barkatullah (1854–1927), edited a magazine titled *The Indian Sociologist* from Tokyo. In 1910 he revived *The Islamic Fraternity*, the English monthly that Abdurreshid Ibrahim had set up, and which the Japanese, yielding to British requests, had closed down. Barkatullah turned it into an explicitly anti-British forum. He also wrote for the influential Japanese pan-Asianist thinker Ōkawa Shūmei, who had begun to outline a Japanese version of the Monroe Doctrine for Asia (in 1946 he would be indicted by the Tokyo War Crimes Tribunal as the main civilian ideologue of Japanese expansionism).

The revolutionary strain of Bengali nationalism was also well represented in Japan by Rash Behari Bose (1886–1945), another Indian associate of Ōkawa Shūmei. At the age of twenty-six, he threw a hand grenade at the then British viceroy as the latter ceremonially entered Delhi on the back of an elephant. He missed. Escaping India, he ended up in Japan in 1915, where he lived buoyed by the pan-Asianist sentiment and the financial assistance of many members of the Japanese elite until his death from natural causes in January 1945. When the hero of Indian revolutionaries, Lala Lajpat Rai, visited Japan in November 1915, Ōkawa and Bose organized a reception for him. Speaking on the occasion, Rai exhorted his hosts to work for the liberation of Asia. British pressure led to deportation orders being issued for Bose the next day, but the Indian nationalists and Ōkawa then successfully lobbied Toyama Mitsuru, the most influential of the pan-Asianists, to intervene on Bose's behalf. Ōkawa would write his first book on Indian nationalism after Tagore's visit to Japan, selectively quoting the latter to support his contention that it was Japan's 'mission to unite and lead Asia'. In 1917, he would also encourage the Bengali revolutionary Taraknath Das to write a book claiming that conflict between the white and yellow races was inevitable.

But Tagore, like Gandhi, had little time for militant nationalists, and he was alarmed in 1916 to see a country that was then in the midst of an extraordinary growth of national self-confidence and imperialist expansion, and preparing, too, for more battles ahead with both old enemies and new friends. The previous year, 1915, Japan had annexed Chinese territories in Shandong. In 1905 Japan had declared Korea a protectorate, and in 1910 had forced it to surrender its sovereignty. The United States had supported Japan's move then; Theodore Roosevelt was reported to have said, 'I should like to see Japan have Korea.'[26] But relations between Japan and the United States had been deteriorating since the 1890s, over the latter's big move into the Pacific and its occupation of Hawaii. And American treatment of Japanese immigrants enraged nationalist Japanese like Tokutomi Sohō.

Sohō also worried that the First World War, which he saw as an internecine struggle between Western European powers for global dominance, would bring trouble to Japan's neighbourhood, no matter who won. Japan had to move first in East Asia to forestall European and American influence there, he wrote, echoing Ōkuwa Shūmei's Asian Monroe Doctrine. Those pan-Asianists who were also ultranationalists were beginning to dream of an Asia liberated from its European masters and revitalized by Japan, and they saw Tagore as a likely collaborator in a pro-Japan freedom movement across Asia.

But Tagore was set to disappoint. He had developed some doubts about Japan's progress well before he left India. 'I am almost sure that Japan has her eyes on India,' he wrote to an English friend in June 1915. 'She is hungry – she is munching Korea, she has fastened her teeth upon China and it will be an evil day for India when Japan will have her opportunity.'[27] His mood soured throughout the long journey that took him, tracing the route of his opium-trading grandfather, via Rangoon, Penang and Singapore. The polluting chimneys and lights and noise of these port cities made him inveigh against the 'trade monster' which 'lacerates the world with its greed'.[28] In Hong Kong, he was appalled to see a Sikh beating up a Chinese worker.

Watching Chinese labourers diligently at work in the port city, he made a canny prophecy about the future balance of power in international relations: 'The nations which now own the world's resources fear the rise of China, and wish to postpone the day of that rise.'[29] But

Tagore seemed to derive no comfort from the prospect of any country rising in the manner prescribed by the modern West. 'The New Japan is only an imitation of the West,' he declared at his official reception in Tokyo, which included the Japanese prime minister among other dignitaries. This did not go down well with his audience, for whom Japan was a powerful nation and budding empire, and India a pitiable European colony.

Tagore had received most of his impressions of the country from Okakura, but Japan had changed rapidly in the period between 1900 and 1916. In such books as *The Awakening of Japan* (1904) and *The Book of Tea* (1906), Okakura himself had begun to advocate a more assertive Japanese identity. 'When will the West understand, or try to understand, the East?' he had asked exasperatedly in *The Book of Tea*:

> We Asiatics are often appalled by the curious web of facts and fancies which has been woven concerning us. We are pictured as living on the perfume of the lotus, if not on mice and cockroaches. It is either impotent fanaticism or else abject voluptuousness. Indian spirituality has been derided as ignorance, Chinese sobriety as stupidity, Japanese patriotism as the result of fatalism. It has been said that we are less sensible to pain and wounds on account of the callousness of our nervous organization![30]

Tagore agreed with Okakura on most counts. Nevertheless, the vogue for patriotism depressed him. Writing his lectures on nationalism in the West, which he planned to deliver in the United States, Tagore concluded:

> I have seen in Japan the voluntary submission of the whole people to the trimming of their minds and clipping of their freedoms by their governments ... The people accept this all-pervading mental slavery with cheerfulness and pride because of their nervous desire to turn themselves into a machine of power, called the Nation, and emulate other machines in their collective worldliness.[31]

In a long letter home, Tagore mentioned caustically how the Japanese who dismissed his exhortations as the 'poetry of a defeated people' were 'right': 'Japan had been taught in a modern school the lesson of how to become powerful. The schooling is done and she must enjoy the fruits of her lessons.'[32]

In China in 1924, torn apart by civil war and ravaged by warlords, Tagore's invoking of Asia's spiritual traditions was never likely to go down well. The May Fourth Movement had expanded since 1919. Returning from their studies in Berlin, Paris, London, New York and Moscow, young men introduced and discussed a range of ideas and theories. By general consensus, they rejected their country's Confucian traditions. As Chen Duxiu wrote, 'I would much rather see the past culture of our nation disappear than see our race die out now because of its unfitness for living in the world.'[33]

For the May Fourth generation, the egalitarian ideals of the French and Russian revolutions and the scientific spirit underlying Western industrial power were self-evidently superior to an ossified Chinese culture that exalted tradition over innovation and kept China backward and weak. They wished China to become a strong and assertive nation using Western methods, and they admired such visitors as Bertrand Russell and John Dewey, whose belief in science and democracy seemed to lead the way to China's redemption. In 1924, few of them were ready to listen to an apparently otherworldly poet from India hold forth on the problems of modern Western civilization and the virtues of old Asia.

In 1923, a debate erupted among Chinese intellectuals as soon as Tagore's visit was announced. Radicals such as the novelist Mao Dun, who had once translated Tagore, worried about his likely deleterious effect on Chinese youth. 'We are determined', he wrote, 'not to welcome the Tagore who loudly sings the praises of eastern civilization. Oppressed as we are by militarists from within the country and by the imperialists from without, this is no time for dreaming.'[34] Tagore's host, Liang Qichao, was already under attack from young radicals, who also kept up a barrage of insults against the romantic poet Xu Zhimo, Tagore's interpreter in China.

In Shanghai and Hangzhou Tagore spoke to large gatherings of students. As always he cut an impressive figure in his robes and long white beard. He attended garden parties and music concerts, often accompanied by Liang Qichao and Zhang Junmai. In Nanjing he met the reigning warlord and pleaded with him to cease fighting. The warlord served champagne to his guests, and assured Tagore he was fully in agreement with his message of peace. (A few months later, he launched an assault on the warlord of Zhejiang.)

Lecturing in Beijing, Tagore returned to his favourite theme:

> The West is becoming demoralized through being the exploiter, through tasting of the fruits of exploitation. We must fight with our faith in the moral and spiritual power of men. We of the East have never reverenced death-dealing generals, nor lie-dealing diplomats, but spiritual leaders. Through them we shall be saved, or not at all. Physical power is not the strongest in the end ... You are the most long lived race, because you have had centuries of wisdom nourished by your faith in goodness, not in mere strength.[35]

The Chinese radicals grew alarmed as Tagore praised Buddhism and Confucianism for nurturing a civilization 'in its social life upon faith in the soul'. The Communist Party and Chen Duxiu had already decided to campaign against Tagore through its various magazines. Chen worried that Chinese youth were vulnerable to Tagore's influence: 'We warn them not to let themselves be *Indianized*. Unless, that is, they want their coffins to lie one day in a land under the heel of a colonial power, as India is.'[36]

The propaganda campaign seems to have worked. At one meeting in Hankou, Tagore had been greeted with the slogans, 'Go back, slave from a lost country! We don't want philosophy, we want materialism!' The vociferous hecklers had to be physically restrained lest they assaulted him. But it was in Beijing, the centre of youthful Chinese radicalism, that Tagore faced organized hostility in the form of primed questioners and boos and heckles. At one of his meetings, where he attacked modern democracy itself, which he claimed benefited 'only plutocrats in various disguises', leaflets denouncing him were handed out.[37] 'We have had enough of the ancient Chinese civilization.' They went on to attack Tagore's hosts, Liang Qichao and Zhang Junmai, who used 'his talent to instill in Young China their conservative and reactionary tendencies'.[38] The communist poet Qu Quibai summed up the general tone of Tagore's reception in China when he wrote,

'Thank you, Mr. Tagore, but we have already had too many Confuciuses and Menciuses in China.'[39]

In retrospect, Tagore, angrily recoiling from the main intellectual and political trends in Japan and China, seems to have misunderstood their context. He may have been too influenced by the Indian model, in which the British were in charge of military and political affairs, and the Indians could devote themselves to spiritual leadership. From the perspective of the Chinese and the Japanese, who had to build their nations from scratch, a people who did not worry about their political subjugation and spoke instead of spiritual liberation were indeed very 'lost'.

At the same time, to see Tagore as an uncompromising foe of Western knowledge was to seriously misread his worldview. As late as 1921, he was writing disparagingly about Gandhi's freedom movement to a friend: 'Our present struggle to alienate our heart and mind from the West is an attempt at spiritual suicide.'[40] Nor was Tagore an apolitical mystic from a lost country. He was more than alert to the Chinese sense of shame and humiliation. Passing through Hong Kong on his way to Japan in 1916, he had deplored the 'religion of the slave' that made a Sikh assault a Chinese labourer. Speaking of Indian collaborators with British imperialists, he lamented that 'when the English went to snatch away Hong Kong from China, it was they who beat 'China ... they have taken upon [themselves] the responsibility of insulting China'.[41] He felt the pain of the destruction of the Summer Palace no less keenly than Chinese nationalists, remembering 'how the European imperialists had razed [it] to dust ... how they had torn to pieces, burned, devastated and looted the age-old art objects. Such things would never be created in the world again.'

He followed the stalemate between England and Ireland, remarking that the former 'is a python which refuses to disgorge this living creature which struggles to live its separate life'.[42] Received by dignitaries during his visit to Persia and Iraq in 1932, he was not indifferent to the new form of warfare being tried out on hapless villagers:

the men, women and children done to death there meet their fate by a decree from the stratosphere of British imperialism – which finds it easy to shower death because of its distance from its individual victims. So dim and insignificant do those unskilled in the modern arts of killing appear to those who glory in such skill![43]

Moreover, unlike the caricature of him among Chinese radicals, Tagore was ready, too, to appreciate new social and political experiments like the Russian Revolution. Years after Tagore left China Lu Xun acknowledged, 'I did not see this clearly before, now I know that he is also an anti-imperialist.'[44] His brother Zhou Zuoren denounced Tagore's critics who 'think they are scientific thinkers and Westernizers, but they lack the spirit of scepticism and toleration'. But in 1924 the young radicals had succeeded in popularizing their misperceptions; deeply shaken by the assaults on him, Tagore cancelled the rest of his lectures. In his last public appearance, he addressed the controversy caused by his visit. Young people, he conceded, are attracted by the West. But he worried that 'the traffic of ideas' was one way, leading to the 'gambling den of commerce and politics, to the furious competition of suicide in the area of military lunacy'. Tagore insisted that 'in order to save us from the anarchy of weak thought we must stand up today and judge the West'; 'We must find our voice to be able to say to the West: "You may force your things into our homes, you may obstruct our prospects of life – but we *judge* you!"'[45]

Moving on to Japan from China in June 1924, Tagore had another opportunity to judge the West rather severely. After years of informal restrictions, the United States had finally banned Japanese immigration altogether, triggering one of the first waves of anti-Americanism that were to sweep across the country repeatedly for the next two decades. Tagore joined them in their sense of outrage over the American decision. Speaking to a large audience at the University of Tokyo, he claimed that 'the materialistic civilization of the West, working hand in hand with its strong nationalism, has reached the heights of unreasonableness'.[46] He said that on his previous trip the Japanese people had scorned his critique of nationalism, but it had been validated by the many urgent reflections worldwide on the catastrophe of the Great War. 'Now after the war,' he said, 'do you not hear everywhere the denunciation of this spirit of the nation, this collective egoism of the people, which is universally hardening their hearts?'[47]

He spoke of those in the West who claim 'sneeringly' that 'we in the East have no faith in Democracy', and feel morally superior. 'We who do not profess democracy,' he asserted, 'acknowledge our human obligations and have faith in our code of honour.' 'But,' he asked, 'are you also going to allow yourselves to be tempted by the contagion of this belief in your own hungry right of inborn superiority, bearing the false name of democracy?'[48]

Tagore may have been misled by the applause his words received. Japan by 1924 was a much more nationalistic country than the one he had first visited in 1916. (In fact, Tagore managed to misjudge the country's mood on every visit except his very last in 1929, when at last he sensed it, and recoiled.) But on the whole, Tagore found the sober Japanese mood more to his taste on this second trip in 1924.

He met Toyama Mitsuru, the ultra-nationalist leader of the Black Dragons, who was dedicated to expanding Japan into the Asian mainland, and repeated his message of a spiritual revival spearheaded by Asia. Tagore had no idea that these Japanese proponents of pan-Asianism meant something far more aggressive. Passing through Japan on his way to Canada in 1929, he again spoke of the 'hopes of Asia', even as he warned that the Japanese 'are following the Western model' and getting lost in the 'mire of Western civilization'.

Returning to Japan later the same year, Tagore began to realize the full extent to which Japan was becoming an imperialist power on the 'Western model'. Students from Korea described to him Japanese brutality in their country, and first-hand Chinese reports revealed to him Japan's aggressive designs on what, in 1929, had become an almost prostrate country. Meeting Toyama Mitsuru on this occasion, Tagore launched into a furious tirade: 'You have been infected by the virus of European imperialism.' Toyoma tried to calm him down, but Tagore declared he would never visit Japan again. His resolve was hardened by the Japanese invasion of Manchuria in 1931 and then its extension into China proper in 1937: the early shots in the conquest of Asia – what Japanese militarists would soon call the Greater East Asian Co-Prosperity Sphere.

When in 1935 an old Japanese friend of his, the poet Yonejiro Noguchi, wrote to ask him to endorse Japan's war in China, since it was the means for 'establishing a new great world in the Asiatic continent', a war of 'Asia for Asia', Tagore replied to say that he thought

Noguchi's conception of Asia would be 'raised on a tower of skulls'. 'It is true,' he added, 'that there are no better standards prevalent anywhere else and the so-called civilized peoples of the West are proving equally barbarous.'[49] But 'if you refer me to them, I have nothing to say'. Noguchi persisted, pointing to the threat of communism in China. Tagore responded by 'wishing the Japanese people, whom I love, not success, but remorse'.[50]

Thus ended the dream of a regenerated Asian spiritual civilization. Certainly 'spirituality' had proved too vague a word; it could readily indicate the warrior spirit of the samurai as well as the self-control of the Brahman. There was also something fuzzy about the notion that Asian countries were joined together by immemorial cultural links established by the export of Buddhism or Chinese culture from their origin countries to the furthest peripheries of Asia.

In 1938, nearing the end of his life, Tagore despaired: 'We are a band of hapless people, where would we look up to? The days of staring at Japan are over.'[51] Three years later, he was dead. His host in China, Liang Qichao, had passed away in 1929, still relatively young at fifty-six. Four years previously, Kang Youwei had died, and Liang had delivered the funeral oration, hailing his old mentor as the pioneer of reform. The Vietnamese Phan Boi Chau, nearly executed and then politically neutered by the French, died in the old imperial city of Hué in 1940. In their last decades, most of these early advocates of internal self-strengthening had become unsympathetic to the rise of hard-edged political ideologies, and politically isolated within their own countries. Elsewhere – in Egypt, Turkey and Iran – disenchanted Islamic modernists were being pushed aside by hard-line communists, nationalists and fundamentalists. In colleges, seminaries and official trade unions, as well as in secret societies and organizations across Asia (and in the coffee houses of Paris, Berlin and London) a new kind of militant nationalist and anti-imperialist was emerging. Many of these were the over-eager 'schoolboys of the East' that Tagore warned against in one of his last essays:

> The carefully nurtured yet noxious plant of national egoism is shedding
> its seeds all over the world, making our callow schoolboys of the East

rejoice because the harvest produced by these seeds – the harvest of antipathy with its endless cycle of self-renewal – bears a western name of high-sounding distinction. Great civilizations have flourished in the past in the East as well as the West because they produced food for the spirit of man for all time . . . These great civilizations were at last run to death by men of the type of our precocious schoolboys of modern times, smart and superficially critical, worshippers of self, shrewd bargainers in the market of profit and power, efficient in their handling of the ephemeral, who . . . eventually, driven by suicidal forces of passion, set their neighbours' houses on fire and were themselves enveloped by flames.[52]

These may have seemed melodramatic words in 1938. But Tagore had remained preternaturally alert to, and fearful of, the violent hatreds still to be unleashed across Asia, beginning with the Japanese invasion of the Asian mainland. Addressing a dinner-party audience in New York in 1930 that included Franklin D. Roosevelt, Henry Morgenthau and Sinclair Lewis, Tagore had conceded that 'the age belongs to the West and humanity must be grateful to you for your science'. But, he added, 'you have exploited those who are helpless and humiliated those who are unfortunate with this gift'.[53] As events in the next decade would prove, liberation for many Asians would be synonymous with turning the tables and subjecting their Western masters to extreme humiliation. This extraordinary reversal would occur more quickly than anyone expected, and more brutally than Tagore feared. And Japan would be its principal agent.

'Comrade Anying, I have come to see you on behalf of the people of the motherland. Our country is strong now and its people enjoy good fortune. You may rest in peace.'

Chinese premier Wen Jiabao, addressing a stone statue of Mao Anying, Mao Zedong's favourite son, in October 2009, shortly after the sixtieth anniversary of the founding of the People's Republic of China.

THE STING IN THE TAIL: PAN-ASIANISM AND MILITARY DECOLONIZATION

Speaking to a full house at Carnegie Hall in New York in 1930, Rabindranath Tagore claimed that Americans ignored Britain's domination of India, and worried about Japan only because the latter 'was able to prove she would make herself as obnoxious as you can'.[1] It was his final message to the West, greeted, according to the *New York Times*, by 'considerable laughter and hand-clapping'.

Writing after the Russo-Japanese war in 1905, Kakuzo Okakura, too, had mocked 'the average Westerner', who 'was wont to regard Japan as barbarous while she indulged in the gentle arts of peace: he calls her civilized since she began to commit wholesale slaughter on Manchurian battlefields.'[2] Tagore was, of course, aware that Japan's 'obnoxiousness' was itself a reaction to the nationalistic and imperialist West and its 'unreasonableness'. The intellectual history of Tokutomi Sohō, one of Japan's most important journalists and publicists, richly illustrates his nation's tragic political trajectory.

Born into a rich peasant family in 1863, Sohō developed classically liberal notions of Japan's progress, including the gradual emergence of a nation-building middle class that consisted of former peasants turned bourgeoisie like himself. Sohō believed that freedom and democracy was indispensable for this new class of people attempting to make a strong nation. Greatly influenced by his readings in Western philosophy and literature, he even briefly converted to Christianity.

In the late 1880s his popular books argued that Japan could become wealthy and powerful through economic and industrial production. But during the high noon of Western imperialism in the 1890s, Sohō began to discard his notions of democratic reformism. In particular, European insistence that Japan return some of its gains from its war with China in 1895 angered Sohō. American immigration laws discriminating against Japanese workers in 1913 and 1920 further alienated Sohō from his Western liberal inspirations. By the 1930s, he had settled, like many Japanese, into resentment of the West. He was furious when Japan's incursions into Manchuria in the early 1930s provoked widespread condemnation from Europe and the United States. Western objections to Japan doing what Western imperialists had been doing for centuries struck him as deeply hypocritical.

'Today', he wrote in 1931, 'is a time of domination by the white races ... they think that the world is the private possession of the white races. They control other people's lands, take their resources, turn them into manufactured goods which are then sent back and sold at high prices.' And, he added, 'the unbridled tyranny of the white races exists because there are no powerful people other than the white races. By breaking through this condition, we can make a positive contribution to all mankind.' Commenting in 1933 on Japan's decision to withdraw from the League of Nations, Sohō wrote that 'it teaches Europeans and Americans that the world is not a place for them to monopolize, and it also shows Asians they can be free of domination by Europeans and Americans'.[3]

The pan-Asian and pan-Islamic activist Abdurreshid Ibrahim, now back in Tokyo after finding Atatürk's insular Turkey not to his taste, supported Sohō, claiming that the League of Nations was a Western plot aimed at preventing Japan from liberating Asia. Working with the logic that Japan's self-interest was also Asia's, Sohō had little trouble rationalizing Japan's full-scale invasion of China in 1937. Like many Japanese intellectuals at the time, he believed that Japan had to face down expansionist Soviet Communism in China. American oil embargoes, which threatened to cripple Japan's economy, also fitted neatly into a pattern of unappeasable Western hostility. 'Americans act,' he suggested, 'as if they are the highest authority for judging the rest of the world – their actions manifest the greatest arrogance.'[4]

Bogged down in China, and punitively encircled by Western powers, Japan could avoid collapse only by grabbing the commodities of the Asian mainland and Java. Writing on the eve of the attack on Pearl Harbor, Sohō justified a pre-emptive strike: 'Japan cannot sit idly by and be resigned to the fate of confinement while being strangled to death. It is entirely appropriate for us as a nation to act freely in order to live.'[5] Commenting on the elaborate list of grievances Japan offered as a rationale for declaring war on Britain and the United States, Sohō described the war as a just campaign of expulsion against an 'immoral West led by a moral and magnanimous Japan'.

Japanese writers commonly contrasted Western depravity with Japan's selflessness. The American-educated poet Yonejiro Noguchi, who fell out with his friend Tagore in the 1930s, published a poem in 1944 rejecting his earlier obeisance to Western ideals as profoundly mistaken:

America and England in the old days were for me countries of Justice:
America was the country of Whitman,
England the country of Browning:
But now they are dissolute countries fallen into the pit of wealth,
Immoral countries, craving after unpardonable dreams.[6]

Soho summed up the larger rationale for the war that many Japanese sincerely believed in: 'We must show to the races of East Asia that the order, tranquility, peace, happiness, and contentment of East Asia can be gained only by eradicating the evil precedent of the encroachment and extortion of the Anglo-Saxons in East Asia.'[7]

In this programme of eradication, Japan succeeded beyond the most garish militarist fantasy. In about ninety days, beginning on 8 December 1941, Japan overran the possessions of Britain, the United States and the Netherlands in East and South-east Asia, taking the Philippines, Singapore, Malaya, Hong Kong, the Dutch East Indies, much of Siam and French Indochina, and Burma with bewildering swiftness to stand poised at the borders of India by early 1942. There are few examples in history of such dramatic humiliation of established powers.

As it progressed, the war also set new standards in brutality. Beginning with the skirmishes in Manchuria in 1931, it lasted for much longer, and was bloodier, than the Second World War in Europe, claiming 24 million lives, including 3.5 million Indians who died in the famine of 1943. It had its own abominations too, such as the killing of hundreds of thousands of Chinese civilians in Nanjing; atrocities of slave labour, torture and mass rape became commonplace across a broad geographical region.

Revenge for decades of racial humiliation motivated many Japanese in the battlefield. A pamphlet distributed to troops on the eve of the Asian war was titled 'Read This Alone – and the War Can Be Won': 'These white people may expect, from the moment they issue from their mothers' wombs, to be allotted a score or so of natives as their personal slaves. Is this really God's will?'[8]

The photograph of the Japanese general brusquely demanding the surrender of the commander of British forces in Singapore was widely circulated. This rough treatment was one of the signs that Japan was no longer going to observe the protocol it had accorded to defeated enemies in its pre-1914 wars against China and Russia. As one of the Japanese colonels put it, 'At the time of the Russo-Japanese War we worshipped the West, but now we are doing things in the Japanese way.'[9]

The Japanese set up friendly regimes across almost all of occupied Asia as part of their blueprint for a Greater East Asian Co-Prosperity Sphere, which placed Japan at the centre of countries which each had a differing political status. The big words were often meant to give cover to old-style imperial exploitation of local resources with the assistance of native collaborators. Military commanders single-mindedly pursuing war objectives treated local populations with great brutality, making a mockery of the popular slogan 'Asia for Asians'. What seemed benign forms of imperialism gave way to pure plunder as the war progressed, and Japan's situation worsened. In Burma, a local uprising by Japan's own protégés eventually challenged Japanese control of the country.

Yet many Japanese officials brought sincerity and determination to the liberation of Asia, actively boosting nationalist movements in Burma and Indonesia, besides galvanizing anti-Western feeling in countries such as India, with Subhas Chandra Bose, the leader of the Indian National Army (INA) against the British briefly becoming the most popular anti-imperialist icon in his country. Colonel Suzuki Keiji, a staff officer at the Imperial General HQ in Japan, who helped train young Japanese in foreign-language schools and was the crucial contact for Asian freedom fighters in Japan, was genuinely motivated to advance what he called 'racial movements of coloured people against their European masters'. Often called Japan's Lawrence of Arabia, Suzuki encouraged radical young nationalists such as Aung San, the father of Aung San Suu Kyi, even before the Second World War erupted in Asia.

The Japanese trained the first generation of postcolonial Burmese leaders on the island of Hainan. In Malaya, the nationalist journalist Ibrahim bin Haji Yaacob (1911–79) set up the League of Malay Youth with Japanese help, and then assisted in Japan's invasion of the British-held peninsula. In Java, the Japanese promoted young nationalists such as Sukarno (1902–70), later Indonesia's first president. As early as 1904 the Egyptian nationalist Mustafa Kamil had predicted that the Japanese, extending their empire to the Dutch colonies, would be warmly welcomed by his fellow 'Easterners' in Java.[10] So it happened: the Japanese were initially greeted with enthusiasm in many parts of Indonesia that had previously been under the iron heel of the Dutch.

As in Vietnam where they discouraged the use of French, the Japanese granted official recognition to the Malay language. During the long occupation from 1942 to 1945, groups of highly motivated and romantic young nationalists in Malaya, Burma and Indonesia, often supported by the Japanese, began to articulate the sense of national community. Before the war, this process was stunted in places like Burma and Indonesia, where, for instance, there was no substantial local bourgeoisie to underpin nationalist politics and the Dutch had easily squashed the smallest steps towards an anti-colonial mass movement by exiling or incarcerating its nascent leaders. In that sense, the Japanese invasion, which placed budding native elites into positions of prominence and power, was the turning point for local nationalisms across East Asia.

In April 1943, the 'liberation of Asia' became Japan's official war objective; later that year, the Greater East Asia Congress in Tokyo revealed that pan-Asianism was more than a Japanese fantasy.[11] Jawaharlal Nehru had spoken often of how 'we feel as Asiatics a common bond uniting us against the aggression of Europe'.[12] Writing from a British prison in 1940, just seven years away from India's freedom from colonial rule, Nehru said, 'My own picture of the future is a federation which includes China and India, Burma and Ceylon, Afghanistan and possibly other countries.'[13]

In Tokyo, Subhas Chandra Bose, surrounded by adoring Indian students, described the congress as a 'family party' where all the guests were Asians.[14] The Philippines' ambassador to Japan claimed that 'the time has come for the Filipinos to discard Anglo-Saxon civilization and its enervating influence ... and to recapture their charm and original virtues as an oriental people'.[15] The Burmese leader Ba Maw (1893–1977) felt the 'call of Asiatic blood'.[16] 'We were Asians,' he later recalled, 'rediscovering Asia.'[17]

Ba Maw later said that the congress of 1943 created the spirit that then went into the Bandung Conference of 1955, where some of Asia's greatest leaders gathered and subsequently formed the Non-Aligned Movement. What energized this spirit in the 1940s most vigorously was the discovery of European weakness. The slow, frustrating efforts of al-Afghani, Liang Qichao and other first-generation intellectuals and activists across Asia – all those many periodicals with tiny circulations, and late-night conversations in dingy rooms – were finally bearing fruit. The Japanese had revealed how deep the roots of anti-Westernism went, and how quickly Asians could seize power back from their European tormentors.

Shortly before Singapore fell to the Japanese in early 1942, the Dutch prime minister in exile, Pieter Gerbrandy, spoke to Churchill and other Allied leaders:

> Our Eastern peoples were, for the greater part, still subject to racial instincts and inferiority complexes. The Japanese slogan 'Asia for the Asiatics,' might easily destroy the carefully constructed basis of our cultural synthesis . . . Though a lengthy Japanese occupation of important parts of the Pacific Territories might not necessarily turn the final victory of the Western powers into virtual defeat, it would at least prove a formidable obstacle to a real peace in the Far East. Japanese injuries and insults to the White population – and these were already being perpetrated by the detestable Asiatic Huns – would irreparably damage white prestige unless severely punished within a short time.[18]

This was a shrewd prophecy. After a long and hard struggle, the Japanese were finally 'punished', fire- and nuclear-bombed into submission, realizing the dark premonition Tagore had in Japan in 1916 that 'nations who sedulously cultivate moral blindness and the cult of patriotism will end their existence in a sudden and violent death'.[19] Still, in most countries they occupied, the Japanese deeply undermined the European power that kept the natives in a permanent state of submission.

The Europeans returned to their former colonies in a state of shock and incomprehension; and their first impulse was to circle the wagons. In Vietnam, the commander of French forces, Philippe Leclerc, who had taken part in the liberation of Paris from the Nazis in 1944, warned that 'any signs of weakness or lack of agreement [among the Allies] would play the game of the Japanese and lead to grave consequences for the future of the white races in Asia'.[20] Racial and cultural solidarity were also high in the minds of the British generals who tried, with the help of Indian soldiers, to restore French rule over Vietnam, and hold Indonesia for the returning Dutch colonialists.

However, everywhere they came up against the new communal identities forged during the long war, when the Europeans were absent or slaving in prison camps. Japanese victories over European powers had crystallized a sharp political awareness among many Western-educated Asians. Soon after the Russo-Japanese War in 1905, Nehru had spoken of how it had diminished the feeling of inferiority that many of his compatriots suffered from. Two decades after Japan's defeat in 1945, Lee Kuan Yew, Singapore's long-serving prime minister, recalled similar lessons freshly learnt by the post-Second World War generation of Asians:

> My colleagues and I are of the generation of young men who went through the Second World War and the Japanese Occupation and emerged determined that no one – neither the Japanese nor the British – had the right to push and kick us around. We were determined that we could govern ourselves and bring up children in a country where we can be proud to be self-representing people. When the war came to an end in 1945, there was never a chance of the old type of British colonial system ever being recreated. The scales had fallen from our eyes and we saw for ourselves that the local people could run the country.[21]

Even the Japanese were forced to recognize this sentiment as in a mostly empty gesture they accorded a measure of self-rule to Burma in 1943. In Indonesia in August 1945, they made a show of accepting Sukarno's declaration of independence, which came two days after Japan's surrender to Allied Forces. Accustomed to deferential natives, European powers mostly underestimated the post-war nationalism that the Japanese had unwittingly or deliberately unleashed. They also misjudged their own staying power among populations un-remittingly hostile to them. This led to many disastrously futile counter-insurgency operations and full-scale wars, many of which still scar nations across Asia.

Nevertheless, the speed of decolonization was breathtaking. Japan's conquest of Asia had sapped British will to hold on to India; a cata-strophic partition of the subcontinent marked Britain's half-panicked departure in 1947. Burma became free in 1948, after many an injury and insult to the white population. The Dutch in Indonesia resisted, but Indonesian nationalists led by Sukarno finally threw them out in 1949. Post-war chaos plunged Malaya and Singapore into prolonged insurgencies, but the British withdrawal was never in doubt.

In 1951, arguing his case for the nationalization of Iran's British-run oil industry at the United Nations, Mohammad Mossadegh spoke of how the Second World War had changed 'the map of the world'. 'In the neighbourhood of my country,' he said, 'hundreds of millions of Asian people, after centuries of colonial exploitation, have now gained their independence and freedom.' Speaking of countries that had 'struggled for the right to enter the family of nations on terms of free-dom and equality', the Iranian prime minister asserted that 'Iran demands that right'. He received a tremendous ovation. Even Taiwan, ushered into the UN through the back door by the United States, was moved to remind the British that 'the day has passed when the control of the Iranian oil industry can be shared with foreign companies'.[22]

Two years after this speech, which is still remembered in Iran, Mos-sadegh was toppled by an Anglo-American coup. Iran would be made to wait longer – and fight harder – for its right to enter the family of nations on terms of equality, like many other Asian countries. Propped up by the United States, French colonialists persisted in fighting a guerrilla war with Ho Chi Minh's popular Viet Minh. They struggled for nine years, losing their protectorates, Cambodia and Laos, in the process. The comprehensive defeat of the French at Dien Bien Phu in 1954 brought the most powerful country in the world – the United States – into Indochina. But this only bloodily prolonged the inevit-able. The United States continued to maintain bases in the Philippines and Japan, projecting a formidable military power across the Pacific. But the last stubborn Western illusion in Asia – the conviction that brute power would provoke obedience and compliance from the natives – was shattered in 1975 with the disorderly retreat from the roof of the American embassy in Saigon. Four years later, Iranians overthrew their pro-American despot, storming the American embassy in Tehran and taking the occupants hostage in another symbolic destruction of Western influence over their country.

By then Japan, economically resurgent under an American security umbrella, had long been in retreat from its pan-Asian ambitions. And the new confrontations of the Cold War in Asia obscured the fact that Japan had changed much of Asia for ever – economically as well as politically. The prominent Malay nationalist Mustapha Hussain spoke for many Asians when he said that, 'Although the Japanese occupation was described as one of severe hardship and brutality, it left something positive, a sweet fruit to be plucked and enjoyed only after the surrender.'[23] In that sense pan-Asianism was important not in what it did for Japan but in what it allowed others to do, and in the unintended consequences that flowed from Japan's actions, starting with its defeat of Russia in 1905.

INTELLECTUAL DECOLONIZATION: THE RISE OF NEO-TRADITIONALISTS

Writing after the end of the war in Asia, a grudgingly self-critical Tokutomi Sohō compared Western powers to cormorants that 'dived into the water and caught fishes big and small'. Japan followed suit, he added, 'but failed to catch any fish and drowned herself'. Sohō attributed Japan's folly to the fact that

> the history of Japan from the latter half of the nineteenth century to the early half of the twentieth century was not of her own [making] but closely interwoven with that of the world. It shows that Japan was constantly imitating what the senior powers had done, though she might have been clumsy in playing her part compared with the other powers. There is a Japanese saying, 'People ruin themselves by trying to ape their betters.'[24]

But the saying was also applicable to the European imitators of

Britain and France. In the twentieth century, the previous century's logic of expansion for the sake of resources and territory led to new rivalries. Thinkers as varied as Nehru, Simone Weil and Hannah Arendt were to observe how by the 1930s, the barbarities inflicted on native populations in Asia and Africa – concentration camps, poison gas attacks, systematic murder – were transplanted to the heart of Europe, and unleashed on Europeans themselves during the search for *Lebensraum*. However bitter, Tagore couldn't have been more prescient in warning against the 'special modern enthusiasm for Western progress and force': the kind of modernization that inevitably led to a sad mimicry of Western imperialism.

> We have for over a century been dragged by the prosperous West behind its chariot, choked by the dust, deafened by the noise, humbled by our own helplessness, and overwhelmed by the speed. We agreed to acknowledge that this chariot drive was progress, and that progress was civilization. If we ever ventured to ask 'progress towards what, and . . . for whom?' it was considered to be peculiarly Oriental . . . [yet] of late, a voice has come to us bidding to take count not only of the scientific perfection of the chariot but of the depth of the ditches lying across its path.[25]

Tagore may seem to be one of the many Western-educated intellectuals trying to find a way to claim moral superiority over their colonial masters, even as they conceded political and economic defeat. 'The spell of white prestige,' Kakuzo Okakura had exhorted fellow Asians in 1904, 'must be completely broken that we may learn our own possibilities and resources . . . History must be written so presenting our past glories and our present woes that every student shall burn with the longing to avenge and save.'[26] This meant that the greater the scale of humiliation by the West, the more intense was the desire to posit an idealized image of the East. Nevertheless, Tagore and Liang Qichao represented a strong early trend, still visible today, of Asian intellectuals defining Western modes of politics, economics, science and culture as inhumanly utilitarian.

Liang Shuming was typical in his critique of two tendencies of Western culture: individual self-interest, which he claimed both liberal democracy and communism shared, and the Faustian will and hunger for knowledge of nature, which had produced modern science but had also created the Machine, which, following Gandhi (whom he admired), Liang termed the 'devil of the modern world'.[27]

This critique of modernity was widely shared in Asia, often by liberal intellectuals, Islamic modernists and Marxist revolutionaries as well as traditionalists. Growing out of a shared experience of Western domination, it not only responded to the common set of dilemmas posed by the global ascendancy of Western cultural, political and economic norms, but it also rephrased the questions raised by Western philosophers for hundreds of years: What is the good life? What is the nature of authority and of justice and equality? What binds an individual to society? This rephrasing put these questions into a broader human perspective. As Tagore wrote:

> When organized national selfishness, racial antipathy and commercial self-seeking begin to display their ugly deformities in all their nakedness, then comes the time for man to know that his salvation is not in political organization and extended trade relations, not in any mechanical rearrangement of social systems, but in a deeper transformation of life, in the liberation of consciousness in love, in the realization of God in man.[28]

Often contemptuously dismissed in their own time, Tagore and Liang and al-Afghani created the vocabulary in which many Asians would phrase their aspirations and frustrations for the next century.

Politically the most prominent of these critics of Western modernity and reinventors of tradition was, of course, Gandhi. Gandhi could see how the unprecedented moral disasters of the modern age – the Western scramble for colonies in Asia and Africa, the world wars between rival nations and empires, the rise of totalitarianism – worked out the nihilist logic of a purely secular and materialistic outlook: that nothing is sacred in the battle for worldly power, and that nation-states with economies built around the endless multiplication of individual desires are likely to wage the most destructive wars in order to maintain their chosen ways of life.

China produced its own thinkers keen to preserve and propagate some if not all the norms and ideals of their country's long Confucian tradition. Like many Asians who started out as Western-style liberals, Yan Fu did a U-turn, signing a petition in 1916 for Confucianism to be made the state religion:

> Western culture, after this European war, has been corrupted utterly. Formerly, when I heard our scholars of the old school say that there would come a day when the teachings of Confucius would be practiced by all mankind, I thought they were talking nonsense. But now I find that some of the most enlightened men in Europe and America seem to be coming gradually to a like opinion ... It seems to me that in three centuries of progress the people of the West have achieved four principles: to be selfish, to kill others, to have little integrity, and to feel little shame. How different are the principles of Confucius and Mencius, as broad and deep as Heaven and Earth, designed to benefit all men everywhere.[29]

Liang Qichao himself never overcame his distrust of the modern West and his regard for Chinese tradition. And the vehement rejection of Confucianism by May Fourth radicals did not end its intellectual and moral prestige in China. During Guomindang rule from 1927 to 1937, Chiang Kai-shek tried to restore the Confucian system as part of his attempt to reunite a fractious country. His campaign for the regeneration of China – grandly titled the New Life movement – was based on Confucian ideas of propriety, justice, integrity and self-respect.

Liang Qichao died in 1929, a believer to the last in Confucianism despite many attacks on him by younger intellectuals. The most famous Confucian of the 1920s and 1930s was Liang Shuming, who envisioned Gandhian-style self-sufficient and moral village communities across China. He actually put his theory into practice in Shandong province where he started a rural reconstruction programme designed to Confucianize the Chinese countryside. In 1938, Mao Zedong, another rural activist, visited Liang and they held long discussions about Liang's work. Mao himself never seems to have shaken off his early Confucian moralism despite his public and virulent criticism of Confucianism. His utopian socialism carried more than a tinge of Kang Youwei's fantasy of a harmonious world. Speaking in 1949, Mao was convinced that 'Western bourgeois civilization, bourgeois democracy and the plan for a bourgeois republic have all gone bankrupt in the eyes of the Chinese people'. A 'people's republic', he asserted, would now 'abolish classes and enter a world of Great Harmony' – one that Kang Youwei 'did not and could not find the way to achieve'. In 1958, party cadres were instructed to learn from Kang's book as they set out to establish 'People's Communes' across the country.

As much as Liang Qichao and other Confucianists (and indeed Ho Chi Minh), Mao believed that the moral and spiritual transformation of individuals and collective virtuous action were the prerequisites for larger social and political changes. In the end, Mao succeeded where Liang Qichao failed in reviving and unifying China around a shared ethic. During their first three decades in power, the Chinese Communists tried to root out Confucianism from China, denouncing it as 'feudal' and reactionary. But as the appeal of communism has declined, party officials have returned to upholding Confucianism. Chinese culture, Mao insisted, should have its own form, its 'own national form'.[30] And the Chinese government seems to be striving towards this in a wholly unexpected way as it promotes Chinese culture abroad through the building of Confucius Institutes – Chinese versions of the Alliance Française and Goethe-Institut. Chinese leaders have also taken to using words like 'harmonious society' to burnish their credentials as mitigators of social and economic inequality.

The Counter-Moderns of the Islamic World

Nowhere were traditionalist ideals so strenuously invoked against the onslaught of modernity as in the Muslim world. Crisis convulsed the world of Islam from the moment it was confronted and then penetrated by the West. The course of history, which white men presumed to direct, seemed to violate the Muslim sense of a world order shaped exclusively by God. Malaise gripped the most intelligent and sensitive Muslims; it was what Jamal al-din al-Afghani expressed most passionately as he moved from a liberal interpretation of Islam to nationalism, and then to pan-Islamism.

'Islam' and 'the West': those were the dichotomies al-Afghani invented. They attested to no simple opposition but a fundamental imbalance of power. Internally weak, the world of Islam was threatened from outside. Yet its own belief in the divinely guided society and prescribed notions of social good survived the confrontation with a socio-economic order predicated on individual self-interest.

Nostalgia for the old world of Islam overcame some of the most brilliant and cosmopolitan men in the Muslim world, such as the Indian Muslim poet Muhammad Iqbal, the intellectual and spiritual father of Pakistan. Born in 1876 into an illiterate family, Iqbal came under the influence of the anti-British poet Akbar Illahabadi. In 1905 he travelled to Europe, where he studied philosophy in Britain and Germany. Impressed by Europe's manifold achievements, Iqbal was nevertheless disturbed by its racist and ultra-competitive cultures. Anticipating Tagore and Liang and other post-Great War critics of the West's materialist culture, he was already warning in 1908:

> O, dwellers of the cities of the West,
> This habitation of God is not a shop,
> And that which you regard as true coin,
> Will prove to be only a counterfeit.
> Your civilization will commit suicide
> With its own sword.[31]

Iqbal had started out as an Indian nationalist in the Akbar Illahabadi mould. But while in Europe, the history of Islam acquired new meanings for him. Returning to India in 1908, his sighting of the coast of Sicily, the setting of one of Islam's greatest triumphs in Europe, brought forth a lament for what was now a 'tomb of Muslim culture':

> Whose story is hidden in your ruins?
> The silence of your footfall has a mode of expression.
> Tell me of your sorrow – I too am full of pain;
> I am the dust of that caravan whose goal you were.
> Paint over this picture once more and show it to me;
> Make me suffer by telling the story of ancient days.
> I shall carry your gift to India;
> I shall make others weep as I weep here.[32]

While in Europe Iqbal also became an admirer of Nietzsche – specifically of the latter's idea of the Superman, of self-creation and self-assertion – even as he became hyperconscious of his Muslim identity and increasingly convinced that the progress of Indian Muslims lay not in imitating Europe but in reforming and reviving the religious community they had been born into. To this end, he began to exalt Nietzschean-style masculine vigour and the great Islamic past in his writings. Like many Islamic modernists who harked back to classical Islam, Iqbal became a critic of Sufism and the mystical and folk traditions within Islam that advocate the rejection of the ego and the self, and even of Islamic sects like the Ahmadi. Europe, he believed, would destroy itself through excessive materialism; Islam, which concealed the principle of true individualism, would then emerge as a saviour of humanity.

Iqbal was to greatly influence a generation of Iranian thinkers who created the intellectual basis of the Islamic Revolution of 1979. In his book *We and Iqbal* on the Indian thinker, Ali Shariati compared him to both al-Afghani and Tagore: 'He fights with colonialism for the liberation of Muslim nations as Sayyid Jamal had done. He endeavors to save civilization as Tagore had tried to do from the tragedy of calculating reason and the pest of ambition.'[33] Shariati claimed that Iqbal 'gave ideological consistency' to the Islamic movement al-Afghani began.[34] Speaking in 1986 at a conference on Iqbal in Tehran, Iran's Supreme Leader Sayyid Ali Khamenei went even further, claiming that the Islamic Republic of Iran was 'the embodiment of Iqbal's dream'. 'We are,' Khamenei added, 'following the path shown to us by Iqbal.'[35]

Shariati and Khamenei are correct in one sense, even though the enforced rituals and forms of Islamic ideologies and states in the modern era have little in common with Iqbal's notion of spiritual freedom and the community of Islam. Towards the end of his life, Iqbal's ideas, insisting on a 'pure' Islam, increasingly concerned with upholding the Sharia and contemptuous of Western political systems and ideologies, had much to offer to Islamic revivalists – especially those just beginning to posit a necessary conflict between Islam and un-Islam. In his magnum opus, a Dantean book of poems titled *Jawid Nama* ('The Book of Eternity'), Iqbal invented a series of dialogues with famous figures. One of his interlocutors is al-Afghani; the two range across the ideologies of capitalism and socialism and the idea of the good, divine sovereign. For al-Afghani in the poem – and Iqbal – Western democracy is an opiate forced by the rich upon the poor:

The West's republicanism is the same old instrument,
In its strings there are no tunes but those of Kaiserism.
The demon of exploitation dances in republican garb,
And you suppose that it is the fairy of liberty.
Constitutional bodies, reforms, privileges, rights,
Are sweet-tasting western soporifics.[36]

The conversation ends with al-Afghani sending a message to Soviet Communists to abandon *Das Kapital* and make the Koran the intellectual inspiration of their socialism. 'What is the Koran? For the capitalist, a message of death; / It is the patron of the propertiless slave.'

This Islam-centred thought attracted to Iqbal a young writer called Abul Ala Mawdudi (1903–79). Three years after Iqbal's death in 1938, Mawdudi founded Jamaat-e-Islami, the first Leninist-style revolutionary vanguard party anywhere in the Islamic world. Mawdudi, who was opposed to nationalism as well as socialism and capitalism, created the first coherent and consistent programme for an 'Islamic' state in which God was the absolute sovereign. Mawdudi's initial lack of political success in Pakistan belies the great influence of his quasi-theocratic ideology upon a wide range of Muslim thinkers and activists, including Iran's Ayatollah Khomeini who translated many of the South Asian writer's works into Persian. Aiming to turn Pakistan into an Islamic state, Mawdudi would posthumously receive official patronage from Pakistan's brutal military despot Zia-ul-Haq in the 1980s.

No Islamic leader described an entirely secular utopia. The Indonesian communist party, the PKI, did acquire widespread support in the Muslim-majority country from 1921 to 1965, when it was violently eradicated. Still, radical atheists like Mao Zedong had little chance of flourishing in Islamic societies. And even secular nationalist parties like the Baath in Iraq and Syria could not ignore the mobilizing power of Islam. In Indonesia, Sukarno's own ruling ideology – 'nasikom' – was a composite of nationalism, Islam and communism. The revolutions that succeeded in Muslim countries were launched in the name of Islam not Marx or Paine. Liberalism, defined in the broadest sense, had a tenuous hold in the Muslim world.

Muslims initially admired Western-style liberalism for having created, at least in Europe, a humane civilization. But this prestige began to crumble in the last quarter of the nineteenth century; liberalism was discredited by its apparent complicity with imperialism, and its failure to sympathize with liberal nationalistic elements in Muslim society. Liberalism in Europe resolutely failed to amount to liberalism in the colonies. It seemed too much a sort of racially segregated liberalism. Mohammed Abduh summed up a widespread sentiment when, after successive disappointments, he confessed in 1895 that, 'We Egyptians believed once in English liberalism and English sympathy; but we believe no longer, for facts are stronger than words. Your liberalness we see plainly is only for yourselves, and your sympathy with us is that of the wolf for the lamb which he deigns to eat.'[37]

But even indigenous and reformist liberalisms proved to have shallow roots. Men like Sir Sayyid Ahmad Khan, the Indian educationist, Taha Husayn, the Paris-educated liberal Egyptian disciple of Abduh, or Namik Kemal, the Young Ottoman thinker accomplished the vital work of focusing Muslim minds on a world ordered by more than just the Islamic God. However, they remained peripheral in their own societies, unable to give them an enduringly original way forward. They could insist, as Taha Husayn did, that 'I am pleading for a selective approach to European culture, not wholesale and indiscriminate borrowing.'[38] Yet Western intellectuals thought they were not secular enough, while traditionalists suspected them of further hollowing-out Muslim societies with Westernizing ideologies of humanism and rationalism. At best, liberal constitutionalism, as al-Afghani espoused it, could be a tool to strengthen Muslim societies against the West. But a liberal Muslim like Sir Sayyid, who went so far as to challenge the basic tenets of Islam, invited the wrath of al-Afghani himself.

Among ideologies imported from – and then used against – the West, nationalism had more purchase, especially as old empires crumbled in the first half of the twentieth century and the idea of self-determination came into vogue. Someone like Iqbal, who was initially suspicious of nationalism which he blamed for the 'suicide of the West', and more inclined to al-Afghani's pan-Islamism, bowed to the former's political logic. 'For the present,' he admitted in the early 1930s, 'every Muslim nation must sink into her own deeper self, temporarily focus her vision on herself alone, until all are strong and powerful to form a living family of republics.'[39] Al-Afghani's own exhortations to local nationalisms were prescient in this regard; they proved more practical than his pan-Islamism which, as the doomed campaign for the restoration of the caliphate proved, was a romantic idea. The Egyptians and Indian Muslims trying to over-come the British, the Syrians struggling against the French, the Iranians resisting Anglo-Russian designs on their country, the Indonesians ranged against the Dutch, and even the Turks expelling the Greeks from Anatolia in 1922 borrowed from the armoury of Western ideas and institutions. Many of the leaders of these nationalist movements – Mustafa Kamil, Saad Zaghlul, Jinnah, Atatürk, Nasser, Sukarno – belonged to the Westernized minorities in their respective countries, and left-wing ideals of socialism often played a major role in these anti-imperialist campaigns. Yet the entry of the Muslim masses into anti-imperialist politics inevitably gave an Islamic tinge to these various nationalisms.

Decolonization, and the gradual lessening of Western influence, did not undercut the power of popular Islam. In Pakistan the notion of Islam defining a national community eventually complicated – and compromised – the secular intentions of the country's founder, Jinnah. In countries like Iraq, Syria, Egypt and Iran, Muslim groups energized by anti-Westernist nationalism, such as Egypt's Muslim Brotherhood, had to be suppressed with brute force by quasi-socialist nationalist leaders. Yet neither the modernizing shah of Iran nor Saddam Hussein of Iraq could abandon the imagery and symbolism of popular Islam. Even the ideologically secular Atatürk introduced a state-sponsored Islam while carefully negotiating with Islamic leaders.

The most striking aspect of the Muslim world in the second half of the twentieth century has been the outbursts, frequently fanatical, of deeply politicized Islam in both Sunni and Shiite lands. During this time, Pakistan's Jamaat-e-Islami and Egypt's Muslim Brotherhood moved from the political margins of their societies to the mainstream. An Islamic Revolution erupted in Iran, and its aftershocks travelled as far as the Malay Peninsula and Java, transforming politics in these regions. Three years later, in 1981, an Islamic militant assassinated the president of Egypt. Within a decade transnational militant groups, often upholding hard-line Salafi versions of Islam, declared jihad against despotic Arab regimes in Tunisia, Egypt, Algeria, Syria and Libya.

Despite different political contexts, these Islamist groups had in common an idea of Islam as a framework for moral reform as well as a revolutionary ideology and an identity. They identified their adversaries as repressive indigenous state and local elites, which in turn were seen as part of a larger, remote and menacing entity called 'the West'. In the Islamist worldview, not only liberalism, nationalism and socialism are seen to have failed, but the progenitor of these ideologies, the West itself, is also judged to have failed. As Sayyid Qutb (1906–66), the most influential of modern Islamist thinkers, wrote – echoing, among others, Gandhi's radical strictures against modern civilization:

> At this time an outcry has arisen everywhere, a warning alarm about the fate of humankind in the thrall of a materialist civilization devoid of faith and human spirit – the white man's civilization. The alarms are various; at times they warn of the descent of all humanity into the abyss; others warn of its descent into Marxism; still others have made various suggestions to prevent these manifold dangers. But all of these attempts are futile because they do not deal with the foundation of the problem, they do not attack the vast and extensive roots of the problem which lie buried beneath European soil. All these outcries and all these remedies just make clear to us the deficiencies and myopia of the European mentality and its vision.[40]

The West is no longer the source of good as well as bad things, deep in material benefits but shallow in spiritual matters; it has to be rejected *in toto*. This conviction had been building up over decades among many Muslims. Two destructive world wars and the Great Depression had revealed serious structural flaws in the Western models of politics and economy. Decolonization further undermined the political power of Western countries; and desperate attempts to regain it – in Suez in 1956, and in Algeria and Vietnam – destroyed any fragments of remaining political and moral authority. A further devastating blow to the reputation of the West was the creation of the state of Israel on

Palestinian lands in 1948. It confirmed the duplicity that the West had shown with the secret 1916 Sykes–Picot agreement (revealed to the world by Lenin after the Bolshevik Revolution) by which the British and French planned to divvy up the Arabic-speaking countries between them after the First World War; and the racial arrogance revealed at the Paris Peace Conference seemed to have been institutionalised by the imposition of a European settler nation on the Middle East.

Events occurring in far-off lands may have affected only elite perceptions of the West in Muslim countries. But internal changes exposed much larger populations to political tumult and an angry awakening to inequality and injustice. The overall population of Muslim countries increased dramatically in the second half of the twentieth century, forcing many people out of rural areas into crowded cities and towns; the proportion of Muslims living in urban areas rose exponentially between 1950 and 1990. Exposed to the new communications media, the conspicuous consumption of the elites and rampant inequality, many Muslims embraced Islam with a new fervour. Mosques and madrasas sprang up across the new urban landscape. Cheap books and magazines made Islamic piety more widely available and popular Muslim journalists and preachers (few of whom had received the traditional education of the *ulema*) began to offer a new do-it-yourself Islam to people uprooted from traditional social structures. The pluralization of Islamic authority, of which al-Afghani and Abduh and many other members of the lay Muslim intelligentsia had been the harbingers, was never so accelerated as it was in the last half of the twentieth century.

This new Islam was boosted, too, by the ideological logic of modern nation-building programmes. In countries like Turkey and Egypt, where top-down reforms were imposed by despots, modernization became synonymous with the removal of Islam from the centre of public life, the devalidation of Islamic education and law, and the marginalization of Islamic scholars. As al-Afghani had observed during his travels in the Muslim world, the imperatives of modernization and economic growth imposed by Western powers had radically disrupted the old cohesion of Islamic societies by producing new classes and redistributing power among them.

New urban elites emerged from modern educational institutions and bureaucracies, and they tended to have little time for traditional sources of authority. Many of them enriched themselves at the expense of the rural poor. A reservoir of discontent built up, especially among the people most marginalized by this process, such as the clergy, small-town merchants, provincial officials and men from semi-rural backgrounds – the kind of people who hung around al-Afghani.

What gave anti-Westernism a broader mass base and intellectual foundation was the failure of secular nationalist programmes in post-colonial Muslim countries. In many instances – Egypt, Tunisia, Indonesia, Algeria – the postcolonial Muslim state followed the colonial state's policies, especially in its suspicion of popular Islam, and tried to restrict if not eliminate altogether the latter's role in public life. But the vast majority of people in Muslim countries never stopped believing in Islam. They also failed to develop the habit of seeing Islam as a purely *religious* phenomenon, separate from economics, politics, law and other aspects of collective life.

Westernized and secular postcolonial elites saw Islam as an obstacle to the national task of secular development and economic consolidation; they often cracked down brutally on Islamic groups. But when such modernizing endeavours failed, as they were bound to in many cases, or caused mass suffering, the prestige of Islam was further enhanced. Not only that: in the eyes of their victims, the failures of modernization and secularization diminished the credibility and authority of local elites in Muslim countries and their ideologies of modernization.

Sayyid Qutb witnessed the severe deficiency of both Western-style liberalism and socialism in Egypt; he was also an early critic of nationalism, which he saw as an aspect of the intellectual colonialism suffered by Egypt. Not surprisingly, Qutb, whose life and ideas dramatized the widespread recoil from secular Western ideologies to Islamism, went on to become the inspiration for several generations of radical Islamists in Egypt, Saudi Arabia, Syria, Iraq and Turkey.

Born into a once-prosperous rural family that had fallen on hard times (a background shared by many radicals across Asia), Qutb came of age in an Egypt energized by the post-1919 nationalism of Saad

Zaghlul's nationalist Wafd party. He studied at a secular college in Cairo; his first mentor was a journalist of a fairly conventional liberal bent, and Qutb served as a teacher for many years in Egypt's modern education system. Indeed, as a literary critic and early admirer of Egypt's greatest novelist, Naguib Mahfouz, Qutb ranged himself against the more religious writers of his time.

But as the Wafd party failed to make any headway against the pro-British monarch, and the impotence of Western-style liberalism became clear against a background of British gunboat-aided encroachments on Egyptian sovereignty, Qutb began to change his mind. Salafist Islam, of which he was to become a prominent spokesperson, was still a minor current in the secular nationalist Egyptian mainstream. Rashid Rida had turned the pan-Islamism of al-Afghani into a major international force through his magazine *al-Manar*, and influenced by him, Hasan al-Banna would form the Muslim Brotherhood in 1928, giving Salafism an organizational basis. But it was men like Saad Zaghlul and Mustafa Kamil who, assisted by Christian and Jewish Arabs, largely led the project of fighting British imperialism and inculcating a sense of Arab nationalism in the first three decades of the twentieth century.

Prevented from presenting the Egyptian case at the Paris Peace Conference in 1919, Saad Zaghlul's Wafd party led a major uprising against British rule. Secular symbols marked the revolt. a Coptic priest demanded independence from the pulpit of the al-Azhar mosque. Peasants participated in large numbers. The British seemed to give in by unilaterally declaring Egypt a sovereign state in 1922. However, this turned out to be a charade. The British held on to their special privileges in the country, making it impossible for the Wafd government, which came to power in Egypt's first elections in 1924, to function. Britain's major collaborator – the monarch – helped by dismissing the parliament on the first day it met in 1925. The British controlled almost every ministry in Egypt. Political self-expression for Egyptians was limited to an appointed Legislative Council, which merely rubber-stamped British decisions. The British occupation forces held the real power in the country, exercising it in 1926 with an actual gunboat that forced the Wafd out of the government.

Relations between the Arab world and the West were never so

fraught as they were between the two world wars. Muslim intellectuals who stressed Western ideologies of nationalism, secularism and democracy felt cruelly betrayed by Europe's refusal to support their aspirations for national independence. Now demarcated by European-style borders, the old boundary-less *Dar al-Islam* of the Ottoman Empire became an obstacle course for Muslims, even for those going on pilgrimage to Mecca. Working secretly together, Britain and France had already parcelled out among themselves bits of Ottoman territory they had seized after the Great War, creating arbitrary new states in the form of Iraq, Jordan and Lebanon and promising a separate homeland to European Jews in British-ruled Palestine. Fuelled by anti-Semitism in Europe, Jewish immigration to Palestine picked up during the inter-war years, when Egyptians were preoccupied with domestic politics.

While Arabs everywhere protested against the appropriation of Palestinian lands, European businessmen extracted Egypt's resources, degrading its original inhabitants into cheap labour. The Wafd party kept being elected with large majorities but was thwarted from holding political office since it was seen by the British as an 'ultra-democratic, anti-foreign revolutionary regime'.[41] As Nehru, who observed the case of Egypt from India, caustically commented in 1935 'democracy for an Eastern country seems to mean only one thing: to carry out the behests of the imperialist ruling power and not to touch any of its interests. Subject to that proviso, democratic freedom can flourish unchecked.'[42]

Powerful anti-imperialist agitations and uprisings finally reduced British control of Egypt and Sudan in 1936, confining it to the occupation of the corridor of the Suez Canal. The continuing political uncertainty did not help economic reconstruction, especially in the countryside where a rising population and pressure on agricultural land increased poverty. In the eyes of many Egyptians, an overly Westernized ruling elite assumed a colonialist posture towards the mass of poor and illiterate people; these disaffected Egyptians would soon form the bulk of the Islamist Muslim Brotherhood.

In the 1930s, Sayyid Qutb emerged as a critic of British interference, the growing inequalities in Egypt, and the Egyptian inability to support Palestinian Arabs against Zionist settlers. He broke with his liberal mentors, and as anti-colonial movements intensified in India, Vietnam, Malaya, Indonesia and Kenya Qutb despaired at Egypt's 'native collaborators'.[43] His anguish deepened with the establishment in 1948 of the state of Israel, which the systematic murder of 6 million Jews had made a moral imperative for many Western nations. In the war that followed, the Zionists defeated the combined Arab armies, expelled hundreds of thousands of Arab inhabitants of Palestine, and proclaimed an independent state. This constituted a radical defeat for Egypt in particular – the most modern of Arab nations – and Israel became, and has remained, a symbol of Arab impotence against Western power.

Israel's victory and Egypt's military humiliation in 1948 were major milestones in Qutb's new thinking, as was his trip later that same year to the United States, then the embodiment of post-war modernity. This was where Qutb first began to develop his larger critique of Western civilization as unhealthily obsessed with material and technological progress to the detriment of moral freedom and social justice.

Like Liang Qichao, Qutb found little in the American model of politics and society to recommend back home. Democracy was unworkable in his view, not because it assumed an educated and aware citizenry but because it made human beings the final source of sovereignty, rather than God. Furthermore, the idea that the good life was to be defined in terms of economic well-being became repugnant to Qutb, and also discredited Marxism in his eyes. American expressions of social liberalism and individualism – sexual freedom in particular – appalled him even more. Racism, of which he encountered the anti-Arab variant as well as the traditional version, struck Qutb as an essential feature of America's material plenitude, generated by the 'conceit' that this was 'the White Man's endowment'.[44] He freely employed the words 'white man' as an epithet thereafter: 'We must nourish in our school-age children sentiments that open their eyes to the tyranny of the white man, his civilization, and his animal hunger.'[45]

Qutb had already been inspired by the idea of a vanguard Islamist party and Islamic state floated by the Pakistani thinker Abul Ala Mawdudi. Soon after his return from America in 1950, he became a member of the Muslim Brotherhood, and aggressively began to espouse an Islamist view of politics, society and economy, exhorting Muslims to replace secular regimes with the divine laws as manifested in the Sharia. Like al-Afghani and Abduh before him, Qutb was indifferent to exegetical traditions of Islam, preferring to focus on the Koran and the sayings of the Prophet. Unlike al-Afghani, however, Qutb felt no need to reconcile Islam with reason or science. As he saw it: 'He who feels a need to defend, justify and apologize is not capable of presenting Islam.' He deplored the fact that many Muslims exposed to the modern West felt as though 'Islam stood accused, in need of defending itself, like a prisoner on trial'.[46] Qutb had previously included non-Muslim Asia in his broad anti-imperialist front. 'It seems,' he had written in 1943, 'that Eastern civilization and its spiritual treasures is the sanctuary for the world in its present crisis.'[47] But now he focused on the 'bloc of Islam, which, strengthened by the new states of Pakistan and Indonesia, represented the dignity of the Muslim East'.[48]

Convinced that modern secular life posed more problems than solutions, Qutb began to inveigh against Egypt's political and social development, which under the auspices of British imperialism had proceeded along mostly Western lines. An opportunity came for Qutb to put his ideas into practice when anti-imperialist Egyptian army officers, led by Gamal Abdel Nasser, staged a coup against the Egyptian king in 1952. Nasser invited Qutb to submit his ideas for a righteous polity but the army officers, who were of a secular and socialist bent, rejected Qutb's blueprint for an Islamic state. For Qutb, this was a clear sign that Nasser's regime was, notwithstanding its strident anti-Zionism and pan-Arabism, a mere clone of godless Western imperialists. Relations between the Muslim Brotherhood and the army deteriorated quickly, to the point where the organization was proscribed; Qutb soon found himself imprisoned and tortured. Accused of conspiring against the revolution, he was arrested three times, and kept in prison for most of the next ten years, during which time he suffered from a variety of ailments. The publication of his seminal book, *Milestones*, landed him in prison for the last time in 1964.

Qutb was given a brisk trial in 1966, after which he was hanged and then buried in an unmarked grave. His relatively brief life belies his influence, which was immense and endures to this day. Just a year after his death, Israel comprehensively defeated Arab armies in the Six-Day War, and the humiliation finally discredited the secular Arab nationalism espoused by Nasser. Though forced underground by the secularist despots who followed Nasser in Egypt, Qutb's ideas now travelled all over the Muslim world.

His influence spread because Qutb did not just politically challenge the West and Westernizing elites; he also repudiated their epistemological and metaphysical worldview. As he asserted in *Milestones*:

> Humanity is standing today at the brink of an abyss, not because of the threat of annihilation hanging over its head – for this is just a symptom of the disease and not the disease itself – but because humanity is bankrupt in the realm of 'values', those values which foster true human progress and development. This is abundantly clear to the Western World, for the West can no longer provide the values necessary for [the flourishing of] humanity.[49]

Qutb extended a conventional critique of corrupt Middle Eastern regimes and failed modernization into an indictment of all those Western ideologies – whether nationalism, liberalism or socialism – that banished religion and morality from the realm of politics, and exalted human reason above God.

'Those who say that religion has nothing to do with politics do not know what religion means,' Gandhi wrote in the last pages of his autobiography. Qutb, who greatly admired Rabindranath Tagore for his emphasis on spirituality, would no doubt have concurred. Qutb's ideological heirs, the Sunni Islamic radicals who in recent decades have tried to topple secular dictatorships in Egypt, Syria and Algeria, were motivated by the same desire to reinstate Islam's centrality in human life.

However, the radical implications of Qutb's critique of Western secularism were nowhere as clearly worked out as in Shiite Iran. As Ayatollah Khomeini wrote, using words seemingly borrowed from Qutb (or, with some modifications, Liang Qichao and Tagore):

> For the solution of social problems and the relief of human misery require foundation in faith and morals; merely acquiring material power and wealth, conquering nature and space, have no effect in this

regard. They must be supplemented by and balanced with, the faith, the conviction, and the morality of Islam, in order to truly serve humanity, instead of endangering it . . . So as soon as someone goes somewhere or invents something, we should not hurry to abandon our religion and its laws, which regulate the life of man and provide for his well-being in this world and the hereafter.[50]

Khomeini was referring to the most ambitious programme to catch up with the West since Muhammad Ali's nineteenth-century reforms in Egypt. This was the shah's 'White Revolution' of 1963. Not surprisingly, it was also Iran that hosted what Michel Foucault called the 'first great insurrection against global systems, the form of revolt that is the most modern and the most insane'. According to Foucault, 'Islam, which is not simply a religion, but an entire way of life, an adherence to a history and a civilization – has a good chance to become a gigantic powder keg, at the level of hundreds of millions of men.'[51] The Iranian Islamic Revolution became the prime example of how, in the absence of any democratic politics, Muslims could use Islamic themes of sacrifice and martyrdom to challenge despotic and corrupt rulers who claimed legitimacy both domestically and in the West as modernizers and secularizers.

Although never a European colony, oil-rich Iran had been dominated by British and Russian imperialists since the nineteenth century. Al-Afghani had witnessed the first of the great anti-imperialist movements in 1891. There were more to come after the First World War. Not content with appropriating large parts of the Ottoman Empire, Lord Curzon, then the British foreign minister, hatched a scheme to annex Iran, convinced, as his early biographer Harold Nicolson put it, that 'God had personally selected the British upper class as an instrument of the Divine Will'. Iranian nationalism strengthened throughout the early half of the twentieth century against a backdrop of such blatant foreign interference. Its galvanizing moment came in 1953 when the CIA, working alongside British intelligence officers, toppled the elected nationalist government of Mohammad Mossadegh that had threatened to nationalize Western oil interests, and re-installed Shah Reza Pahlavi. With a Western-backed despot at its head, Iran seemed to be going backwards in the age of decolonization, and the shah obliged his supporters in the West by undermining all nationalist, socialist and liberal organizations in the country, paving the way, as it turned out, for an explicitly Islamic movement.

At a time when the ideals of democracy and republicanism inspired masses as well as intellectuals in most postcolonial countries, Iran under the shah seemed to be actively working to depoliticize its citizenry. In lieu of a nation-building ideology, the Pahlavi regime offered a mix of Persian chauvinism, the cult of the shah, and a tarted-up version of Iran's pre-Islamic history. But it attracted neither the traditionalist masses nor the expanding middle class. The grandiose schemes of land reform, industrialization and urbanization the shah imposed on his largely peasant population led to an ever-deeper discontent. The attempt to push Iran into the twentieth century created a small middle class, but it also uprooted millions of people from their traditional rural homes and exposed them to the degradations of urban life. Inequality increased as a small urban elite prospered and acquired the symbols of a modern consumer economy.

In the early 1960s, Iranian intellectuals began to republish with new introductions works by al-Afghani; he was a hero among Islamic radicals at Tehran University in the 1970s, the Islamic counter to the icons of Marx, Mao and Che Guevara cherished by left-leaning students – 'the man', as Ali Shariati put it in 1970, 'who first raised the voice of awareness in the dormant East'.[52] Building on the visceral anti-Westernism of men like al-Afghani, Iranian intellectuals had by the late 1970s developed a systematic critique of the political and economic systems and ideologies – industrial capitalism, the bureaucratic nation-state, Marxism – created by the revolutions of the West and spread by Western imperialists round the world in the previous two centuries.

The most prominent among these intellectuals was Jalal Al-e Ahmad (1923–69), whose neologism *gharbzadegi* ('Westoxification', or more literally 'West-struckness', which connotes both bewitchment and sickness), popularized in 1962 in a book that often reads like an Iranian version of Gandhi's *Hind Swaraj*, became synonymous with the pathology of mindless imitation of the West. According to Al-e Ahmad, it was a symptom of rootlessness: 'the aggregate of events in the life, culture, civilization, and mode of thought of a people having no supporting traditions, no historical continuity, no gradient of transformation.'[53] Initially a communist and secular nationalist, Al-e Ahmad claimed (anticipating a Marxist critique that was to become well known in the 1970s) that the global economic system was designed to benefit the West and keep the rest of the world in a perpetual state of underdevelopment. The old world of East–West parity and exchanges had given way to one in which countries that were rich, industrialized, and exporters of finished products and culture lorded it over those that were still largely poor, agricultural, producers of raw materials, and helpless consumers of Western products as well as of Western culture. And development, even if miraculously achieved by Asian countries like Iran and India, was only going to lead to the drab consumerist dystopia of the West.

Meanwhile, Western oil companies that controlled Iran's oil were making the country's economy wholly dependent on the West. Recycling petrodollars for tractors, the West was forcing the mechanization of agriculture; the result was extensive and unmanageable rural migration to the cities. The industrialization championed by the West and its local agents in Iran was also destroying local handicrafts, causing massive unemployment. Echoing al-Afghani, Al-e Ahmad lamented that Iranians received news of the world through such unreliable filters as Reuters, and that an uprooted generation of Westernized or West-returned Iranians had become handmaidens to Western power.

Initially, Al-e Ahmad thought that *gharbzadegi* could be countered by sending Iranian students to Japan and India rather than the West: the East-struck Iranians would balance the West-struck ones. Islam played no role at all in this scheme. However, a visit to the then new nation-state of Israel in 1962 impressed upon him the power of political solidarity built upon a shared religion: 'I as an Easterner [prefer] an Israeli model over all other models of how to deal with the West,' he wrote in his diary.[54] Israel had turned into a modern and independent nation without losing its religious and cultural identity, unlike Turkey. Al-e Ahmad became convinced of the importance of developing an indigenous approach to Iran's economic and political problems. He identified Shiite Islam as the right kind of vaccine for *gharbzadegi*, and the *ulema* as the appropriate doctors to administer it. As he saw it, the clergy were the only group of people in Iran not to be intoxicated by the West, and hence likely allies of secular intellectuals. They were men of learning of mostly lower-class backgrounds who spoke the language of, and were therefore trusted by, the masses. Of course, Al-e Ahmad had in mind the tobacco rebellion in which al-Afghani had played a role in bringing about an alliance between the clergy and nationalist intellectuals that mobilized the Iranian masses in a popular movement.

Imprisoned by the shah in the early 1960s, Mehdi Bazargan (1907–95), a distinguished scientist who was later appointed by Ayatollah Khomeini as the first prime minister of post-revolution Iran in 1979, wrote a history of India's freedom movement. Bazargan revered al-Afghani and Muhammad Iqbal, but he was particularly attentive to the role of popular religiosity in Gandhi's mass campaign against the British. It began, he wrote, 'by a spiritual and mental revolution and conviction, with a pure spiritual force' and 'penetrated the hearts and minds of the educated class', creating 'leaders and sympathizers'.[55] India was now as West-struck as Iran, but for Bazargan its liberation from Western rule together with the charismatic figure of Gandhi, who appealed to the masses as well as to intellectuals, held up an inspiring example to Iranians aspiring to revolutionary change through religion.

The Paris-educated Ali Shariati went even further in the direction of making Shiite Islam seem a mass-mobilizing ideology. Less intellectually rigorous than Al-e Ahmad, Shariati described in more emotive terms the West's domination of Iran:

My friend, I live in a society where I face a system which controls half of the universe, maybe all of it. Mankind is being driven into a new stronghold of slavery. Although we are not in physical slavery, we are truly destined with a fate worse than yours! Our thoughts, hearts, and will powers are enslaved. In the name of sociology, education, art, sexual freedom, financial freedom, love of exploitation, and love of individuals, faith in goals, faith in humanitarian responsibility and belief in one's own school of thought are entirely taken away from within our hearts! The system has converted us into empty pots which accommodate whatever is poured inside them.[56]

Shariati greatly admired the political activism of al-Afghani, but faulted him for depending too much on conservative ruling classes and for failing to see the revolutionary potential of young masses. The translator of Frantz Fanon and Che Guevara, Ali Shariati nevertheless expanded their conventionally anti-imperialist critiques to include the Western secular ideologies of salvation: socialism and communism. He was inspired by, among other Islamic thinkers, Sayyid Qutb, Iqbal and Abul Ala Mawdudi, whose writings had begun to be translated into Persian in the 1950s. 'Marxism itself', he wrote, 'is utterly a product of the history, social organization, and cultural outlook of this same West' that it sought to negate.[57]

Shariati combined a Western tradition of historical determinism with a Shiite millenarian tradition to argue for Islam as an ideology of emancipation. Such thinkers as Shariati and Morteza Motahhari (1920–79), an erudite cleric and activist, laid the intellectual foundations of the Iranian Islamic Revolution in 1979 by arguing that the history of Shiite imams furnished everything from a specific 'political strategy' to a 'tradition of party campaign and organization'.[58]

As it turned out, most Iranians, who saw the corrupt and repressive shah as a tool of American interests, sought political redemption through their faith. The experience of deprivation, loneliness and anomie had made many Muslims in urban centres turn towards rather than away from Islam. The shah alienated them even further with his brutal attempt to create a dictatorship, following the then-fashionable theory outlined by the American social scientist Samuel Huntington, according to which premature democracy in modernizing Third World countries created chaos rather than political stability, undermining the rule of law and the possibility of economic and social development.

When the revolt finally erupted in Iran in the late 1970s, every major socio-political organization outside the state joined it – secular communists and nationalists as well as religious radicals. Millions of demonstrators and strikers appeared united by their hatred for the American-backed shah. But it was an exiled cleric, Ayatollah Khomeini, the charismatic figure dreamt of by Bazargan in the 1960s, who emerged as the most visible face of protest by deftly using the idiom of Shiite Islam – and anti-imperialism: 'Islam is the religion of militant individuals who are committed to truth and justice. It is the religion of those who desire freedom and independence. It is the school of those who struggle against imperialism.'[59]

A referendum held weeks after his triumphant return to Iran in 1979 overwhelmingly endorsed Khomeini; 99 per cent of Iranians voted in favour of Iran being made into an Islamic Republic. 'Come friends,' Ali Shariati had paraphrased Frantz Fanon in the 1960s, 'let us abandon Europe; let us cease this nauseating apish imitation of Europe. Let us leave behind this Europe that always speaks of humanity, but destroys human beings wherever it finds them.'[60] Revolutionary Iran seemed to be fulfilling the wildest dreams of such anti-Western radicals as Shariati. Certainly the clerics, while using an explicitly religious idiom to get the Iranian masses on their side, did not just address religious issues. At a dark time in twentieth-century Muslim history, the devil speaking in Muhammad Iqbal's poem *Iblees Ki Majlis-e-Shura* ('The Parliament of Satan') had lamented:

> I know that this community no longer cherishes the Qur'an
> That capitalism is now also the Faith of the Believer.
> I know too, that in the dark night of the East
> The defenders of faith no longer possess Moses' illuminating hand
> But the imperatives of the present age make me apprehensive
> That the path of the Prophet may yet reveal itself to the people.[61]

So it now seemed to happen. The Iranian clerics used an explicitly Islamic vocabulary with a left-wing programme to propose revisions of property ownership, expropriate the wealth of the bourgeoisie, secure freedom from foreign economic and military domination, control vulgar consumption and promise social welfare to the poor. (It was no accident that two of the main left-leaning intellectuals – Jalal Al-e Ahmad and Ali Shariati – had clerical fathers.)

As it turned out, Khomeini kept the shah's authoritarian state more or less intact. Far from expressing a political spirituality, he installed clerics in powerful positions and began to use the shah's methods – secret police, torture, execution – against his real and perceived opponents, and on a larger scale than the shah. (Opposed to the creeping clerical despotism, Mehdi Bazargan first resigned from the government, and then became an intrepid critic of the Iranian regime.) The long war with Iraq (1980–88), initiated by the Western-backed

Saddam Hussein, tightened the hold of religious radicals over the levers of state power.

The early ferocity of the Revolution has abated since then. The regime has relied more upon development fuelled by oil revenues and mass literacy drives than terror for its legitimacy. And there have been reformist trends within the regime. The intellectual Abdolkarim Soroush has rejected Ali Shariati's description of Islam as an ideology and has called for an 'Islamic secularism'; he is a major influence upon the country's pro-democracy Green Movement. The generational shift within Iranian Islam was articulated most cogently by Sayyid Muhammad Khatami, who was twice elected president in the 1990s and 2000s. But even Khatami, who emphasizes a 'dialogue of civilizations' and concedes many positive aspects to the West, believes that Western civilization is 'worn out and senile' and is trying to preserve its dominance by 'adapting neo-colonialism' to the new age.[62] It is largely due to the Islamic Revolution in Iran that today the basic principles of the first Muslim Westernized elites – that development entails the rejection of Islamic values in favour of Western ones – lie discredited from Tunisia to Xinjiang, and that Islam continues to serve as a focal point of resistance to authoritarian regimes in the Muslim world.

Khatami's successor, Mahmoud Ahmadinejad, vends much cruder versions of his ideas, directing populist nationalism against Israel, the old bugbear of politicized Muslims in the region. He supports anti-Western forces across the Middle East, and his obsession with nuclear power, which is backed by all sections of political opinion in Iran including those opposed to the Islamic regime, carefully manipulates the potent sentiments of Iranian nationalism. His populism represents the democratization of anti-Westernism in Muslim countries.

That resentment has also been globalized, and channelled into acts of spectacular violence in the past two decades by al-Qaeda and its affiliates. It's no accident that militants from Morocco to Sumatra and Xinjiang to Mozambique found a hospitable home in Afghanistan, another country where Westernized elites violently imposed their ways on a large majority. In the 1970s a communist regime in Afghanistan, propped up by the Soviet Union, tried to modernize hastily and brutally what it saw as a feudal and backward society, uprooting people from their traditional cultures and forcing them into Western-style cities and occupations. There were many who resisted, and within just a few months, 12,000 people considered anti-communist, many of them members of the country's educated elite, were killed in Kabul alone; many thousands more were murdered in the country-side.

The rest of this appalling story of Afghanistan's destruction is better known. The subsequent backlash from radical Islamists was supported by the United States, and turned, with the help of Pakistan's Islamist dictator General Zia-ul-Haq and Saudi Arabia, into the first global jihad in Islam's long history. Wherever there were Muslims, Saudi petrodollars underwrote Wahhabist mosques, madrasas and clerics. Victory against Soviet Communism – a godless ideology of the amoral West – emboldened radical Islamists, and expanded their anti-Western agenda.

In Pakistan, Egypt, Algeria, Tunisia, and many other countries, Islamists had often articulated popular opposition to Western imperialists, and then acquired greater support as postcolonial elites, which claimed to be nationalist and socialist, proved to be corrupt and despotic. The Islamists invoked, too, the plight of Palestinian refugees and the standing insult the presence of Israel in the Middle East posed to Muslim pride. But it was the experience of training and fighting together during the decade-long anti-Soviet jihad in Afghanistan that bound the Islamists together into an international community. It defined their enemy more clearly than before – the materialist and imperialist civilization of the West in which both communists and capitalists were complicit – and stoked their fantasy of a global caliphate. In the 1990s, such Afghanistan-trained Islamists declared jihad against Westernized and Westernizing elites in their respective countries, and were brutally crushed.

Many strands and tendencies merged in this joint revolt against local tyrants and their Western allies. Abu Musab al-Zarqawi, who later became notorious for his brutality as leader of al-Qaeda in Iraq, spent five years in a Jordanian prison for conspiring to overthrow the monarchy and replace it with a caliphate. Osama bin Laden was outraged by the Saudi support for the American-led war on Iraq in 1991.

Extremist Wahhabism, in the person of bin Laden, joined with Sayyid Qutb's Egyptian Islamism in the person of Ayman al-Zawahiri, a refugee from a long-running Western-backed secular dictatorship in Egypt who became bin Laden's deputy. These were the ideological heirs of Qutb, whom they claimed as their inspiration for jihad (they were also indebted to Mawdudi for their idea of a 'vanguard' revolutionary movement). Qutb had indeed prophesized a global combat between Islam and the West, and exhorted Muslims to shed their passivity and become self-motivated individuals fulfilling God's will. But his zealous followers went way beyond anything their mentor advocated in targeting civilians, including Muslims. Failure to topple their own regimes, and news of atrocities committed against the devout in Palestine, Kashmir and Chechnya by pro-Western countries like Israel, India and Russia, made them determined to strike the apparent puppet-master, the United States, and set off a worldwide clash between Muslims and the West. After a series of abortive attempts, the militants finally succeeded on 11 September 2001.

It now seems grotesquely apt that the attack was led by a radicalized young man from Cairo. Mohammed Atta exemplified all the major trends of Muslim countries in recent decades: demographic explosion, urbanization, and the rise of a DIY Islam which is as radical as it is private and political. In many countries, especially in the Middle East and South Asia where modernization failed or was not even properly attempted, hundreds of millions of Muslims have long inhabited a netherworld fantasy of religious-political revenge. Trying and failing to enter the modern world defined by the West, they ended up not only uprooting themselves but also hating the West – the source of so much upheaval and trauma in their lives. So it is not surprising that the vicious perpetrators of mass murder on 9/11 had millions of silent supporters. Recalling the collapse of the World Trade Center towers, the Muslim narrator of Mohsin Hamid's *The Reluctant Fundamentalist* evoked a widely felt sentiment when he said, 'I *smiled*. Yes, despicable as it may sound, my initial reaction was to be remarkably pleased.'

Remarking on a similar feeling of gratification among Turks in Istanbul, Orhan Pamuk argued that 'the Western world is scarcely aware of this overwhelming feeling of humiliation that is experienced by most of the world's population'. 'The problem facing the West', he wrote, 'is not only to discover which terrorist is preparing a bomb in which tent, which cave, or which street of which city, but also to understand the poor and scorned and "wrongful" majority that does not belong to the Western world.'[63]

The catastrophically misconceived 'global war on terror' sparked an even bigger conflagration, intensifying, as Pamuk feared, 'the hostility toward the West felt by millions of people in the Islamic countries and poverty-stricken regions of the world – people living in conditions that give rise to feelings of humiliation and inferiority'.[64] Unwittingly parodying many earlier Western interventions in Asia, in 2002 the Bush administration pledged to bring 'democracy, development, free markets and free trade to every corner of the world', a mission that, informed by neither history nor irony, soon met with fierce local resistance and universal opprobrium. In particular, the Anglo-American invasion of Iraq in 2003, which caused the deaths of hundreds of thousands of people, radicalized Muslims across a vast swathe of territory. Opening up new theatres of conflict within Africa, Europe and East Asia, the global war on terror seemed to ring in a fully fledged 'clash of civilizations'. A survey conducted by the Pew Research Center found that many 'in predominantly Muslim nations in 2006 expressed ill will toward the United States and other Western countries, frequently ascribing to them such traits as "violent" and "selfish"'.

Such rage against the West has diminished since then, together with the ideological intensity of Western interventions in Iraq and Afghanistan which have become more about saving face than about spreading freedom and democracy. Yet the widespread conviction among many Muslims today is that the West failed in its many aggressive wars on Islam and bankrupted itself in the process. It has given a new boost to the preachers of global Islam whose ideology, disseminated through TV evangelists, YouTube videos, web sites and audio recordings, seems to have as many takers among Muslim immigrants in Europe as among their home populations. Indeed, millenarian Islam has a special appeal among Muslims in the West who are convinced that their host countries are moral as well as political failures and who now look to Islam for new sources of moral and religious authority in their secular surroundings.

Though it has benefited few Muslims, economic globalization has, paradoxically, boosted old Islamic ideals of integration by shrinking time and space. Besides, the failure of nationalism has meant that for many people in Muslim countries, transnational networks override national loyalties. Wahhabi Islam continues to make inroads in places as far off as Malaysia and Indonesia. Austere versions of Arabian Islam continue to gain ground among the lower-middle classes in Pakistan through its new electronic media. Revolutionary Iran – and political Islam in general – plays a major role in the internal politics of Iraq and Lebanon. With overwhelmingly young populations, Arab countries such as Egypt and Tunisia are now trying to build representative democracy. Failure, which is not inconceivable, will provoke yet another generational shift to hardline Islamist ideas and organizations. Islam remains a gigantic powder keg, likely to blow up any time.

THE TRIUMPHS OF THE NATION-STATE: TURKEY, THE SICK MAN, REVIVES

By evolving into a strong modern nation, Turkey seems to have been the exception to the main trends of extremism and chaos in the Muslim world. Rather, it seems to have pre-empted most of them. Confronted with Western encroachments on its territory and sovereignty, it underwent the pangs of modernization early in the nineteenth century with the Tanzimat regulations. It then seems to have fortuitously lost the burdensome flab of a multinational empire and worked itself into a lean nation-state, ensuring its survival and dignity in a West-ordained global order.

This self-renewal was accomplished by a new energetic ruling class of educated and secular-minded Turks rather than the more tradition-minded sultans and viziers. The central figure was an army officer, Mustafa Kemal 'Atatürk', the hero of Turkish resistance to the European powers during and after the First World War. Born in a European province of the Ottoman Empire and exposed to the simplistic notions of nationalism and science common among educated Turks of his generation, Atatürk wanted, as he wrote in 1918, 'to carry out the social revolution in our social life in the form of a sudden coup'.[65] It helped that until his late thirties he had barely set foot in Anatolia – the heartland of conservative Turkish Islam – and he moved briskly and brutally after consolidating power in 1922. He dissolved the caliphate, the symbolic seat of Islamic authority, in 1924; shut religious organizations and schools in the following year; replaced Sharia with Western legal codes in 1926; and amended the constitution in 1928 to dethrone Islam as the state religion. This ferocious assault on traditional practice was followed by the substitution of the Latin for the Arabic alphabet and of Turkish for the Arabic call to prayer, and by the banning of fezzes, veils and other icons of Islamic culture.

The end of the caliphate, the holy office that the Ottoman sultans had revived in the last decades of their rule, shocked and appalled Muslims all over the world. They had hoped for a Turkish ruler to lead them to victory and vindication against the foreign infidels. But Atatürk, who had not been above using pan-Islamism to consolidate the fragile nation-state of Turkey against the West, now refused to oblige. As he saw it, Turkey's spiritual leadership of the Muslim community was impractical. How could Turkey with its few million Muslims hope to determine the internal affairs of India and the Malay Peninsula, both places still under Western rule? His drastic measures were also partly based on a growing Young Turkish impatience with the clergy, who had resisted the reforms of Ottoman rulers, and Sultan Abdulhamid's own futile flirtation with pan-Islamism. 'Islam, this absurd theology of an immoral Bedouin,' Atatürk once blurted out, 'is a rotting corpse that poisons our lives.'

Atatürk saw modernization as synonymous with wholesale secularization and Westernization, and he went to absurd lengths to promote Western dress and 'reform' Turkish music. One of his adopted daughters, who bombed Kurdish rebels wearing a military uniform, was turned into the model 'Republican' woman. He hoped naively that science would eventually vanquish religion, and that nationalism would step in to provide new identities to Turkish Muslims. Still, the contrast with Arabs idly fantasizing about the past glory of Islam, beseeching God for the return of his favours and complacently blaming the West for their ills couldn't be greater. Not surprisingly Atatürk, criticized by neo-traditionalists like Muhammad Iqbal, had many fervent admirers among modernizers in the Muslim world: Nasser, the shah of Iran, Jinnah and Sukarno were among those who wanted to imitate him.

He has had even more influential devotees among Western believers in a teleological or purpose-led model of history, who believe that the non-West has no choice but to move (or be pushed) into convergence with the West, using the West's own patented techniques like secularization and constitutional democracy. The historian Bernard Lewis, whose scholarship on modern Turkey made his reputation, became a welcome visitor in the Bush White House with his fantasy that Iraq could be strong-armed, just as Turkey was, into becoming a modern democracy.

But this conventional Western view, in which Turkey quickly ascends to modernity after cutting the Gordian knot of Islam, suppresses a lot of inconvenient facts. Atatürk and the rest of Turkey's revolutionaries consisted of a tiny bourgeois elite, mostly nurtured abroad, and their military techniques of modernizing and secularizing Turkish society empowered another secular military and bourgeois elite. The great mass of Turkey's population, mostly peasants concentrated in Anatolia, did not reject Islam (nor did the mass of people do so in Tunisia, Algeria or indeed Iran, despite aggressive state-backed secularization programmes). And in retrospect, even the modernizers seem to have not so much abandoned Islam as set it off on a new phase in its distinctive Turkish history.

They discarded many of the old ingrown and cumbersome aspects of Islam, such as the *ulema* who had become a powerful barrier to even the Tanzimat modernizers. Religious feeling didn't weaken. As though bowing to this fact, the Turkish government reintroduced religious education in the late 1940s, and Turks were again permitted to go on pilgrimage to Mecca and visit the shrines of sultans and saints. The military regimes that periodically ruled the country after 1961 made more concessions to the essentially Islamic nature of Turkey's population, especially after the military coup of 1980. Greater democratization was always bound to empower the traditionalist masses of Anatolia and marginalize the old dictatorial, if secular, ruling class – and so it has happened since the mid-1990s with the rise of the Islamic Justice and Development Party (AKP).

This development is often feared and scorned in the West as the 're-Islamization' of Turkey. A less alarmist way of putting it would be that the part of the Turkish population that had long played a passive role in their country's transformation from above has now found its voice. It tends to be devout, inclined to embrace Islamic symbols banned by Atatürk (such as the headscarf), while remaining a participant in the global economy in which Turkey is a major figure.

The Indian poet Iqbal, who believed that 'the morning breeze is still in search of a garden / Ill lodged in Atatürk, the soul of the East is still in search of a body',[66] expressed some broad optimism for the Turkish experiment in the early 1930s when he wrote:

> She [Turkey] alone has claimed her right of intellectual freedom; she alone has passed from the ideal to the real – a transition which entails keen intellectual and moral struggle. To her the growing complexities of a mobile and broadening life are sure to bring new situations suggesting new points of view, and necessitating fresh interpretations of principles.[67]

Some of these hopes have been realized. Turkey is the first Muslim country to have developed a model of indigenous modernity that not only does not depend on the original Western one but also seems to rival it. Furthermore, this Islamic modernism is rooted in lived experience rather than, as has been the case elsewhere, pure imagination. Western ideas remain important but they are now assessed on the basis of their effectiveness, rather than simply swallowed whole. And a certain abject attitude towards the West has been replaced by a renewed pride in Turkishness. As Necmettin Erbakan, Turkey's first openly Muslim prime minister and an early mentor to the leaders of the AKP, wrote in 1970, mocking decades of the Turkish state's imitation of the West:

> Thus the European, by making us copy him blindly and without any understanding, trapped us in this monkey's cage and, as a result, forced

us to abandon our personality and nobility. That is to say, he was successful in this because he used agents recruited from within, who felt inferior
and disgusted with themselves, bringing to his knees the Turk who for
centuries could not be defeated by the crusades and external blows.[68]

For Muslims elsewhere, Turkey's success confirms the validity of
an 'Islamic' solution to the problem of adapting to Western modernity, and the geopolitical implications of this unique achievement are
immense. By its own reckoning, Turkey has resoundingly answered
the question that haunted the Tanzimatists: can a Muslim country
modernize itself enough to be counted as a member of Western
civilization? The isolationist nationalism of Atatürk reflected this
determination to enlist Turkey into the only club that mattered. While
secluding itself from its Muslim neighbourhood, Turkey went on to
propose itself as a reliable partner to NATO. Joining other anti-
communist Cold War alliances it also befriended Israel, the outcast
state for Muslims around the world.

But Turkey, like Meiji Japan before it, may have finally come up
against an explicitly racially motivated disinclination in the West
against granting it full membership to their club. As its efforts to join
the European Union are rebuffed, and anti-Muslim-immigrant sentiment rises in Europe, Turks have begun to wonder whether, although
a modernized Islam seems to have adjusted itself to the West, the West
may still be reluctant to include Islam in its self-perceptions.

This frustration of Turkey's oldest geopolitical ambition has coincided with the country's long-delayed reckoning with its geographical
destiny, or its long history as the ruler of the Middle East. Growing
economic ties bind it to the Arab Middle East and Iran. The rise of
pro-Palestinian sentiment within the Turkish population has led to
diplomatic confrontations with Israel. Despite being offered a lucrative deal, Turkey refused to allow its territory to be used by American
troops during the war on Iraq in 2003. It also opposes the Western
regime of sanctions against Iran. One result is that after Nasser,
Saddam Hussein and Hezbollah's Hassan Nasrallah, the fierce anti-
Western passions of the Arab street have been focused, more
respectably, on the AKP leader, Prime Minister Recep Tayyip Erdoğan.
After nearly a century of Western-style modernization, Turkey, under

an Islamic leader, finds itself holding the banner of pan-Islamism yet again; and this is not all.

Elections across the Arab world, which have enfranchised millions of people for the first time, are bringing parties with an explicitly Islamic orientation to power. Even before the Arab Spring, many Muslim countries had made new ideological and political beginnings with leaders from non-secular and non-elite backgrounds. In Indonesia, the world's largest Muslim country, Abdurrahman Wahid, the leader of one of the world's biggest Islamic organizations, helped his country's transition from a dictatorship to representative government. For Arabs seeking to rebuild their political systems battered by decades of despotic rule, there is no clearer precedent than nearby Turkey, where many previously underrepresented people have been politically empowered by the AKP.

Nearly a century ago, Atatürk seemed to be the Muslim world's greatest visionary as he hectically remade his country in the image of the West. His attempts at large-scale secularization – which essentially created a small authoritarian elite – were to be admired and imitated by many rulers of Muslim countries, most recently Pakistan's deposed dictator Pervez Musharraf. But Turkey itself shows that Atatürk's political and cultural experiment succeeded only partially and that some selective borrowings from Western modernity cannot relegate Islam to the private sphere – let alone ensure social and economic justice for the majority of the population. Rather, many Muslims, suffering from a secular and kleptocratic despotism, decided to experiment with a more Islamic polity. In the future there will be many more politicized Muslims desiring accountable governments that guarantee civil rights and a degree of egalitarianism – and they will express their aspirations less through secular Western ideologies than through the old ideal of a moral community of believers.

'THE CHINESE PEOPLE HAVE STOOD UP'

China's own evolution into a strong, centralized nation-state has been much messier and bloodier, involving the premature deaths of tens of millions of people, and the persecution and displacement of many more. But its success lies at the heart of China's assertiveness today. The pressures on China in the early twentieth century were, if anything, greater than those suffered by the doddering Ottoman Empire. The collapse of the Qing dynasty, the Japanese invasion of the country, and protracted civil war between Sun Yat-sen's Guomindang and the Chinese Communist Party made it imperative, even from a perspective other than the Social Darwinian one, for China to form a strong nation-state or perish. In this, it succeeded beyond the wildest dreams of its founders, and, as in Turkey, the selective repudiation of the past and the appropriation of Western ideologies like secular nationalism and communism were crucial.

Successive humiliations by foreigners shaped Chinese nationalism. Chinese schoolchildren still learn about Western vandalism during the Opium War in great detail, and the indoctrination began well before the Communists seized power: 'The Opium War', one history textbook of the late 1920s declared, 'branded the iron hoofprint of imperialism on the bodies of our people.'[69] A book on the conflict published in 1931 openly confessed to inciting 'bitter hatred of the common enemy' among its Chinese readers. It was left to Mao to redefine the conflict as a 'national war against imperialism';[70] he also used it to explain why neither revolution nor nation-building was a dinner party. 'In the face of such enemies,' he declared in 1951, 'the Chinese revolution cannot be other than protracted and ruthless.'[71]

In 1990, a year after the Chinese army killed unarmed protestors near Tiananmen Square, a commemorative symposium organized by Communist authorities focused on evil foreigners, describing the Opium War as a plot to 'enslave our people, steal our wealth and turn a great nation that had been independent for thousands of years into a semi-feudal semi-colony'. Many Chinese looked forward to 1997 – the year the British lease on Hong Kong, exacted from the hapless emperor after the Opium War, was to expire – as a likely salve for a 'century of humiliation'; and anyone appearing to stand in their way – Margaret Thatcher, the British prime minister, or Chris Patten, the last British viceroy of Hong Kong – or seeming to display the old British attitude of condescension and superiority was attacked, often viciously. Nothing revealed British weakness in Chinese eyes (and gladdened Chinese hearts) more than a widely distributed picture of Mrs Thatcher emerging from a blunt talking-to by Deng Xiaoping and then stumbling on the steps of Beijing's Great Hall of the People and ending up on her knees.

The handover of 1997 came and went. The British retreated; Hong Kong returned to Chinese control. But Chinese nationalism, inflamed again in 1999 by NATO's accidental bombing of the Chinese embassy in Belgrade and by other real and imagined slights from the West, remains a potent force. One of the entrances to the parklands of the Summer Palace still displays a sign saying: 'Do not forget the national shame, rebuild the Chinese nation.'

For the early generations of Chinese leaders, this was of course easier said than done. The idea of restoring China's old glory motivated the masses as well as its elite, and the best way, it seemed to a wide range of thinkers from Yan Fu and Liang Qichao to Mao Zedong, was to replace the old dynastic state and its politically passive subjects with a centralized nation-state. But in order to mobilize active and efficient citizens in the service of a nation-state China needed new and common institutions: schools, the law, and military service. And, after several abortive experiments, it was eventually the ideology of communism that helped create the necessary political community for the creation of a modern nation-state.

In many ways, the humiliations at the Paris Peace Conference, and the subsequent May Fourth Movement which exalted Western thought and violently repudiated Confucianism, enshrined Marxism-Leninism as the main ideological outlook of Chinese thinkers and revolutionaries. The Russian Revolution, Lenin's voluntary renunciation of Russia's territories and special privileges in China, and a resurgent communist movement in Europe all helped convince Chinese activists of the validity and inevitable triumph of communism.

Lenin's influential theory of imperialism called for liberation movements in countries oppressed by imperialist forces, so Marxism-Leninism could seem to complement the fierce nationalism of the May Fourth generation. Lenin's idea of a vanguard of dedicated revolutionaries appealed not only to men like Chen Duxiu or Mao but also

Sun Yat-sen, who reorganized his Nationalist Party, the Guomindang, along Leninist lines, and set up, with Soviet assistance, the famous Whampoa Military Academy where many of China's leaders were trained. Shortly before he died in 1924, Sun stressed the need for revolutionary glue in China:

> Why are Chinese like a sheet of loose sand? What makes them like a sheet of loose sand? It is because there is too much individual freedom. Because Chinese have too much freedom, therefore China needs a revolution . . . Because we are like a sheet of loose sand, foreign imperialism has invaded, we have been oppressed by the commercial warfare of the great powers, and we have been unable to resist. If we are to resist foreign oppression in the future, we must overcome individual freedom and join together as a firm unit, just as one adds water and cement to loose gravel to produce something as solid as a rock.[72]

The problem in China, Sun recognized, was one of mobilizing the Chinese masses into a revolutionary movement. He even allied himself with the Communists to achieve this. By 1924, Sun had also become aware that his political programme must meet the economic challenge of China – the agrarian crisis in particular. But he died too early, and his successor, Chiang Kai-shek, though a self-styled military tactician, had little interest in land reform. Allied with landlords, urban financiers and businessmen, he failed to keep up Sun's radical initiative, which passed to Mao Zedong and the Communists.

'Whoever wins the support of the peasants,' Mao said, 'will win China; whoever solves the land question will win the peasants.'[73] And so it happened. Mao's stress on rural mobilization was initially opposed by doctrinaire Marxists within his own party. Eventually, however, through a series of agrarian revolutions – land redistribution, local government by peasants – the Communists under Mao welded Chinese peasants into a revolutionary army, and made their victory in 1949 possible.

Analytically, a theory suffused with the assumptions of Western history proved disastrous for China. Here Liang Qichao's critique of the earliest socialist ideas of class struggle in China was to prove prescient.

China, he had argued, did not have the particular social and economic conflicts that made socialism so necessary in the West. Sticking to textbook Marxism, however, the Communists misleadingly characterized the Chinese past as 'feudal': a built-in bias towards urban industrial growth and against agrarian life led to a condescending attitude towards the mass of Chinese peasants; 'poor and blank', as Mao called them. And the search for class enemies led to campaigns of mass killings in the 1930s and 1940s in the remote country areas into which the Communists had been forced by their rivals, the Nationalists and the Japanese.

Organizationally, however, communism worked much better than the warmed-over Confucianism of the Nationalists. Eventually it helped Mao build up a mass base for the CCP in the countryside. Unlike his rivals, Mao himself provided a compelling narrative of China to the Chinese masses. As he wrote in his 1940 essay, 'On New Democracy':

> Since the invasion of foreign capitalism and the gradual growth of capitalist elements in Chinese society, that is, during the hundred years from the Opium War until the Sino-Japanese War, the country has changed by degrees into a colonial, semi-colonial, and semi-feudal society. China today is colonial in the enemy-occupied areas and basically semi-colonial in the non-occupied areas, and it is predominantly feudal in both . . . It is precisely against these predominant political, economic, and cultural forms that our revolution is directed.[74]

The Japanese invasion helped Mao's cause as much as the corruption and brutality of the Nationalists; the Communists tapped directly into the anti-imperialism of the Chinese masses, and appeared the natural leaders of the Chinese resistance even when their actual military contribution to Japan's defeat was minor. Class struggle was another of their preferred catalysts for the reorganization of Chinese society. They pursued, often brutally, land reform and other class-based social and economic policies, even as they fought a civil war with the Nationalists after 1945. Moreover, the same organizational skills helped the CCP to rebuild a political and administrative system remarkably quickly after their victory in 1949 (which forced the

Nationalists to retreat to Taiwan), and to lead their young nation-state into a major war with the United States in Korea in 1951.

Together with Soviet and Korean communist forces, China fought the United States to a stalemate in Korea by 1953 at the cost of nearly half a million Chinese dead. For the fledgling People's Republic of China it was a bloody initiation into the Cold War, and its century-long suspicion of Western powers was confirmed when the United States successfully isolated China, arming Nationalist Taiwan and giving the small island China's seat at the United Nations.

Yet Marxism-Leninism continued to reveal its intellectual inability to deal with Chinese realities. The view (deriving from the May Fourth radicals) that the Chinese were irrevocably tainted by their backward past and needed urgent guidance from a vanguard was never going to encourage political democratization in China. The problem of concentrating excessive power in the apparently wise 'vanguard' became more and more apparent as China embarked on rapid economic growth.

Wanting China to catch up with the West as quickly as possible, Mao Zedong set fantasy targets: he asked his compatriots in the mid-1950s, for instance, to match Britain's industrial production in fifteen years. The blunders resulted in a series of catastrophes which brought China to its knees. Food shortages followed by famine killed more than 30 million people between 1959 and 1961. Mao's Cultural Revolution, which aimed, initially at least, to start the Chinese revolution afresh in the 1960s degenerated into civil war.

It was the death of Mao in 1976 that enabled a fresh beginning on principles that, though presented as purely pragmatic, seemed to owe less to orthodox communism than to Mencius's economic ideals of public ownership combined with free trade. In retrospect, communism in China seems more and more to have been an effective ideology for mobilizing and unifying the Chinese masses. Chinese activists in the early twentieth century tried and failed to create a unified nation-state that could launch China's search for wealth and power in the modern world. It was the Communists who succeeded in creating a broad-based participatory nationalism that included peasants as well as urban workers. They created a new army, giving a new sense of purpose and energy to demoralized peasants, and went on to build a powerful state bureaucracy that combined party and administrative officials to reach down into every urban neighbourhood and village.

This is partly why, though communism led to a calamitous misinterpretation of Chinese realities and has lost its intellectual appeal, the Chinese Communist Party seems in little danger of going the way of its East European and Russian counterparts. It no longer insists on doctrinal orthodoxy – indeed it has tried to replace communism with Confucian notions of the 'harmonious society' – but it remains unchallenged in its role as the sole guarantor of China's stability, security and growing prosperity.

Partly out of noble intentions, and partly out of vanity, malice and ineptitude, Mao unleashed one disaster after another on his people. But his heirs still rule the country, and millions continue to invest their faith, despite successive tragedies and disasters, in what they see as the good intentions and wisdom of their remote rulers in Beijing.

Founding the People's Republic of China in 1949, Mao Zedong had said, 'The Chinese have always been a great, courageous and industrious nation; it is only in modern times that they have fallen behind. And that was due entirely to oppression and exploitation by foreign imperialism and domestic reactionary governments.' Mao went on to declare that 'the Chinese people, comprising one quarter of humanity, have now stood up'.

The words now have a prophetic resonance, confirming that the old vision of wealth and power dreamt of by Yan Fu as well as Liang Qichao is a reality. 'We will have not only a powerful army but also a powerful air force and a powerful navy,' Mao promised in 1949. 'Ours will,' he warned, 'no longer be a nation subject to insult and humiliation.' In less than six decades, history seems to have fulfilled Mao's hopes.

There still exists a great and restless Chinese mass in the countryside, cruelly shut out from the new urban prosperity to which their labour and taxes have contributed so much. Social unrest, environmental decay, corruption and other ills feed on China's new affluence. Yet China, the biggest exporter and the largest holder of foreign-exchange reserves in the world, increasingly drives the global economy, boosting

GDP rates across the world with its hunger for resources and markets. Western Europe and America have no option but to pay court to it; the small commodity-producing countries of Africa and Latin America form the new periphery to China's metropole; its formerly hostile neighbours – Japan, South Korea, Vietnam, Mongolia – now cower in its shadow, seeking favourable trade deals.

The CCP's hold on state power remains unchallenged; it keeps key industries under its control; it promotes the rhetoric of egalitarianism and maintains a remarkable ideological cohesiveness on foreign policy, ensuring that China presents a united face to the world. China doesn't seem close to embracing liberal democracy; rather, its one-party state seems to have ensured the political stability that Samuel Huntington regarded as imperative for Third World societies undergoing modernization.

As previous pages have shown, the idea of individual rights was never deeply rooted in even the most liberal strains of modern Chinese thought, which always had a collectivist orientation. Democracy was seen as essential to the modern nation-state that China had to become in order to survive. 'The strength of a nation', Liang Qichao wrote, 'stems ultimately from democracy.' But democracy for Liang was 'simply public-mindedness', as opposed to the selfishness of monarchism.[75]

In this formulation of democracy, individual rights enshrined by Western liberal ideologies were always subordinate to the imperatives of national solidarity and a strong state, especially in the context of the permanent external threats China faced in the first half of the twentieth century. The cults of the state and a loyal citizenry that were manifest even in Liang Qichao's writings were to be elaborated at length by the Communists, notwithstanding Marxist predictions about the 'withering away of the state'.

During his debates with his radical rivals, Liang Qichao asserted that Western-style liberalism might weaken the state by promoting individual and group interests. What China may well need, he said, is state socialism which controls the economy and works to diminish inequality, while making the country a serious combatant in the jungle of international competition. 'The economic policy I advocate', he wrote, 'is primarily to encourage and protect capitalists so that they can do their best to engage in external competition. To this policy all other considerations are subordinate.' Liang's inadvertent prophecy is confirmed by contemporary China, which the West increasingly accuses of being mercantilist in its economic policies, and where an all-powerful state is quick to suppress, often brutally, freedom of expression and other civil rights if they seem to be undermining the all-important national tasks of high economic growth and political stability.

THE RISE OF THE 'REST'

Praising European energy and initiative in 1855, de Tocqueville added, 'European races are often the greatest rogues, but at least they are rogues to whom God gave the will and the power and whom he seems to have destined for some time to be at the head of mankind. Nothing on the entire globe will resist their influence.'[76] This turned out to be true in more ways than de Tocqueville could predict.

White men, conscious of their burden, changed the world for ever, subjecting its great diversity to their own singular outlook and in the process reducing potentially rich encounters with other peoples and countries to monologues about the unassailable superiority of modern Western politics, economy and culture. Successfully exporting its ideas to the remotest corners of the world, the West also destroyed native self-confidence, causing a political, economic and social desolation that can perhaps never be relieved by modernity alone.

In the end, Western efforts to modernize supposedly backward Asians, however sincere or altruistic, incited more resentment than admiration or gratitude. Expelled from their old social and political orders and denied dignity in a West-dominated world, aggrieved natives always wanted to beat the West at its own game. This is the point that the Chinese intellectual in André Malraux's prophetic novel *The Temptation of the West* (1926) makes when he says, 'Europe thinks she has conquered all these young men who now wear her garments. But they hate her. They are waiting for what the common people call her "secrets".'[77] Many of these secrets are now in Asian hands.

Television and the internet, and in particular the growth of virtual communities, have helped stoke an unprecedented intensity of political emotion around the world. It is no exaggeration to say that millions, probably hundreds of millions of people in societies who have grown up with a history of subjection to Europe and America – the Chinese software engineer and the Turkish tycoon, as well as the unemployed Egyptian graduate – derive profound gratification from the prospect of humiliating their former masters and overlords, who appear uncompromisingly wedded to their right to dictate events around the world. The images from Guantanamo Bay and Abu Ghraib, the deep Western financial crisis, and the brutal but inept military actions in Afghanistan and Pakistan all sustain a powerful sense of Western hypocrisy, failure and retrenchment.

This loss of the West's moral prestige and the assertiveness of the East may appear a recent phenomenon. But, as this book has shown, the less uneven global order coming into being was outlined as early as the nineteenth century by Asian intellectuals who rejected the West's racial and imperial hierarchies and its right to define the rules of international politics. The historical resentments and frustrations of non-Western societies, whose periodic eruptions come as a shock to many Europeans and Americans, have long been central to Asia's political life in which memories of past religious and political grandeur despoiled by European imperialists still have not faded.

These different national subjectivities now combine to remake the modern world; it is impossible to ignore them. Assumptions of Western supremacy remain entrenched even among intelligent people; indeed, they routinely dictate the writing of newspaper editorials as well as the making of foreign and economic policy in the United States and Europe. However, for many others, the Western nations long ago squandered much of their moral authority – as early as the First World War – even though they retained their power to dictate the course of history. But even this power, rarely admired and mostly feared, leaked away steadily throughout the Cold War's many cynical hot wars. Nor was it boosted by the downfall of the West's communist rival. Blighted by the calamitous 'war on terror', it has been profoundly discredited by the collapse of the 'Washington Consensus', the West's vaunted model of unregulated financial capitalism.

Globalization, it is clear, does not lead to a flat world marked by increasing integration, standardization and cosmopolitan openness, despite the wishful thinking of some commentators. Rather, it reinforces tribalist affiliations, sharpens old antipathies, and incites new ones while unleashing a cacophony of competing claims. This can be seen most clearly today within Europe and the United States, the originators of globalization. Inequality and unemployment grow as highly mobile corporations continually move around the world in search of cheap labour and high profits, evading taxation and therefore draining much-needed investment in welfare systems for ageing populations. Economic setbacks, the prospect of long-term decline and a sense of political impotence stoke a great rage and paranoia among their populations, directed largely at non-white immigrants, particularly Muslims.

As the West retreats into parochial neuroses, Asian countries appear more outward-looking, confident and optimistic. Turkey and Japan seek to move out from under the Western security umbrella they have huddled beneath for decades. Longstanding territorial disputes between old rivals in the Pacific – such as China and its neighbours – remain unresolved, leaving the United States with many military and diplomatic options in the region. But economic trends tell a different story. Trade with China anchors the economy of Brazil as well as those of Indonesia and Australia, bypassing the United States and the European Union. New trade agreements and regional blocs – such as the one between ASEAN countries (the Association of South-east Asian Nations) and China that creates the world's largest combined market – informal groups like BRICS (Brazil, Russia, India, China and South Africa) and the G20, and revolts against despotic clients of the United States and Europe in the Middle East and North Africa – all these developments attest to a widespread desire to defrost the remaining divisions left over from the Cold War, and to create an international order less dependent on the United States and Western Europe.

Modernizing China, in particular, poses a formidable challenge to the West, and a much greater one than that presented by radical Islamists who mostly embody the rage of permanent losers in the international economic system. Observing a humiliated country in 1889, Kipling had wondered, 'What will happen when China really wakes up, runs a line from Shanghai to Lhasa, and controls her own gun-factories and arsenals?' This old anxiety now has a strong basis as an aggressively nationalistic China rises swiftly, and, with Turkey, India, Egypt and Iran all going their own way, the long revolt against the West that began in the late nineteenth century seems to be approaching a historical watershed. Certainly, the dominance of the West already appears just another, surprisingly short-lived phase in the long history of empires and civilizations.

Epilogue: An Ambiguous Revenge

*It is abundantly clear who are the strong and who the weak,
who the fit and the unfit, in today's world . . . In the future, a
condition of prosperity without equality, wealth without
peace, will probably prevail.*

Zhang Junmai, 1923

*We are not going to follow the West in competition, in selfish-
ness, in brutality.*

Rabindranath Tagore, in Beijing 1924

The growth of historical and internationalist awareness during the
late nineteenth and early twentieth centuries now seems truly astonishing. Only a few years after al-Afghani rebutted British claims to
have civilized India, Tagore was debating the vices of nationalism
with the Japanese, and Liang Qichao was reflecting on the corrup-
tions of American democracy and capitalism. In many ways, the
insights Asian thinkers produced into their own and the larger human
condition at this time are still transforming the world's intellectual
and political landscape and shaping individual and collective
consciousness.

It was a small group of thinkers in every Asian country whom education and experience exposed to a larger view of their societies and
the world. Marginal men by virtue of that education and experience,
they were particularly sensitive to change; though isolated from the

mass of their ordinary compatriots, they were the first, nevertheless, to articulate their deepest predicaments, needs and aspirations.

It took much private and public tumult, and great physical and intellectual journeys, to bring these thinkers to the point where they could make sense of themselves and their environment, and then the knowledge they achieved after so much toil was often full of pain and did not offer hope. They often seemed to change their minds and contradict themselves. As some of the first to break with tradition, they were faced with the Sisyphean task of finding their bearings in the modern world and reorienting their minds to new problems of personal and collective identity. They were conscious of belonging to civilizations that had not so long ago been great and self-contained but were now growing infirm against a successful and vigorous West. So the manifold adjustments to a new and largely painful historical situation led them into apparent inconsistencies: a figure like Liang Qichao, for instance, upheld Chinese tradition, then rejected it *in toto* before embracing it again; al-Afghani went through phases of bitterly arraigning Islam and then passionately defending it; Sayyid Qutb was a fervent secular nationalist before he turned into an uncompromising Islamist. Even the most conservative of Asian intellectuals and activists – Gandhi, Kang Youwei, Mohammed Abduh – were forced to radically interpret their own traditions – Hindu, Confucian and Islamic.

Personally powerless, they lurched between hope and despair, vigorous commitment and a sense of futility. Still, there is a striking unity to be observed in their perceptions, and this is because as traditionalists or iconoclastic radicals, these thinkers and activists were struggling to articulate a satisfying answer to the same question: how to reconcile themselves and others to the dwindling of their civilization through internal decay and Westernization while regaining parity and dignity in the eyes of the white rulers of the world.

This was the fundamental challenge for the first generation of modern Asian intellectuals, and many of the ideologies embraced by modern Asian peoples – secular nationalism, revolutionary communism, state socialism, Arab nationalism, pan-Islamism – developed as a response to the same stubborn challenge of the West. It links not only the Muslim Jamal al-Din al-Afghani to the Chinese Liang Qichao, but also al-Afghani to Osama bin Laden, Liang to Mao Zedong, the Ottoman Empire to present-day Turkey and pre-Communist China to the capitalist China of today.

Many of these thinkers judged Western-style politics and economics to be inherently violent and destructive forces. They knew that borrowing technical skills through a modern system of education from Europe wasn't enough; these borrowings brought with them a whole new way of life. They demanded an organized mass society whose basic unit was the self-reliant individual who pursues his economic self-interest while progressively liberating himself from guild rules, religious obligations and other communal solidarities – a presupposition that threatened to wreck the old moral order. These thinkers sensed that, though irresistible and often necessary, the modern industrial society and social freedoms pioneered by Europe would destroy many of their cherished cultures and traditions, just as they had in Europe itself, and leave chaos in their place. In the 1920s Zhang Junmai, the disciple of Liang Qichao and Tagore's host in China, summed up some widely shared fears about the coming confrontation between two opposed modes of life:

> The fundamental principles upon which our nation is founded are quietism, as opposed to [Western] activism; spiritual satisfaction, as opposed to the striving for material advantage; a self-sufficient agrarianism, as opposed to profit-seeking mercantilism; and a morally transforming sense of brotherhood rather than racial segregation ... A nation founded on agriculture lacks a knowledge of the industrial arts, [but] it is likewise without material demands; thus, though it exists over a long period of time, it can still maintain a standard of poverty but equality, scarcity but peace. But how will it be hereafter?

As people like Zhang feared, the process of modernization was to have a drastic impact at the very least. It was to disrupt old economies of agriculture and handicrafts, barter and trade, and draw young people away to the squalor of new urban centres, sundering or loosening the religious and communal attachments that gave meaning to their lives and exposing their raw nerves to extremist politics. And all this was for a process which did not lead directly, even in the West itself, to a clear destination of happiness and stability, and which

despite producing mass education, cheap consumer goods, the popular press and mass entertainment had only partly relieved a widely
and deeply felt rootlessness, confusion and anomie.

Fearing or suspecting this fate for their societies, many Asian intellectuals became some of the most eloquent – and earliest – critics of
modernity, using their own traditionalist conceptions of the meaning
and purpose of human life to counter the assumption that economic
liberalism, individual self-interest and industrialization could be the
cure-all for the manifold problems of the human condition. Often
drawing upon philosophical and spiritual traditions in Islam, Hinduism and Confucianism they developed a refined suspicion of the 'brave
new world' of science and reason, insisting on the non-rational,
non-utilitarian aspects of human existence. With their anti-modern
sensibility, which transcended conventional political categories and
divisions, they anticipated Europe's own thinkers, who were forced to
re-examine their nineteenth-century belief in a progressively rational
world by the slaughter of the First World War.

The richness of their ideas and imagination continues to be a
resource for societies faced with the crisis of modernity. Still, it should
be admitted: the course of history has bypassed many of their fondest
hopes. In fact, it was European principles of nationalism and civic
patriotism that almost all native elites embraced in order to beat (or
at least draw level with) the West in what seemed a Darwinian struggle for the future. Even someone as spiritually minded, anti-political
and critical of modern state-building as Gandhi could not avoid
becoming a nationalist leader; he even flirted with pan-Islamism early
in his political career. Impatient to reorient China's traditionalist
masses towards nationalism, Chinese intellectuals felt compelled to
vilify over two millennia of Confucian tradition. The Ottoman Turks
went so far as to abolish the office of the Islamic caliphate altogether,
renounce their leadership of the Muslim *umma*, and then disestablish
Islam itself in order to turn Turkey into a modern nation-state.

Other Western ideas also seemed crucial in stealing some of the
wealth and power of the West. Liberal democracy – elected parliaments, an independent judiciary and press – initially appeared as
important as science and technology in mobilizing a modern economy

along rational and utilitarian lines. Indeed, as one indigenous modernizer after another in Japan, Turkey, China and India conceded, resistance to the West required urgent adaptation to Western ideas of organizing state and society. At the very least, it called for the expedient overthrow of the apparently moribund empires and dynasties of the East.

There was one Western idea in particular that proved irresistible to Muslim as well as Communist anti-imperialists. Endorsed by the success of Europe, it was embraced by postcolonial elites almost everywhere in Asia. This revolutionary recipe for self-strengthening and pride, generous in its emancipatory promise, consisted of the institutions and practices of the nation-state: clear boundaries, orderly government, a loyal bureaucracy, a code of rights to protect citizens, rapid economic growth through industrial capitalism or socialism, mass literacy programmes, technical knowledge and the development of a sense of common origins within a national community.

Fulfilling either some or the barest minimum of these conditions, an assortment of new nation-states filled the immense vacuum created by the dissolution of European empires. In the period following the end of the Second World War, many Asian countries achieved independence from colonial rule; and more than fifty new states with new names, borders and currencies appeared in just two decades after 1945.

Formal decolonization itself was always unlikely to guarantee true sovereignty and dignity to Asian nations. In the 1950s, Nehru often stressed the urgent task facing postcolonial leaders like himself: 'What Europe did in a hundred or a hundred and fifty years, we must do in ten or fifteen years.' Catching up with the West's economic and political power remained as imperative for Egypt's Abdel Gamal Nasser, who desperately sought foreign assistance for the Aswan Dam project in the 1950s, as for Mao Zedong, who while exhorting the Chinese to match Britain's industrial capacity in fifteen years during the Great Leap Forward, led his country into a catastrophic famine in the early 1960s.

Ideologies such as communism and socialism were mobilized to enable the formation of new nations. Leaders with resonant names – Nehru, Mao, Ho Chi Minh, Nasser, Sukarno – not only supervised these political transformations and identified goals of material progress for their new nations; they also gave them their symbolism of radical nationalism and solidarity against Western imperialism.

But the transition from criticizing foreign rule and instigating mass movements to establishing a stable basis for self-determination proved to be very difficult. The idealist impulses behind revolt and national independence soon faded before the sheer magnitude of such nation-building tasks as sustained economic growth and territorial consolidation. Stumbling out of long decades of colonial exploitation into a world bitterly divided by the Cold War, the new states had to urgently find aid and capital for weak, often pre-industrial economic systems; set fiscal policy; institute land reforms; build such political institutions as parliaments, electoral commissions and parties; make national citizenship more attractive than local loyalties to ethnic, religious, linguistic and regional groupings; codify a legal order; make primary education and health care accessible; attack poverty and crime; and maintain roads and railways. And, as if this wasn't enough, they also had to equip their countries with a professional army and bureaucracy, check population growth, and establish a foreign policy that regulated relations with the old imperial metropole and also guaranteed the maximum benefits from the main protagonists of the Cold War.

Such manifold and arduous tasks, and (not surprisingly) cruel disappointments, mixed successes, tragic setbacks and vicious conflicts marked the first three decades after 1945 in almost all Asian countries. Ryszard Kapuściński once summed up the tragic 'drama' of the honest and patriotic postcolonial leader by describing the

> terrible *material resistance* that each one encounters on taking his first, second and third steps up the summit of power. Each one wants to do something good and begins to do it and then sees, after a month, after a year, after three years, that is just isn't happening, that it is slipping away, that it is bogged down in the sand. Everything is in the way: the centuries of backwardness, the primitive economy, the illiteracy, the religious fanaticism, the tribal blindness, the chronic hunger, the colonial past with its practice of debasing and dulling the conquered, the blackmail by the imperialists, the greed of the corrupt, the unemployment, the red ink. Progress comes with great difficulty along such a

road. The politician begins to push too hard. He looks for a way out through dictatorship. The dictatorship then fathers an opposition. The opposition organizes a coup.

And the cycle begins anew. [1]

The imported ideological passions of the Cold War aggravated political tensions in many countries, such as Pakistan and Indonesia. Separatist movements broke out in Kashmir, Aceh, East Pakistan, Tibet and Sri Lanka. Hard-fisted rulers – Suharto of Indonesia, Ayub Khan in Pakistan, Indira Gandhi in India – came to the fore, often accompanied by much violence and disorder. For a while at least, the Third World, as a large part of the postcolonial world was inaccurately called, seemed doomed from a Western point-of-view, the site of obscure civil wars and the source of needy immigrants.

The picture is a lot clearer and multifarious after more than half a century of change, when many of the ideological blinkers of the Cold War no longer exist. Moral idealism rather than practicality and effectiveness seems to have defined such broad transnational groupings as the Non-Aligned Movement, which almost all postcolonial Asian nations joined in an attempt to build an alternative to the crude polarities of the Cold War. We can see that the seemingly wholesale adoption of Western ideologies (Chinese communism, Japanese imperialism) did not work. Attempts at syntheses (India's parliamentary democracy, Muslim Turkey's secular state, China's state capitalism) were more successful, and violent rejections of the West in the form of Iran's Islamic Revolution and Islamist movements continue to have an afterlife.

Many new nations, such as Pakistan, never recovered from birthing traumas; their liberationist energies dispersed into political-religious movements of an increasingly militant nature. Others, such as the populous nations of China, India and Indonesia, despite some serious setbacks, managed their economic growth and sovereignty to the point where their cumulative heft now seems to pose a formidable challenge to the West itself.

Recent history tells us that there are more such challenges – political, diplomatic and economic – still to arise from large parts of Asia. More than half a century after decolonization began, we continue to live in what the American writer Irving Howe called a 'revolutionary age'.

> The revolutionary impulse has been contaminated, corrupted, debased, demoralized ... but the energy behind that revolutionary impulse remains. Now it bursts out in one part of the world, now in another. It cannot be suppressed entirely. Everywhere except in the United States, millions of human beings, certainly the majority of those with any degree of political articulateness, live for some kind of social change ... These are the dominant energies of our time and whoever gains control of them, whether in legitimate or distorted forms, will triumph.[2]

Replacing Europe's power with its own, America, Howe wrote, was 'sincerely convinced that only by the imposition of its will can the world be saved. But the world resists this will; it cannot, even if it would, surrender its own mode of response.' Written in 1954, these words sound no less convincing a year after the Arab Spring and the collapse of several pro-Western dictatorships. Chaos and uncertainty may loom over a wide swathe of the Arab world for some years. But the spell of Western power has finally been broken. If uprooted Muslims defy it contemptuously, others such as the Chinese have adopted its 'secrets'. The sense of humiliation that burdened several generations of Asians has greatly diminished. The rise of Asia, and the assertiveness of Asian peoples, consummates their revolt against the West that began more than a century ago; it is in many ways the revenge of the East.

Yet this success conceals an immense intellectual failure, one that has profound ramifications for the world today and the near future.

It is simply this: no convincingly universalist response exists today to Western ideas of politics and economy, even though these seem increasingly febrile and dangerously unsuitable in large parts of the world. Gandhi, their most rigorous critic, is a forgotten figure within India today. Marxism-Leninism lies discredited and, though China's rulers increasingly make gestures towards Confucian notions of harmony, China's own legacy of ethical politics and socio-economic theory remains largely unexplored. And even if it is exportable to other Muslim countries, Turkey's Islamic modernity doesn't point to any alternative socio-economic order.

The 'Washington Consensus' may lie in tatters, and Beijing's Communist regime mocks – simply by persisting as long as it has – Western claims of victory in the Cold War and the inevitability of liberal democracy. But the 'Beijing Consensus' has even less universal application than its Washington counterpart; it sounds suspiciously like merely a cynical economic argument for the lack of political freedom.

The earliest Asian modern intellectuals were beholden to European ideas. Working in a world shaped by European actions, or 'blinded by the dust-storm of modern history', as Tagore put it, they naturally embraced the nation-state as the prerequisite for modernity. And though these 'derivative' and synthetic varieties of nationalism had some uses in a geopolitical situation fraught with perils for newly sovereign countries, their limitations and problems are now more clearly visible.

It was never going to be easy for internally diverse societies like India and Indonesia to find a social, political and cultural identity without violence and disorder. Europe itself took hundreds of years to develop and implement the concept of a sovereign nation-state, only to then plunge into two world wars that exacted a terrible toll from ethnic and religious minorities. The European model of the ethnically homogenous nation-state was a poor fit in Europe itself. That it was particularly so for multi-ethnic Asian societies has been amply proved by the plight of Kashmiri Muslims, Tibetans, Uighurs, the Chinese in Malaysia, Sunni Muslims in Iraq, Kurds in Turkey and Tamils in Sri Lanka.

The countries with restive minorities may seem to hold together. But they do so at great human cost which future generations will find too steep. Furthermore, the nation-state is fundamentally unable to deal on its own with such problems as climate change, environmental degradation and water scarcity, which spill across national borders. China's damming and proposed diversion of the rivers that originate in the Tibetan plateau threaten catastrophe in South and South-east Asia.

Much of the 'emerging' world now stands to repeat, on an ominously larger scale, the West's own tortured and often tragic experience of modern 'development'. In India and China, the pursuit of economic growth at all costs has created a gaudy elite, but it has also widened already alarming social and economic disparities. It has become clear that development, whether undertaken by colonial masters or sovereign nation-states, doesn't benefit people evenly within a single territory, not to mention across larger regions.

Certainly China's and India's new middle classes have done very well out of two decades of capitalism, and their ruling elites can strut across the world stage like never before. But this apparently wildly successful culmination to the anti-colonial revolution has coincided with a veritable counter-revolution presided over by political and business elites across the world: the privatization and truncation of public services, de-unionization, the fragmentation and lumpeniza-tion of urban working classes, and the ruthless suppression of the rural poor. As instructed by the Chinese premier, Mao's son may well rest in peace in North Korea since his father's great dream of national regeneration has been fulfilled. But there is no doubt that not just Mao but all the leaders of the Chinese Revolution would have rejected this strange denouement to their great venture, in which some Chin-ese people stand up while most others are forced to stand down, and the privileged Chinese minority aspire to nothing higher than the con-veniences and gadgets of their Western consumer counterparts.

Sixty years after independence, India, with its stable and formally democratic institutions and processes, seems to have come closer to fulfilling the nationalist project of the first postcolonial elites. The Indian nation-state has grown stronger, with a voice in the inter-national arena. It is an increasingly attractive place for Western corporate and speculative capital. Indian elites, like their Asian coun-terparts in Japan, are still content to make themselves a junior partner to the United States, implicitly affirming that the post-war inter-national order will survive.

These Asian beneficiaries of globalization project an image of a confident and self-aware people moving as one towards material ful-filment and international prominence. But India displays even more garishly than China the odd discontinuities induced by economic globalization: how by fostering rapid growth in some sectors of the economy it raises expectations everywhere, but by distributing its benefits narrowly, it expands the numbers of the disenchanted and the frustrated, often making them vulnerable to populist and ethnocratic politicians. At the same time the biggest beneficiaries of globalization find shelter in such aggressive ideologies as Hindu nationalism.

The feeling of hopelessness and despair, especially among landless peasants, has led to militant communist movements of unprecedented vigour and scale – the Indian prime minister describes them as the greatest internal security threat faced by India since independence. These Mao-inspired communists, who have their own systems of tax collection and justice, now dominate large parts of central and northern India, particularly in the states of Andhra Pradesh, Jharkhand, Bihar, Chhattisgarh and Orissa. Their informal secessionism has its counterpart among the Indian rich. Gated communities grow in Indian cities and suburbs. The elite itself seems to have mutinied, its members retreating into exclusive enclaves where they can withdraw from the social and political complications of the country they live in. This is deeply troubling as up to a third of Indians live in conditions of extreme poverty and deprivation. More than half the children under the age of five in India are malnourished; failed crops and spiralling debt drove more than a hundred thousand farmers to suicide in the past decade.

The disasters occasionally described in the Western media – the violence in Kashmir that has claimed more than 80,000 lives in the last decade and a half; the destruction of the environment and the uprooting of nearly 200 million people from their rural homes in China – can no longer be explained away with reference to the logic of development as manifested in Europe's history. The West itself has begun to feel the pain of the emerging world's transition to modernity, as China's hunger for energy and resources raises the price of commodities and its cheap exports undermine the once-strong economies of Europe and put workers out of jobs in America.

Of course, as some of Asia's intellectuals pointed out, Europe's own transition to its present state of stability and affluence was more than just painful. It involved imperial conquests, ethnic cleansing and many minor and two major wars involving the murder and displacement of countless millions. As India and China rise with their consumerist middle classes in a world of finite energy resources, it is easy to imagine that this century will be ravaged by the kind of economic rivalries and military conflicts that made the last century so violent.

The war on terror has already blighted the first decade. In retrospect, however, it may seem a mere prelude to greater and bloodier conflicts over precious resources and commodities that modernizing as well as already modern economies need. The hope that fuels the pursuit of endless economic growth – that billions of consumers in

India and China will one day enjoy the lifestyles of Europeans and Americans – is as absurd and dangerous a fantasy as anything dreamt up by al-Qaeda. It condemns the global environment to early destruction, and looks set to create reservoirs of nihilistic rage and disappointment among hundreds of millions of have-nots – the bitter outcome of the universal triumph of Western modernity, which turns the revenge of the East into something darkly ambiguous, and all its victories truly Pyrrhic.

Bibliographic Essay

The idea for this book came to me in 2005, while reading a book by William Pfaff and Edward Stilman called *The Politics of Hysteria*. Written in 1962, as the United States worked hard to export the ideologies of the 'free world' and beat back communism, Pfaff and Stilman invoked the tormented history of European imperialism in Asia, warning that 'the radical and disruptive remaking of [Asia's] life and society – the challenge to Asians' understanding of existence itself, made by the West's four century-long intrusion – is ignored or simply not understood by Western policymakers and observers.' This ignorance, Pfaff and Stilman could have added, was also widespread among Asians themselves, especially those brought up, like myself, on histories of nation-building – triumphalism in a local key. I grew up with the stirring story of India's emergence as a free nation-state from Western rule, but I knew next to nothing about what had happened in other Asian countries, about the writers, leaders and activists who had expressed similar ideas and aspirations.

The previous pages are a result of serendipitous reading. I went from book to book, appalled by my growing knowledge of how little I knew, and anxious to alleviate my ignorance by reading more. There were lucky discoveries along the way, books that opened up large vistas. Among these are two exceptional books: Cemil Aydin's *The Politics of Anti-Westernism: Visions of World Order in Pan-Islamic and Pan-Asian Thought*, and Erez Manela's *The Wilsonian Moment: Self-Determination and the International Origins of Anticolonial Nationalism*.

This book's building blocks are not only such authoritative overviews and, indeed, many national histories, but also much more tightly focused scholarship. To name all of them would take up too many pages, and leave the reader no less uncertain where to begin his own journey into these still obscure realms of modern history. Rather than list all the books I consulted, I decided to mention those that a general reader might find useful.

PROLOGUE

Given its world-historical significance, the Russo-Japanese War has had relatively few books in English devoted to it. The diplomatic wrangles leading up to it are covered in Ian Hill Nish's *The Origins of the Russo-Japanese War* (London, 1986). A short account of its major battles can be found in Geoffrey Jukes' *The Russo-Japanese War 1904–1905* (Oxford, 2002). Constantine Pleshakov provides a gripping narrative of the doomed Russian effort at the Battle of Tsushima in *The Tsar's Last Armada: The Epic Voyage to the Battle of Tsushima* (New York, 2003). Vladimir Nabokov registers the impact of the war in the opening pages of his memoir, *Speak, Memory* (New York, 1966), and the biographies and memoirs of Gandhi, Nehru, Atatürk, Sun Yat-sen and Mao Zedong rarely fail to do likewise. On the battle's international ramifications, see Rotem Kowner's *The Impact of the Russo-Japanese War* (London, 2009) and Cemil Aydin's *The Politics of Anti-Westernism* (New York, 2007).

I. ASIA SUBORDINATED

Juan Cole's *Napoleon's Egypt: Invading the Middle East* (New York, 2007) is the best recent account of the French megalomaniac's misadventures in Egypt. Edited by Irene Bierman, *Napoleon in Egypt* (Reading, 2003) has scholarly essays on specific aspects of the French invasion and occupation, while *Napoleon in Egypt: Al-Jabarti's Chronicle of the French Occupation, 1798* (Princeton, 1993) cannot be beaten as a record of the Muslim response to the French intrusion.

Post 9/11, the literature on Islam and Islamic history has proliferated. There is much rich material to choose from, but the three volumes of Marshall Hodgson's *The Venture of Islam* (Chicago, 1974) remain the most stimulating panoptic account. His *Rethinking World History: Essays on Europe, Islam and World History* (Cambridge, 1993) offers an equally bracing way to think about a less West-centric history. An account of travels in the fourteenth century, the *Travels of Ibn Battutah* (London, 2003) gives the clearest sense of the geographical extent and cultural influence of the Muslim world. An interesting companion piece might be *Westward Bound: Travels of Mirza Abu Taleb* (Delhi, 2005), a description of travels undertaken at the turn of the nineteenth century by a Muslim witnessing Europe's assumption of superior power. K. M. Panikkar's *Asia and Western Dominance: A Survey of the Vasco da Gama Epoch of Asian History, 1498–1945* (London, 1953) is a

somewhat dated but still entertaining broad history of the West's slow pene-
tration of Asia. Some notable though under-regarded contributions to this
field are by Sanjay Subrahmanyam, whose *The Portuguese Empire in Asia,
1500–1700: A Political and Economic History* (Oxford, 2012) and *Three
Ways to Be Alien: Travails and Encounters in the Early Modern World*
(Brandeis, 2011) are essential reading.

The Opium Wars (London, 2011) by Julia Lovell ably replaces the classic
studies of the subject by Maurice Collis and Arthur Waley; it is especially
good on the uses of the opium wars by Chinese nationalists over the decades.
Jonathan Spence, in his masterpiece *The Search for Modern China* (New
York, 1999), gives a characteristically elegant account of the opium tangles
in addition to much else, while John K. Fairbank's early contribution to
Sinology – *Trade and Diplomacy on the China Coast* (Palo Alto, Calif.,
1953) – retains the capacity to surprise. The nascent Chinese sense of the out-
side world is captured in Rebecca Karl's *Staging the World: Chinese
Nationalism at the Turn of the Twentieth Century* (Durham, N.C., 2002) and
Theodore Huters' *Bringing the World Home: Appropriating the West in Late
Qing and Early Republican China* (Hawaii, 2005).

The military aspects of the Indian Mutiny are described in Saul David's
The Indian Mutiny (London, 2003) and Christopher Hibbert's *The Great
Mutiny: India 1857* (London, 1982). For it ideological, social and political
reasons, see Eric Stokes's *English Utilitarians and India* (London, 1959) and
The Peasant Armed: The Indian Rebellion of 1857 (New York, 1986), and
Rudrangshu Mukherjee's *Awadh in Revolt, 1857–1858: A Study in Popular
Resistance* (Delhi, 1984). A broader account of rural revolts against British
rule is provided by Ranajit Guha's seminal book, *Elementary Aspects of
Peasant Insurgency in Colonial India* (Durham, N.C., 1999). Ayesha Jalal's
Partisans of Allah: Jihad in South Asia (Cambridge, Mass., 2008) offers an
important ideological backdrop to the Mutiny as well as antidotes to crude
prejudices about jihad, especially in the chapter titled 'The Martyrs of Balakot'. For Indian perspectives of the Mutiny, see Amaresh Misra's *Lucknow:
Fire Of Grace – The Story of its Renaissance, Revolution and the Aftermath*
(Delhi, 1998) and the edited volume by Mahmood Farooqui, *Besieged: Voices
from Delhi 1857* (Delhi, 2010). Abdul Halim Sharar's *Lucknow: The Last
Phase of an Oriental Culture* (Delhi, 1975) is an outstanding evocation of a
city in decline. Satyajit Ray's script and film of *The Chess Players*, the short
story by Premchand, gives a vivid sense of the culture of Awadh in the 1850s.
On nineteenth-century Delhi, see Mushirul Hasan's *A Moral Reckoning:
Muslim Intellectuals in Nineteenth-Century Delhi* (Delhi, 2007), William
Dalrymple's *The Last Mughal* (New York, 2007), Pavan K. Varma's biog-

raphy of the city's greatest poet *Ghalib: The Man, The Times* (Delhi, 1989) and the edited volume by Ralph Russell and Khurshidul Islam, *Ghalib 1797–1869: Life and Letters* (Delhi, 1997). The Indian Muslim predicament is sensitively described by M. Mujeeb, *Indian Muslims* (Delhi, 1962) and Rajmohan Gandhi's *Understanding the Muslim Mind* (Delhi, 1988).

The literature rebutting triumphalist accounts of the West's 'superiority' over Asia grows all the time. Christopher Bayly's *The Birth of the Modern World 1780–1914. Global Connections and Comparisons* (Oxford, 2003) is a magisterial account of recent scholarship on the subject. Andre Gunder Frank's *Reorient: Global Economy in an Asian Age* (Berkeley, 1998), Janet L. Abu-Lughod's *Before European Hegemony: The World System A.D. 1250–1350* (New York, 1989) and Kenneth Pomeranz's *The Great Divergence: China, Europe, and the Making of the Modern World Economy* (Princeton, 2001) are now acknowledged classics in their field. Prasannan Parthasarthi's *Why Europe Grew Rich and Asia Did Not: Global Economic Divergence, 1600–1850* (Cambridge, 2011) complicates the story further. Hamashita Takeshi's *China, East Asia and the Global Economy: Regional and Historical Perspectives* (New York, 2008) places China in the centre of a vast Eurasian network of trade and tributary relations. The general reader may find Stewart Gordon's *When Asia was the World: Traveling Merchants, Scholars, Warriors, and Monks Who Created the 'Riches of the East'* (Philadelphia, 2009), Jerry Brotton's *The Renaissance Bazaar: From the Silk Road to Michelangelo* (New York, 2003) and Jack Goody's *The East in the West* (Cambridge, 1996) more accessible. John Darwin's *After Tamarlene: The Global History of Empire* elegantly performs the necessary task of reorientating world history. V. G. Kiernan's *The Lords of Human Kind: European Attitudes Towards the Outside World in the Imperial Age* (London, 1969) is a more informative account of its subject than Edward Said's complex polemic *Orientalism* (New York, 1978). On how 'whiteness' became an ideology and a form of political solidarity against the 'rest', see Marilyn Lake and Henry Reynolds's book *Drawing the Global Colour Line: White Men's Countries and the International Challenge of Racial Equality* (Cambridge, 2008) and Bill Schwarz's first volume of what promises to be a remarkable trilogy, *The White Man's World* (New York, 2012).

2. THE STRANGE ODYSSEY OF JAMAL AL-DIN AL-AFGHANI

Nikki Keddie's *Sayyid Jamal Ad-Din 'Al-Afghani': A Political Biography* (Berkeley, 1972) remains the most authoritative source of information about al-Afghani's life and ideas. Elie Kedourie's *Afghani and 'Abduh: An Essay on*

Religious Unbelief and Political Activism in Modern Islam (London, 1966) is marred by some conspiracy-theorizing but is still useful. Ibrahim Abu-Lughod's *The Arab Discovery of Europe: A Study in Cultural Encounters* (Princeton, 1963) describes the first generation of Muslims initiated into the mysteries of Western power. Albert Hourani's *Arabic Thought in the Liberal Age 1798–1939* (Oxford, 1962) covers more terrain, and has a superb chapter on al-Afghani.

Caroline Finkel's *Osman's Dream: The History of the Ottoman Empire* (New York, 2007) and Carter Vaughn Findley's *The Turks in World History* (New York, 2004) are helpful primers on a big subject. M. Şükrü Hanioğlu's *A Brief History of the Late Ottoman Empire* (Princeton, 2008) is a very accessible account of nineteenth-century Turkey, whose intellectual currents are described in Şerif Mardin's *The Genesis of Young Ottoman Thought: A Study in the Modernization of Turkish Political Ideas* (Princeton, 2000), while Philip Mansel's *Constantinople: City of the World's Desire, 1453–1924* (London, 1995) and *Sultans in Splendour* (London, 2002) richly evoke the world the Ottoman sultans made.

Juan Cole's *Colonialism and Revolution in the Middle East: Social and Cultural Origins of Egypt's Urabi Movement* (Cairo, 1999) is the best single book on the restless country al-Afghani knew in the 1870s. On the broader political history of nineteenth-century Egypt, see K. Fahmy, *All the Pasha's Men: Mehmed Ali, His Army and the Making of Modern Egypt* (Cairo, 2002). David Landes' *Bankers and Pashas: International Finance and Economic Imperialism in Egypt* (Cambridge, Mass., 1980) covers the antics of the elites while Michael Ezekiel Gasper provides a view from the streets in *The Power of Representation: Publics, Peasants, and Islam in Egypt* (Stanford, 2009). The Cairo of that era is beautifully evoked in Max Rodenbeck's *Cairo: The City Victorious* (London, 2000) and Trevor Mostyn's *Egypt's Belle Epoque: Cairo and the Age of the Hedonists* (London, 2006).

David Lelyveld, *Aligarh's First Generation: Muslim Solidarity in British India* (Delhi, 2003) is a useful study, and for an interesting take on Sayyid Ahmed, see the chapter by Faisal Devji, 'Apologetic Modernity', in Shruti Kapila's edited volume, *An Intellectual History for India* (Cambridge, 2010). Jacob M. Landau's *The Politics of Pan-Islam: Ideology and Organization* (Oxford, 1990) is an authoritative account, while Cemil Aydin has a fascinatingly discussion of the original motivations of pan-Islamism in *The Politics of Anti-Westernism*.

3. LIANG QICHAO'S CHINA AND THE FATE OF ASIA

On the Ottoman Turkish and Arab fascination with Japan, see Renée Worringer (ed.), *The Islamic Middle East and Japan: Perceptions, Aspirations, and the Birth of Intra-Asian Modernity* (Princeton, 2007). The best long and short introductions to Japan's modern history are Marius B. Jansen, *The Making of Modern Japan* (Cambridge, Mass., 2000) and Ian Buruma's *Inventing Japan* (New York, 2003) respectively. American views of Japan and the Pacific have more recently been described in Bruce Cumings's *Dominion from Sea to Sea: Pacific Ascendancy and American Power* (New Haven, Conn., 2010).

Liang Qichao's thought has been well-served by three major monographs: Joseph R. Levenson, *Liang Ch'i-ch'ao and the Mind of Modern China* (Cambridge, Mass., 1959), Hao Chang, *Liang Ch'i-ch'ao and Intellectual Transition in China, 1890–1907* (Cambridge, Mass., 1971), and Xiaobing Tang, *Global Space and the Nationalist Discourse of Modernity: The Historical Thinking of Liang Qichao* (Stanford, 1996). Jonathan Spence movingly describes Liang's and Kang Youwei's parallel lives in *The Gate of Heavenly Peace: The Chinese and their Revolution, 1895–1980* (New York, 1982). On Yan Fu, see Benjamin Schwartz's *In Search of Wealth and Power: Yen Fu and the West* (Cambridge, Mass., 1964).

Broader descriptions of the Chinese intellectual scene can be found in Hao Chang's *Chinese Intellectuals in Crisis: Search for Order and Meaning (1890–1911)* (Berkeley, 1987) and Merle Goldman and Leo Ou-fan Lee (eds.), *The Intellectual History of Modern China* (Cambridge, 2002). Rana Mitter's *A Bitter Revolution: China's Struggle with the Modern World* (Oxford, 2005) is a superbly written account of the debates and controversies leading up to and beyond the May Fourth Revolution. The clash of generations in the 1910s and 1920s is also well-illustrated in Vera Schwarcz's *The Chinese Enlightenment: Intellectuals and the Legacy of the May Fourth Movement* (Berkeley, 1986). Good general studies of the subject include T. C. Wang's *Chinese Intellectuals and the West 1872–1949* (Chapel Hill, 1966), Paul Cohen's *Discovering History in China* (New York, 1984) – especially the subtle insights of the chapter titled 'China's Response to the West' – and Jerome B. Greider's *Intellectuals and the State in Modern China: A Narrative History* (New York, 1981). For two excellent essays on Liang Shuming and Zhang Taiyan see Charlotte Furth (ed.), *The Limits of Change* (Cambridge, Mass., 1976). Wang Hui's forthcoming *The Rise of Modern Chinese Thought* will contain essays on all major Chinese writers and philosophers. Joseph W. Esherick's *The Origins of the Boxer Uprising* (Berkeley, 1988) is an unsurpassed account of the motivations of the Boxers.

Eri Hotta, in *Pan-Asianism and Japan's War 1931–1945* (New York, 2007), lucidly details the broad range of Pan-Asianist traditions in Japan. Also see the provocative and stimulating essay 'The Discourse of Civilization and Pan-Asianism' by Prasenjit Duara in *Journal of World History*, Vol. 12, No. 1

(Spring, 2001). Marius B. Jansen's *The Japanese and Sun Yat-sen* (Princeton, 1970) captures the precarious situation of Chinese exiles in Japan. On the political and intellectual crisis in Europe Liang wrote about, the best summary account is Mark Mazower's *Dark Continent: Europe's Twentieth Century* (London, 2000).

4. 1919, 'CHANGING THE HISTORY OF THE WORLD'

The Paris Peace Conference has invited close attention from scholars and writers. David Fromkin's *A Peace to End all Peace: The Fall of the Ottoman Empire and the Creation of the Modern Middle East* (New York, 1989) is a fair-minded account of the break-up of the Ottoman Empire and the creation of the Middle East. Margaret MacMillan's *Paris 1919: Six Months That Changed the World* (New York, 2002) covers the actual proceedings at the conference. But it is Erez Manela's *The Wilsonian Moment: Self-Determination and the International Origins of Anticolonial Nationalism* (New York, 2009) that reconstitutes 1919 as the seminal year for all major Asian countries striving for independence. The recent series by Haus Publishing, London, 'Makers of the Modern World', contains revealing monographs on all the leading participants at the conference. As a brief and illuminating history of American foreign policy-making, Walter A. McDougall's *Promised Land, Crusader State: The American Encounter with the World since 1776* (New York, 1997) is without peer. The story of the Comintern is entertainingly told in Peter Hopkirk's *Setting the East Ablaze: Lenin's Dream of an Empire in Asia* (New York, 1985), and the official histories of individual communist parties in China, India and Vietnam are widely available. But the in-depth account of the making of Asian nationalisms-cum-communisms is yet to be written; it exists piecemeal in specialist monographs: Michael Williams' article 'Sneevliet and the Birth of Asian Communism', in *New Left Review* I/123, September-October 1980, has some useful information. Suchetana Chattopadhyay's *Early Communist: Muzaffar Ahmad in Calcutta 1913–1929* (Delhi, 2011) is a revealing account of the world of an early Indian communist. As is Kris Manjapra's *M. N. Roy: Marxism and Colonial Cosmopolitanism* (Delhi, 2010).

5. RABINDRANATH TAGORE IN EAST ASIA, THE MAN FROM THE LOST COUNTRY

Tagore's worldview is best observed through his own lucid prose writings, most of them available in English from diverse sources. The best biography of him in English is Krishna Dutta and Andrew Robinson's *Rabindranath Tagore: The Myriad-Minded Man* (London, 1995). Few have written as well as Amit Chaudhuri on Tagore's aesthetic; see his introduction to *The Essential Tagore* (Cambridge, Mass., 2011) and the essays collected in *On Tagore* (Delhi, 2012). Nirad C. Chaudhuri wrote with rare piety about Tagore in *Autobiography of an Unknown Indian* (London, 1951). Amartya Sen's essay on Tagore, collected in *The Argumentative Indian: Writings on Indian History, Culture and Identity* (Delhi, 2005) first alerted me to his political thought – though I had dutifully read about it at school. Sabyasachi Bhattacharya's *Rabindranath Tagore: An Interpretation* (Delhi, 2011) is a sensitive intellectual biography.

The best academic study of Tagore's political thought is Michael Collins's *Empire, Nationalism and the Postcolonial World: Rabindranath Tagore's Writings on History, Politics and Society* (New York, 2011). On his differences with Gandhi, see Sabyasachi Bhattacharya (ed.), *The Mahatma and the Poet: Letters and Debates Between Gandhi and Tagore, 1915–1941* (Delhi, 1997). See also Sugata Bose, *A Hundred Horizons: The Indian Ocean in the Age of Global Empire* (Delhi, 2006) and Ramachandra Guha's introduction to Tagore's *Nationalism* (Delhi, 2010). Tagore's intellectual background is described in David Kopf's *British Orientalism and the Bengal Renaissance: The Dynamics of Indian Modernization, 1773–1835* (Berkeley, 1969). See also the essays of Tapan Raychaudhuri in *Europe Reconsidered: Perceptions of the West in Nineteenth-century Bengal* (Delhi, 2002), *Perceptions, Emotions, Sensibilities: Essays on India's Colonial and Post-colonial Experiences* (Delhi, 1999) and Sudipta Kaviraj's *The Unhappy Consciousness: Bankimchandra Chattopadhyay and the Formation of Nationalist Discourse in India* (Delhi, 1995).

For India's links with China, see Madhavi Thampi (ed.), *Indians in China, 1800–1949* (Delhi, 2010) and Kalidas Nag, *Discovery of Asia* (Calcutta, 1993). Tagore's visits to East Asia were first described at length in Stephen N. Hay's *Asian Ideas of East and West: Tagore and his Critics in Japan, China, and India* (Cambridge, Mass., 1970). A recent volume edited by Amiya Dev and Tan Chung, *Tagore and China* (Delhi, 2011), contains both Indian and Chinese perspectives. The important figure of Aurobindo Ghose has been much traduced by Hindu nationalists and his prose writings have hardly received much scholarly examination, with the exception of Peter Heehs's writings, in particular his biography, *The Lives of Sri Aurobindo* (New York, 2008). Ashis Nandy writes about Aurobindo with characteristic sensitivity in *The Intimate Enemy: Loss and Recovery of Self Under Colonialism* (New Delhi, 1988). See also the chapter by Sugata Bose, 'The Spirit and Form of an Ethical Policy: A Meditation on Aurobindo's Thought', in *An Intellectual*

History for India (Delhi, 2010) edited by Shruti Kapila. The Aurobindo Ashram's website has all his prose works in easily downloadable PDF format. And B. Parekh's *Colonialism, Tradition and Reform* (London, 1989) and Dennis Dalton, *Mahatma Gandhi: Non-Violent Power in Action* (New York, 2000) still stand out from among the mass of books on this subject.

6. ASIA REMADE

John D. Pierson's *Tokutomi Sohō, 1863–1957: A Journalist for Modern Japan* is an excellent introduction to Japan's geopolitical trajectory in the late nineteenth and early twentieth centuries. Shogo Suzuki's *Civilization and Empire: China and Japan's Encounter with European International Society* (New York, 2009) analyses how Japan's socialization into the European system of states was inevitably tainted with violence. John Keay's *Last Post: The End of Empire in the Far East* (London, 1997) is, like most of this underrated author's work, a wholly absorbing study about the last days of European empires in Asia. Japan's occupation of Asia is well described in Nicholas Tarling's *A Sudden Rampage: The Japanese Occupation of Southeast Asia, 1941–1945* (Hawaii, 2001), William Newell (ed.), *Japan in Asia, 1942–45* (Singapore, 1981) and Shigeru Satō's *War, Nationalism, and Peasants: Java under the Japanese Occupation, 1942–1945* (Armonk, 1994). The two volumes by Christopher Bayly and Tim Harper, *Forgotten Armies: The Fall of British Asia, 1941–1945* (London, 2007) and *Forgotten Wars: Freedom and Revolution in Southeast Asia* (London, 2007), set a new standard in history-writing.

Vijay Prashad's *The Darker Nations: A People's History of the Third World* (New York, 2007) is the only book of its kind. Readers interested in Bandung can do no better than consult the volume of essays edited by Christopher Lee, *Making a World After Empire: The Bandung Moment and Its Political Afterlives* (Athens, Ohio, 2010), particularly the chapter by Dipesh Chakraborty, 'The Legacies of Bandung'. See also Prasenjit Duara (ed.), *Decolonization: Perspectives from Now and Then* (New York, 2004).

Iqbal has been inadequately translated into English; the one exception is V. G. Kiernan's *Poems from Iqbal* (Karachi, 2005). Iqbal Singh's *The Ardent Pilgrim: An Introduction to the Life and Work of Iqbal* (Delhi, 1997) is still the best account of him in English. Ayesha Jalal talks abut the poet and thinker bracingly in *Self and Sovereignty: Individual and Community in South Asian Islam since 1850* (New York, 2000). Mawdudi's work and influence has received extended analysis in Vali Nasr's *Mawdudi and the Making of Islamic Revivalism* (New York, 1996). Ali Shariati's reputation in English has benefitted from a capable biographer in Ali Rahnema, *An Islamic Utopian: A Political Biography of Ali Shariati* (London, 1998). Hamid Algar has translated and introduced two volumes of Shariati's essays, in *On the Sociology of Islam* (Berkeley, 1979) and *Marxism and Other Western Fallacies: An Islamic Critique* (Berkeley, 1980). Also see Nikki Keddie, *Iran: Roots of Revolution* (New Haven, Conn., 1981), especially Yann Richard's chapter on Shariati.

John Calvert's *Sayyid Qutb and the Origins of Radical Islamism* (London, 2010) cuts through all the post-9/11 clichés about his subject. Elegantly written, Roy Mottahedeh's *The Mantle of the Prophet: Religion and Politics in Iran* (London, 1985) is the most accessible general introduction to the place of religion in Iranian society before 1979. Ervand Abrahmanian's *Iran Between Two Revolutions* (Princeton, 1982) is indispensable to anyone wishing to understand Iranian politics up to 1979. And Khomeinism is also best understood through the same author's *Khomeinism: Essays on the Islamic Republic* (Berkeley, 1993). Hamid Dabashi's *Theology of Discontent: The Ideological Foundation of the Islamic Revolution in Iran* (New Brunswick, N.J., 2006) remains as fresh and revelatory as ever. See also his *Shi'ism: A Religion of Protest* (Cambridge, Mass., 2011). Jalal Al-e Ahmad's *Occidentosis: A Plague from the West* (Berkeley, 1984) anticipates many contemporary critiques of modern capitalism.

Some refreshingly unprejudiced and suggestive views on Islamic modernism can be found in Mansoor Moaddel's *Islamic Modernism, Nationalism, and Fundamentalism: Episode and Discourse* (Chicago, 2005) and Roxanne Euben's, *Enemy in the Mirror: Islamic Fundamentalism and the Limits of Modern Rationalism: A Work of Comparative Political Theory* (Princeton, 1999). Atatürk's rigidly secular worldview is carefully explained in M. Şükrü Hanioğlu, *Atatürk: An Intellectual Biography* (Princeton, 2011). Bernard Lewis's later political absurdities do not mar his early achievement, *The Emergence of Modern Turkey* (Oxford, 1968), but a more interesting take on his subject exists in Carter Vaughn Findley's *Turkey, Islam, Nationalism, and Modernity: A History* (New Haven, Conn., 2011).

Mao Zedong's own writings, edited by Stuart Schram in several volumes, are the best guide to his intellectual and political evolution – and catastrophes. The scholarly contributions to Timothy Cheek (ed.), *A Critical Introduction to Mao* (Cambridge, 2010) do well to rescue him from sensationalist biographers. Thomas A. Metzger's *Escape from Predicament: Neo-Confucianism and China's Evolving Political Culture* (New York, 1986) is a provocative look at the Confucian underpinnings of Communist China. On the Confucian revival, see Daniel Bell, *China's New Confucianism: Politics and Everyday Life in a Changing Society* (Princeton, 2008).

Notes

PROLOGUE

1. Quoted in Rotem Kowner (ed.), *The Impact of the Russo-Japanese War* (London, 2006), p. 20.
2. Gandhi, *The Collected Works of Mahatma Gandhi*, vol. 4, http://www .gandhiserve.org/cwmg/VOL004.PDF, p. 470.
3. Jawaharlal Nehru, *Autobiography* (1936; repr. edn New Delhi, 1989), p. 16.
4. Ibid., p.18.
5. Marius B. Jansen, *The Japanese and Sun Yat-sen* (Princeton, 1970), p. 117.
6. John D. Pierson, *Tokutomi Sohō 1863–1957: A Journalist for Modern Japan* (Princeton, 1980), p. 143.
7. Ibid., p. 279.
8. Benoy Kumar Sarkar, 'The futurism of young Asia', *International Journal of Ethics*, 28, 4 (July 1918), p. 536.
9. Quoted in Cemil Aydin, *The Politics of Anti-Westernism: Visions of World Order in Pan-Islamic and Pan-Asian Thought* (New York, 2007), p. 76.
10. Quoted in Kowner (ed.), *Impact of the Russo-Japanese War*, p. 242.
11. Philip Short, *Mao: A Life* (London, 2004), p. 37.
12. Ibid., p. 38.
13. Kowner (ed.), *Impact of the Russo-Japanese War*, p. 230.
14. Sun Yat-sen, 'Pan-Asianism', *China and Japan: Natural Friends – Unnatural Enemies* (Shanghai, 1941), p. 143.
15. Gandhi, *Collected Works*, vol. 4, p. 471.

I. ASIA SUBORDINATED

1. Quoted in Juan Cole, *Napoleon's Egypt: Invading the Middle East* (New York, 2007), p. 17.
2. Ibid., p. 11.
3. Ibid., p. 128.
4. Ibid.
5. Trevor Mostyn, *Egypt's Belle Epoque: Cairo and the Age of the Hedonists* (London, 2006), p. 18.
6. Ibid., p. 14.
7. Bernard Lewis, *A Middle East Mosaic: Fragments of Life, Letters and History* (New York, 2000), p. 41.
8. Shmuel Moreh (trans.) *Napoleon in Egypt: Al-Jabarti's Chronicle Of The French Occupation, 1798* (Princeton, 1993), p. 71.
9. Ibid., pp. 28–9.
10. Ibid., p. 28.
11. Ibid., p. 31.
12. Ibid., pp. 109–10.
13. Lewis, *A Middle East Mosaic*, p. 42.
14. Quoted in Bernard S. Cohn, *Colonialism and its Forms of Knowledge: The British in India* (Princeton, 1996), p. 112.
15. K. M. Panikkar, *Asia and Western Dominance: A Survey of the Vasco da Gama Epoch of Asian History, 1498–1945* (London, 1953), p. 74.
16. Tapan Raychaudhuri, *Europe Reconsidered: Perceptions of the West in Nineteenth-century Bengal* (Delhi, 2002), p. 185.
17. Edmund Burke, *Selected Writings and Speeches* (New Brunswick, 2009), p. 453.
18. Nicholas B. Dirks, *The Scandal of Empire: India and the Creation of Imperial Britain* (Cambridge, Mass., 2006), p. 292.
19. Nirad C. Chaudhuri, *Autobiography of an Unknown Indian* (London, 1951), p. 408.
20. Christopher Hibbert, *The Dragon Wakes: China and the West, 1793–1911* (London, 1984), p. 32.
21. Ibid., p. 53.
22. Julia Lovell, *The Opium War* (London, 2011), p. 89.
23. Jonathan Spence, *The Search for Modern China* (London, 1990), p. 123.
24. Ibid., p. 129.
25. Lovell, *The Opium War*, p. 52.
26. William Theodore De Bary, Richard John Lufrano, Wing-tsit Chan and

Joseph Adler (eds.), *Sources of Chinese Tradition, From 1600 Through the Twentieth Century*, vol. 2 (New York, 2000), p. 203.

27. Ibid., p. 204.

28. John K. Fairbank, *Trade and Diplomacy on the China Coast: The Opening of the Treaty Ports, 1842–1854* (Palo Alto, Calif., 1953), p. 173.

29. Madhavi Thampi (ed.), *Indians in China, 1800–1949* (Delhi, 2010), p. 89.

30. Lovell, *The Opium War*, p. 227.

31. Patricia Buckley Ebrey, *The Cambridge Illustrated History of China* (Cambridge, 1996), p. 240.

32. Hibbert, *The Dragon Wakes*, p. 264.

33. Ibid., p. 226.

34. Ibid., p. 265.

35. Rebecca E. Karl, *Staging the World: Chinese Nationalism at the Turn of the Twentieth Century* (Durham, N.C., 2002), p. 12.

36. Ibid., p. 14.

37. Theodore Huters, *Bringing the World Home: Appropriating the West in Late Qing and Early Republican China* (Hawaii, 2005), p. 65.

38. Krishna Dutta and Andrew Robinson, *Rabindranath Tagore: The Myriad-Minded Man* (London, 1995), p. 81.

39. Raychaudhuri, *Europe Reconsidered*, p. 73.

40. Rudrangshu Mukherjee, *Awadh in Revolt, 1857–1858: A Study of Popular Resistance* (Delhi, 1984), p. 32.

41. William Dalrymple, *The Last Mughal: The Fall of Delhi 1857* (London, 2009), p. 96.

42. Emily Eden, *Up the Country: Letters Written to Her Sister from the Upper Provinces of India* (Cambridge, 1866), p. 139.

43. Dalrymple, *The Last Mughal*, p. 104.

44. Raychaudhuri, *Europe Reconsidered*, p. 38.

45. Karl Marx, *Early Writings* (Harmondsworth, 1975), p. viii.

46. Mahmood Farooqui (ed. and trans.), *Besieged: Voices from Delhi 1857* (Delhi, 2010), p. 352.

47. Ibid., pp. 382–3.

48. Mukherjee, *Awadh in Revolt*, p. 81.

49. Ibid., p. 148.

50. Narayani Gupta, *Delhi Between Two Empires, 1803–1930: Society, Government and Urban Growth* (Delhi, 1981), p. 21.

51. Lovell, *The Opium War*, p. 260.

52. Abdul Halim Sharar, *Lucknow: The Last Phase of an Oriental Culture*, trans. E. S. Harcourt and Fakhir Husain (Delhi, 1975), p. 66.

53. Ibid., p. 62.
54. Benoy Kumar Sarkar, 'The futurism of young Asia', *International Journal of Ethics*, 28, 4 (July 1918), p. 532.
55. John D. Pierson, *Tokutomi Sohō, 1863–1957: A Journalist for Modern Japan* (Princeton, 1980), p. 130.
56. Alan Macfarlane, *The Making of the Modern World: Visions from the West and East* (London, 2002), p. 35.
57. Alexis de Tocqueville, *'The European Revolution' and Correspondence with Gobineau* (New York, 1959), p. 268.
58. Raychaudhuri, *Europe Reconsidered*, p. 90.
59. Macfarlane, *The Making of the Modern World*, p. 36.
60. Stephen N. Hay, *Asian Ideas of East and West: Tagore and his Critics in Japan, China, and India* (Cambridge, Mass., 1970), p. 82.
61. Amiya Dev and Tan Chung (eds.), *Tagore and China* (Delhi, 2011), p. 170.
62. Joseph R. Levenson, *Liang Ch'i-ch'ao and the Mind of Modern China* (Cambridge, Mass., 1959), p. 155.

2. THE STRANGE ODYSSEY OF JAMAL AL-DIN AL-AFGHANI

1. Ali Rahnema, *Ali, An Islamic Utopian. A Political Biography of Ali Shariati* (London, 1998), p. 98.
2. Nikki R. Keddie, 'The Pan-Islamic appeal: Afghani and Abdülhamid', *Middle Eastern Studies*, 3, 1 (Oct. 1966), p. 66.
3. Ali Shariati and Sayyid Ali Khamenei, *Iqbal: Manifestations of the Islamic Spirit*, trans. Laleh Bakhtiar (Ontario, 1991), p. 38.
4. Janet Afary and Kevin B. Anderson, *Foucault and the Iranian Revolution: Gender and the Seductions of Islamism* (Chicago, 2005), p. 99.
5. Shariati and Khamenei, *Iqbal: Manifestations of the Islamic Spirit*, p. 38.
6. Nikki R. Keddie, *Sayyid Jamal Ad-Din 'Al-Afghani': A Political Biography* (Berkeley, 1972), p. 138.
7. Ibrahim Abu-Lughod, *The Arab Discovery of Europe: A Study in Cultural Encounters* (Princeton, 1963), p. 102.
8. Ibid., p. 120.
9. Bernard Lewis, *The Emergence of Modern Turkey* (Oxford, 1968), p. 146.
10. Keddie, *Sayyid Jamal Ad-Din 'Al-Afghani'*, p. 45.
11. Ibid., p. 104.
12. Ibid., p. 46.

NOTES

13. Ibid., p. 54.

14. Aziz Ahmad, 'Sayyid Aḥmad Khān, Jamāl al-dīn al-Afghānī and Muslim India', *Studia Islamica*, 13 (1960), p. 66.

15. Narayani Gupta, *Delhi Between Two Empires, 1803–1930: Society, Government and Urban Growth* (Delhi, 1981), p. 22.

16. William Dalrymple, *The Last Mughal: The Fall of Delhi 1857* (London, 2009), p. 9.

17. Ibid., p. 24.

18. Ralph Russell and Khurshidul Islam, 'The satirical verse of Akbar Ilāhābādī (1846–1921)', *Modern Asian Studies*, 8, 1 (1974), p. 8.

19. Ibid., p. 9.

20. Christopher Shackle and Javed Majed (trans.), *Hali's Musaddas: The Flow and Ebb of Islam* (Delhi, 1997), p. 103.

21. Gail Minault, 'Urdu political poetry during the Khilafat Movement', *Modern Asian Studies*, 8, 4 (1984), pp. 459–71.

22. Keddie, *Sayyid Jamal Ad-Din 'Al-Afghani'*, p. 250.

23. Rajmohan Gandhi, *Understanding the Muslim Mind* (Delhi, 1988), p. 23.

24. Ibid., p. 25.

25. Ralph Russell (ed.), *Hidden in the Lute: An Anthology of Two Centuries of Urdu Literature* (Delhi, 1995), pp. 185–6.

26. Keddie, *Sayyid Jamal Ad-Din 'Al-Afghani'*, p. 107.

27. Russell (ed.), *Hidden in the Lute*, p. 202.

28. Keddie, *Sayyid Jamal Ad-Din 'Al-Afghani'*, p.103.

29. Ibid., p. 105.

30. Jawaharlal Nehru, *Autobiography* (1936; repr. edn New Delhi, 1989), p. 435.

31. Philip Mansel, *Constantinople: City of the World's Desire, 1453–1924* (London, 1995), p. 291.

32. Ibid., p. 288.

33. Ibid., p. 277.

34. M. Şükrü Hanioğlu, *A Brief History of the Late Ottoman Empire* (Princeton, 2008), p. 6.

35. Mansel, *Constantinople: City of the World's Desire*, p. 248.

36. Ibid., p. 265.

37. Feroz Ahmad, *From Empire to Republic: Essays on the Late Ottoman Empire and Modern Turkey* (Istanbul, 2008), p. 43.

38. Şerif Mardin, *The Genesis of Young Ottoman Thought: A Study in the Modernization of Turkish Political Ideas* (Princeton, 2000), p. 79.

39. Ibid., p. 115.

40. Lewis, *The Emergence of Modern Turkey*, p. 139.

41. Mardin, *The Genesis of Young Ottoman Thought*, p. 167.

42. Cemil Aydin, *The Politics of Anti-Westernism: Visions of World Order in Pan-Islamic and Pan-Asian Thought* (New York, 2007), p. 36.

43. Mansel, *Constantinople: City of the World's Desire*, p. 11.

44. Keddie, *Sayyid Jamal Ad-Din 'Al-Afghani'*, p. 64.

45. Ibid., p. 69.

46. Juan R. I. Cole, *Colonialism and Revolution in the Middle East: Social and Cultural Origins of Egypt's Urabi Movement* (Cairo, 1999), p. 195.

47. Gustave Flaubert, *Flaubert in Egypt: A Sensibility on Tour*, trans. Francis Steegmuller (Harmondsworth, 1996), p. 28.

48. Stanley Lane Poole, *The Story of Cairo* (London, 1902), p. 27.

49. Trevor Mostyn, *Egypt's Belle Epoque: Cairo and the Age of the Hedonists* (London, 2006), p. 126.

50. Mansel, *Constantinople: City of the World's Desire*, p. 9.

51. Ibid., p. 73.

52. Mostyn, *Egypt's Belle Epoque*, p. 127.

53. Lady Duff Gordon, *Letters from Egypt* (London, 1865), p. 59.

54. Ibid., p. 309.

55. Mostyn, *Egypt's Belle Epoque*, p. 46.

56. Cole, *Colonialism and Revolution in the Middle East*, p. 193.

57. Lucie Duff Gordon, *Last Letters from Egypt: To Which Are Added Letters from the Cape* (Cambridge, 2010), p. 108.

58. Cole, *Colonialism and Revolution in the Middle East*, p. 46.

59. Elie Kedourie, *Afghani and 'Abduh: An Essay on Religious Unbelief and Political Activism in Modern Islam* (London, 1966), p. 25.

60. Flaubert, *Flaubert in Egypt*, p. 79.

61. Keddie, *Sayyid Jamal Ad-Din 'Al-Afghani'*, p. 90.

62. Ibid., pp. 116–17.

63. Ibid., p. 94.

64. Michael Gaspe, *The Power of Representation: Publics, Peasants, and Islam in Egypt* (Stanford, 2009), p. 101.

65. Keddie, *Sayyid Jamal Ad-Din 'Al-Afghani'*, p. 94.

66. Ibid., p. 95.

67. Cole, *Colonialism and Revolution in the Middle East*, p. 146.

68. Duff Gordon, *Letters from Egypt*, p. 105.

69. Keddie, *Sayyid Jamal Ad-Din 'Al-Afghani'*, p. 104.

70. Ibid., p. 106.

71. Ibid., p. 110.

72. Ibid., p. 111.

73. Kedourie, *Afghani and 'Abduh*, p. 29.
74. Keddie, *Sayyid Jamal Ad-Din 'Al-Afghani'*, pp. 121–2.
75. Ibid., p. 118.
76. Ibid., p. 125.
77. Flaubert, *Flaubert in Egypt*, p. 81.
78. Keddie, *Sayyid Jamal Ad-Din 'Al-Afghani'*, p. 133.
79. Rajmohan Gandhi, *Understanding the Muslim Mind* (Delhi, 1988), p. 26.
80. Mardin, *The Genesis of Young Ottoman Thought*, p. 60.
81. Ibid.
82. Kedourie, *Afghani and 'Abduh*, pp. 50–51.
83. Ahmad, 'Sayyid Aḥmad Khān, Jamāl al-dīn al-Afghānī and Muslim India', p. 59.
84. Keddie, *Sayyid Jamal Ad-Din 'Al-Afghani'*, pp. 164–5.
85. Ahmad, 'Sayyid Aḥmad Khān, Jamāl al-dīn al-Afghānī and Muslim India', p. 66.
86. Nehru, *Autobiography*, p. 478.
87. Ahmad, 'Sayyid Aḥmad Khān, Jamāl al-dīn al-Afghānī and Muslim India', p. 65.
88. Russell (ed.), *Hidden in the Lute*, p. 205.
89. Ibid., p. 203.
90. Russell and Islam (trans.), 'The satirical verse of Akbar Ilāhābādī', p. 11.
91. Russell (ed.), *Hidden in the Lute*, p. 205.
92. Keddie, *Sayyid Jamal Ad-Din 'Al-Afghani'*, p. 167.
93. Ibid., p. 135.
94. Russell and Islam (trans.), 'The satirical verse of Akbar Ilāhābādī', p. 56.
95. Keddie, *Sayyid Jamal Ad-Din 'Al-Afghani'*, p. 160.
96. Russell (ed.), *Hidden in the Lute*, p. 207.
97. Keddie, *Sayyid Jamal Ad-Din 'Al-Afghani'*, p. 183.
98. Mark Sedgwick, *Muhammad Abduh: A Biography* (Cairo, 2009), p. 51.
99. Stéphane A. Dudoignon, Hisao Komatsu and Yasushi Kosugi (eds.), *Intellectuals in the Modern Islamic world: Transmission, Transformation, Communication* (New York, 2006), p. 9.
100. Keddie, *Sayyid Jamal Ad-Din 'Al-Afghani'*, pp. 202–3.
101. Ibid., p. 202.
102. W. S. Blunt, *Gordon at Khartoum, Being a Personal Narrative of Events in Continuation of 'A Secret History of the English Occupation of Egypt'* (London, 1911), pp. 208–9.
103. Keddie, *Sayyid Jamal Ad-Din 'Al-Afghani'*, p. 208.
104. Kedourie, *Afghani and 'Abduh*, p. 43.

105. Keddie, *Sayyid Jamal Ad-Din 'Al-Afghani'*, p. 191.

106. Ibid., p. 196.

107. Sedgwick, *Muhammad Abduh*, p. 39.

108. Keddie, *Sayyid Jamal Ad-Din 'Al-Afghani'*, p. 250.

109. Ibid.

110. Ibid., p. 263.

111. Ibid., p. 285.

112. Ibid., p. 286.

113. Ibid., p. 304

114. Ibid.

115. Ibid., p. 317.

116. Renée Worringer (ed.), *The Islamic Middle East and Japan: Perceptions, Aspirations, and the Birth of Intra-Asian Modernity* (Princeton, 2007), p. 16.

117. George Nathaniel Curzon, *Persia and the Persian Question*, vol. 1 (London, 1966), p. 480.

118. Keddie, *Sayyid Jamal Ad-Din 'Al-Afghani'*, p. 324.

119. Ibid.

120. Ibid., p. 339.

121. Ibid., p. 343.

122. Ibid., p. 363.

123. Ibid., p. 362.

124. Ibid., p. 400.

125. Ibid., p. 382.

126. Ibid., p. 391.

127. Sayid Jamāl al-Dīn al-Afghānī and Abdul-Hādī Hā'irī, 'Afghānī on the decline of Islam', *Die Welt des Islams*, New Series, 13, 1/2 (1971), pp. 124–5.

128. Christopher De Bellaigue, *Patriot of Persia: Muhammad Mossadegh and a Very British Coup* (London, 2012), p. 17.

129. Keddie, *Sayyid Jamal Ad-Din 'Al-Afghani'*, p. 411.

130. Ibid., p. 420.

131. Charles Crane, 'Unpublished Memoirs', Institute of Current World Affairs, pp. 288–9.

132. http://www.martinkramer.org/sandbox/2010/02/america-and-afghani/

133. Charles Kurzman (ed.), *Modernist Islam, 1840–1940: A Sourcebook* (New York, 2002), p. 78.

134. Ruhollah Khomeini, *Islamic Government* (Washington, D.C., 1979), p. 35.

135. Wilfred Cantwell Smith, *Islam in Modern History* (Princeton, 1977), p 49.

136. Keddie, *Sayyid Jamal Ad-Din 'Al-Afghani'*, p. 419.

137. Ibid.

3. LIANG QICHAO'S CHINA AND THE FATE OF ASIA

1. Renée Worringer (ed.), *The Islamic Middle East and Japan: Perceptions, Aspirations, and the Birth of Intra-Asian Modernity* (Princeton, 2007), p. 34.
2. William Theodore De Bary (ed.), *Sources of East Asian Tradition: The Modern Period* (New York, 2008), p. 545.
3. Ibid., p. 46.
4. Ibid., p. 47.
5. Renée Worringer, '"Sick Man of Europe" or "Japan of the near East"? Constructing Ottoman modernity in the Hamidian and Young Turk eras', *International Journal of Middle East Studies*, 36, 2 (May 2004), p. 207.
6. Ibid.
7. Marius B. Jansen, *The Making of Modern Japan* (Cambridge, Mass., 2000), p. 274.
8. Bruce Cumings, *Dominion from Sea to Sea: Pacific Ascendancy and American Power* (New Haven, Conn., 2010), p. 85.
9. John D. Pierson, *Tokutomi Sohō, 1863–1957: A Journalist for Modern Japan* (Princeton, 1980), p. 233.
10. Ian Buruma, *Inventing Japan* (New York, 2004), p. 50.
11. Pierson, *Tokutomi Sohō*, p. 235.
12. William Theodore De Bary, Carol Gluck and Arthur E. Tiedemann (eds.), *Sources of Japanese Tradition, 1600–2000*, vol. 2 (New York, 2006), p. 133.
13. Pierson, *Tokutomi Sohō*, p. 237.
14. Ibid., p. 239.
15. Ibid., p. 241.
16. Joseph R. Levenson, *Liang Ch'i-ch'ao and the Mind of Modern China* (Cambridge, Mass., 1959), p. 112.
17. Ibid., p. 117.
18. William Theodore De Bary, Richard John Lufrano, Wing-tsit Chan and Joseph Adler (eds.), *Sources of Chinese Tradition, From 1600 Through the Twentieth Century*, vol. 2 (New York, 2000), p. 205.
19. Levenson, *Liang Ch'i-ch'ao and the Mind of Modern China*, p. 49.
20. Rudyard Kipling, *From Sea to Sea: Letters of Travel* (New York, 1920), p. 274.
21. Levenson, *Liang Ch'i-ch'ao and the Mind of Modern China*, p. 297.
22. Hao Chang, *Liang Ch'i-ch'ao and Intellectual Transition in China, 1890–1907* (Cambridge, Mass., 1971), p. 60.

23. Levenson, *Liang Ch'i-ch'ao and the Mind of Modern China*, p. 49.

24. Ibid., p. 45.

25. Ibid., p. 44.

26. Theodore Huters, *Bringing the World Home: Appropriating the West in Late Qing and Early Republican China* (Hawaii, 2005), p. 50.

27. Levenson, *Liang Ch'i-ch'ao and the Mind of Modern China*, p. 37.

28. Julia Lovell, *The Opium War* (London, 2011), p. 298.

29. Benjamin Schwartz, *In Search of Wealth and Power: Yen Fu and the West* (Cambridge, Mass., 1964), p. 55.

30. Lovell, *The Opium War*, p. 298.

31. Levenson, *Liang Ch'i-ch'ao and the Mind of Modern China*, p. 30.

32. Ibid., p. 33.

33. Ibid., p. 116.

34. Ibid., p. 83.

35. Ibid., p. 117.

36. Pierson, *Tokutomi Sohō*, p. 241.

37. Sven Saaler and Christopher W. A. Szpilman (eds.), *Pan Asianism: A Documentary History, Vol. 1, 1850–1920* (Lanham, Md., 2011), p. 166.

38. Pierson, *Tokutomi Sohō*, p. 241.

39. Prasenjit Duara, 'Asia Redux: conceptualizing a region for our times', *Journal of Asian Studies*, 69, 4 (November 2010), p. 971.

40. Rebecca E. Karl, 'Creating Asia: China in the world at the beginning of the twentieth century', *American Historical Review*, 103, 4 (Oct. 1998), pp. 1115–16.

41. Ibid., p. 1107

42. Ibid., p. 1108.

43. Rebecca E. Karl, *Staging the World: Chinese Nationalism at the Turn of the Twentieth Century* (Durham, N.C., 2002), p. 141.

44. Ibid., p. 89.

45. Hao Chang, *Liang Ch'i-ch'ao and Intellectual Transition in China*, p. 164.

46. Levenson, *Liang Ch'i-ch'ao and the Mind of Modern China*, p. 117.

47. Madhavi Thampi (ed.), *Indians in China, 1800–1949* (Delhi, 2010), p. 160.

48. Robert Bickers and R. G. Tiedemann (eds.), *The Boxers, China and the World* (Lanham, Md., 2007), p. 57.

49. Jasper Becker, *City of Heavenly Tranquility: Beijing in the History of China* (Oxford, 2008), p. 115.

50. Aurobindo Ghose, *Bande Mataram, Early Political Writings*, vol. 1 (Pondicherry, 1972), p. 312.

51. Edgar Snow, *Red Star Over China* (Harmondsworth, 1972), p. 159.

52. Tsou Jung, *The Revolutionary Army: A Chinese Nationalist Tract of 1903*, trans. John Lust (Paris, 1968), pp. 58–9.

53. De Bary, Lufrano, Wing-tsit Chan and Adler (eds.), *Sources of Chinese Tradition*, vol. 2, p. 312.

54. Hao Chang, *Chinese Intellectuals in Crisis: Search for Order and Meaning (1890–1911)* (Berkeley, 1987), p. 113.

55. De Bary, Lufrano, Wing-tsit Chan and Adler (eds.), *Sources of Chinese Tradition*, vol. 2, p. 313.

56. Zhang Yongle, 'The future of the past: on Wang Hui's rise of modern Chinese thought', *New Left Review*, 62 (2008), p. 81.

57. Jonathan Spence, *The Gate of Heavenly Peace: The Chinese and their Revolution, 1895–1980* (New York, 1982), p. 74.

58. Levenson, *Liang Ch'i-ch'ao and the Mind of Modern China*, p. 121.

59. Ibid., p. 116.

60. David G. Marr, *Vietnamese Anticolonialism, 1885–1925* (Berkeley, 1971), p. 121.

61. Lu Xun, *Diary of a Madman and Other Stories*, trans. William A. Lyell (Hawaii, 1990), p. 23.

62. Stéphane A. Dudoignon, Hisao Komatsu and Yasushi Kosugi (eds.), *Intellectuals in the Modern Islamic World: Transmission, Transformation, Communication* (New York, 2006), p. 278.

63. Ibid., p. 277.

64. Marr, *Vietnamese Anticolonialism*, p. 137.

65. Ibid., p. 114.

66. William Appleman Williams, *The Tragedy of American Diplomacy* (New York, 1972), p. 72.

67. R. David Arkush and Leo O. Lee (eds.), *Land Without Ghosts: Chinese Impressions of America from the Mid-Nineteenth Century to the Present* (Berkeley, 1989), p. 87.

68. Ibid., p. 89.

69. Ibid., p. 90.

70. Hao Chang, *Liang Ch'i-ch'ao and Intellectual Transition in China*, p. 245.

71. Arkush and Lee (eds.), *Land Without Ghosts*, p. 91.

72. Ibid.

73. Benoy Kumar Sarkar, 'Americanization from the viewpoint of young Asia', *The Journal of International Relations*, 10, 1 (July 1919), p. 42.

74. Arkush and Lee (eds.), *Land Without Ghosts*, pp. 61–2, 65.

75. Ibid., p. 92.

76. Ibid., p. 83.

77. Ibid., p. 93.
78. Jerome B. Greider, *Intellectuals and the State in Modern China: A Narrative History* (New York, 1981), p. 167.
79. Pierson, *Tokutomi Sohō*, p. 267.
80. Hao Chang, *Liang Ch'i-ch'ao and Intellectual Transition in China*, p. 269.
81. Ibid., p. 270.
82. Huters, *Bringing the World Home*, p. 20.
83. Philip Short, *Mao: A Life* (London, 2004), p. 79.
84. Spence, *The Gate of Heavenly Peace*, p. 144.
85. Peter Zarrow, *China in War and Revolution, 1895–1949* (New York, 2005), p. 135.
86. Spence, *The Gate of Heavenly Peace*, p. 142.

4. 1919, 'CHANGING THE HISTORY OF THE WORLD'

1. http://www.firstworldwar.com/source/wilson1917inauguration.htm.
2. Erez Manela, *The Wilsonian Moment: Self-Determination and the International Origins of Anticolonial Nationalism* (New York, 2009), p. 21.
3. Walter A. McDougall, *Promised Land, Crusader State: The American Encounter with the World since 1776* (New York, 1997), p.136.
4. Manela, *The Wilsonian Moment*, p. 45.
5. Ibid., p. 71.
6. Stéphane A. Dudoignon, Hisao Komatsu and Yasushi Kosugi (eds.), *Intellectuals in the Modern Islamic World: Transmission, Transformation, Communication* (New York, 2006), p. 190.
7. Iqbal Husain, 'Akbar Allahabadi and national politics', *Social Scientist*, 16, 5 (May 1988), p. 38.
8. Iqbal Singh, *The Ardent Pilgrim: An Introduction to the Life and Work of Mohammed Iqbal* (Karachi, 1997), p. 39.
9. Amiya Dev and Tan Chung (eds.), *Tagore and China* (Delhi, 2011), p. 190.
10. Manela, *The Wilsonian Moment*, pp. 91–2.
11. Jean Lacoutre, *Ho Chi Minh* (Harmondsworth, 1967), p. 35.
12. Sven Saaler and Christopher W. A. Szpilman (eds.), *Pan Asianism: A Documentary History, Vol. 1, 1850–1920* (Lanham, Md., 2011), p. 136.
13. Benoy Kumar Sarkar, 'The international fetters of young China', *The Journal of International Relations*, 11, 3 (Jan. 1921), p. 355.
14. Geoffrey Barraclough, *An Introduction to Contemporary History* (Harmondsworth, 1967), p. 215.

15. Ibid., p. 176.
16. Sarkar, 'The international fetters of young China', p. 355.
17. William Appleman Williams, *The Tragedy of American Diplomacy* (New York, 1972), p. 72.
18. Benoy Kumar Sarkar, 'Americanization from the viewpoint of young Asia', *The Journal of International Relations*, 10, 1 (July 1919), p. 47.
19. Ibid.
20. Manela, *The Wilsonian Moment*, p. 29.
21. McDougall, *Promised Land, Crusader State*, p.127.
22. Ibid.
23. David Fromkin, *In the Time of the Americans: FDR, Truman, Eisenhower, Marshall, MacArthur – The Generation That Changed America's Role in the World* (New York, 1996), p.143.
24. Manela, *The Wilsonian Moment*, p. 137.
25. Jonathan Clements, *Prince Saionji* (London, 2008), p. 120.
26. Ibid., p. 32.
27. Manela, *The Wilsonian Moment*, p. 75.
28. Hugh Purcell, *The Maharaja of Bikaner* (London, 2010), p. 27.
29. Manela, *The Wilsonian Moment*, p. 194.
30. Ibid., p. 149.
31. Christopher De Bellaigue, *Patriot of Persia: Muhammad Mossadegh and a Very British Coup* (London, 2012), p. 53.
32. Lacoutre, *Ho Chi Minh*, p. 32.
33. Krishna Dutta and Andrew Robinson, *Rabindranath Tagore: The Myriad-Minded Man* (London, 1995), p. 216.
34. Kedar Nath Mukherjee, *Political Philosophy of Rabindranath Tagore* (Delhi, 1982), p. 43.
35. Manela, *The Wilsonian Moment*, p. 217.
36. Dudoignon, Komatsu and Kosugi (eds.), *Intellectuals in the Modern Islamic World*, p. 62.
37. M. Şükrü Hanioğlu, *Atatürk: An Intellectual Biography* (Princeton, 2011), p. 91.
38. Cemil Aydin, *The Politics of Anti-Westernism: Visions of World Order in Pan-Islamic and Pan-Asian Thought* (New York, 2007), p. 134.
39. Hanioğlu, *Atatürk*, p. 57.
40. Charles Kurzman (ed.), *Modernist Islam, 1840–1940: A Sourcebook* (New York, 2002), p. 8.
41. Jonathan Spence, *The Gate of Heavenly Peace: The Chinese and their Revolution, 1895–1980* (New York, 1982), p. 172.
42. Jonathan Clements, *Wellington Koo* (London, 2008), p. 95.

43. Guoqi Xu, *China and the Great War: China's Pursuit of a New National Identity and Internationalization* (Cambridge, 2005), p. 271.

44. Ibid., p. 273.

45. Tse-tsung Chow, *The May Fourth Movement: Intellectual Revolution in Modern China* (Cambridge, Mass., 1967), p. 127.

46. Deng Maomao, *Deng Xiaoping: My Father* (New York, 1995), p. 81.

47. Ibid., p. 61.

48. John Fitzgerald, *Awakening China: Politics, Culture, and Class in the Nationalist Revolution* (Stanford, 1996), p. 93.

49. Manela, *The Wilsonian Moment*, p. 190.

50. Ibid.

51. Clements, *Wellington Koo*, p. 96.

52. Stuart R. Schram (ed.), *Mao's Road to Power: Revolutionary Writings 1912–1949. Vol. 1, The Pre-Marxist Period, 1912–1920* (New York, 1992), p. 389.

53. Paul Valéry, *The Outlook for Intelligence* (New York, 1963), p. 115.

54. Xiaobing Tang, *Global Space and the Nationalist Discourse of Modernity: The Historical Thinking of Liang Qichao* (Stanford, 1996), p. 177.

55. Spence, *The Gate of Heavenly Peace*, p. 152.

56. Jerome B. Greider, *Intellectuals and the State in Modern China: A Narrative History* (New York, 1981), p. 252.

57. Dev and Tan (eds.), *Tagore and China* (Delhi, 2011), p. 79.

58. Aurobindo Ghose, *Bande Mataram, Early Political Writings*, vol. 1 (Pondicherry, 1972), p. 561.

59. Ibid., p. 422.

60. Muhammad Iqbal, *A Message From the East* [Payam-e-Mashriq], trans. M. Hadi Hussain (first published 1924; Lahore, 1977), pp. 90–91.

61. Joseph R. Levenson, *Liang Ch'i-ch'ao and the Mind of Modern China* (Cambridge, Mass., 1959), p. 203.

62. Ibid., p. 200.

63. W. Franke, *China and the West* (Oxford, 1967), p. 124.

64. Levenson, *Liang Ch'i-ch'ao and the Mind of Modern China*, p. 207.

65. Ibid., p. 201.

66. Greider, *Intellectuals and the State in Modern China*, p. 254.

67. Levenson, *Liang Ch'i-ch'ao and the Mind of Modern China*, p. 203.

68. Kakuzo Okakura, *The Book of Tea* (New York, 1906), p. 4.

69. Greider, *Intellectuals and the State in Modern China*, p. 23.

70. Bertrand Russell, *The Problem of China* (London, 1922), p. 194.

71. Greider, *Intellectuals and the State in Modern China*, p. 263.

72. William Theodore De Bary, Richard John Lufrano, Wing-tsit Chan and

Joseph Adler (eds.), *Sources of Chinese Tradition, From 1600 Through the Twentieth Century*, vol. 2 (New York, 2000), p. 322.

73. Sven Saaler and Christopher W. A. Szpilman (eds.), *Pan Asianism: A Documentary History, Vol. 2, 1920–Present* (Lanham, Md., 2011), p. 81.

74. Ibid., pp. 188–90.

5. RABINDRANATH TAGORE IN EAST ASIA, THE MAN FROM THE LOST COUNTRY

1. Rebecca E. Karl, 'China in the world at the beginning of the twentieth century', *American Historical Review*, 103, 4 (Oct. 1998), p. 1110.

2. Rabindranath Tagore, *Letters to a Friend* (Delhi, 2002), p. 110.

3. Aurobindo Ghose, *Bande Mataram, Early Political Writings*, vol. 1 (Pondicherry, 1972), p. 820.

4. Ibid., p. 931.

5. Tapan Raychaudhuri, *Europe Reconsidered: Perceptions of the West in Nineteenth-century Bengal* (Delhi, 2002), p. 275.

6. Tapan Raychaudhuri, *Perceptions, Emotions, Sensibilities: Essays on India's Colonial and Post-colonial Experiences* (Delhi, 1999), p. 36.

7. Raychaudhuri, *Europe Reconsidered*, p. 77.

8. Ghose, *Bande Mataram*, vol.1, p. 362.

9. Ibid., p. 550.

10. Amiya Dev and Tan Chung (eds.), *Tagore and China* (Delhi, 2011), p. 242.

11. Robert Bickers and R. G. Tiedemann (eds.), *The Boxers, China and the World* (Lanham, Md., 2007), p. 148.

12. Dev and Tan (eds.), *Tagore and China*, p. 170.

13. Stephen N. Hay, *Asian Ideas of East and West: Tagore and his Critics in Japan, China, and India* (Cambridge, Mass., 1970), p. 32.

14. Mohit Kumar Ray (ed.), *The English Writings of Rabindranath Tagore*, vol. 4 (Delhi, 2007), p. 443.

15. Ibid., p. 631.

16. Ibid., p. 496.

17. Gandhi, *Hind Swaraj and Other Writings*, ed. Anthony Parel (Cambridge, 1997), p. xxii.

18. Aurobindo Ghose, *Early Cultural Writings*, vol. 1 (Pondicherry, 2003), p. 545.

19. Dev and Tan (eds.), *Tagore and China*, p. 35.

20. Krishna Dutta and Andrew Robinson, *Rabindranath Tagore: The Myriad-Minded Man* (London, 1995) p. 202.

21. Hay, *Asian Ideas of East and West*, p. 43.
22. Sven Saaler and Christopher W. A. Szpilman (eds.), *Pan Asianism: A Documentary History,* Vol. *1, 1850–1920* (Lanham, Md., 2011), p. 96.
23. Ibid., p. 98.
24. Dev and Tan (eds.), *Tagore and China*, p. 349.
25. Ibid., p. 343.
26. David Wolff and John W. Steinberg (eds.), *The Russo-Japanese War in Global Perspective: World War Zero* (Leiden, 2007), p. 478.
27. Dutta and Robinson, *Rabindranath Tagore*, p. 200.
28. Hay, *Asian Ideas of East and West*, p. 61.
29. Sugata Bose and Kris Manjapra (eds.), *Cosmopolitan Thought Zones: South Asia and the Global Circulation of Ideas* (New York, 2010), p. 103.
30. Kakuzo Okakura, *The Book of Tea* (New York, 1906), p. 4.
31. Hay, *Asian Ideas of East and West*, p. 73.
32. Ibid., pp. 78–9.
33. Ibid., p. 136.
34. Ibid., p. 200.
35. Dev and Tan (eds.), *Tagore and China*, p. 30.
36. Hay, *Asian Ideas of East and West*, p. 227.
37. Ibid., p. 168.
38. Ibid., p. 170.
39. Jonathan Spence, *The Gate of Heavenly Peace: The Chinese and their Revolution, 1895–1980* (New York, 1982), p. 216.
40. Tagore, *Letters to a Friend*, p. 110.
41. Dev and Tan (eds.), *Tagore and China*, p. 79.
42. Tagore, *Letters to a Friend*, p. 118.
43. Krishna Dutta and Andrew Robinson (eds.), *Rabindranath Tagore: An Anthology* (New York, 1997), p. 127.
44. Dev and Tan (eds.), *Tagore and China*, p. 37.
45. Hay, *Asian Ideas of East and West*, p. 172.
46. Ibid., p. 316.
47. Dutta and Robinson, *Rabindranath Tagore*, p. 252.
48. Ibid.
49. Ibid., p. 347.
50. Hay, *Asian Ideas of East and West*, p. 320.
51. Dev and Tan (eds.), *Tagore and China*, p. 76.
52. Rabindranth Tagore, *Crisis in Civilization* (Delhi, 2002), p. 260.
53. Dutta and Robinson, *Rabindranath Tagore*, pp. 300–301.

6. ASIA REMADE

1. Krishna Dutta and Andrew Robinson, *Rabindranath Tagore: The Myriad-Minded Man* (London, 1995), p. 301.

2. Kakuzo Okakura, *The Book of Tea* (New York, 1906), p. 2.

3. John D. Pierson, *Tokutomi Sohō 1863–1957: A Journalist for Modern Japan* (Princeton, 1980), p. 371.

4. Ibid., p. 375.

5. William Theodore De Bary, Carol Gluck and Arthur E. Tiedemann (eds.), *Sources of Japanese Tradition, 1600–2000*, vol. 2 (New York, 2006), p. 136.

6. Donald Keene (ed.), *So Lovely a Country Will Never Perish: Wartime Diaries of Japanese Writers* (New York, 2010), p. 14.

7. De Bary, Gluck and Tiedemann (eds.), *Sources of Japanese Tradition*, vol. 2, p. 137.

8. Christopher Bayly and Tim Harper, *Forgotten Armies: The Fall of British Asia, 1941–1945* (London, 2007), p. 7.

9. Keene (ed.), *So Lovely a Country*, p. 30.

10. Rotem Kowner (ed.), *The Impact of the Russo-Japanese War* (London, 2006), p. 230.

11. Keene (ed.), *So Lovely a Country*, p. 41.

12. Jawaharlal Nehru, *Autobiography* (1936; repr. edn New Delhi, 1989), p. 488.

13. Ibid., p. 632.

14. Keene (ed.), *So Lovely a Country*, p. 40.

15. Ibid., p. 43.

16. Bayly and Harper, *Forgotten Armies*, p. 356.

17. Keene (ed.), *So Lovely a Country*, p. 41.

18. Eri Hotta, *Pan-Asianism and Japan's War 1931–1945* (New York, 2007), p. 217.

19. Stephen N. Hay, *Asian Ideas of East and West: Tagore and his Critics in Japan, China, and India* (Cambridge, Mass., 1970), p. 70.

20. Christopher Bayly and Tim Harper, *Forgotten Wars: Freedom and Revolution in Southeast Asia* (London, 2007), p. 149.

21. Hotta, *Pan-Asianism and Japan's War*, p. 218.

22. Christopher De Bellaigue, *Patriot of Persia: Muhammad Mossadegh and a Very British Coup* (London, 2012), p. 179.

23. Bayly and Harper, *Forgotten Wars*, p. 18.

24. De Bary, Gluck and Tiedemann (eds.), *Sources of Japanese Tradition*, vol. 2, p. 138.

25. Mohit Kumar Ray (ed.), *The English Writings of Rabindranath Tagore*, vol. 7 (Delhi, 2007), p. 970.
26. Sven Saaler and Christopher W. A. Szpilman (eds.), *Pan Asianism: A Documentary History, Vol. 1, 1850–1920* (Lanham, Md., 2011), p. 98.
27. Charlotte Furth and Guy Alitto, *The Limits of Change: Essays on Conservative Alternatives in Republican China* (Cambridge, Mass., 1976), p. 229.
28. Michael Collins, *Empire, Nationalism and the Postcolonial World: Rabindranath Tagore's Writings on History, Politics and Society* (New York, 2011), p. 67.
29. Herlee G. Creel, *Chinese Thought: From Confucius to Mao Tse Tung* (Chicago, 1971), p. 237.
30. Furth and Alitto, *The Limits of Change*, p. 197.
31. Ayesha Jalal, *Self and Sovereignty: Individual and Community in South Asian Islam since 1850* (New York, 2000), p. 170.
32. Muhammad Iqbal, *The Call of the Caravan Bell*, trans. Umrao Singh Sher Gil, http://www.disna.us/files/The_Call_of_The_Caravan_Bell.pdf, p. 47.
33. Ali Shariati and Sayyid Ali Khamenei, *Iqbal: Manifestations of the Islamic Spirit*, trans. Laleh Bakhtiar (Ontario, 1991), p. 31.
34. Ibid., p. 75.
35. Javeed Majeed, *Muhammad Iqbal: Islam, Aesthetics and Postcolonialism* (Delhi, 2009), p. xxiii.
36. Wilfred Cantwell Smith, *Modern Islam in India* (Lahore, 1943), p. 111.
37. Reza Aslan, *No God but God: The Origins, Evolution, and Future of Islam* (New York, 2005), p. 232.
38. Taha Hussein, *The Future of Culture in Egypt* (Washington, D.C., 1955), p. 17.
39. Muhammad Iqbal, *The Reconstruction of Religious Thought in Islam* (Lahore, 1944), p. 159.
40. Roxanne Euben, *Enemy in the Mirror. Islamic Fundamentalism and the Limits of Modern Rationalism: A Work of Comparative Political Theory* (Princeton, 1999), p. 49.
41. Nehru, *Autobiography*, p. 519.
42. Ibid., p. 520.
43. John Calvert, *Sayyid Qutb and the Origins of Radical Islamism* (London, 2010), p. 117.
44. Ibid., p. 154.
45. Ibid., p. 149.
46. Euben, *Enemy in the Mirror*, p. 68.

47. Calvert, *Sayyid Qutb*, p. 105.

48. Ibid., p. 161.

49. Sayyid Qutb, *Milestones* (Delhi 1973), p. 3.

50. Said Amir Arjomand, 'Iran's Islamic Revolution in comparative perspective', *World Politics*, 38, 3 (Apr. 1986), p. 407.

51. Janet Afary and Kevin B. Anderson, *Foucault and the Iranian Revolution: Gender and the Seductions of Islamism* (Chicago, 2005), p. 4.

52. Shariati and Khamenei, *Iqbal: Manifestations of the Islamic Spirit*, p. 38.

53. Jalal Al-e Ahmad, *Occidentosis: A Plague from the West*, ed. Hamid Algar (Berkeley, 1984), p. 34.

54. Ali Mirsepassi, *Intellectual Discourse and the Politics of Modernization: Negotiating Modernity in Iran* (Cambridge, 2000), p. 113.

55. Hamid Dabashi, *Theology of Discontent: The Ideological Foundation of the Islamic Revolution in Iran* (New Brunswick, N.J., 2006), p. 355.

56. Ali Shariati, *Reflections of a Concerned Muslim: On the Plight of Oppressed Peoples*, trans. Ali A. Behzadnia and Najpa Denny (Houston, Tex., 1979), pp. 9–10.

57. Ali Shariati, *Marxism and Other Western Fallacies: An Islamic Critique*, trans. R. Campbell (Berkeley, 1980), p. 49.

58. Ali Gheissari, *Iranian Intellectuals in the Twentieth Century* (Austin, Tex., 1998), p.101.

59. Hamid Algar (trans.), *Islam and Revolution: Writings and Declarations of Imam Khomeini* (Berkeley, 1981), p. 28.

60. Ali Shariati, *On the Sociology of Islam*, trans. Hamid Algar (Berkeley, 2000), p. 23.

61. Translated from the Urdu by Ali Mir (unpublished).

62. Daniel Brumberg, *Reinventing Khomeini: The Struggle for Reform in Iran* (Chicago, 2001), p. 198.

63. Orhan Pamuk, 'The anger of the damned', *New York Review of Books*, 15 November 2001.

64. Ibid.

65. M. Şükrü Hanioğlu, *Atatürk: An Intellectual Biography* (Princeton, 2011), p. 205.

66. Rajmohan Gandhi, *Understanding the Muslim Mind* (Delhi, 1988), p. 62.

67. Muhammad Iqbal, *The Reconstruction of Religious Thought in Islam* (Lahore, 1944), p. 162.

68. Feroz Ahmad, *From Empire to Republic: Essays on the Late Ottoman Empire and Modern Turkey* (Istanbul, 2008), p. 323.

69. Julia Lovell, *The Opium War* (London, 2011), p. 321.

70. Ibid., p. 330.
71. Ibid., p. 331.
72. Timothy Cheek (ed.), *A Critical Introduction to Mao* (Cambridge, 2010), p. 31.
73. Shao Chuan Leng and Norman D. Palmer, *Sun Yat-sen and Communism* (New York, 1961), p.157.
74. Stuart R. Schram (ed.), *Mao's Road to Power: Revolutionary Writings 1912–1949. Vol. 7 New Democracy, 1939–1941* (New York, 2005), pp. 330–69.
75. Peter Zarrow, *China in War and Revolution, 1895–1949* (New York, 2005), p.15.
76. Alexis de Tocqueville, *'The European Revolution' and Correspondence with Gobineau* (New York, 1959), p. 268.
77. André Malraux, *The Temptation of the West*, trans. Robert Hollander (New York, 1974), p. 104.

EPILOGUE: AN AMBIGUOUS REVENGE

1. Ryszard Kapuściński, *The Soccer War* (London, 1990), p. 106.
2. Nicolaus Mills and Michael Walzer (eds.), *50 Years of Dissent* (New York, 2004), p. 35.

Acknowledgements

This book rises from the shoulders of many specialist studies and general global histories. But it is also a collaborative work in another sense. Moving from the Ottomans to late Qing China, I was more than aware that I was breaching disciplinary boundaries and academic protocols. My occasionally impudent forays were enabled by generous friends both in academia and outside it. They suggested books and papers and read my manuscript, alerting me to errors of fact and interpretation. Those that remain in the finished book should not be blamed on Tabish Khair, Jonathan Shainin, Ananya Vajpeyi, Manan Ahmad, Hussein Omar, Masoud Golsarkhi, Wang Hui, Suzy Hansen, Siddhartha Deb, Alex Travelli, Adam Shatz, Nader Hashemi, Jeff Kingston, Jason Epstein, Shashank Kela or Jeffrey Wasserstrom, all of whom read different parts of the work-in-progress and frankly expressed their opinions. I was also very fortunate to have such sceptical, challenging and well-informed editors as Simon Winder and Paul Elie. Gratitude is also due to the staff at the Bleibtreu Hotel, Berlin, where I started working on this book; the London Library, which supplied so many materials for it; and the Sharmas at Mashobra, who have afforded me, for two decades now, that vital sanctuary in which to write – and, more important, daydream.

Index

Babism 53
Balakot, Battle of 37
al-Banna, Hasan 266
Baqar, Maulvi 37
Barakatullah, Maulvi 169, 232
Bazargan, Mehdi 123, 274, 276
Beijing Consensus 306
Bengal 5–6, 23–4, 221–2
bin Laden, Osama 121, 278–9
Blunt, Wilfrid Scawen 87, 94, 96,
    99–100, 102–103
Boer War 158, 159, 210
Bose, Rash Behari 232
Bose, Subhas Chandra 248, 249
Boxer Rising 6, 161–3
Britain
    in Afghanistan 54–5, 104–5
    al-Afghani's distrust 110–11
    and China 24–5, 28–30, 140–41
    conquests in Asia 22–3
    hatred of 59
    in India 23–4, 33–6, 59–60, 83–4,
        158, 160
    and Japan 128, 129
    Opium Wars with China 28–31,
        32–3, 287
    Royal Navy 41
    Sykes–Picot Agreement 194,
        264, 267
Buddhism
    in China 131, 149, 157, 212, 215
    from India to Japan 230
    shared legacy 231
Burke, Edmund 24, 83
Burma 22, 138, 248, 251, 252
al-Bustani, Butrus 52, 84

Cahid, Hüseyin 66–7
Chatterji, Bankim Chandra 23,
    221, 226

Chen Duxiu 182–3, 197, 215,
    235, 236
Chiang Kai-shek 164, 256, 289
China
    anti-Manchuists 164–6, 176–7
    army modernization 164, 180
    Boxer Rising 6, 161–3
    and Britain 25–6, 28–30, 140–41
    Buddhism 131, 149, 157,
        212, 215
    civil service exams 135, 137, 138,
        142, 145, 163
    civil war 289, 290–91
    Communist Party 208, 209, 290,
        292, 293
    Confucianism see Confucianism
    cultural heritage 136–7
    early Western contact limited
        135–6
    economic policy 292–4
    economic strength 137, 296
    education 163
    environmental issues 307
    exiles in Japan 152–8
    in First World War 180, 192, 205
    foreign debts 140, 178–9
    Great Leap Forward 303
    Hong Kong 28, 29, 234, 237,
        287–8
    Hundred Day reforms 32, 149–51
    India viewed as lost country 219
    inequality in 307
    Korean war 291
    Mao regime 290–92
    Marxism-Leninism 288–9, 291
    May Fourth Movement/New
        Culture 182–3, 206–7, 211–12,
        215, 235
    Middle Kingdom 24
    modernization 139–40, 163–4